SOCIAL SELF, GLOBAL CULTURE

An
Introduction
to
Sociological
Ideas

edited by

Allan Kellehear

Melbourne

OXFORD UNIVERSITY PRESS

OXFORD UNIVERSITY PRESS AUSTRALIA

Oxford   New York
Athens   Auckland   Bangkok   Bombay
Calcutta   Cape Town   Dar es Salaam   Delhi
Florence   Hong Kong   Istanbul   Karachi
Kuala Lumpur   Madras   Madrid   Melbourne
Mexico City   Nairobi   Paris   Singapore
Taipei   Tokyo   Toronto

and associated companies in
Berlin   Ibadan

OXFORD is a trade mark of Oxford University Press

National Library of Australia
Cataloguing-in-Publication data:

Social self, global culture: an introduction to sociological ideas.
  Bibliography.
  Includes index.
  ISBN 0 19 553740 8.

  1. Sociology. I. Kellehear, Allan.

301

Indexed by Brett Lockwood
Copy-edited by Lucy Davison
Cover design by Kirsten Lowe
Text design by Sarn Potter
Typeset by Desktop Concepts P/L, Melbourne
Printed through Bookpac Production Services, Singapore
Published by Oxford University Press,
253 Normanby Road, South Melbourne, Australia

SOCIAL SELF,

GLOBAL CULTURE

This book is to be returned on
or before the date stamped below

1 5 JUN 2001	2 2 MAR 2004
− 2 APR 2002	
− 3 APR 2002	
3 0 OCT 2002 1 1 FEB 2003	
1 1 DEC 2003 − 2 FEB 2004	

UNIVERSITY OF PLYMOUTH

PLYMOUTH LIBRARY

Tel: (01752) 232323

This book is subject to recall if required by another reader
Books may be renewed by phone
CHARGES WILL BE MADE FOR OVERDUE BOOKS

Contents

Introduction

The Social Self

Community

Nation

Globalisation

Appendix

Contributors

LUCINDA ABERDEEN is a sociologist with a background in social research in both academic and non-academic settings. Initially a research sociologist with the Victorian Government, she has conducted studies on the social impact of road planning, disability, human rights, and racism. More recently, she has lectured in the anthropology of indigenous and immigrant health. She is currently teaching and researching in the School of Sociology and Anthropology at La Trobe University in the area of Aborigines and the State.

IAN ANDERSON is Chief Executive Officer of the Victorian Aboriginal Health Service. In 1993 he was one of seven indigenous presenters involved in the ABC's Boyer Lectures. Apart from his training as a medical practitioner, Ian has also been a postgraduate student in sociology and anthropology at La Trobe University. He is the author of *Koorie Health in Koorie Hands* (1988).

PETER BEILHARZ has taught at Monash University, the University of Melbourne, and the Phillip Institute, and is currently a reader in sociology at La Trobe University. A co-founder of the international journal of social theory, *Thesis Eleven*, he is the author of *Labour's Utopias* (1992) and *Transforming Labor* (1994).

KEN DEMPSEY is presently a reader in sociology at La Trobe University. He has taught at the University of New England in New South Wales, and at Simon Fraser and Concordia universities in Canada. He was at one time joint editor of the *Australian and New Zealand Journal of Sociology*. Author of *Smalltown: A Study of Social Inequality, Cohesion and Belonging* (1990) and *A Man's Town: Inequality Between Women and Men in Rural Australia* (1992), he is currently writing a book on marital inequality in Australia, which is to be published by Oxford University Press in late 1996.

DAVID DE VAUS is an associate professor of sociology at La Trobe University, and Head of Research and Senior Principal Research Fellow at the Australian Institute of Family Studies. He is the author of *Surveys in Social Research* (1990) and *Letting Go: Relationships Between Adults and Their Parents* (1993). His current research is on the sociology of the family, in which he examines later-life families, demographic changes in families, applied family policy research, and designs for social research.

CHRIS EIPPER is a senior lecturer in sociology and anthropology at La Trobe University. He has undertaken ethnographic research in both Ireland and Australia. His publications include *The Ruling Trinity: A Community Study of Church, State and Business in Ireland* (1986) and *Hostage to Fortune: Bantry Bay and the*

Encounters with Gulf Oil (1989). He is also the author of two novels: *Dieback* (1990) and *Shadowing Secrets* (1990).

DOUG EZZY is currently a lecturer in sociology at La Trobe University. He has also taught at the University of Tasmania and Deakin University, and is the editor of *SocHealth*, an email newsletter for social sciences working in the field of Australian health. His current research focuses on the meaning of work, the consequences of unemployment, and the hermeneutics of the self.

JULIE FINLAYSON is a social anthropologist with extensive research experience in Aboriginal Australia. Her work as a consulting anthropologist for Aboriginal organisations and communities has taken her to central Australia, north Queensland, and parts of south-eastern Australia. Formerly an associate lecturer at La Trobe University, Julie now works for the Centre for Aboriginal Economic Policy Research at the Australian National University. Julie's current interests focus predominantly on policy issues in relation to indigenous socio-political circumstances.

ALBERTO GOMES is a senior lecturer in the School of Sociology and Anthropology at La Trobe University. Trained as an anthropologist at the University of Malaya in Malaysia and the Australian National University, he has done extensive research on economic, social, and demographic change among Malaysian Aborigines. He is the editor of *Modernity & Identity: Asian Illustrations* (1994).

BRIAN GRAETZ is an associate professor in the School of Sociology and Anthropology at La Trobe University. His main research interests are in the fields of education, health, social stratification, and political behaviour. He is author of *Images of Class in Australia* (1987), *Dimensions of Australian Society* (1994, with Ian McAllister), and numerous articles in national and international journals. He has been a consultant to a number of organisations, and has taught in social research methods programs conducted by the Australian Consortium for Social and Political Research Inc.

SUSAN HARVEY has taught courses on the sociology of migration, education, and language at La Trobe University in the School of Sociology and Anthropology for twenty-two years. Her research interests and activities have included a study of language maintenance in children of Dutch- and Polish-born immigrants; a study of Dutch immigrants to Australia who returned to the Netherlands; a study of Greek students and their tertiary education in Melbourne; and, more recently, the relevance of 'ethnic' diaspora churches to national identity, migrant communities, and cultural maintenance. Her publications have appeared in *Racism, La Trobe Sociology Papers, The Victorian Yearbook*, and in several edited collections.

TREVOR HOGAN is a lecturer in sociology at La Trobe University, where he first arrived as a postgraduate student and tutor in 1989. Throughout the 1980s he worked as a social researcher and teacher in a diverse range of institutional settings, both in Australia and internationally. He is an editor of the international journal of social theory *Thesis Eleven*, and his research interests and publications traverse theology, history, and social and political theory.

ROWAN IRELAND has been at La Trobe University since late 1970 and is now a reader in sociology. Occasionally he escapes to pursue his research interests in Brazil. These have included investigations into the political implications of varieties of religious life and his current project on urban social movements. He has taught units in the sociology of religion and on social movements, as well as offering units for the program of studies coordinated by La Trobe's Institute of Latin American Studies. His books include *Kingdoms Come: Religion and Politics in Brazil* (1991).

ALLAN KELLEHEAR works in Fitzroy, Melbourne, where he is Head of Research Development at Turning Point Alcohol & Drug Centre, as well as being an honorary visiting professor in the School of Sociology and Anthropology at La Trobe University. He has taught introductory sociology in several Australian universities, and is a researcher and writer in the sociology of health and illness, death and dying, and research methodology. His latest book, *Experiences Near Death: Beyond Medicine and Religion* (1996), is published by Oxford University Press.

BERYL LANGER is a senior lecturer in the School of Sociology and Anthropology at La Trobe University. Her specialist area of research and teaching is in the sociology of cultural production, consumption and representation. Her current research and publications are on the globalisation and commodification of Australian children's culture, and on the implications of globalisation for multiculturalism. She is also involved in Canadian studies, where her research and publications are on literary production, and her current project deals with Canadian crime writing as a case study of the localising of global culture.

FIONA MACKIE teaches sociology at La Trobe University, where she is a senior lecturer. She has taught and researched in the area of immigrant experience for many years, and this research is linked to her interest in contemporary pressures towards a limited form of subjectivity. Her research and teaching draw on the themes in her book *The Status of Everyday Life: A Sociological Excavation of the Prevailing Framework of Perception* (1985), as well as on postmodern theory and new science. Her current work will appear in two books that explore spacetime as a vital issue in social life.

KEVIN McDONALD teaches in the sociology program at the University of Melbourne. He holds a doctorate from Ecole des Hautes Etudes en Sciences Sociales. His current research explores questions of action and identity, with an emphasis on linking theoretical production with sociological fieldwork that reconstructs social logics. He has recently undertaken a sociological 'intervention' with young people, confronting questions of social and cultural transformation.

KERREEN REIGER is a senior lecturer in the School of Sociology and Anthropology at La Trobe University, having formerly taught at Phillip Institute (now Royal

Melbourne Institute of Technology) for many years. Her research and teaching interests are in historical and social policy studies, especially issues relating to women as mothers. She is the author of *The Disenchantment of the Home* (1985) and *Family Economy* (1991).

KATY RICHMOND is a senior lecturer in sociology at La Trobe University. Her research and writing have focused on women's place in paid employment, homosexuality in prisons, health promotion, and women's health. A founding member of the Australian Sociological Association's Women's Section, she was later elected President of the Association in 1991–92.

ROSEMARY WEARING is currently a senior lecturer in sociology at La Trobe University. Over the past eight years she has been researching the impact of the law and policing in the area of domestic violence. She has published several major reports and two articles on this topic, and is presently writing a book.

EVAN WILLIS is an associate professor in the School of Sociology and Anthropology at La Trobe University. He is Co-convenor of the Health Sociology Research Group there. His interests are in medical sociology, and the sociology of work and technology. His recent books include *The Sociological Quest* (1995), *Illness and Social Relations* (1994), and (with Jeanne Daly and Ian McDonald) *Researching Health Care* (1992).

Acknowledgments

The basic part and chapter topics of this book grew out of several group meetings with colleagues. My thanks go to Peter Beilharz, Ken Dempsey, Rowan Ireland, Kerreen Reiger, Katy Richmond, David de Vaus, and Evan Willis, all of whom were dedicated and imaginative members in these initial, creative meetings. Later we were joined by Alberto Gomes, Trevor Hogan, and Kevin McDonald. The additional input of these people into the development and formulation of the book's structure reflects their years of experience, and their commitment to and enthusiasm for first-year teaching in this subject.

A volunteer group of first-year sociology students also read many of the chapters and provided invaluable suggestions and criticism. I thank the following students for their wonderful effort, especially since this work was performed in addition to their other reading commitments: Cindy Tatarskyj, Rebecca Riseley, Agostino 'Gus' Carfi, Kate Neilson, Maria Sernia, Michelle Beard, Jason Odering, Lucy Brancato, Tina Kyriakos, Johanna Reed, Amelia Colarusso, Melba Gasparro, Stuart Hughes, Karli Denier, Christiana Eid, Kaleroi 'Roula' Kourabas, Nigel Rohde, Mark Cucchiara, Fiona Anderson, Mark Baker, David Gonzalez, Nari Kennedy, Leigh Taylor, Maree Van den boom, and Lynn Woodgate.

I would also like to extend my personal thanks to Beth Robertson — not only a good typist, but also a trusted confidante and patient friend. Finally, I would also like to thank Jill Lane. A book that attempts to be imaginative in its approach needs a publisher to match. I had one in Jill Lane.

The following people and institutions also kindly agreed to give permission to reproduce photos, poems, or other textual materials, and I gratefully acknowledge their assistance and cooperation: Jenny Joseph, 'Warning', from *Selected Poems*, Bloodaxe Books Ltd, Newcastle-upon-Tyne, Copyright© Jenny Joseph 1992; photograph by P. Lyssiotis (1986), from the *Shadows* series, reproduced in *Arena*, no. 76, p. 35; extract from Adrian Dixon, 'Adrian Finds His Avalon', in G. Wotherspoon© 1986, *Being Different*, Hale & Iremonger, Sydney; Cathy Freeman photograph by Tony Feder courtesy of Sporting Pix Australia© 1994; Helen Gow, 'Open Letter to the Victorian Minister of Health Services', *Health Forum*, no. 32, December 1994, pp. 24–5; extract from Isaacs' *Idols of the Tribe*, reprinted with permission of the publisher from *Idols of the Tribe: Group Identity and Political Change* by Harold Robert Isaacs, Cambridge, Mass.: Harvard University Press, Copyright© 1975 by Harold R. Isaacs; photograph of King Peter — Mona Mona 1930s Donahne reproduced with permission of the John Oxley Library, State Library of Queensland; Fran Winant, 'Dyke Jacket', in *Dyke Jacket: Poems and Songs*, Violet Press, New York, Copyright © Fran Winant 1976.

Preface

How are we to understand ourselves as Australians? In this book we attempt to address this question through a series of reflective essays, organised around four key sociological ideas: self, community, nation, and globalisation. We begin with the idea of self, so as to distinguish sociological ideas about the individual from psychological and biological explanations. But we also take the self as our departure point in introducing important sociological ideas to do with the self — socialisation, representation, and identity, for example. Each of these chapters discusses its insights against the background of specific concerns to do with gender, ethnicity, or consumption and popular culture.

Under the heading of community, we examine issues of religion, work, or deviance in the context of contested meanings of community and locality. And when we move on to discuss the nation, whether in relation to the health or welfare system, or while discussing social inequality, we do so with an eye to how current problems can be understood as outcomes of history and contemporary globalising influences. This background comes to the foreground in the final part, when processes of urbanisation, revolution, or development are taken up.

Each of these parts are drawn together with a sum-up chapter, which attempts to comment and reflect on the previous chapters. Some of these sum-up chapters, particularly in the latter half of the book, also attempt to make links, not only to previous chapters in their part, but also to previous parts. The appendix takes a practical look at future graduate possibilities for students who major in sociology, particularly within Arts or Social Science degree programs.

Our aim in designing this book as a series of reflective discussions was to move away from a traditional didactic approach to first-year sociology texts. We wanted to engage readers; encourage their involvement with some basic ideas; send them willingly and expectantly to the further reading, hopefully with an interest ignited by these chapters.

Not all sociologists who browse these chapters will agree with the approaches, knowledge, or reading bases that some of our contributors have employed as the basis of their arguments and reflections. Even as I edited each contribution separately, and as I received feedback from other colleagues about other contributor's chapters, it was very clear that many people wanted to write other people's chapters differently, *their* way.

Sociologists work in many different traditions of literature, favour different 'heroes' and periods of theorising, and have different visions about what constitutes 'good sociology'. You see it all here. We have chosen to show the reader the diversity of contemporary Australian sociology. Sometimes we have written about this explicitly, and when we have done this, we highlight this diversity by referring to 'perspectives'.

But the better examples are the divergent styles of the authors themselves. These are living examples of the plurality of sociological thinking in Australia, such as it is.

And at the end of the day, the destination in first-year sociology is not the sociological textbook, but rather the further reading, and discussion with other students and lecturers. We believe that it is important to encourage the reader to think about the chapters, rather than studying them for any pieces of information within them. We hope readers will be curious about the differences and styles of opinion, imagination, and message within each. In this way, the reader may see that sociologists are ordinary men and women who are similar to the reader, but whose work life is dedicated to understanding how the workings of our society shape our everyday experience.

Sociology is about interpreting the world (theory); about checking these interpretations against experience (research); and about being careful not to be deceived by superficial appearances (criticism). Sociology is a conversation, an informed argument, about the way things are, sometimes even about the way things might be. Personally challenging and relevant, sociology is a journey into our organisations, history, politics, knowledge, and, ultimately, ourselves.

Allan Kellehear
La Trobe University, Melbourne

Introduction

Sociologists have been interested in
the study of society in a special way.
Allan Kellehear, Chapter 1

Chapter 1

Social Self, Global Culture: A Personal Introduction to Sociological Ideas

Allan Kellehear

As a boy, not more than twelve years of age, I used to spend most afternoons after school at Folly's place. Folly was an old widow of sixty-something who had the most interesting house and garden I had ever seen. She had flowers of every colour and an enormous vegetable patch. She even grew pineapple plants and harvested fruit from a cactus vine that grew, like a snaking beanstalk, around a bleached, white, English-style pergola. Folly had aviaries of canaries, finches, and quails. And she also had part of her yard cordoned off for chickens. The inside of her house was even more interesting.

There seemed always to be the faint smell of tea and buttered toast. And when you sat in her giant velvet club lounge, it would offer up the smells of the dogs and cats, both past and present, who lived with Folly. There was always a clear ticking noise emanating from her art deco clock on the lounge room mantle and regularly punctuating the quiet loneliness of the lounge room when Folly was absent. Keeping that clock company were several photos in old wooden frames dotted along a mantle too tall for me to reach. We had nothing like any of these things at my house.

I seldom thought much about *why* Folly's house was so different from mine. When I did, I think I used to assume that it was because she was 'old', and I supposed that all 'old people' had houses, gardens, furniture, and photos like Folly's. But one day, out of idle curiosity, I asked about one of the photos on the mantle, which was of some men in uniform. She explained to me, with a strange mixture of pride and hesitation, that the photo was of her sons. They were both soldiers in the Second World War and had fought the Japanese in the Pacific area. At that point we both fell silent, immersed in our thoughts.

That night I went home to look at our family album because I was interested to see if I had relatives in uniform too. In one of our many photo albums I came across many pictures of many relatives in uniform: school uniforms. But these were not the school uniforms that were commonly seen in Australia. These were *Japanese* school uniforms. This was one of several experiences during my childhood that reminded me that my family was 'different' from 'other' Australian families.

But having a Japanese parent and an Irish-Australian parent was, as I later learnt, only one way in which culture and history have conspired to create me and my experiences. However, for every discordant or ill-fitting experience that I have had as a result of daily encounters with Anglo-Australians and their assumptions, there have been opportunities to share the story with other Australians who have had similar or identical experiences. If you have a non-Anglo background — Italian, Jewish, or Vietnamese perhaps — then you will know only too well that awkwardness of occasionally 'not quite fitting'. But ethnic differences are only one way, and merely one obvious way, in which the history and culture of distant events and places shape you.

The fact is, as I came to realise later in life, the historical and cultural forces that cause me to experience an occasional moment of strangeness among fellow Australians is something shared by almost all Australians. Anglo-Australians also occasionally feel 'the odd one out' — when walking down an Australian street where most of the faces are Asian, such as some of those in Cabramatta in Sydney, or Richmond in Melbourne, for instance. Anglo and non-Anglo-Australians jointly feel awkward about the plight of the Australian Aborigine. Remember that, as recently as the 1960s, Aboriginal children were still being separated from their families in the belief that integrating Aborigines would be better for their long-term 'welfare'.

However, if the whole country were populated by only one ethnic group, there would still be social differences that would contribute to genuine feelings of strangeness and that would lead to corresponding differences in aspirations, feelings, attachments and needs. People from different social classes or age groups, or with different genders or sexual preferences — even people with different occupations, lifestyles, or professional rank — make 'others' appear different to 'us'. The various ways of studying the social conditions that give rise to our personal experiences are called the social sciences, and playing an important role in the social sciences are sociological explanations.

The relevance of sociology

Sociologists have been interested in the study of society in a special way. Sociology's preoccupation has been with the processes by which people are made, regulated and controlled; how and why societies change and use people; and the nature of conflict and power in all these social processes. In all this, students of sociology have shown a particular interest in the peculiar social conditions that promote and encourage the development of certain types of men and women over other types.

Folly's sons fought in a war that gave Folly a particular view of the Japanese that was foreign to me. It also made her the mother not simply of two men, but of two men who were soldiers who had seen active military service. Today, few men and women under the age of forty can say that they have seen active military service or, just as importantly, would even want to say that.

Ten years after Australians fought the Japanese, they found themselves fighting another Asian war, this one in Korea. Only, this time, Japan was used as a friendly base for Australian soldiers, for recreation and for medical repatriation. Those abstract occurrences created the circumstances for my parents meeting and, further in time, my birth and later meeting with Folly. For my parents' generation, and their parents' generation, war had been Australians' most common introduction to their Asian neighbours. Clearly it was not a meeting under 'ideal conditions'.

And yet, although all the Australians of my childhood were products of that history and those cultural circumstances, we all occupied different positions within Australian society, giving each of us different, highly individual experiences of it. That experience, whatever else may have been born of it, gave Folly and me something very personal in common that few Australians before us had had. Folly and I were linked, despite our age differences, to a time and place in which mothers had military sons who had seen battles. Wives went to work in weapons factories. People married, or became, 'war brides' in countries they had only previously read about: the USA, Japan, France, or Italy.

These kinds of men and women are no longer created, because the conditions that promoted their creation no longer exist. Australia has not had a major military involvement since the Vietnam War. Still people are being 'made' by contemporary society, fashioned by the social circumstances of the day: by the present experiences of refugee migration; by economic opportunity or unemployment; by rising rates of university participation; by diversification and change inside Australian marriages and families; by what some have called the Americanisation of Australian cultural life; by increasing economic and political links with Asia; by the growing tide of republicanism; and by the many other changes in Australian society today.

According to C. Wright Mills (1959), the peculiar type of thinking style or imagination that characterises the sociologist who examines all this is the ability to link individual biography with history, and to trace this link to current social circumstances. A study of current social circumstances leads us to an examination of our institutions, such as the family, religion or work.

It will also tend to lead us to an examination of the less tangible, but no less potent, influences and pressures behind those organisations: interest groups, the power of authority and tradition, the disempowering consequences of lack of resources and social position, the distracting but ambiguous immediacy of modern media and its transformative role in turning all experiences, all values and desires, into commodities for sale.

The methods by which sociology investigates its interests and expresses its imagination are varied. Some sociologists conduct studies that involve active research work. These are the sociologists who conduct surveys and interviews (Minichiello et al. 1990; de Vaus 1990). There are also sociologists who study archives and analyse the content of social policies on education or media images of masculinity, for instance (Kellehear 1993). But there are other ways of working in sociology too. Working quietly in another corner of the workaday world are sociologists who are concerned with the practical without immersing themselves in it. These are the social theorists who attempt to describe the 'big picture' of society's workings, or the social creation of the individual self.

Why do any of these things matter? There are two major reasons why sociology matters in everyday life. First, people tend to view their personal world as private and psychological, rather than historical and cultural. Some people persist, for example, in believing that migrants are the only ones who have 'culture'. However, there is an influential culture, a store of unique experience, that shapes every person's values and conduct, whether it is the experience of being disabled or able-bodied, being a woman or a man, or being educated or uneducated. These are sources of culture that are every bit as influential as having a Maltese or Irish family background.

The choices we make in life are so often based on the range of options that are, or are not, available to us. Most people depend on the limits of their experience for a sense of these options. Many people have no idea that the life they lead is only one possible way that they could live. What may be possible is nevertheless inconceivable if one has not encountered it in some way.

A sociological appreciation of these personal limits helps to extend one's imagination and knowledge beyond these barriers to private understanding. This is because sociology, in making the link between personal experience and social position, is able to show how the former is dependent on the latter, in families, neighbourhood, nation, and time. It is also able to make these connections by constantly examining people who live lives different from our own. And when we regularly see how other people's lives are determined by their place in the cultural scheme of things, we can more easily acknowledge the influence of culture and social position on our own life and experience.

Second, as modern individuals, we are no longer simply affected by what happens in the local community or state. Our houses and cars are linked up to world media. Our local economies are dependent on overseas ones. The very atmosphere we breath is affected by events in Brazilian rainforests or aerosol industries in Sydney. There is a greater need to understand these interdependencies than ever before. The attempt to understand these global problems and their solutions, or barriers to their solution, is not simply an academic exercise. A sociological style of thinking is clearly the most relevant and practical equipment for the challenge of globalisation facing us all, academic or not.

And in the context of all this talk about globalisation there are two further insights that are worth noting. In the first place, the transformation of the local by the foreign is a process that has had a long history. Folly's butter and toast, and her chickens were all European in origin. In more contemporary terms, her tea, her art deco clock, and all her photos were, in one way or another, imported products from North America, Great Britain or Ceylon (as Sri Lanka was called then). Also the mass movement of people from the continents of Europe, Asia, or Africa, movements that brought both Folly and myself to this country, is a comparatively recent phenomenon. These movements are linked to global social changes as diverse as the Industrial Revolution, the French Revolution, European colonialism and the two world wars.

In the second place, and just as relevant to our present concerns, it was these processes themselves that gave rise and impetus to the development of sociology itself. Sociology was born of the strong desire to understand the political ruptures and social changes that began sweeping Europe in the nineteenth century. In this way, sociology is particularly well equipped in studying and monitoring the processes that have created various types of modern people and globalising influence.

Some historical and intellectual background

In the nineteenth century, as a result of the industrial changes sweeping Europe, a massive migration of workers from rural areas swelled the new urban factories. Farmers became factory workers, and then clerks, in the new industrial order. Community ties weakened as people left their villages to work in the cities. Families became isolated and dependent on each other like never before. In that context, the values of privacy and sentimentality became more widespread, as did the experience of anonymity, appalling work conditions, and urban squalor (Nisbet 1966).

Religious influence began to radically wane as Church property was confiscated by the State. Intellectuals also increased their enlightenment project of criticism of all things that did not conform to the principles of reason. Key among these targets of criticism were traditional authorities, such as monarchy and religion. And because of increasing levels of literacy, more people every year became able to read this criticism.

These changes to economy and society attracted major interest from the moral philosophers of the day, and these people became the forerunners of today's sociologists. A great interest developed in the topics of migration, secularisation, community, property and capital, labour conditions, and the nature of work (Nisbet 1966, pp. 24–31). Theorists such as Karl Marx, Max Weber, Émile Durkheim, Georg Simmel, Ferdinand Tönnies, and Auguste Comte were among the many who attempted to theorise about these new living conditions. Many saw these changes as largely negative. Some, however, saw them as ultimately for the good.

Theorists, such as Marx, concentrated on the structure of social classes and their relationship to one another. He was a critic of capitalist culture (Beilharz 1991a, p. 173), a culture that, he believed, upheld the idea of the production of wealth as the central most important human value. The negative consequences of privileging the idea of wealth production are further taken up by more contemporary theorists, such as Louis Althusser or members of what was known as the Frankfurt School. Theodor Adorno, Herbert Marcuse, Erich Fromm, and others were members of this famous European institute. These ideas are also sometimes discussed as a perspective or an approach called 'conflict theory' or 'critical social science'.

Other theorists, such as Max Weber, believed that capitalism was only part of our problem; the increasing bureaucratisation of modern life was also crucial in constraining free will and action (Beilharz 1991b, p. 226). Weber's work placed more emphasis on the role of ideas as people conceive of them, the different types of authority to which we are daily subject, and how organisations undermine participation and democracy.

Theorists such as Émile Durkheim, and more recently Talcott Parsons and his followers, took a more conservative view of modern culture. Parsons argued that industrialisation was not necessarily destructive, but was merely evidence of social change from one form of society to another. Conflict and disorientation were adjustment problems or difficulties that arose when some of these changes produced 'abnormal' responses (Langer 1991, p. 73). This view is sometimes called a 'functionalist' approach because it assumes conflict to be a transitional, rather than normal, state of social affairs.

Most of the above theorists tend to treat social life as if all human meaning stems from economy, politics, and large-scale organisation alone. They also believe that sociology can identify social processes in 'factual' ways, similar to the way natural scientists attempt to identify 'laws' of nature. They have all contributed in their own way to the belief, in evidence in so many sociology textbooks, that sociology is a science. But not all sociologists see things that way.

For one thing, there are many sociologists who do not believe in the 'grand theory' that politics and economy are the main motivators of individual behaviour. Irving Goffman (1967), and Peter Berger and Thomas Luckmann (1966), for example, believe that people are driven by meanings that they discover in face-to-face interactions. People develop a theory of what to do and how to act by copying and analysing what others around them do and say. This approach is sometimes labelled 'symbolic interactionist' or 'phenomenological'.

Other sociologists believe that the idea of accurately representing the 'other' in society presents a problem. How do we ever really know what others mean by their actions? At best, perhaps, we can say that our social theories about the world ('sociological' ones or 'lay' ones) are stories that we share for a time to help us feel that we are in control and 'know' the world.

The world then, in this way, may be a product of a series of changing stories that were agreed upon and then discarded when their ability to convince us weakened substantially. In that way, perhaps, modern history is merely the history of our attempts at surveillance and control. Michel Foucault is one of the key inspirations for this line of thought, but it is also characteristic of the body of ideas called 'poststructuralism' (Aggar 1991).

Another interesting observation about most sociologists is that they have tended to be men. The male point of view that has dominated sociology has tended to take the male body, emotions, self, politics, or social experience as the norm. This is clearly not a valid view, and feminist perspectives now represent ongoing critical voices in most sociological analysis and debate.

The changes that introduced sociology to Europe were similarly, but more recently, to introduce sociology to Australia. The Australian social sciences experienced their greatest growth after 1945, having been battered by the Great Depression, startled by the declining power of the United Kingdom in the Pacific region, and having experienced the rapid program of postwar industrialisation, urbanisation, and immigration that began in that period.

Although sociology subjects were variously offered by the University of Sydney between 1910 and 1930, the first professor of sociology in Australia finally took up his chair as recently as 1958 at the University of New South Wales (Encel 1984).

Since then, most universities in Australia have established sociology de except perhaps some of the more conservative and older universities.

As was the case in Europe, most of the initial interest and staff came losophy, anthropology, and education. And in all the departments establis then, the theoretical ideas of these disciplines continue to proliferate in one ... or another. Sometimes the ideas of these intellectuals are present as 'perspectives', 'camps', or 'factions' of thought among academics. More commonly these ideas are somewhat blended. They will appear in individual sociologists' work as 'influences' on their personal ideas and writing.

Contemporary concerns of Australian sociology

Sociology contains a diverse array of specialities: the sociology of marriage and the family; the sociology of media and cultural studies; the sociology of migration; the sociology of sexuality and gender; the sociology of health and medicine; and many more besides these. But what each of these specialised fields have in common is an interest in four *levels* of analysis. Most sociologists work at one or more of these levels within their particular fields of expertise. These levels, which also constitute the major sections of this book, are the social self, community, nation, and globalisation.

The social self

It is common to view the individual self in psychological terms, but as parts of this chapter have already suggested, there is another way. The formation of identity may be seen as being influenced by the major groups to which one is exposed in the family, at school and at work. In addition to this, the role of one's social position within any of these environments is also important to the kinds of values and attitudes one may come to hold. Being the oldest in the family is a different experience from being the youngest. Being on the assembly line in a Ford car plant will give a person a different view of working for Ford than being one of its white-collar executives.

An important key to understanding the social processes operating at this level is the identification of how others treat you in that social position, because it is the variable ways that others treat you that shape one's experience of being in a certain social class, or being a member of a certain gender or ethnic group, or holding a certain status at work. Because we rarely pan back to see and think about the context of people's treatment of us, we often see these matters in terms of individual personality and character instead of culture and socialisation.

Community

The idea of community has been a popular concern of sociologists all over the world, especially since a romantic, rural notion of community is believed to have been destroyed by the social effects of industrialism and modern urbanisation. In Australia, the idea of community is regularly explored through sociological studies of whole towns and suburbs. There is much debate about what this word *community* actually means.

A popular term with nostalgic connotations, it is also used as a political device to gloss over the internal differences of groups. For example, who is the Chinese community in Australia? Is it the Chinese from Hong Kong? those from Singapore? or the Australian-born Chinese whose great-grandparents mined the gold fields around Bendigo in the last century? Do Christian Chinese identify with their Muslim counterparts? Do any of these people want to be lumped together as if they 'naturally' shared the same aspirations and values? Who is calling them 'the Chinese community' and for what purposes? What, then, is valuable and problematic about attempting to examine the 'idea of community' in Australia?

Nation

The idea of nationhood has its problems too. Who are these people called 'Australians'? What is this thing called 'the Bronzed Aussie'? Is Australia the egalitarian society that it projects itself as? That Australians have no 'culture', or at least no 'unique' culture, has been a long-standing lament. Is this true? Can this be true? And now, for several years, there has been talk about the republic and changing the flag. Cathy Freeman, a Commonwealth Games track and field gold medallist, ran with two of our flags (the national and the Aboriginal flags) and was castigated for not flying the flag with the Union Jack in the left-hand corner only. What does any of this say about our conflicting sentiments and ideas about nationhood?

And the increasing number of Asian immigrants from Vietnam and China in the last few years has regularly raised debate about migration and cultural identity, as has similar migration to all Western countries. As traveller Bill Bryson reflected on his trip through the USA when he nostalgically drove up to what he thought was a British icon, a BP petrol station: 'it wasn't really like England — it didn't have a man with a turban at the cash register!' (Bryson 1989). Both British and Australian identity are in the process of change.

Globalisation

No consideration of life in Australia, and no understanding of how we are created as individuals, is complete without tracing how the forces outside Australia have shaped us. In this respect, we must look not only at the politics of the environment and our economic dependencies, but also at the media images and social movements that have influenced us. In 1995, 'Mighty Morphin Power Rangers' influenced children in similar ways to *Mutant Ninja Turtles* a few years before them, or as 'Astroboy', 'Prince Planet' or 'The Samurai' had for generations before that.

The international Green movement, the women's movement, and Amnesty International are bringing about quiet revolutions that shape us as much as do the 'McDonaldisation' of Australia and the development of information superhighways. Events in the former Soviet Union and in East Timor are felt by political allies and critics here to be urgent problems that are relevant to Australian environmental concerns and our decisions to sell arms to neighbouring powers.

To finish where we began

Folly had never heard of 'Astroboy', and the 'Mighty Morphin Power Rangers' were some thirty years from karate-chopping their way onto our television screens. She had some notion that beetles were not only the bugs on her plants and that four musicians in England had adopted a different spelling of that name. UB40 and the Crash Test Dummies would surely have confused her even more than the Beatles had then with their name. She was, as most of the kids in my street wisely pronounced, 'old fashioned'.

This is the common attitude of people everywhere. Here are 'we', and there stands the outsider, 'the other'. Historical events, social circumstances, and individual biography all conspire to create conditions that promote our tendency to see the differences in each other. What is it about these conditions, however, that allow us to see ourselves in the other so that, at the end of the day, two remarkably different people can sit together on an old club lounge and discuss photos?

Ironically, the answer is not to be found in any conditions as such. Rather, it is in the way that these events and experiences can be understood. With careful and sympathetic attention to what is common and what is unique in history, in organisations, in interpersonal relations, and in the movement of ideas, it is possible to acquire understanding, however modest. The systematic attempt to gain such an understanding can be seen in the thoughts and arguments of all the best sociological writing. I hope that you are also able to discern such an understanding and imagination in the following chapters, as the authors introduce their respective areas.

Discussion questions

1   What is sociology, and how is it different from your understanding of other social sciences such as, for example, economics or politics?
2   What is the sociological imagination, and does this 'quality of mind' exist in the other social sciences?
3   What is the relationship between social position and social opportunity? To help you think about the answer to this, try to answer the following questions first:
    •   How has being a man or a woman hindered your opportunities in certain circumstances or within certain groups?
    •   How has it helped?
4   What is the relationship between social change and an individual life? To help you think about the answer, try to answer these questions first:
    •   In what ways are the behaviour and values of people between eighteen and twenty-five similar to their counterparts twenty years ago?
    •   How are they different?
    •   What are the sociological reasons for these similarities and differences?
5   What is the relationship between authority and social control? To help you answer this question, think about the following:

- How has educational philosophy in Australia shaped what you think you understand about the world? (Did you study fishing or hunting at school? Why not?)

Or try thinking about these questions:

- How has the media, television or popular music shaped or validated your experience and/or values?
- Could you have ignored or shut out these influences?
- If not, what control do you believe you have in respect of them?

Recommended reading

For nice brief introductions to some of the major sociological theorists try dipping and browsing through:

- Beilharz, P. (ed.) 1991, *Social Theory: A Guide to Central Thinkers*, Allen & Unwin, Sydney.
- Cuff, E. C. and Payne, G. C. F. 1984, *Perspectives in Sociology*, George Allen & Unwin, London.

For some discussion of local men and women of sociology, try:

- Austin, D. J. 1984, *Australian Sociologies*, Allen & Unwin, Sydney.

There are also some brief primers of sociology (100 pages or so) that may be worth a look. The following one is satisfactory but does not have significant discussions of feminist or poststructural approaches:

- Willis, E. 1995, *The Sociological Quest: An Introduction to the Study of Social Life*, Allen & Unwin, Sydney.

If you have time for a broader and more reflective introduction, you might try:

- Lynd, R. S. 1946, *Knowledge For What?*, Princeton University Press, Princeton.
- Mills, C. Wright 1959, *The Sociological Imagination*, Oxford University Press, New York.

For a good introduction to some feminist ideas in sociology, see:

- Smith, D. 1987, *Everyday Life as Problematic: A Feminist Sociology*, Northeastern University Press, Boston, chs 2 and 3.
- Miller, C. and Swift, K. 1976, *Words and Women*, Doubleday, New York, chs 2 and 7.

Trying to find a good, clear introduction to the ideas of postmodernism or poststructuralism *and* one that might be accessible to people new to the social sciences is near impossible. You may gain some useful impressions from:

- Game, A. 1991, *Undoing the Social*, Open University Press, London, preface and ch. 1.
- Aggar, B. 1991, 'Critical Theory, Poststructuralism, Postmodernity: Their Sociological Significance', *Annual Review of Sociology*, vol. 17, pp. 105–31.

New sociology students often find they are unfamiliar with many of the terms and concepts used by sociologists. For help in deciphering the 'language' of sociology, refer to:

- Kellehear, A. 1990, 'Jargonbusters', in *Every Student's Guide to Sociology*, Thomas Nelson, Melbourne, pp. 75–82.
- Marshall, G. 1994, *The Concise Oxford Dictionary of Sociology*, Oxford University Press, Oxford.

The Social Self

'Who are you?'
'Who are *You?*' said the Caterpillar
This was not an encouraging opening
for a conversation. Alice replied,
rather shyly, 'I — hardly know, Sir,
just at present — at least I know who I
was when I got up this morning, but I
think I must have been changed
several times since then.'

Lewis Carroll
Alice's Adventures in Wonderland

Chapter 2

The Self in Families

Kerreen Reiger

The questions 'Who am I?' and 'Where do I fit in?' are important to most of us. Take the story of Fluffy the porcupine, for example (Lester 1986). His parents had chosen what they thought was 'such a pretty name', much better than the more common Spike or Pokey. However, after trying hard by rolling in marshmallow and shaving cream, Fluffy knew he 'simply wasn't'. He became quite despondent until he came across another misfit: a rhinoceros whose parents had called him Hippo. As friends, they could laugh together about their identity problems.

One of the most important starting points for developing a sociological understanding is ourselves. In modern Western society we take for granted certain ideas about what an individual identity or a self is, as well as about how families affect our development. In this chapter we will explore these assumptions and the extent to which they reflect particular aspects of Western history.

Since the origins of sociology in the nineteenth century, social scientists have struggled to make sense of the relationship between individual and society, while paying attention to groups such as families, which fall somewhere in between. In this project, they have not been alone. Not only some of the West's most famous social and political theorists, but also politicians and clergy, and even ordinary people themselves, have asked some fundamental questions concerning the 'modern' way of life that emerged with industrial capitalist society. A central question has been 'What has been happening to the ties that hold people together in groups, including families?'. A further and closely related question is whether there is anything distinctive about 'modern' individuals, or to put it another way, whether 'modern' people are any different than those in traditional, pre-industrial societies. These questions then create the difficult tasks of explaining and evaluating any changes in behaviour and ways of life.

Already we are asking basic sociological questions, and in doing so, we both reflect and go against some trends in modern society. On the one hand, issues of individuality are peculiarly modern; they are not of much concern in many non-industrial, close-knit communities. Most of us are interested in questions of the self or the individual, or what recent theorists call 'subjectivity': the condition of being a human subject. Articles in the popular press, television shows, and movies all depict characters 'searching for themselves', with the questions of 'Who am I?' and 'Who can I become?' being typical themes. However, while sociology too shares this interest in individuality, it also regards it with a certain scepticism. Why are we so commonly preoccupied with personal identity and immediate family relationships, with the quality of our interaction with parents, children or partners? Has this been true of other generations and cultures? Before considering sociological accounts of the self and its formation, especially in family life, there are two other points to be made. We need, first, to look more closely at our assumptions about what it is to be an individual or have a self. Second, we must briefly inspect the theories of individuality derived from biology and psychology, because these tend to dominate public discussion of this issue.

What is the self?

So how do we usually think about our selves or individuality? It is commonly taken for granted that identity consists of basic, intrinsic characteristics that emerge during life. Some people conceive of this in spiritual terms as a 'soul'; others as a combination of a particular body with its own personality. One way or another, it is commonly believed that we are unique selves with a capacity for reasoning and acting. Indeed, our laws and values are based on concepts of individual freedom and responsibility for behaviour. If you commit a crime, you are held accountable. You are expected to be able to say why you did it, just as in everyday life we expect others to be able to explain the motivations for their actions. In other words, we take it for granted that human beings' behaviour has meaning that can be shared with others.

However, these concepts of what it is to be a person are not universal, but vary historically and from one culture to another. Take, for instance, nineteenth-century debates about whether women were legal 'persons', able to own property, have custody of children, or receive formal education (Bacchi 1990, pp. 7–14). Many of these arguments reflected specific Western assumptions that to be a 'person' was to be a 'rational' individual, and women were seen as essentially emotional. To be a citizen was also to be capable of holding possessions and fighting to defend them: to be, in short, a property owner and a potential warrior. Similarly, Aboriginal Australians were not counted in censuses until after 1961 and had few legal rights, even over their own children (Burgmann 1993, p. 29). Like slaves in the supposed 'democracy' of ancient Athens, they were not considered citizens, because they were not regarded by those in power as real 'people'. Their own concepts of personhood certainly contrasted with those of White society, for Aboriginal people derive their identity from their kin or tribal network.

We can contrast our ideas of individuality with those of non-Western and pre-modern cultures. In some Melanesian cultures it is not uncommon for 'personhood' to be conceived of as something that you develop through living a good life, rather than a quality you are born with. It is through the giving of goods to others, and the moral qualities that are therefore gained, that you can become a 'a big man'. In non-Western societies there is usually much more interest in, and concern for, the group than the individual. Selfhood is part of clan, tribe, or lineage identity (Macintyre 1986, pp. 250–3). Whether someone does right or wrong brings honour or shame on everyone connected to him or her. In other societies, and even in the West in the Middle Ages, we can see different notions from those surrounding modern individuality. People were not assumed to be naturally acquisitive in the Middle Ages; indeed, taking interest on a loan was a serious sin in the eyes of the Church. Community standards and needs were placed above those of individuals. This, of course, meant little personal freedom in choice of occupation or marriage partner, but people were not thought to be at emotional or psychological risk because of such restrictions. Instead, they were the norms or rules that tied the society together.

It has only been as a result of the many changes in Western society over the last five hundred years that our current ideas of the individual self have developed. They can only be understood in the context of the economic changes associated with the rise of capitalist commerce and industrial production, and the accompanying movement towards more widespread political rights. Furthermore, as family systems were affected by the changes in everyday life, new notions of domestic life, and of individuality, arose. Much production of clothing and foodstuffs was taken over by industry, so households lost their economic basis in that their members no longer worked together. Rather, individual members went out to work, often in towns, for wages paid to them as individuals. In the nineteenth century, new ideas about the family and about the home as a place of retreat from the world of business and industry emerged along with the changes taking place in the organisation of work. For men especially, home was to become the little 'castle' in which they could be most truly themselves. For women, of course, it continued to be a centre of everyday work. It is out of this series of economic, political, and social developments that modern concepts of what it is to be an individual and to have a self have arisen. Along with these historical developments, we need to understand the impact of new forms of knowledge about people's make-up and behaviour.

Biological and psychological theories of the individual

In the twentieth century we have been influenced, on the one hand, by the growth of biological sciences, especially of genetics, and on the other, by psychology. Both claim to offer crucial interpretations of what it is to be an individual, and we will examine some of their ideas before turning to sociological understandings. What is known as 'social Darwinism' pervaded the emergence of the natural and social sciences in the late nineteenth and early twentieth centuries. Ideas of natural selection and the survival of the fittest were applied to human populations, usually in colonial settings and in racially oppressive ways. The 'White Australia' policy of denying legal rights to non-Whites merely reflected widespread beliefs about the superiority of Western culture and the greater intelligence of the White race. It was in this setting that the modern science of genetics originated, with its stress on the individual's inherited genetic make-up as the primary influence on human behaviour. Debates on the respective input of parents and grandparents, and on whether intelligence was evident in the shape of one's head, now sound naive. Controversy about the effects of 'nature' or heredity versus 'nurture' or social environment have continued throughout the subsequent decades (Murphy 1986, p. 16). In recent years the greater sophistication of modern genetics has given us much more credible information about the role of bodily factors in making a person who they are. They have also, though, given an aura of scientific authority to some claims that are more dubious. Sociobiology, established by zoologist E. O. Wilson in the 1960s, has attempted to explain behaviour primarily in terms of individuals' attempts to maximise their genetic advantage and pass it on to offspring. This line of thinking emphasises the effect of evolutionary patterns and sees individuals mainly as self-interested animals, determined overwhelmingly by their biological traits. These ideas have had considerable popular appeal and have attracted a good deal of media attention.

Such extreme biological determinism has largely gone out of academic and political fashion, however, along with its social Darwinist underpinnings. Nazism showed the dangers of the 'science of eugenics' — the study of the supposed 'quality' of the population. However, the idea that people are no more than the product of their genes, and can be ranked accordingly, still has appeal, especially to those who want to maintain others in positions of social inequality. It also is making a comeback, therefore, in situations of national conflict, and the term 'ethnic cleansing' has given new political meaning to determining people's status on the basis of biological characteristics. Since the 1970s, other developments have also raised new questions about the physical nature of individuals. Procedures in medical science, such as *in vitro* fertilisation, associated reproductive technologies, organ transplants, and forms of genetic engineering still being developed, give rise to new conceptions of what it is to be a person. That as an adult you are merely the grown version of what you were when born is no longer necessarily so. We have not yet come to terms with the implications of organ transplants and other ways in which bodies can be altered — not even cosmetic surgery. What we can say is that our understanding of what it is to be a self is still undergoing considerable change in the light of contemporary technological developments.

The second major influence on our concept of the individual in the twentieth century has been the emergence of psychology. This social science discipline has carved out its territory primarily as a method for studying the individual, but just as there are many forms of human behaviour, there are many psychologies. Casting his shadow over all of us, though, has been the figure of Sigmund Freud, founder of psychoanalysis and one of the main contributors to a fundamental change in our thinking about human beings. Thanks largely to Freud's subversive influence, we tend to look beneath the surface of behaviour, seeking hidden motives and conflicts, including those stemming from childhood. The preoccupation with the private lives of royalty and politicians, as shown by the huge sales of 'tell all' biographies, has only developed in recent decades. This suggests that the popular perception of individuals has been affected by Freud's refusal to take them at face value. Even if psychoanalytic therapy is not everyone's 'cup of tea', Freud has shaped our thinking very profoundly. He saw the individual as an unstable mixture of biological drives or instincts, unconscious desires, and social constraints, and his concepts have profoundly shaped much professional practice. However, not only counsellors, teachers, and social workers have been influenced. Terms such as *inferiority complex*, *the ego*, and *libido* have passed into common usage. Parents have been bombarded since the 1930s with psychologists' advice about rearing children. Many of these disagree with Freud's ideas about the formation of the self within the dynamics of family life in early childhood, offering alternative theories. Some, such as behaviourist theorists, seek general rules or laws of human behaviour. They claim that, like other animals, humans respond to stimuli that influence patterns of learning. Other 'humanist' psychologists prefer to see people as intrinsically motivated by a search for self-fulfilment or self-realisation. They emphasise the progressive stages of development in the life process.

Sociology has been influenced by all the developments discussed so far: economic, social, and intellectual changes affecting the formation of the individual in modern society. It also has its own contribution to make, however, particularly through its focus on the self as intrinsically a 'social' self, one formed by society. Rather than assuming that the individual is a predetermined entity ready to unfold from birth onwards according to biological factors, a sociological perspective stresses that we are inherently social. We are born into a network of other human beings who already have an existing way of life — a culture that is strongly affected by the physical environment, whether it be desert, tropical rainforest, or industrial city.

Forming our selves within families: sociological views

Clearly children are born with certain temperamental dispositions stemming from their genetic constitution as well as from the general condition of being human. We are, after all, creatures inhabiting our bodies first and foremost. We must take in nourishment, eliminate wastes, and maintain bodily functioning. A range of particular capacities or potentials are present at birth, but even these are already affected by social factors. The organisation of the society into which we are born, and the resources available, will impact upon our nutrition and our care as infants. Whether women as mothers are physically healthy will be influenced not only by natural conditions, such as drought or famine, but also by the social conditions of working life and family arrangements. These too can cause mother and child to be short of adequate food and shelter. Mothers then not only can be emotionally stressed, but can also suffer problems of blood pressure and experience difficult childbirth, with associated health problems later. Their babies can be underweight and undernourished, their bodies already damaged by social conditions. This was the situation faced by poor women bearing children outside marriage only a couple of generations ago (Evans and Saunders 1992). These problems still confront young women with drug addiction now, as well as many mothers and children in impoverished, Third-World conditions, including some Aboriginal Australians. It is extremely naive, therefore, to polarise 'biological' and 'social' factors. Rather, a complex interaction takes place between the human organism and its physical and social environment.

One of the main factors in this process, and the importance of the family in it, is the long dependency period of human beings. Relative to other animals, we are born in a remarkably undeveloped state, taking many months to achieve the capacity even to feed ourselves, let alone move around. This means that learning is critical to our capacity to become human — in other words, to be able to interact and communicate with others. We are born not just into some abstract 'society', but also into a particular network of people who share ties of kinship and culture. Different networks may organise household units in very different ways, and often these are not based on a nuclear family. A child inevitably enters some system of social relationships. The cultural patterns are felt very quickly. In some societies birth is secluded, and only women are involved; in others it is a noisy, community celebration; and in most modern hospitals, it is a highly technological, professionalised event (Reiger 1991, pp. 19–23). How the baby is cared for already stamps the imprint of society on the emerging self. As American sociologist Peter Berger puts it, 'Graphically, society not only imposes its patterns upon the infant's behaviour but reaches inside him to organise the functions of his stomach' (Berger 1976, p. 57). In other words, whether babies are fed 'on demand' or on a rigid schedule, as doctors advised in the 1930s in Western countries, and whether they are fed by breast or bottle are social factors that influence the development of both physical and emotional capacities.

One important sociological perspective on the formation of the social self and the significance of the family originated in anthropological studies of small-scale societies. Here the significance of culture could readily be seen. Members learnt the approved ways of behaviour through specific training as children within the family group, whether it was a large clustering of relatives or a small structure of parents and children. Families' socialisation of the next generation was said to be 'functional' in the operation of the entire social system, making individuals behave in accordance with approved traditions. This is, of course, only one approach to considering how the self is shaped, and it tends to emphasise the perspective of society: that there is some system 'out there' that 'needs' people to behave in particular ways. This viewpoint tends to assume that social rules are imposed on a passive self so that the child will learn to fit into approved roles.

The term *role* is important in this tradition of sociology; it refers to the position of an individual within a sub-system of the larger society, such as the family. All the various kin terms — *mother, father, sister, cousin*, and so on — indicate the relative statuses or positions that people are in with respect to each other. Of course these vary widely in their actual meaning. In modern Western society cousins frequently have little to do with each other; in others they are regarded as the equivalent of siblings, part of the mother's kinship bonds. Similarly, modern uncles usually have minimal responsibility for nieces and nephews, whereas in some other cultures they play the 'role' of social father to their sisters' children: they are responsible for their financial support and moral upbringing (Macintyre 1986, pp. 252–6). Whatever the variation in the details of family roles, though, they involve a pattern of expected behaviour that makes social life reasonably predictable and orderly.

There are several aspects to considering how we attain selfhood from within this viewpoint. Humans' great capacity for learning how to behave is shaped first within the intimate environment of early child-rearing. Children imitate and identify with the social roles, including both the tasks and personal characteristics, of adults, especially those of the same sex. They are seen as 'internalising', or taking into themselves, the appropriate ways to behave. This occurs at both conscious and unconscious levels. Some behaviours, such as eating patterns, ways of speaking to elders, and so on, are clearly taught, with a system of rewards and punishment. They vary in detail from one culture to another though. On the Pacific island of Tube Tube, which was studied by Martha Macintyre, for example, children were rarely directly punished, either physically or verbally, but were removed from company until their unacceptable behaviour ceased (Macintyre 1986, p. 255). By contrast, it was not long ago that children in Western societies were regularly subjected to harsh canings, both in household and school settings. Training of children also varies within and between different groups in contemporary Western society (Berger 1976, pp. 109–10).

However, much internalisation of social rules is not so overt. It occurs without conscious learning, merely through the influence and example of those we interact with (see Chapter 3). Other sociologists, then, have focused more on the interpersonal processes associated with growing up. They are more interested in how people interact with each other, and how the child's identity comes to reflect the general ways of behaving in different family contexts. For example, learning about sexual matters and ways of handling emotions are usually absorbed through subtle means, such as tones of voice and the way a baby or young child is physically handled. If we grow up in a family context in which anger is felt to be dangerous and unacceptable, chances are we will have difficulty handling our own angry feelings and those of others, even as an adult. Similarly, if affection has not been expressed openly towards us as children, we are unlikely to find it easy to demonstrate affection towards others. The expression of all emotions is culturally shaped and variable, from wailing noisily with grief to maintaining a traditional English reserve in the face of death. Aspects of our deepest being, though, reflect the power of both unconscious influences and explicit social learning.

Whereas some sociologists give greatest emphasis to the 'interactive' nature of the developing self, others are more interested in examining how the family operates 'in between' the larger society and the individual. The social processes through which the self is formed are specific to time and place — that is, to the circumstances of a given society. They also reflect its power imbalances. In understanding the formation of our selves in the context of families in modern Western societies, several historical developments are significant. The economic and technological changes associated with the industrial revolution and development of a capitalist economy profoundly altered everyday life and family relationships. In pre-industrial times, as in many parts of the world now, all members of the household, even young children, contributed their labour to the family economy. Women and men had different work roles on the farm or in workshops, but marriage was fundamentally an economic, as well as sexual, arrangement. Partners were mutually interdependent and children were a labour resource (Gittins 1985, pp. 4–30). They were not seen as having 'special needs', such as for toys or entertainment. However, the mechanisation of farms and the introduction of factories took away many of their jobs. Men, working-class women, and for a while, their children, went 'out' from home, into a new sphere of life called 'work'. Home eventually became associated with women and children, with leisure (for men), and private life.

This development had profound implications. The separation of home and work meant that children, and many women, came to be seen as men's economic dependants rather than contributors to the household. In middle-class families particularly, a new emphasis was placed on the moral and educational, eventually even the psychological, development of children. Mothers' duties became defined more in terms of children's perceived needs, fathers had less daily contact with other family members, and children became the focus of new attention. By the early twentieth century, compulsory schooling limited children's labour in the home, although it was not uncommon to keep children home at harvest time or to mind younger children. By the interwar years, a new market for toys emerged, which has now flourished (see chapter 6). New values came to influence child-rearing as greater stress was laid on individuality. During the 1930s, experts such as doctors and psychologists emphasised regularity of routine and strict discipline, but by the 1960s this gave way to more lenient 'child-centred' approaches.

Under the influence of American paediatrician Dr Spock, mothers were encouraged to give children more freedom of speech and activity. As most Western families by the later twentieth century had fewer children, emotional patterns were established that were significantly different from those established in pre-industrial families. There were fewer adults to relate to, as well as fewer siblings, because households were less likely to include either relatives, boarders, or servants. Both affection and power became more concentrated. Furthermore, an increased stress on family privacy meant that violence towards women and children remained relatively hidden until recently (Scutt 1983). Although there are now a range of family types, including single-parent families and step-families, the intensity of our family relationships tends to be greater than in other societies (Macintyre 1986, pp. 251–5).

As families and households vary historically and culturally, different practices and ideas influence the 'production' of children as social beings. The self is constructed through involvement in relationships with other people, especially those who are emotionally important. In other words, the self formed in any sort of family system is a 'social' self. As the Fluffy and Hippo story with which we started suggested, we are very much what our families make us. We also struggle, however, to shape our own identity over the course of our lives. As modern Western society values individuality and personal achievement, the questions of 'Who am I?', 'Who may I become?' and 'Where do I belong?' have taken on special importance. However, families are basically *groups*, and consequently, too much 'individuality' can undermine the well-being of the collective. This is the conundrum most of us now live with.

Discussion questions

1 How would you define and describe your self?
2 What social changes have produced modern ideas about the self and how it develops?
3 What is distinctive about a sociological view of the individual compared with biological and psychological ones?
4 What are some of the historical influences on the development of individuals in the context of families?
5 In what ways has your own development as a person been affected by growing up in your particular family context?

Recommended reading

For more introductory material on sociology and the concept of socialisation, see:
*   Bilton, T., Bonnett, K., Jones, P., Starworth, M., Sheard, K., and Webster, A. (ed.) 1987, *Introductory Sociology*, Macmillan, Basingstoke, ch. 1, s. 2.

On cross-cultural styles of rearing children, you could try:
*   Murphy, R. 1986, *Cultural and Social Anthropology: An Overture*, 2nd edn, Prentice Hall, Englewood Cliffs, NJ.
*   Stephens, W. N. 1963, *The Family in Cross-cultural Perspective*, Holt, Rinehart & Winston, New York.

For more information concerning the development of the Western form of family life since the emergence of industrial capitalism, and Australian material too, you could well enjoy reading parts of:
*   Shorter, E. 1976, *The Making of the Modern Family*, Basic Books, New York.
*   Stone, L. 1979, *The Family, Sex, and Marriage in England, 1500–1800*, Penguin, Harmondsworth, chs 6 and 13.
*   Poster, M. 1975, *Critical Theory of the Family*, Pluto Press, London (more difficult, but see ch. 7 especially).
*   Gilding, M. 1991, *The Making of the Australian Family*, Allen & Unwin, Sydney.
*   Burns, A., Goodnow, J. and Bottomley, G. (eds) 1983, *The Family in the Modern World*, Allen & Unwin, Sydney.

For critiques of family dynamics and their effects on individuals, particularly women and children, see particularly:
*   Segal, L. (ed.) 1983, *What is to be Done about the Family? Crisis in the Eighties*, Penguin, Harmondsworth.
*   Barrett, M. (ed.) 1988, *Women's Oppression Today*, Verso, London.

Chapter 3

The Gendered Self

Katy Richmond

Lyngstrand [after a moment]
Have you ever thought — I mean, have you ever thought really
seriously about marriage, Miss Wangel?
Boletta [giving him a glance]
About ... ? No.
Lyngstrand
I have.
Boletta
Really?
Lyngstrand
Yes, I often think about things like that — and marriage in particular.
And I've read a great many books on the subject. I think marriage
might almost be regarded as a sort of miracle ... The way the
woman is gradually transformed till she comes to resemble her
husband.

(Ibsen 1965)

We conceive of ourselves as having a fixed sense of self, but in fact it is very much a floating self. We are continually forming and reforming who we are, how we see things, our ideas about where we want to go. Sonia Tolstoy, the wife of the famous Russian novelist Leo Tolstoy, wrote when she was twenty-one, 'I am nothing but a miserable crushed worm, whom no one wants, whom no one loves, a useless creature with morning sickness, and a big belly, two rotten teeth, and a bad temper, a battered sense of dignity, and a love which nobody wants and which nearly drives me insane'. A few years later she wrote, 'It makes me laugh to read over this diary. It's so full of contradictions, and one would think I was such an unhappy woman. Yet is there a happier woman than I?' (Tolstoy 1975, p. 144).

Often we feel dismayed by our 'selves'. We may perceive we have been forcibly assigned an identity by society (which we may or may not like). We may think we have a different 'inner' self from the one we think is apparent to others. And we may feel intimidated by what we think others think about us. We may want to move in a different direction in the future, but we may perceive this future pathway to be blocked by almost insurmountable difficulties. Finally, we may be conscious of wishing to be a certain sort of person, but we may see ourselves as behaving — against our best intentions — in quite a different way.

However our thinking may have locked us unnecessarily into a corner. For one thing, 'society' does not exist (except as a concept to help us think about things). We are not embedded 'in society' but in the context of a network of overlapping social relationships. Some of these may be experienced as oppressive, but others may be liberating and tolerant. Second, we may perceive that others see us in a certain way, but we may be wrong: others may see us differently. In fact, the odds are that there are as many different perceptions of who we are as there are people gazing upon us. Third, we may underestimate our own capacities. We can change how others see us, but more than that, we can institute real changes in our selves. We can change our social relationships and move to new and more supportive friendships. We can find new role models. We can move away from those whom we think perceive us negatively, or wish to mould us in ways we do not want to be moulded. And we can (to some degree at least) modify our public image so that we may appear to be the person others wish us to be. Or better, we can actively strive to force on others another image of ourselves: an image we are happy with. To institute these sorts of changes can be challenging. Yet people can successfully reject the identity thrust upon them by their families.

Judith Okely (1978), for example, says that if her family and school socialisation experiences had succeeded in moulding her successfully she would not have become an anthropologist. She was sent to a top English girls' boarding-school, and the idea was that she was to get 'good' education, but then she would marry a surgeon or a lawyer. If things had worked out the way her parents wanted, her sense of self would be centred around her children, her grandchildren, her beautiful house, and her reputation as an accomplished hostess. But her parents (and the school) failed.

What has sociology said about how we develop a sense of self? Much of sociology has been about building up the 'big picture' by analysing central social institutions and systems of social control. Sociology has been largely dominated by an interest in the public domain: the world of economics and the labour force, politics, religion, law, education, and bureaucracy. Few sociologists have examined the private world of the self in any depth. So, when sociologists have discussed the self, the analysis has often been oblique and general — really suggesting that the broad macrocosmic social structure and processes of social change are what shapes the individual self — and has not been too concerned about the details.

Of the several broad sociological perspectives, only symbolic interactionism has analysed in detail the accomplishment of a sense of self. Functionalist (or social systems) theory and Marxist theory have each concentrated on the 'big picture' (though from vastly different points of view), not the interactions of daily life. On matters of sex and gender, none of these sorts of sociology have had much to say. Symbolic interactionism did not develop any sort of theory about sex and gender; functionalism mirrored the views of conventional patriarchal society; and Marxism (to a large degree) thought all would be well if women just entered the workforce, where they could be liberated. Sociological understanding of gender and the self really only begins with the advent of the 'second wave' of feminism in the late 1960s and early

1970s. The writers who have had most to say about sex, gender, and the self have been feminists, writing within a feminist sociological, historical, or philosophical framework.

Functionalist sociology portrayed human beings as socialised primarily by family life (and only later by school and church). Within this sort of sociology, the work of socialisation was said to be over by early adulthood. Talcott Parsons, for example, pictured boys as being socialised within the home to take up an instrumental role in society: they were to be very goal-directed, they were to be fully employed in the paid labour force, and they were to become the breadwinners for their future families. Girls were trained for 'expressive' roles: their universe would be bounded by the front gate of their homes, they were intended to take on roles as wives and mothers, and their job was largely to socialise young children, and to create harmony and happiness within the home.

Critics of Parsons have commented first on his use of language. Women working at home as wives and mothers also undertake instrumental roles in a very goal-directed way: getting meals, dealing with the laundry, shopping, cleaning, and so on. Women's work can hardly be described as primarily 'expressive'. Other critics of functionalist sociology have claimed that it creates an 'oversocialised' conception of a human being. People, they argue, are not 'determined' by their upbringing to the extent that functionalist sociology suggests. In other words, socialisation is a much more hit-and-miss affair. Parents may disagree about their children's upbringing. The mother may encourage musical talents in a boy while the father may push him to concentrate on sporting skills. Moreover, parental attempts at socialisation could result in a child whose accomplishments diverge markedly from the parents' intentions (a boy might be belted so severely for failing at school that he simply stops studying altogether). Or children can simply pretend to follow their parents' precepts, but maintain a quiet determination to be someone different when they grow up. Paul Bowles, an American writer, describes his view of his upbringing in this way:

> Very early I understood that I would always be kept from doing what I enjoyed and forced to do that which I did not ... Thus I became an expert in the practice of deceit ... [T]he family ... had an idea of how they wanted me to be; but insofar as I resembled it, I should remain subjugated to them, or so it seemed to me then. So, secretly I rejected every suggestion while pretending to accept it.

> Bowles 1972, pp. 17, 22

Still other critics have pointed out that masculinity and femininity are not learnt as general precepts, but are learnt in the context of specific social environments. They say that there is no such thing as 'learning to be a man' or 'learning to be a woman'. The meaning of masculinity and femininity varies enormously from one social context to another, and moreover, this content changes markedly over time. So the argument is that parents (and the broader social environment) do not socialise a girl to be a girl, but rather to be a specific sort of girl — for example, a first-born, working-class, Italian Catholic girl living in Adelaide. Thus concepts of 'appropriate girlhood' can vary enormously. For example, Gillian Bottomley describes a Greek pre-wedding 'bed-making' celebration she went to in Australia in 1971, where the bride had a trousseau that included twenty-three nightdresses, twelve pairs of sheets and pillow-slips, and 'enough kitchen equipment to open a restaurant' (Bottomley 1992, p. 97). This, says Bottomley, was a trousseau much larger in scale than any Anglo-Australian girl would have — if she had a trousseau at all.

To say all this in a different way: the socialising process may involve the learning of a wide variety of cultural norms and values associated with religion, gender, eth-nicity, nationality, and local identity. Children face a variety of different inputs. Moreover, they may be socialised within a household in which there is major dis-agreement about how they are to be trained. And socialisation is often differentiated by birth order: the first-born is often treated differently from later-born children. Children can reject aspects of their upbringing and follow new role models: an aunt, a cousin, a school teacher, for instance.

All of this privileges the family as a site of socialisation. Yet children have a vari-ety of non-familial experiences: crèches, kindergartens, schools, the media, church, neighbourhoods. The experiences of boys often differ significantly from those of girls. Even the physical environment of childhood is gendered. A boy and a girl may live in the same family home on a suburban block, but the real environment for the boy includes the street and neighbouring parks, creeks, and public land; the girl's environment is much more likely to be confined to her home, the home of her friends, and her school yard. Her physical confinement is largely constructed through fear. She is told 'Don't talk to strange men … Hurry on home … Come home before dark … Don't walk down that dark lane'. Later on, at school, the girl and her friends may talk on the margins of the school yard; the boy and his friends control the yard and the playing fields. In church, girls may sit quietly at the front (confined often by their 'good clothes'); the boys may be allowed to play at the back.

However, the gendered nature of the physical environment, neighbourhoods, schools, and churches varies considerably from place to place. Growing up in a White, middle-class, Protestant suburb in a large metropolis is quite different from growing up in a rural community, such as that described by Ken Dempsey (1992). One of the most significant factors of life in a rural town is the high level of interac-tion between members of the community and the high level of visibility each person experiences in everyday life. For these reasons, the subordination of women to men has the following visible result for local boys and girls: 'An analysis of diaries … pro-vided by all 156 secondary-school pupils aged fourteen and older [in Smalltown] … showed that 92 per cent of boys played football and 80 per cent of girls watched it on a Saturday. Only 28 per cent of the girls reported playing any sport on a Saturday … Not one boy reported watching a girl's sport' (Dempsey 1992, p. 56).

But even this story of socialisation makes it sound too simple. Socialisation, as the symbolic interactionists in particular have described it, is not something 'acquired', like a coat, during childhood, but is an ongoing process. We are socialised by our family, resocialised by our school experiences, socialised again by friends, relatives, significant adults, and resocialised later at university, in marriage, during parenting, and later through processes of widowhood and old age. So we can change.

Gender as a social construct

Much of the feminist movement in the late 1960s and early 1970s was focused on constructing a model of women as oppressed by men. The term *patriarchy* was invoked to describe, in general terms, the nature of the social structure through which men controlled women. Feminist writing attempted to understand how men and women were socialised. Nancy Chodorow (1978), for example, in her book *The Reproduction of Mothering*, argued from a Freudian perspective that, because mothers (mostly) undertake the care of children, there is reproduced in girl children a very strong sense of having to play an important role in the bringing together of groups of people in any social group to which they belong (including the family). One of many writers who argue in this way is Jean Baker Miller. She says that 'Women's sense of self becomes very much organized around being able to make and then to maintain affiliations and relationships. Eventually, for many women the threat of disruption of an affiliation is perceived not as just a loss of a relationship but as something closer to a total loss of self' (Miller 1976, p. 87).

Such statements about 'women in general' are now seen as 'essentialist'. These sorts of ideas construe all men as having certain characteristics, and all women as having certain other characteristics. But Judith Grant (among others) has criticised such an approach to the understanding of gender and the self. She argues that this sort of thinking is sometimes useful political rhetoric, but at bottom it 'tends to remain within a binary us-and-them paradigm' (Grant 1993, p. 67). Her argument is that there is no universal experience of 'being a woman' or 'being a man'.

To summarise this point, masculinity and femininity are learnt in social contexts. There is a complex interplay between social constructions of gender identity, sexual identity, class, and ethnicity. Furthermore, social constructions of masculinity and femininity are not fixed: they change forms continuously in historical processes that are often difficult to 'fix' at any moment in time. We will now consider three examples.

Femininity in an English boarding-school

Some of the complex ways in which a particular form of femininity is framed within the context of a particular social class setting are indicated in Okely's discussion of the way young upper-class girls were 'moulded' by an English boarding-school in the 1950s. (The scenario described by Okely, including her description of having to find a secret place to study after 'lights out', was remarkably similar to my experience of a Melbourne girls' boarding-school in the early 1950s.)

Okely's subject is the social construction of femininity, and her data come largely from her own boarding-school experience. She argues that the particular form of 'self' inculcated in upper-class girls centred around making them into adult upper-class women acceptable to upper-class men. The men were presumed to be the bread-winners, and the women, though 'lucky to have a good education', were to have a future as bearers and rearers of children:

> Our lives and potential were presented as those of failed men ... Without a husband, we knew we could not maintain our financial hold in the class system, however exclusive our accent and manners ... The notion of 'char-acter' was contrasted favourably by our instructors with 'personality' — a negative trait because it carried the notion of individuality ... The required behaviour ... included modesty, deference and submission ... We learnt that obedience and good conduct were inseparable from and superior to the intellect and academic knowledge ... To be wearing the diamond engagement ring was the ultimate achievement.
>
> Okely 1978, pp. 121–31 passim

Masculinity in a coal-mining village

Conventional wisdom assumes that gender identity is 'taught' either by parents, by teachers, or by significant others, such as clergymen. However this view overstates not only the purposive nature of socialisation (the presumption that adults 'do it' to children), but also underestimates the extent to which a social setting itself 'teaches' in a multiplicity of ways. Bill Williamson (1982), a British sociologist, describes the ways in which masculinity is 'learnt' in a village in northern England. In his account, learning through parents and teachers is far less significant than the gradual acquisi-tion of 'manliness' through involvement in everyday village life. Through a long process, boys learn to understand the centrality of the mine and mining to the future of 'being a man' in that part of England.

Williamson wrote about the world of his grandfather in an impoverished mining village in the north of England. In this village the boys became miners, but the process of learning to be a miner started very young. Williamson describes the process as 'pit hardening'. It was, he says, a process not of acquiring particular technical skills, but of assimilating certain special attitudes associated with a particular brand of mas-culinity. These attitudes include a strong attachment to the idea of being 'tough' and of not worrying about danger, the development of a sense of fatalism, a belief in hard physical labour, and a vision of themselves as 'real men'. Young boys in this village also acquired attitudes that defined their class position. They learnt that they would be mine workers who worked for a wage, and they understood the authority rela-tionships in the mine dominated by the pit owner (Williamson 1982, p. 29).

What makes Williamson's account of the boys' acquisition of gender identity in this mining village particularly interesting is his focus on the ways in which this ver-sion of masculinity was a requirement for being a mine worker: 'It was ... a subtle process of getting boys used to a whole way of life and to coping with, through suppression, those fears which, if allowed out, would prevent a man ever going underground' (Williamson 1982, p. 36). Williamson argues that the masculine traits fostered in the village boys were exactly the sort of responses required by the coal-mining employers: 'These responses include regular attendance, an acceptance of authority, sustained effort at work and an almost total acceptance of the conditions of work itself, a respect for the dangers of the pit but without too much concern about them, and, finally, a sense of resignation' (Williamson 1982, p. 36).

Williamson's argument, then, suggests that a sense of self is gendered, but much more than that. The gendered self is moulded within the context of a particular time and a particular place (in this instance, a turn-of-the-century mining village). The sense of self that is inculcated in this way has a purpose: the fitting of the individual to the environment (becoming a miner and accepting a life of danger and physical hardship). Working-class men often develop a masculine self of this kind: they tend to grow to adulthood with a strong sense of the importance of group solidarity among men and of the necessity of appearing to be physically tough, and with a real or feigned ability to use machinery (Hearn 1992, p. 164).

Femininity in a girl's bedroom on a British working-class housing estate

Angela McRobbie's argument about the acquisition of femininity among working-class girls in a housing estate in Birmingham in the 1970s does not differ substantially from Williamson's story, though the gender and the location differ. Again, the sense of identity constructed in this context matches the social and economic environment in which the young person will be placed in later life.

Age was a key factor in defining self. At the age of fourteen or fifteen the girls studied by McRobbie are, she argues, in a 'kind of twilight zone sexually'. One girl told McRobbie 'I think it'd make me Mum happy if she saw me with a boyfriend, steady like, by the time I was 16-17' (McRobbie 1978, p. 99). Another girl said, 'I worry a lot about not getting married. I mean what if no one wants me and I had to stay with me Mum and Dad?' (McRobbie 1978, p. 106).

Their social experiences are constrained by their parents' low incomes, and their world is confined to their school, the girls and boys they know, and their own homes, specifically their bedrooms. Their free time is substantially reduced by the amount of domestic labour they do for their mothers. Being almost totally economically depend-ent on men, they would not leave their parents' house until they married.

McRobbie argues that the culture of the girls is constructed around a sexualised, feminine, anti-school culture, where the predominant interests of the girls are their best friends and the local boys. The girls need 'best friends' in order to confide about sexual matters, and the difficulties of being degraded and humiliated by boys if 'you get known for being like that' (McRobbie 1978, p. 107).

McRobbie suggests that the lives of the teenage girls whom she interviewed were determined at least in part by their material position: 'their social class, their future role in production, their present and future role in domestic production and their economic dependence on their parents' (McRobbie 1978, p. 97). She concludes, 'They are both saved by and locked within the culture of femininity' (McRobbie 1978, p. 108).

These three examples vary in time and place. All three are British; two are working-class; and one is middle-class. One example is from the late nineteenth century; another is set around 1950; and the third dates from about 1975. To round off this set of examples, a study of the acquisition of masculinity by a middle-class boy would be ideal. But such studies are not easy to find. However, we do know that middle-class men value independence and interpersonal skills (particularly the ability to provide leadership, and to engender loyalty and obedience from subordinates) (Hearn 1992, p. 164). These sorts of values are inculcated particularly in private school settings, and especially in sports such as cricket.

Construction of a sexual identity

In the discussion so far, I have overstated the ease with which any sort of masculinity or femininity is acquired. Our sense of self as male or female is socially constructed, but our sense of self changes as our social environment changes, and particularly as our bodies change. For some women, the onset of puberty is a matter of great anxiety. Young women with anorexia seem to be holding back the onset of puberty, denying the arrival of breasts, fat on hips, and so on, and trying to maintain the body image of a pre-pubertal girl. Sheila MacLeod (1981) in *The Art of Starvation* describes her growing body in these terms:

> Although I was still 'tiny' ... by any normal standards, when I looked in the mirror, I saw someone who appeared to me to be 'gross' ... I had been a thing of firm, clear outlines; now I seemed to splay out in all directions and to have assumed a shape, thanks to undue accretions of flesh, which bore no relation to the person I believed to exist within it. 'That', I told myself, 'can't be me'.
>
> MacLeod 1981, p. 51

Heterosexuality, homosexuality, and transsexualism

So far it has been assumed that children are socialised to be heterosexual and that this socialisation is successful. In other words, it is assumed that male bodies are linked with male heterosexuality, that female bodies are linked with female heterosexuality, and these sexual identities are acquired unproblematically by socialisation experiences within the family. Yet some boys and girls grow up to be homosexual and some to be transsexual (that is, wanting to change sexual identity entirely). Others want to cross-dress.

The words we use about our selves are grounded in history. Even describing oneself as a homosexual is something that would not have been possible until late in the nineteenth century, because the terms *homosexual* and *homosexuality* did not exist until 1869. They were apparently first introduced by a Hungarian doctor, Karoly

Maria Benkert (Hearn 1992, p. 15). The word *transsexual* was first used in the late 1940s, but did not become a generally recognised term until the 1960s (King 1987, p. 374; Billings and Urban 1982, p. 267).

Heterosexuality is normatively valued. The various non-heterosexual orientations are highly stigmatised, and consequently they are rarely accepted easily as part of one's self. The difficulties here relate not to a wish to have a different body (as in the case of the anorexic young woman described above), but to the often negative consequences of defining oneself as a homosexual. Adrian Dixson reports that he was first called a homosexual by a close friend when he was seventeen:

> The very word shocked me ... Of course, the possibility of my being homosexual had occasionally bothered me ... but I had generally managed to convince myself that it was probably just a passing phase ... Gradually my anguish was overtaken by a sense of bitter resentment. 'Why me?' I wondered. Of all the ugly afflictions that beset the world this was surely the most awful. I certainly hadn't chosen to be a homosexual ... whatever favourable qualities I'd inherited — reasonable intelligence, average good looks — now seemed permanently and incurably blighted by a curse so distasteful and disgusting that society unanimously refused to discuss it ... One thing was clear. I couldn't change my nature but I might change my image. From now on I would allow nothing in my manner or appearance to betray my affliction.
>
> Dixson 1986, pp. 71–3

Even 'knowing' that one is a homosexual does not fully solve the problem of defining oneself, of knowing who one is. Male homosexuality and female homosexuality are also socially constructed within specific social contexts. Fran Winant's (1976) lengthy poem on her leather jacket aptly describes her desperation to achieve a butch image that will be acceptable to her friends, yet without sacrificing her sense of herself as an attractive person. This is part of the poem:

> leaning on the snack bar counter
> I kick the white cardboard box at my feet
> to make sure its still there
> inside is a snappy $8 ski type jacket . . .
> I'm going to take 10 minutes to gloat over
> being able to get my hands on
> such a desirable dyke item
> I'm going to wear it with satisfaction
> fighting off my fears of
> looking tough and ugly
> enjoying my toughness
> building on it not denying it

and if necessary enjoying my ugliness
affirming that too . . .
will I look like a little boy now
or a little girl
or will I finally look like myself
in my particular combination of
the clothes I want
wonder if theres a way to look feminine
in this jacket after all.

Winant 1976, pp. 121–2

Conclusion

In talking about masculinity and femininity, and the way in which they are socially constructed, I have blurred the distinctions between sex and gender. But gender identity and sexual identity are analytically separable. We are brought up to believe in a simple equation of sex and gender: if you are born with female external genitalia then you are a woman, and, similarly, male genitalia determines that you are a man. However, things are more complex. Bob Connell argues that 'We always see the "natural" through social spectacles'. Gender isn't simply an elaboration of biologically constructed social differences (Connell 1986, p. 354). Biology is not a 'given' that we learn about. We construct what biology is. Moreover, biology is not destiny. Consider two examples: biological males can be reconstructed to be females; post-menopausal women, assumed in the past to have bodies that make child-bearing impossible, can now be reconstructed so that they can bear children.

Gender roles are social constructions framed around social constructions of biology, and these sets of social constructions — although connected in diverse ways — are always in flux and differ from one social context to another. This does not mean that the shape of what we know as gender is endlessly flowing in different directions. At this moment in history, for example, the gender of 'woman' is constructed as both heterosexual and White. Grant explains: 'Obviously, this does not mean that women of colour are not women. It only means that the ideology of gender promotes archetypes as normative ideals' (Grant 1993, p. 177).

One of the really interesting issues to do with all this is why we are pulled in the direction of believing that being male and being female is clear-cut and unproblematic. Connell calls this 'the pull of categorical thinking' (Connell 1986, p. 349). One argument is that there is (historically recent) pressure on us all 'to have a clear-cut unchangeable identity as a member of one sex or the other' (Connell 1986, p. 352).

We are now moving towards a more complicated view of gender and the self. We are no longer stuck in the groove of describing the relationships between 'all men' and 'all women' as being based on 'patriarchy' and 'oppression' and 'subordination'. We are looking now to analyse the different ways in which men and women see their bodies (broadly, as heterosexual, homosexual, or transsexual), the different ways in which men and women construct masculinity and femininity, and the ways in which apparent biological 'constraints' are being resisted and reformulated in daily life.

It is evident in our daily lives that people with similar social backgrounds end up differently, with different senses of personal identity. Our selves are largely consti- tuted within our families, which in turn are shaped by wider social contexts. But even within the same family, siblings emerge differently. Some of this can be explained by 'place in the family'. The experience of being the eldest differs from that of being the youngest. But, more than that, children in a family each have a symbolic place, some- times indicated by their names. One child might be named after a much feared grand- father, another named after a Christian saint, and both treated accordingly. Each child experiences the family and its members in a different way. The emergent self cannot be fully 'explained' by reference to broad social processes but is to be under- stood only by knowing the particular setting.

Discussion questions

1   Think of an incident in which you were your 'true self'. What made this incident one in which you felt you were your true self? Can you think of an incident where you behaved in a way that was not an expression of your 'true self'? Go around the group and look for gender differences among the stories of true and false selves.
2   What social pressures have moulded your 'self'?
3   What aspects of your 'self' do you think can be changed?
4   Why were the girls described by McRobbie locked into lives of early marriage?
5   What is essentialism, and why has it been criticised?

Recommended reading

For recent Australian research on how communities construct gender differences see:
•   Dempsey, K. 1992, *A Man's Town: Inequality between Women and Men in Rural Australia*, Oxford University Press, Melbourne.
For a personal account of what it means to be a feminist see:
•   Spender, D. 1986, 'What is Feminism: A Personal Answer', in J. Mitchell and A. Oakley (eds), *What is Feminism?*, Basil Blackwell, Oxford.
For a succinct discussion of some of the major issues confronting recent feminism, see:
•   Ramazanoglu, C. 1989, *Feminism and the Contradictions of Oppression*, Routledge, London, especially chs 1 and 2.
For further discussions of sex and gender distinctions, see:
•   Benjamin, J. 1990, *The Bonds of Love: Psychoanalysis, Feminism and the Problem of Domination*, Virago, London.
•   Chodorow, N. (1978) *The Reproduction of Mothering: Psychoanalysis and the Sociology of Gender*, University of California Press, Berkeley.

- Epstein, C. F. 1988, *Deceptive Distinctions: Sex, Gender, and the Social Order*, Yale University Press, New Haven, ch. 4.
- Grant, J. 1993, *Fundamental Feminism: Contesting the Core Concepts of Feminist Theory*, Routledge, New York.
- Oakley, A. 1972, *Sex, Gender and Society*, Harper and Row, New York, especially ch. 8.
- Pringle, R. 1992, 'Absolute Sex? Unpacking the Sexuality/Gender Relationship', in R. W. Connell and G. W. Dowsett (eds), *Rethinking Sex: Social Theory and Sexuality Research*, Melbourne University Press, Melbourne, pp. 76–101.
- Segal, L. 1990, *Slow Motion: Changing Masculinities, Changing Men*, Virago, London, chs 3, 8, and 10.

Chapter 4

The Ethnic Self

Fiona Mackie

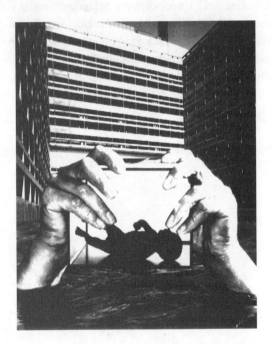

Opening questions

What do we mean by 'the self'? How does the self form? Is there only one self for each person — a clear and unified identity? If we think of an ethnic self, who defines it as 'ethnic'? Is everyone defined in terms of their ethnicity? Is the idea of an ethnic self simply a reflection of the fact that each of us is born into some culture, or with some language or peoplehood, so that everyone is an ethnic self? Or are some people more likely to be thought of as ethnic than others? Is the 'ethnic' label attached by the people themselves, or is it attached from outside? If so, who is ascribing that definition, and in whose interests does it operate?

In this chapter I shall not so much answer these questions as weave together a number of themes that we need to consider if we are interested in these questions. I shall begin with what seems like a straightforward question.

How is the self formed?

First glimpses of culture

'Silly question', you may think. 'Obviously, the self is born.' Certainly, we are born unique, but interestingly it is also the case that we would each be very different if we had been born into a different culture, society, language, or set of circumstances. We are not actually born a self. Instead, our self forms in relation to our surroundings (Mead 1934, part III). We are evoked or called forth by the elements, patterns, and language of the particular world into which we are born. In the early stages, 'significant others' are especially important in forming us: mother, father, sisters, brothers. In a society in which the family is characteristically a nuclear family, influences on the person's earliest phases of development will probably be largely limited to those family members. If an extended family is more customary, then aunts, uncles, grandparents, and cousins may feature in early self-formation as much as the parents. So already we can see an influence arising from culture. The cultural pattern that governs the shape of 'the family', as an institution, will influence the particular 'significant others' who feature in the earliest phases of self-formation.

Gender intersections

Thus, 'ethnic' factors are already operating, in the sense that each of us is shaped by and towards the culture into which we are born. But factors of gender are also operating. In Western cultures, and more broadly, in modernity (characterised by large-scale industrialised societies, whose spread, since the industrial revolution, has been dominated by the Western culture in which they first formed) specific qualities have been ascribed to each sex. These qualities are oppositional. 'Maleness' is characterised as more 'rational', and 'femaleness' as more emotional; 'maleness' as more dominant in culture and public affairs, 'femaleness' as closer to nature and the private sphere. This division of qualities between genders is not neutral. Since our system of knowledge assigns great value to rationality and to the public sphere, men come to be seen as more important than women. The ascription of qualities according to gender thus favours males, as long as they conform to these gender-expectations, and supports their power over women.

I shall not focus directly on gender, since we have looked at it in the previous chapter. But it is vital to notice two things. First, the oppositional characterisation of the two genders has been mirrored by an institutional arrangement, the nuclear family, based also on a dominant expectation of heterosexuality, which prescribed that children be raised by two parents, one of each sex. The gender ascriptions fitted with wider institutional arrangements. In the family formed under capitalism, man was associated with external employment and deemed head of the family, representing it in the public domain. Woman was predominantly characterised as child-bearer and mother, which justified confining most women predominantly to the private sphere of home and child-raising. This arrangement, highly favourable to capitalism, freed males for work and provided unpaid labour — women and mothers — to feed and tend for the male worker and 'his' children.

Thus, the oppositional characteristics ascribed through gender became reflected throughout institutional arrangements. An inequality was cemented that implied a hierarchy: 'man is better than woman'. While in contemporary Australia this assumption no longer stands, and the nuclear family is no longer so predominant, it is taking us a lot longer to dismantle the multiple ways in which these patriarchal assumptions have influenced and shaped our language and institutions. What this means — and this is the second point we need to draw from this brief consideration of gender — is that in the early stages of our self-formation we are also being simultaneously inducted into these dominant gender expectations. As children grow up, they are forced to split their selves according to an enforced division (Benjamin 1988). Human capacities are divided between those apportioned to boys and those apportioned to girls. This halving and partialising of human qualities means that we each risk losing half the universe of possibilities before we begin.

Such oppositional thinking is rooted deeply in the thought patterns of modernity. The assumed opposites are designed to legitimise a hierarchy, one side of the opposition ('maleness') being defined as superior through the exclusion of the other. Woman becomes 'not-man'. Similar operations occur with the dichotomies of civilised/primitive, White/Black, West/East, and adult/child; and each polarisation tends to support the others. Woman, child and primitive, all defined as being closer to nature and the emotions, are thought to be less 'developed' than the rational, civilised assumptions attached to man.

So being seen as an ethnic self may operate in a negative way, affecting our opportunities. This depends on the *kind* of ethnic or racial labelling.

Cultural diversity and the prevailing conception of the world

Each self, then, is shaped according to a particular set of cultural and gender patterns. Similarly, we are each shaped according to a particular thought pattern.

A particular patterning of thought underlies our social institutions: the gender division supporting the nuclear family. The way a parent behaves towards a child from its earliest moments conveys the language of those dominant patterns of thought and culture. A baby at the breast already begins to interpret a language of gestures (Mead 1934). If the baby bites the nipple, the mother's retraction teaches the baby that the milk will cut off, but that smooth sucking tends to mean a relaxed supply. Thus, from the first moments, the baby is encouraged towards certain behaviours learnt through social relationships. As the child grows, the patterns are learnt through play. As play evolves into games involving others, such as cricket or rounders, the child has to be able to take on, in his or her mind, the different roles of each participant. Thus we learn the social roles that we gradually adopt. In doing this, we internalise wider social patterns in, and as, the very structure of our self.

The self becomes divided into two parts. A 'me' is formed as we internalise the authority of our 'significant others' and, later, the authority of the 'generalised other'. Through the latter, we internalise the particular ways people behave towards us and expect us to behave. As well as this 'me', each self is an 'I', reflecting a unique personality and creativity. The 'I' reacts to the 'me' (the governing expectations). 'I' may disagree with those expectations (Mead 1934).

Thus each of us is, at least in part, an 'ethnic' self, shaped according to particular cultural and social patterns that lie at the very heart of our humanness. That being so, why is it, in modernity, that only certain people, and not everyone, seem to be thought of as 'ethnic'? That question requires us to look more closely at the dominant pattern of thought and 'reason' that characterises modernity.

As discussed earlier, one is not born, but becomes, a 'self'; similarly, while an individual thinks, thought does not have its origins in an individual (Mannheim 1976). One takes on the thought pattern of a particular group. Where social groups are relatively small, the dominant thought pattern may be fairly uniform, so that each person comes to learn pretty much the same way of thinking and of seeing the world. As societies grow larger, with a more complex division of labour, different people are in very different life situations, and thus come to develop different patterns of thinking and ways of seeing. At the time Karl Mannheim was writing, the diversity arose from the differences in social classes and occupational groups. Since great migratory movements have drawn people from many different cultures into the large world metropolises in search of employment, the population of each major metropolis now comprises people from many different cultural backgrounds. Thus, today, diversity arises not only from different social class positions, but also from different cultural backgrounds and thus from differently formed ethnic selves.

Mannheim saw this increased diversity as very positive. It extended an understanding of social relativity: that there is not one, absolute set of truths, beliefs, or ways of seeing the world that is the only right, or best, one. Rather, there are many different thought patterns and ways of seeing the world. With increased social mobility, more and more people moved between different life situations and occupations. Thus, different thought patterns came together in people's own minds. People came to realise how they are shaped by the beliefs and patterns of their particular group. If I think of having been a chambermaid, a greengrocer's assistant, a nurse in a mental hospital, and unemployed, as well as a lecturer, I can see how different I was in each situation — how my self changed. Similarly, people who have lived in several different cultures are aware of how their selves alter accordingly. This might have led to increased human cooperation and understanding. Instead of each person being confined to a particular ethnocentric viewpoint — seeing things only from an ethnic perspective and remaining unaware of the ways that our thinking is slanted — we would be able to shift between each others' perspectives, widening our ways of seeing and thinking, and our understanding of the ways society shapes us.

However, issues of power worked against this. Now that religion no longer decrees the governing Western conception of the world, there is increased communication between equal and different viewpoints and perspectives, but powerful interest groups compete over who will control the prevailing conception of the world. Battles are waged between political parties, in advertising, through the media. One can understand why, in a society in which there is a preoccupation with issues of power, there should be a concern to control the dominant conceptions. Through thought, language, and institutions, prevailing conceptions come to influence our very self, from its earliest formation.

We are beginning to build up a picture of the prevailing conception of the world in modernity: it is one shaped by increasing diversity, a relativity of ideas, and a pattern of relations governed by competition. Another aspect seems to be the pervasiveness of dichotomies, operating in the area of gender as a division between public and private, and at the centre of the self as a division between 'I' and 'me', and between the internal and external self.

It is important to trace how this tendency towards polarising dichotomies — which is central to the dominant conception of the world and the thought–language pattern that elevates man (the public, the external) over woman (the private, the internal) — has also profoundly shaped relations between ethnicities. Such tendencies towards divisions and hierarchies are rooted in the specific form of 'rationality' that is taken for granted in modernity and is presented as playing a central role in the 'history' of modernity's development. Both that history and that form of rationality are marked by a racism from which we are only slowly emerging.

Racism and ethnocentrism in the 'history' of modernity and the West

As capitalism developed in the West, its formation and spread depended on the ascendancy of science, particularly those sciences linked to technology. As more advanced engines fuelled developing industry, large numbers of people became 'labourers' (Marx 1918; 1964). Working with machines instead of in agriculture, they became detached from rural patterns of time. The time of the clock became associated with 'efficiency', and through the 'work ethic' (Weber 1968), people's minds became detached from the rhythms of their bodies and their emotions. 'Rational' behaviour came to *mean* this kind of detachment from body, emotion, and personal ties. 'Bureaucracy', as the most 'efficient' and impersonal way of organising large numbers of people, spread into many different social institutions and social relations.

'History' presented modernity as 'development', as if this *particular* form of development represented development *per se*. Societies that were technologically based, industrialised, and driven by a scientific form of rationality came to be seen as 'more developed', the pinnacle of 'civilisation'. Science was seen as the most 'rational' and 'developed' form of reason, supplanting religion or custom, which were labelled 'traditional', 'superstitious', and 'primitive'. *Different* ways of seeing the world were depicted as *pre*-scientific. This thinking has shaped our self-formation, and it is important to notice how it subtly supports a thought system that places our particular cultural pattern, modernity, at the pinnacle of a picture of 'progress'. Thus, it is a very ethnocentric viewpoint, depicting the West's position as the best — the West as superior.

This way of thinking legitimated the colonialism that enabled modernity to spread. The linear notion of human development placed a whole range of cultures, as well as 'Black' people versus 'White', in a kind of frozen past. Black people and their cultures were seen as outmoded, 'primitive'. A warped social Darwinism implied that 'they' were closer to monkeys, while 'we' were the fully developed humans. The very notion of 'civilisation' was formulated through this operation of classing whole segments of humanity as 'primitive'. Only through that contrast could it be made clear what 'civilised' was supposed to mean.

Consequences for the 'ethnic self'

It is disturbing to see how the modern self, by internalising governing patterns of thought, language, and world, incorporates ideas and assumptions (as if they were 'truth') that will cause that self to rank people. Through interlocking, hierarchised dichotomies, the adult, rational, Western, White male is posed as the ideal 'social subject', and one is encouraged to see certain persons and cultures as different, less desirable, inferior, even slightly dangerous, and sometimes scarcely human (Saïd 1978). If I adopt these patterns uncritically — without noticing that they represent only one particular perspective or asking myself how I feel about that bias — all my social relations will be shaped by them. I will be unconsciously inclined to treat certain categories of person, whenever I meet or think of them, as inferior. This tendency will characterise social relations in general, to the benefit of one particular form of self: the self of modernity.

This form of self, as well as being based in racism and ethnocentrism, is highly Eurocentric. Rooted in dominant patterns of thought, which are now global in their influence and taken for granted, this bias tends to go unnoticed, which means that its power is able to operate more freely. We are not alerted to question it. If we do not de-centre this view, so that we can see how it colours everything, then we remain victims of an ethnocentric blindness. Many writers suggest that this blindness has characterised our whole view of ethnicity and the patterns of relations between different ethnicities.

Roberta Sykes, charting the horrific history of White Australia's relations with Aborigines, speaks of how early settlers arrived with a whole history of racist assumptions rooted in their psyches. To them, it was 'evident' that they were superior. Blacks were seen as 'sub-human; non-human; beasts; animals; pestilence', and 'the enemy' (1989, pp. 5 and 6). Colonists thus felt justified in exterminating Aborigines in the name of 'progress'. The lands of Torres Strait Islanders were treated as '*terra nullius*', meaning that no one deemed human occupied them. The culture of the Islanders was falsely assumed to be dead, 'archaic', and destroyed by the arrival of 'civilisation' (Sharp 1993).

While these old, supposedly 'scientific', ideas of race and racial difference have been overturned, they still operate. The basis of argument has shifted in such a way that the modified versions of these ideas have similar social consequences to the old judgments. Barker speaks of a 'new racism', now masked under assumptions of 'cultural' difference. Spurious arguments suggest that it is 'natural' to feel closest to people of one's own 'culture', ignoring all the differences of class, gender, and personality that operate against any notion of cultural homogeneity (Barker 1981; Miles 1988). Through 'internal colonialism', Ashis Nandy suggests, the West is now everywhere, having become a 'psychological category' (1983). As modernity infiltrates India, displacing traditional cultures, the West's categories assert themselves, and the Indian self must now grow up having internalised a Western evaluation of the Indian — a sense of inferiority to be contended with at the very root of the self. Gilane Tawadros says the same thing about Black women artists in the contemporary United Kingdom. They must contend with the governing view of 'Black', which has influenced their very self as they grew up (1989).

Voices from the periphery

Ethnic, as a label, has tended to be attached to people pushed to the periphery or margin by the Western viewpoint of modernity. Since the White, Anglo-Saxon, Protestant male perspective operates as the ideal subject-position, this perspective has tended to appear as if it were *not* 'ethnic'. *Ethnic* becomes a term used for a person who is 'other' than this centred self, as if the latter were a neutral observer, unaffected by any particular ethnic or cultural perspective. The voice of this perspective has tended to pose as 'objective truth', pushing other voices out of language and dominant discourse — marginalising and silencing them.

Voices from the periphery are now taking their place within the contemporary dialogue, displacing and revealing the ethnocentrism that has characterised modernity. People who have been pushed to the margins often have a particularly acute understanding of processes to which those in the centre remain blind (Tawadros 1989). This is because the power necessary to sustain the centre's position has operated *against* those being peripheralised. They can chart the process of these inequalities, because they have lived them — they have experienced them in their own lives

But there are strong forces operating against such insights. The art of people from African and Asian cultures settled in the United Kingdom is marginalised through a new form of 'primitivism' (Araeen 1987). Treated as 'ethnic art', it is excluded from mainstream artistic movements. Similarly, the contemporary circumstances of people of African and Asian descent in the United Kingdom, and the inequality and discrimination they daily contend with, is neatly excluded from consideration. They are seen as people somehow locked in the past, tied to an 'archaic' culture, as if culture were fixed and frozen, instead of constantly growing and changing. The Murray Islanders, in the Mabo case in the Australian High Court, have had to overturn a similar assumption: that their culture had died, remaining fixed in a 'primitive' past, and had failed to go on developing in contemporary circumstances. So unquestioningly does a particular ethnocentric culture of modernity govern our legal system that it was almost impossible for the Murray Islanders to present their case. 'Oral tradition' is regarded by Western legal systems as inferior to written custom — inadmissible evidence unless 'writing' authenticates it (Sharp 1991).

'Ethnics' in Australia

Originally, in the governing view, the most desirable immigrants to Australia were British. The categories of those who subsequently became acceptable followed a clear, but unacknowledged, set of racial and pseudo-racial assumptions. As insufficient numbers of Britons sought to come, Australia turned to Germans, then Northern Italians, Southern Italians, Greeks, Turkish people, and finally those labelled 'Arab', 'Muslim', and 'Asian'.

The rationale for the obviously racist scale of acceptance was that we were moving gradually from cultures thought to be similar to ours towards those perceived as different. As is predominantly the case in modernity, difference is seen as a threat in this scenario. Such an assumption was legitimatised by the governing ideology of 'assimilation', which dominated policy and theory until the adoption of a multicultural rhetoric in 1973. The usual 'either/or' dichotomous model prevailed, decreeing that a 'Greek', for example, must assimilate (become like 'us') as fast as possible. The presumption was that one is *either* Greek *or* Australian.

In the areas of education, health, welfare, and trade unionism, it was not taken into account that Australian social structures might need to be changed in order to deal with such an influx of immigrants with different languages and cultural backgrounds (Martin 1978). Such realisations and responses were slow to come. Generations of children and adults suffered as a result of this indifference to their needs, and an attitude that equated their cultural difference with deficiency. People who could not speak English or fit into Australian institutions were presented as deficient — they had not yet become sufficiently like 'us'. Thus the 'assimilation' policy treated cultural difference or 'ethnic' background as a slur, while an English background was not seen as 'ethnic', but was treated like some neutral gold standard, against which the ethnicity of others was measured.

As was the case with other eloquent voices from the periphery, the ethnic rights movement helped to change Australia (Martin 1978). But a deeper concern arose regarding the emphasis on cultural, rather than structural, issues. As one wave of non-English-speaking immigrants after another entered the manufacturing sector of the workforce, Australia avoided wider critique of structural factors. This critique was deflected into blaming the immigrants (Mackie 1984). For example, when repetitive strain injury developed among Italian and Greek immigrants (often women) working in factories, this was ridiculed as 'Greek back' and, later, 'Lebanese back'. Australians thus failed to learn about an injury that interested them only once it emerged among middle-class workers thought of as 'Australian' rather than 'ethnic'. Later, in a similar instance of historical blindness, the Australian community failed to take heed of insights gained by Lebanese immigrant men, early victims of the process of increasing structural unemployment that later spread across all sectors of Australian society (Mackie 1983). Dismissed as irrelevant, these people were denied a voice, and once again, Australians failed to gain an understanding of the structural problems in their society.

The 'assimilation' model could have been displaced far sooner had we listened to second-generation immigrants. When I spoke to second-generation Australians of Greek background in 1969 (Mackie 1975), they were not making a stark choice between 'Greek' or 'Australian' culture, nor were they engaged in a linear progression from one to the other. Rather, each person brought about a personally meaningful balance between the two cultural influences that had shaped, and continued to shape, their self. Such balance between different cultures is now widespread in the 'selves' who inhabit large-scale contemporary metropolises.

Finally, we shall consider how this balance may facilitate the kind of reflexivity that Mannheim hoped for and saw as increasingly available. Why is reflexivity relevant? It represents a process that can release us from the dangers of blind ethnocentrism.

The reflexive self

As a self, none of us can escape the fact that we are shaped according to a dominant cultural patterning. If people simply remain bound to that patterning, accepting it as the right and best way, without being aware that it is the result of a particular and slanted viewpoint, then they are condemned, by their self-construction, to suffer from an ethnocentric blindness. In a reflexive view, people are still part of that cultural patterning, but they *see* their position within that patterning and how they are shaped according to it. They can partly stand outside that patterning. Then they may be able to exercise choice between those aspects they wish to adopt and those they wish to overcome, jettison, or change in their selves.

Second-generation immigrants, brought up in two different but simultaneous cultures, have a strong opportunity to become reflexive — able to see and choose between the best of both cultures, as they themselves see it. This is how cultures change, and it is an opportunity of which the Murray Islanders have taken advantage (Sharp 1993). In contemporary modernity we are all surrounded by cultural diversity, so that reflexivity, which can release us from our different ethnocentrisms, is widely available, though often sectored off because cultures do not meet, or at least not on equal terms. Nikos Papastergiadis suggests that our multiculturalism needs to develop beyond a mere patronage of 'ethnic' difference as entertainment, while all the main criteria of progress — the work ethic, respectability, and punctuality — are defined by the centre (1986, p. 54). This way, the 'ethnic self' can only be expressed in private; in public, another cultural frame is hegemonic, thus splitting the person. To displace such a hegemony, Gayatri Chatravorty Spivak suggests that the Western self of modernity must strive to 'un-think' its privilege (1990).

Why should we care? Well, why allow ourselves to be robbed of our human heritage of diversity through a fear of difference that has clearly only been induced in the interests of a particular form of power? In coming to see how cultural exclusions operate, one can displace and defuse them. Human beings can communicate their cultures to each other, instead of their cultures operating to bring about a mutual silencing through the fear of difference.

The ethnic self

The self, then, is 'ethnic' for all of us. The question seems to be whether the self is also allowed to be multi-ethnic in its experience, or whether it must remain either blinded to its ethnicity or bound in an ethnocentrism that deprives it of access to the diversity of human cultures: the one or the many. Reflexivity clears a space for choice, in a situation where a thousand intersecting pressures constantly seek to claim the self. That choice may be held open, to avoid closure. Myself, I am many selves. I keep them simultaneously alive by a balance of my 'me' — my ethnic and cultural shaping and expectations, both original and ongoing — and my 'I' — my creative and critical reaction to that shaping, which is constantly changing it.

Discussion questions

1   What are some of the ways that you feel you have been constructed as an 'ethnic self'?
2   Is there only one form of 'ethnic self' in each culture?
3   Consider how dichotomies, operating in dominant thought patterns and institutions, have constructed inequalities based on ethnicity and race.
4   How can we counteract ethnocentric blindness?
5   Give some examples of how 'old racism' may operate in new forms.

Recommended reading

All the recommended reading discusses and critiques the bias and ethnocentrism that haunt dominant (usually Western, Anglo-Saxon) ideas, beliefs, and social practices, unmasking their claims to be neutral, factual, and objective. The writings of Jean Martin (1978), Stephen Castles and Mary Kalantzis, and Roberta Sykes act as practical introductions to the issues, while Nonie Sharp's articles illustrate a contemporary challenge to the old inequalities. Robert Miles and Fiona Mackie present an underlying theoretical approach, which Edward Saïd and Rasheed Araeen deepen by speaking from the perspective of 'the other'. Nawal El Saadawi and Jeannie Martin (1984) consider what has been done to women through this governing, patriarchal, and ethnocentric frame.

- Araeen, R. 1987, 'From Primitivism to Ethnic Arts', *Third Text*, vol. 1, Autumn, pp. 6–25.
- Castles, S., Kalantzis, M., Cope, B. and Morrissey, M. (eds) 1990, 'A Nation Without Nationalism', 'Race, Ethnicity and Socio-Economic Position', and 'Nationalism', in *Mistaken Identity: Multiculturalism and the Demise of Nationalism in Australia*, 2nd edn, Pluto Press, Sydney, pp. 1–13, 36–9, 103–7.
- El Saadawi, N. 1982, 'Distorted Notions about Femininity, Beauty and Love', in *The Hidden Face of Eve: Women in the Arab World*, trans. and ed. S. Hetata, Beacon Press, Boston, pp. 74–90.
- Gendzier, I. L. 1982, 'Foreword' in El Saadawi, *The Hidden Face of Eve: Women in the Arab World*, trans. and ed. S. Hetata, Beacon Press, Boston, pp. vii–xix.

- Mackie, F. 1984, 'Blind Ethnocentrism', *Arena*, no. 67, pp. 93–104; or (for a shortened version) see Mackie, F. 1991, 'Blind Ethnocentrism', in K. Eggerking and D. Plater (eds), *Signposts: A Guide to Reporting Aboriginal, Torres Strait Islander and Ethnic Affairs*, University of Technology, for Australian Centre for Independent Journalism, Sydney.
- Martin, J. I. 1978, 'Definitions' and 'Overview', in *The Migrant Presence: Australian Responses 1947–1977*, Research Report for the National Population Inquiry, Studies in Society, no. 2, Allen & Unwin, Sydney. pp. 15–26, 27–69.
- Martin, J. 1984, 'Non English-Speaking Women: Production and Social Reproduction', in G. Bottomley and M. De Lepervanche (eds), *Ethnicity, Class and Gender in Australia*, Studies in Society, no. 24, Allen & Unwin, Sydney, pp. 109–22.
- Miles, R. 1988, 'Beyond the "Race" Concept: The Reproduction of Racism in England', in M. De Lepervanche and G. Bottomley (eds), *The Cultural Construction of Race*, Sydney Studies in Society and Culture, no. 4, Meglamedia, Sydney, pp. 7–31.
- Saïd, E. 1978, 'Introduction', in *Orientalism*, Routledge & Kegan Paul, London pp. 1–28.
- Sharp, N. 1991, 'A Landmark: The Murray Island Case', *Arena*, no. 94, pp. 78–93; or Sharp, N. 1992, 'Scales from the Eyes of Justice', *Arena*, no. 99/100, pp. 55–61.
- Sykes, R. 1989, 'Blacks, Whites and Racism' and 'Human Rights, Land Rights', in *Black Majority*, Hudson, Melbourne, pp. 5–23, 215–31.

Chapter 5

The Aboriginal Self

Julie Finlayson and Ian Anderson

JF   When I first began formal anthropological research in Australian Aboriginal communities, I was living with an extended Aboriginal family in a small rural town on the central coast of New South Wales. On pension day in each fortnight we embarked on a ritual journey to a nearby country town to do our shopping and to lunch in a local café. During one of these visits, my companion called out to someone in the street who she recognised as a member of the local Aboriginal community, explaining to me in passing that 'you can always tell an Aboriginal person by the way they walk, how they talk, and the way they dress'.

For many non-Aboriginal people, clues to contemporary Aboriginal identity are practical means to recognising an Aboriginal person; but why are clues necessary? The need for cultural clues is directly related, in my view, to the emphasis in Australia on *colour* as *the* definitive racial and cultural marker of Aboriginality. How then should we understand the Aboriginal self?

Who speaks for whom?

In this chapter, Ian and I look at Aboriginality, the self, and identity as related, yet problematic, concepts. The meanings of these concepts are contested, especially in forums where Aboriginal peoples engage (or not) with the State. A number of themes are developed in this chapter. Notions of the Aboriginal self are discussed; in particular, the ways in which difference or 'otherness' is represented, the role of the State in defining the Aboriginal self, and the colonial processes that emphasised essentialism (specific factors argued to be characteristic of race). To best illustrate these issues, our discussion refers to regional contexts and histories.

Readers may be aware of current debates in the social sciences about representation when writing and discussing issues centred on difference. The idea that writing about other peoples and cultures is a legitimate enterprise is currently debated among European academics. But Aboriginal people also (Cowlishaw 1990; Langton 1993) challenge the 'right' of 'experts' to write and speak on their behalf.

To engage with the critique of representation, this chapter has been deliberately constructed as a collaborative enterprise. Increasingly, Aboriginal people are writing and describing the ways in which they and others see themselves, and the terms in which they reflect on their lives and identity. Such writing is widely accessible to the interested reader in the form of plays, novels, and autobiographies (Langford 1988; Weller 1981; 1986; J. Davis 1993; Huggins and Huggins 1994; Narogin 1990).

IA Julie and I have attempted to reproduce a dialogue in this discussion. Our strategy is to introduce you, as a reader, to a discussion between two academics whose histories derive from different sides of the colonial frontier. More importantly, it is our desire to challenge some of the ideas you may have about Aboriginal people, by demonstrating the sociological processes fundamental to constructions of Aboriginality. My objective in writing is to produce works in which indigenous people have an active, rather than passive, voice. This approach challenges those colonial attributes of Aboriginality that enslave the Aboriginal self within what the Native American Vine Deloria called 'conceptual prisons' between 'two worlds' (1973, pp. 131–7).

My journey is the reverse of Julie's. I came to the social sciences as an Aboriginal person who wanted to unlock some of the secrets of academic writing about Aboriginal people. In part, this was stimulated by a curiosity that drives much intellectual work. But I also had a, perhaps arrogant, certainly idealistic, desire to correct some of the prevailing misconceptions to be found in writing about Aboriginal people. The experience has been challenging and enlightening, as well as provocative and infuriating. What continues to drive and shape my thinking has essentially been my experience outside the academy. Intellectual activity has become a point of reflection: an opportunity to think about those issues that affect the lives of myself, my family-mob, and my community.

I argue that it is difficult for writers to write on Aboriginal issues without their readers perceiving that they speak for Aboriginal people. The notion of representation implies creating images to substitute for people or experience. It also involves a political act. Consequently, it is sometimes difficult to distinguish a text or a visual image from the political act of presuming to speak for, or represent, a group of people. For most Australians, face-to-face encounters with Aboriginal people are fleeting, if they occur at all. Consequently, cultural products, such as writing or visual images, play a vital role in making social connections between Aboriginal and non-Aboriginal people. Many non-Aboriginal people invest authority in these forms of representation, uncritical of the fact that these symbols actually constitute their entire experience of Aboriginal people.

Additionally, colonial representations of colonised peoples present them as passive and voiceless. This increases the opportunity for 'experts' to play a pivotal role in colonial relations. Historically, the colonisers' perceptions of Aboriginality were so alien that an expert was necessary to 'make sense' of it.

Indigenous Australians do write about Aboriginal issues from a different social position from that of the non-Aboriginal author. Nevertheless, publication is a dynamic process, in which the act of reading is as important as the intent of the writer. To an extent, it is difficult, regardless of the writer's own background, to avoid being seen as 'an expert'. Neither is it entirely possible for indigenous writers to divorce themselves from the stereotypes that shape people's perception of Aboriginality. Such stereotypes enabled the coloniser to develop and maintain a 'self assured knowledge of "them" (Aborigines)', (Rowse 1993, p. 129).

I too have grown up in a world in which many people still perceive certain qualities, such as colour or cultural practices, as the essential markers of Aboriginality. When we write as indigenous Australians, we should, nevertheless, critically deal with the potent colonial constructions of Aboriginality in order to identify and challenge the stereotypes.

JF The wider story of how the Aboriginal self is constructed must be understood as a dialogue of competing ideas about the self. The State played an instrumental role in shaping Aboriginality, as much as it established, regularised, and legitimated Aboriginal participation in the wider social world. It was the State's intention to control indigenous socialisation processes and their content. State concern focused on colour as the emblem of social and racial identity. In legal discourse and social practices, gradations of colour were made the yardstick of Aboriginality and, inversely, of non-Aboriginality. The individual was measured against a conceptual scale that placed 'Black' people at one end and 'White' people at the other. The scale implied judgements of social status.

IA Colour has operated as a metaphor for specific qualities that are seen as the defining characteristics of Aboriginal people — what are termed the essentialised qualities of Aboriginality. Similarly, certain aspects of culture are seen as typical of an 'authentic' Aboriginality. Traditional Aboriginal kinship systems, totems, hunting, and gathering are all examples of practices argued to be essential features of Aboriginal culture. The idea of essential features of culture corresponds to the colour continuum: the blacker the Aboriginal skin, the more authentically Aboriginal. During the era of assimilation policy, Aboriginal people with fair skins were therefore identified as being the most likely to succeed in becoming members of the wider society.

Anthropological ideas of the Aboriginal self

JF In this section, I argue that government policies and legislation directly contributed to an Aboriginal identity. In Queensland, legislation regulated Aboriginal lives for almost a century. Today, many Queensland Aboriginal people feel the State continues to deny them documentation of their cultural and personal histories. They argue the persistence of Aboriginality as a contested realm in State political discourse and legislation.

Certainly there is a history of scrutiny to accommodate. European anthropologists and social theorists have been intrigued by Australian Aboriginal peoples (see Peterson 1990). Social theorists like E. B. Tylor, J. G. Fraser, and, later, Émile Durkheim, Geza Roheim, and Sigmund Freud traced the history of Western social institutions (such as marriage and the family) as a developmental progression, citing Australian Aboriginal societies as significant case studies. However, their view of Aboriginal societies was ahistorical. They imagined, first, that Aboriginal communities were frozen in time and, consequently, that they mirrored unchanged and unchanging social traditions. Second, they believed indigenous societies reflected greater affinities with a 'primitive' existence.

In the early twentieth century, anthropology was primarily an arm-chair discipline embedded in an antiquarian concern with exotic details about non-European peoples. Few theorists had direct contact with Australian Aboriginal peoples. Field data was collected in Australia by people who interviewed Aboriginal people according to questions and interviews worked out in advance and mailed to them from Europe.

However, academic interest continued to focus on Australian Aboriginal groups, even after field work became central to social anthropology as an academic discipline. The impetus to work in Australia resulted from a widely held view that 'primitive peoples' and their societies were unlikely to survive post-colonial contact. Consequently, from the early nineteenth century onwards, social anthropologists embarked on field work in Australia, and when the first department of Anthropology was established at the University of Sydney in 1926, research on Australian Aborigines was a priority. However, policy issues in the administration of Aboriginal affairs were dominated by State bureaucrats, like A. B. Neville (Western Australia) and C. Cook (Northern Territory). Gillian Cowlishaw (1990) argues that the close, unproblematic alliance between academics, acting as advisers on Aboriginal matters, and State bureaucracies is an unacknowledged and unresolved legacy within academe.

IA The Armidale conferences (held in 1959 and 1960) were good examples of the close relationship between anthropology and the State administration of Aboriginal affairs. These gatherings featured speakers such as mission managers, welfare officers, and educators. The tone was pro-assimilationist. A. P. Elkin, a leading figure in Australian anthropology at the time, opened both conferences.

Years earlier he had argued (1931, p. 30) that 'we should endeavour to understand the Aborigine in order that, as a custodian of a primitive race, we might do more for him, and incidentally for ourselves, in that difficult process of culture-transition through which he is passing'. In this speech, Elkin summarises the alliance between the systematic study and analysis of Aboriginal people, and the development of regimes of Aboriginal administration that administered in the interests of a colonial state.

State construction of the Aboriginal self: Queensland and Tasmania

JF By the 1870s, unlike the southern and eastern Australian states, colonial expansion in north Queensland was just beginning, as frontiers were broached at different times and in different places in response to resource exploitation in fisheries, timber, and mining. Around Cooktown the development of pastoral industry and the Palmer River gold-rush in the mid-1870s exposed Aboriginal groups to dispersal, dispossession, and diseases — all concomitants of European contact. By the 1880s and 1890s, tin mining at Mt Amos and Helenvale, and agricultural and pastoral enterprises at Butcher's Hill and King's Plains made Aboriginal co-residence with Europeans impossible. The countryside was depopulated, partly because Aboriginal people moved to centres of European activities and partly through high Aboriginal death rates. In south-eastern Queensland, a similar history of dispossession occurred as, first, Stradbroke Island in the 1830–60s, then Moreton Bay, and the Redcliffe and Ipswich districts were settled.

By the 1890s, as a consequence of the Queensland *Aborigines Protection and Prohibition of the Sale of Opium Act, 1897*, indigenous people were progressively institutionalised. A new social identity was constructed for them through the categorisation of people by colour. Colour was equated with descent and was used to determine social distance from the source of contamination, identified as traditional culture.

IA Colonial expansion was not a uniform process. Local factors — such as the historical context of occupation and dispossession, economic pressures, the impact of disease and death, prior contact, and relations between the frontier and the centre of colonial power — played a role. Consider the colonisation of Tasmania and the Bass Straits in comparison with north Queensland.

In 1798 Flinders and Bass had sailed in the *Norfolk* and demonstrated that Tasmania was an island separate from the Australian mainland. Accompanying them was Charles Bishop in the *Nautilus*. Bishop remained in the Furneaux Islands to harvest seals from the Strait. He sailed back to Port Jackson in

December 1798 with some 5200 seal skins and 350 gallons of seal oil (Plomley and Henley 1990, p. 39).

The subsequent development of merchant-funded sealing operations provided much of the initial impetus for rapid expansion into Bass Strait. To understand the precise effect of colonial processes on the development of the Aboriginal self, it is important to attend to the nuances of the regional context.

The emerging economy in the Strait had a profound impact on the Aboriginal people of Tasmania. Over one decade, large-scale gang sealing essentially depleted the seal population of the entire Bass Strait. Eventually, independent operators replaced the merchant-funded gangs. Unlike their predecessors, these men lived on the islands and exploited remnant seal populations found on outlying islands and rocks. These seals were accessible from small boats. However, Bass Strait sealing was ultimately transformed through exploitation of the labour of *Pallawah* (Tasmanian Aboriginal) women (see Ryan 1981; Plomley and Henley 1990). Aboriginal women were abducted primarily from north-east *Pallawah* clans, but also from mainland Australia, and the sealing economy depended on their cheap labour. In 1815–16 Captain James Kelly recorded the following observation: 'the custom of the sealers in the Straits was that every man should have from two to five of these native women for their own use and benefit [including those thought] proper to cohabit with as their wives' (as quoted in Plomley and Henley 1990, p. 59). In Tasmania, the fate of Aboriginal people was thus intertwined with the history of both British transportation and the Bass Strait sealing economy. Sealers were often ex-seamen or ex-convicts.

JF European settlement and resource exploitation made it impossible to sustain a hunter-gatherer lifestyle in the long term. Aboriginal people formed kin-related groups on the edges of frontier towns and stations. These camps supplied Europeans with human resources — primarily sex and cheap labour. Henry Reynolds (1990) argues that Aboriginal people's labour in north Queensland made the development of colonial primary industries possible (see also May 1994).

However, relationships in frontier towns were problematic, particularly in regard to law and order. A major concern of government in Queensland was miscegenation and opium-use among indigenous people. Because Aboriginal people were considered child-like and easily led, the State intervened to protect them from contact with undesirable Europeans, although Chinese men were considered equally undesirable. The establishment of missions and reserves in north Queensland was often a response to perceived threats of contact between Aboriginal and Chinese peoples. Nevertheless, contact between Aboriginal and Chinese peoples did occur. Aboriginal people worked for Chinese men on coffee and banana plantations in the Cairns and Innisfail districts. Nor was it uncommon for Chinese men and Aboriginal women to form relationships; many Aboriginal people in north Queensland today are descendants of these partnerships.

IA Frontier histories are littered with examples of colonial centres attempting to assert administrative control at the margins of their influence. Bass Strait was perceived to be a lawless place (Plomley 1987, p. 13). The colonial history of the Islands has had a profound influence on Aboriginal people descended from these communities. This legacy is reflected in aspects of contemporary *Pallawah* life and includes the continued participation in a coastal economy through mutton-birding, but also continuity through Aboriginal women's cultural practices (see, for example, Ryan 1981, ch. 15). However, a sustained colonial presence in the islands did not occur until the establishment of an Aboriginal reserve in the early 1830s. This happened thirty years after sealing began. Consequently, relations between the centres and margins of colonial power have operated as important factors in the institutional development of Aboriginal identity.

JF The Aborigines Protection and Prohibition of the Sale of Opium Act throughout Queensland enabled the State to restrict relationships between Chinese and Aboriginal peoples. While all Aboriginal marriages were subject to official sanction, few applications for marriage between Aboriginal and Chinese partners were approved. The 1897 Act also enabled the State to constrain the mobility of Queensland's indigenous people as their everyday life was progressively subject to the decision-making of the local police chief, or the mission or reserve superintendent.

Restrictive legislation presumed that the Aboriginal subject had an infantile nature, was unable to act responsibly, had an unbridled sexuality, was susceptible to gambling and drinking, and generally lacked self-control. No acknowledgment was made of the impacts of colonial contact or massive social and cultural change on the Aboriginal subject. The Aboriginal self was treated as a static, fixed cluster of racial qualities, rendering Aboriginal people incapable of accommodating change or negotiating a position in the wider community.

IA The 'otherness' of Aboriginal people emerged within the context of colonial regimes of power. Since Australian frontiers were populated with people of diverse ethnic, religious, political, and legal status, any notions of the distinctive differences of Aboriginal people were buried by other categories of difference. In Tasmania Aborigines were grouped with the community of Straitsmen, while in Queensland they were seen as merging with the Chinese community.

Changing the Aboriginal self

JF: Policies to resocialise Aboriginal people presumed that they lacked autonomy and self-management. This was a deliberate misinterpretation of the Aboriginal self, which had little resemblance to the realities as documented by historians (Reynolds 1990; May 1994; McGrath 1987; Loos 1982). A state-wide network of institutions (reserves and missions) was established under the Queensland Protectorate. All decisions relating to indigenous people — and after 1904 this included Torres Strait Islanders — were made by the Protectorate. Those who infringed institutional rules of conduct, or who resisted State authority, were forcibly exiled to other reserves or missions.

IA Regulations were a central device used by the State apparatus to produce a sense of Australian nationhood. Until the late 1960s Aboriginal people were perceived to be outside the Australian nation (and its antecedent pre-federal forms). In marginalising Aboriginal people, protectionist policies fulfilled the dual function of preventing atrocities against Aboriginal people, as well as preserving the colonies, and later the Australian Federation, from Aboriginal people. In a sense, these policies were mechanisms for regulating movement and social relations across a multitude of remnant frontiers scattered across the Australian continent and its islands.

JF Church and State shared a common view of the need for systematic social training of Aboriginal people, although different strategies were used to achieve this (Swain and Rose 1988; Evans and Saunders 1992; Thomson 1989; Maushart 1993). In training establishments such as missions, conformity was encouraged through emphasis on the virtues of hard manual work and religious worship. Formal education was minimal. Limited opportunities existed for indigenous people outside institutions. Some individuals were able to live in non-institutional settings through Exemption Certificates issued between 1940 and the 1960s.

Labour was the key to the social legitimation of Aboriginal people (Huggins 1987/88; Huggins and Huggins 1994). Mixed-descent Aboriginal people, in particular, were targeted for vocational training, and work placements were arranged for them on district farms, pastoral stations, and in middle-class, non-Aboriginal homes. Between 1920 and the 1930s, censuses carried out in Queensland indicated an increase in the proportion of mixed-descent people within the Aboriginal population. To address the situation, policy stressed the importance of educating Aboriginal people for a useful role within the wider community. However, education was a problematic solution, since it was commonly thought that the Aboriginal self was basically an artefact of race and racial characteristics (Austin 1993). It was also widely believed that the 'European blood' in mixed-descent Aboriginal children provided the capacity for change, but to achieve this, children had to be isolated from their Aboriginal mothers.

Legislators worked with a fixed idea of the Aboriginal character. Their ideas were biologically based and founded on the premise that the 'Aboriginal nature' is innate. This is essentialism: a view that denies that Aboriginality is shaped by either cultural meanings or social processes. Nor does it allow for interplay between biology and culture; such interplay was only thought possible for mixed-descent people.

An exempt Aboriginal person, usually of mixed descent, was entitled to a number of rights, including the right to live outside a mission or reserve, to negotiate employment, to control their own wages, and to marry without the permission of the Chief Protector — in short, to live *as if* they were a White person. Exemptees were prohibited from associating with other Aboriginal people, including relatives. Applicants required the support of a reputable and sympathetic European to verify their ability to meet the requirements of an exempted lifestyle (see Huggins and Huggins 1994).

IA The shift towards an assimilationist colonial regime in Queensland, which Julie has documented, typified a broader national shift in the policies of Aboriginal administration that had been occurring throughout Australia since the 1930s. A new consensus towards this approach predominated at the first conference of Commonwealth and State officials in Aboriginal administration, held in 1937 (Rowley 1970, p. 389). However, there were key differences in the strategies that underpinned the essentialist views held about Aborigines. On this biological premise, men like A. O. Neville in West Australia, and anthropologist Norman Tindale (McGregor 1993), advocated systematic biological and cultural assimilation.

However, the implementation of programs varied. Victoria, for example, did not officially legislate for assimilation until after the release of the 1957 McLean Report. The Report advocated the creation of the Aborigines Welfare Board and the absorption of Aboriginal people into the 'Australian' community (Lyons 1983). By contrast, following the death of Tru-Ger-Nan-Ner in Tasmania in 1876, the State declared that there were no Aboriginal people remaining in Tasmania.

In general, segregationist practices and assimilation policies formed a complementary partnership. In 1886, during the heyday of the reserve settlements in Victoria, legislation gave the officials of the Aborigines Protection Board the power to exclude 'half castes' from Victorian Aboriginal missions (Barwick 1985). This was an early attempt at assimilation. But the most potent instrument of State intervention was the construction of the notion of the 'hybrid'. The various labels used to describe mixed-descent people in legislation (half-castes, quarter-castes, quadroons, octoroons) collapsed categories of race and culture onto each other. Simultaneously, these terms signified both a liminal (or in-between) status and, equally, the Aboriginality of the groups. Mixed-descent people were thought of as a fragmented people inhabiting an incoherent world and posing a significant moral danger to the Australian state (Beckett 1988). The presence of a rapidly expanding community of mixed-descent Aboriginal people was thought to threaten the purity of a White Australian national identity.

After the Second World War, ethnographers examined the social worlds of mixed-descent communities in south-eastern Australia (Anderson 1994). In these studies, Aboriginal people are represented in dichotomous terms: as straddling Aboriginal and White cultures, tradition and history, camp and town, Black and White bodies. Ethnographers also began to identify the colonial and historical contexts in which Aboriginalities were formed. Rather than seeing mixed-descent people as a jumble of Black and White bits, ethnographers increasingly perceived them as people connected to their communities and histories, and recognised that Aboriginal people were active agents in their own history: 'it is naive to assume that the dispersal of Kuris in the general community will inevitably lead to individual absorption and assimilation ... some people may disappear in each generation, but individual effort and choice will probably still maintain group ties amongst the majority' (Barwick 1964, p. 30).

Aboriginal people, of course, have always been active agents in the creation of their identities. Throughout the bleakest periods of Australian colonialism, the State was unable to completely regulate Aboriginal socialisation. Aboriginal administration was patchy: it was prone to internal conflict and problems with limited resources. No system of colonial administration was so all-pervasive that it entirely undermined the capacity of Aboriginal people to dynamically respond to their circumstances. By their responses to their circumstances and experience, Aboriginal people continued to be, and still are, actively involved in the ongoing creation of Aboriginal social forms and identities.

A good illustration of these processes can be found in Diane Barwick's biographical account of the life of Louisa Briggs (1985). She was a Victorian Bunerong woman whose life experience spanned many facets of life in the colonial south-east, including life on the Bass Strait Islands, the Victorian goldfields, pastoral work, and mission life. In general, Aunty Louisa Briggs and her family moved in and out of mission life, sometimes contravening the instructions of Aborigines Protection Board officials, and at other times accommodating to their wishes.

Concluding remarks

JF   Understandably, paternalistic legislation had an impact on the experience of Aboriginal people. An overview of State intervention in the lives of indigenous people enables non-Aboriginal people to see the progression by which 'difference' was, and is, used to override indigenous people's control of their own socialisation, including biological reproduction. Further, the history and discourse of race relations in Australia enable us to see that future relations between Aboriginal and non-Aboriginal peoples are fraught with questions about the nature of social relations and the constructions of difference. In our review of the situations in Tasmania and Queensland, we illustrated the following points.

First, Aboriginal social experiences were determined by governments' perceptions of them as members of a racial group. The State intervened in the Aboriginal social world according to sets of assumptions about Aboriginality and racial identity. Second, racially based legislation denied legitimacy to traditional Aboriginality and made the construction of another kind of Aboriginal self, disassociated from indigenous cultural contexts, imperative. The reconstruction and reconstitution of Aboriginal identity was systematically achieved through direct manipulation of Aboriginal socialisation. This entailed confinement on settlements, dividing families, segregating the generations, and prohibiting the use of Aboriginal custom and language in everyday life. Indigenous knowledge and practices were progressively replaced by other sets of social behaviours that emphasised cleanliness, Godliness, and the value of work. Third, colour was used to mark intra-Aboriginal differences. People of mixed ancestry were advantaged because they were thought to be more open to assimilation. These views encouraged mission staff to promote such individuals to special positions within the mission community.

Not all Aboriginal people confirm the success of State efforts at social intervention. Aboriginal people today construct, describe, and represent themselves in ways that uphold their autonomy. We refer you to writings published by Aboriginal men and women about their lived experience of Aboriginality. Indeed, the enthusiasm with which Aboriginal people have lodged claims under the Commonwealth *Native Title Act 1993* may well indicate the strength of feeling about, and continuity of, Aboriginal tradition and custom in the construction of identity.

Discussion questions

1   Does the Australian state in the 1990s continue to have an interest in the production of Aboriginalities? Why or why not?
2   What is the significance of the role of the assimilation program in the development of contemporary Aboriginal identities?
3   Is it possible to have an Aboriginal identity without essentialising?
4   To what extent do you think Aboriginal people have been able to be active agents in the creation of their own identities? How did this change throughout colonial history?
5   Australian foundation myths throughout most of the Federation era were based on imperial notions of settlement and peaceful colonisation. To what extent do you think this has changed, and why?

Recommended reading

- Attwood, B. 1989, *The Making of the Aborigines*, Allen & Unwin, Sydney.
- Brock, P. 1993, *Outback Ghettos: A History of Aboriginal Institutionalisation and Survival*, Cambridge University Press, Melbourne.
- Crawford, E. 1993, *Over My Tracks: A Remarkable Life*, Penguin, Melbourne.
- Edwards, C. and Read, P. (eds) 1989, *The Lost Children*, Doubleday, Sydney.
- Evans, R. and Saunders, K (eds) 1993, *Gender Relations in Australia: Domination and Negotiation*, Harcourt Brace Jovanovich, Sydney.
- Jacobs, P. 1990, *Mister Neville: A Biography*, Fremantle Arts Centre Press, Fremantle.
- Keating, P. 1994, *Worlds Apart*, Hale & Iremonger, Sydney.

- Keen, I. (ed.) 1988, *Being Black: Aboriginal Cultures in 'Settled' Australia*, Aboriginal Studies Press, Canberra.
- Langford, R. 1988, *'Don't Take Your Love to Town'*, Penguin, Melbourne.
- McGinness, J. 1991, *Son of Alyandabu: My Fight for Aboriginal Rights*, University of Queensland Press, St Lucia.
- Miller, J. 1985, *Koori: A Will to Win*, Angus & Robertson, Sydney.
- Reynolds, H. 1981, *The Other Side of the Frontier: An Interpretation of the Aboriginal Response to the Invasion and Settlement of Australia*, James Cook University of North Queensland, Townsville.
- Rintoul, S. 1993, *The Wailing: A National Black Oral History*, William Heinemann Australia, Sydney.
- Rowse, T. 1993, *After Mabo: Interpreting Indigenous Traditions*, Melbourne University Press, Melbourne.
- Somerville, M., Dundas, M., Mead, M., Robinson, J. and Sulter, M. 1994, *The Sun Dancin': People and Place in Coonabarabran*, Aboriginal Studies Press, Canberra.
- Sykes, B. 1992, *Mum Shirl: An Autobiography*, Mammoth Australia, Melbourne.
- Weller, A. 1981, *The Day of the Dog*, Allen & Unwin, Sydney.

Chapter 6

The Consuming Self

Beryl Langer

> Since 1983 there have been cases of American teenagers being shot dead, strangled or stabbed before being robbed of their sports shoes and athletic gear endorsed by heroes such as football quarterback Joe Montana and film-maker Spike Lee and worn as a uniform by gangs.
>
> In Australia, the trend of wearing sports shoes as casual street wear has been quickly adopted — and there have been isolated reports of 'shoe-muggings'. The shoes are an obvious status symbol, as manufacturers obligingly stitch their labels on the outside. So desperate are some kids to be seen wearing the right gear that they are prepared to kill for it.
>
> Evans 1994

Remember 'runners'? They are what Australian school children used to wear before the advent of 'designer label' sneakers, running shoes, basketball shoes, and cross-trainers. They had characteristics that distinguished them from the currently favoured Reeboks, Nikes, and Asics, but for the purposes of our present discussion, the most important features were that they were cheap and interchangeable. Made of canvas and rubber, unchanging in style from one season to the next, they were not the stuff of which envy is made. No one derived status from their 'runners', which were all the same, give or take a bit of wear, tear, and departure from sparkling whiteness from one year to the next. The story of how the world changed from one in which everyone wore cheap runners to one in which the labels on running shoes became so important that people were prepared to kill for them is worth examining, for it highlights some of the processes involved in the formation of what we might call the 'consuming self'. While incidents such as teenagers being mugged for their shoes feed a widespread sense of a social world that is unpredictable and out of control, they can be seen as the logical extension of a consumer culture in which self-esteem and social status are inextricably linked to the capacity to fulfil desires generated by the market. How we are produced as consuming subjects is the question to be considered in this chapter.

In taking up the issue of the consuming self, we shift our focus from the social institutions through which children are initiated into the beliefs and practices of their class, ethnic group, and gender — the family, the school, the peer group, the media — to the broad material and social context in which these institutions are situated. As sociologists we often take this context for granted. It is, after all, the world in which we live, the world in which we ourselves became social beings, and it appears to us to be a 'natural' environment requiring no explanation. While ethnographic studies of 'other' societies necessarily document the social relations through which material life is produced, detailed knowledge of everyday life in our own society makes the question of how basic needs are met seem somewhat superfluous. The material practices of hunter-gatherers and bush gardeners are interestingly 'strange', whereas supermarket shopping seems too tediously familiar to warrant either careful description or theoretical analysis. The fact that ours is a capitalist society, in which most people meet their needs through consumption rather than production, is not, however, a trivial matter. Consumer capitalism not only provides the structural conditions for our existence, but the cultural conditions for our formation as individual subjects. 'Sneaker muggings' testify to the effectiveness of this cultural formation, for children do not come into the world with a 'desire' for Reeboks or a 'need' for Nike Airs. There is nothing new about either mugging or the forced appropriation of shoes by the shoeless, but there is a particularity to the desire for designer sneakers, which can only be explained in terms of the historically specific features of the 'consuming self'.

Mead and Marx: capitalism and the self

George Herbert Mead (1934) conceptualises the formation of the self as a social process involving continuous interaction between the spontaneous and impulsive 'I' and the socially constructed and regulating 'me', which reflects on the 'I' from the standpoint of collective understandings and expectations. According to Mead, we develop a sense of ourselves as individual subjects by viewing ourselves 'as objects', first from the standpoint of 'significant others' in the immediate social environment, and ultimately from the standpoint of the social group as a whole. Mead's analysis provides us with a way of understanding *how* we become social selves, but the question of what kinds of social selves we become can only be answered in historically specific terms. The self does not emerge through interaction with an abstract, universal 'other', but with a particular family situated in a particular place at a particular time in its history, and the character structure of the 'me', whose ongoing conversation with the 'I' constitutes the social self, varies accordingly. Compare, for example, the kind of self that emerges through interaction with 'significant others' in pre-industrial villages with the self that develops through interaction with 'significant others' in Western cities at the end of the twentieth century. The shared understandings and expectations of social groups who produce their own subsistence and entertainment *locally* are qualitatively different from those of people whose material needs are met in shopping centres, and whose electronically mediated sense of the 'social group as a whole' is global. The structure of individual desire, in particular, differs dramatically. There are limits to what people can want in a world constituted by face-to-face relations between 'subsistence-producer' selves, in that the bounds of material possibility are limited by access to land, which is largely determined by birth and marriage. Consumer capitalism, in contrast, is premised on the perpetual stimulation of desire for a constantly changing universe of goods, services, and pleasures, which holds out the promise of what John Berger has called 'the envied future self': the 'new me' that will come into being when I am driving a new car, dressed in this year's 'look', listening to music on my new CD player, jogging in my new designer sneakers, and so on. As Berger (1972, p. 134) puts it:

> The spectator-buyer is meant to envy herself as she will become if she buys the product. She is meant to imagine herself transformed by the product into an object of envy for others, an envy which will then justify her loving herself. One could put this another way: the publicity image steals her love of herself as she is, and offers it back to her for the price of the product.

To understand the 'consuming self' that emerges within this cycle of endless desire, we need to situate Mead's interactionist analysis within the context of consumer capitalism as a social formation.

This is not the place to document either the history of capitalism or how its relation to modernity has been understood within social theory. These are issues that you may take up later in your reading. If, however, we acknowledge that the outcome of the social process of 'role-taking' through which the self emerges cannot be separated from the specific historical conditions under which it occurs, we need at least a summary sketch of the changes that have taken place in everyday life, for which terms like 'consumer capitalism' and 'postmodernism' have come to serve as conceptual shorthand. To simplify, fewer people in countries like Australia produce things in factories or on farms; more people process information and provide services. There are more things to buy, more 'abstract' ways to buy them (credit cards and electronic transfer, rather than cash), and more anonymous relations between buyers and sellers, whose transactions take place in supermarkets and shopping centres rather than corner grocers and local stores. New technologies of information and entertainment blur the distinction between 'public' and 'private' spheres, and create 'virtual' communities connected by electronic networks rather than face-to-face relations. Production is global, and so is culture. Fewer of the things we buy are made in the country we live in — or, indeed, in any one country at all. The component parts of an object assembled in one place can be produced in several others and packaged somewhere else again, as the labels on some of your consumer durables will testify. Information transmission from one part of the world to another is instant, and the same cultural commodities circulate throughout the globe, produced and distributed by multinational publishers and media conglomerates. More of what we eat is prepared outside the home by fast-food franchises like McDonald's, KFC, and Pizza Hut, whose corporate logos are as familiar in the suburbs of Melbourne, Sydney, or Perth as they are in Cleveland, Los Angeles, or Tokyo.

The impact of these changes on daily life is best understood as synergistic rather than cumulative, for changes in the organisation of production, consumption, information, and leisure interact with each other in ways that intensify their effects. For example, work has lost its efficacy as an 'identity hook' for many people, not just because of changes in the organisation of production, but also because these changes intersect with the exponential expansion of consumer 'choices' required to stimulate over-saturated markets, and the emergence of new leisure technologies with transformative effects on the life world. It becomes difficult to construct an identity around 'what I am going to be' when the occupational universe is continuously being restructured by technological change, globalisation, labour market deregulation, and so on.

Until the 1970s substantial numbers of Australians earned a living on family farms or in manufacturing, and clerical workers could count on 'life-long' employment with banks, insurance companies, or the State. Under these conditions, occupational futures could be envisaged in terms of a relatively stable set of options, but as manual jobs are relocated to the 'Third World', and clerical workers are replaced by computers, fewer and fewer people are able to construct their sense of who they are in terms of either the work they do or the firm that employs them to do it. It is difficult to hang your identity on part-time casual employment. At the same time, advertising encourages us to see ourselves not as 'workers' but as Coke- or Pepsi-drinkers, Reebok-wearers, Toyota-drivers, and so on. People's sense of who they are is thus increasingly constructed in terms of consumption rather than production; it is defined less by class position than by the 'lifestyle choices' implicit in such things as the labels on their clothing and sneakers, the logos on their sweatshirts and baseball caps, the houses they live in, the music they listen to, the cars they drive, the food they eat and where they eat it, their leisure activities, and their holiday destinations. The fact that capacity to exercise these choices is not equally distributed (Bourdieu 1984) is obscured by the 'virtual democracy' of the image and the shopping centre. Idealised representations of domesticity, fun, and glamour are projected by television across class lines, and 'window shopping' is accessible even to those who cannot afford the goods on display. Desire, at least, has been democratised. As John Fiske, Bob Hodge, and Graeme Turner (1987) argue in *Myths of Oz*, shopping has become a leisure activity rather than a chore — a fact reflected in the appearance of catch phrases such as 'Shop 'Til You Drop' and 'I Shop Therefore I Am'.

This shift to 'leisure shopping' is underlined by the changed relationship between shopping and tourism, with shopping now a tourist attraction in its own right, rather than just a complement to sight-seeing. Promotional literature on Melbourne as a tourist destination, for example, features a full-page spread headlined 'IN MELBOURNE SHOPPING'S NOT A HABIT IT'S A CAREER'. 'In Melbourne Now', it declares, 'People Are Born To Shop': 'Born to stroll elegant arcades and browse in bric-a-brac bazaars. To saunter along sunny esplanades where local crafts are displayed among swaying palms. To sip cappuccinos and nibble black forest cake. To lunch on fresh sushi, exotic salads or homemade pasta'. What is evoked here is an idyllic fantasy in which we are never short of time or money, never thwarted in our pursuit of a parking spot, never inconvenienced or threatened by the behaviour of others, and never out of place in casually elegant settings by virtue of our size, shape, colour, age, or class. It speaks to us as sophisticated consumers who take material

abundance for granted and are in the market for experience as much as for things —
much 'cooler' customers than the gadget-happy commodity-seekers in Erich Fromm's
ironic account of capitalist culture, *The Sane Society*, which was written in the 1950s.
According to Fromm (1968, p. 135), the consumer capitalist vision of heaven would
'look like the biggest department store in the world, showing new things and gadgets', with ourselves 'having plenty of money with which to buy them': '[We] would
wander around open-mouthed in this heaven of gadgets and new commodities, provided only that there were ever more and newer things to buy, and perhaps that [our]
neighbours were just a little less privileged than [ourselves]'. Both of these texts can
be read as fragmentary 'symptoms' of a shift in capitalist culture over the past forty
years: a shift that not only involves the transformation of conditions under which
social life is produced and reproduced, but of subjectivity — what people think,
want, desire, feel.

Situating the consuming self: a brief history

We tend to think that while 'times' change, 'human nature' is always the same: a universal subject with the same cognitive and emotional structures responding to different historical conditions. When we visit a pioneer village, for example, and try to
imagine what it might have been like to live there a hundred years ago, we picture
ourselves as we are now, but wearing different clothes and using different household
technology — ' me' in a different setting. The 'me' produced under those conditions
would, however, have different cognitive and emotional responses, for social change
is not just about 'modes of production', but about 'modes' of being human. As C.
Wright Mills (1959, p. 40) argues in *The Sociological Imagination*, the personal and
the social are inextricably related, and large-scale structural transformation has consequences for even 'the most intimate features of the human self', and vice versa.
Thus the processes whereby capitalism turned society into a 'gigantic market place'
(Braverman 1974, p. 271) were necessarily transformative of the self, for mass production required mass markets, and these could only come into being if people gave
up self-sufficiency for shopping.

In the first instance, the shift from home production to shopping was a matter of
structural necessity imposed by the conditions of daily life confronted by people who
moved from farm to factory, and who no longer had either the land or the time to
grow things, or to make their own bread, jam, soap, and candles. The practice of
buying rather than making gradually extended to all sorts of domestic goods and
clothing, which meant that the family as an institution was progressively stripped of
its productive role. The family's service role also diminished, with things once
mended at home either discarded or sent out for repairs, cleaning and maintenance
handed over to a burgeoning home-help 'industry', and the care of children and old
people carried out by 'professionals' in institutional settings. Over the course of the
twentieth century, social life has thus been progressively incorporated into the market
through the conversion of services into commodities, and the invention of *new* products and services that become indispensable as the practices they replace are

destroyed by changing conditions. In this way, Harry Braverman (1974, p. 281) argues, 'the inhabitant of capitalist society is enmeshed in a web made up of commodity goods and commodity services from which there is little possibility of escape except through partial or total abstention from social life as it now exists'.

The creation of the 'universal market' is best understood as a complex shift in economic and social logic, rather than a simple exercise in capitalist domination. At the same time, however, as Stuart Ewen (1976) has argued, the 'structural necessity' on which this process turned was less the 'need' of workers for goods than of capitalists for markets. New techniques of mass production could only be sustained by new patterns of mass consumption, and this required the socialisation of individual subjects as consumers. Taken-for-granted assumptions about money, leisure, and pleasure had to be changed, and a new kind of advertising directed at *creating* markets, rather than *informing* them, became an integral part of capitalist production.

The social-psychological insight that self-esteem depends on the esteem of others was strategically deployed in advertising, which linked the promise of social approval to the consumption of manufactured goods, and dismissed age-old habits of thrift and self-reliance as 'old-fashioned'. If making things at home could be defined as retrograde, and 'being modern' tied to the consumption of everything from canned food and toothpaste to cars and appliances, 'workers' could be encouraged to see themselves as 'consumers' (Ewen 1976, p. 37). The conditions of urban modernity associated with industrial capitalism were rich in potential for the manipulation of anxiety to promote consumption: fear of unemployment and loneliness made people vulnerable to feelings of inadequacy, and receptive to products that offered the promise of a more attractive or successful self.

The body, in particular, proved to be a site rich with consumer potential. Ewen (1976, pp. 41–8) documents the ways in which people were encouraged to view their bodies as sources of social embarrassment — a series of danger zones threatening their prospects of employment or romance. Advertising identified 'problems' and offered consumer 'solutions', not just for body odour, bad breath, sallow skin, and dull lifeless hair, but also for personal inadequacies like shyness, socially unacceptable speech patterns, and inability to dance, all of which could be remedied by spending money on products, advice literature, or evening classes. The self was thus constructed not just as consumer, but as prime site of consumption — always capable of improvement if the right purchases were made. Advertising even offered 'liberation' from the alienation and frustration of boring repetitive work in cities beset by problems of pollution and overcrowding — that is, from the conditions of capitalist industrialisation itself (Ewen 1976, pp. 84–7). For example, fantasies of freedom and escape were (and are) used to sell cars to people who wanted to escape the tedium of the assembly lines on which the cars were produced — a classic example of the hermetically sealed circle in which capitalism continuously offers itself as the solution to the problems it generates.

While the techniques of contemporary advertising make the efforts of Ewen's 'captains of consciousness' look clumsy and transparent, the basic strategies he identifies are continuously adapted to the production of new generations of consumers for new generations of products, which both generate and respond to new patterns of family life. Mobile phones, for example, are promoted as the solution to parental concern about children's vulnerability in the public domain, and computers as the solution to anxiety about educational outcomes. Whatever the problem, in other words, caring is linked to spending, and 'good parenting' is defined in terms of consumer solutions.

Socialisation for consumption

Being born into 'the universal market' has implications for children — not just for the repertoire of adult roles available to them for imitation in what Mead (1934) refers to as 'the play stage', but also for what they *become* as they develop an organised sense of their place in relation to the normative expectations of 'the generalised other'. At the level of everyday experience, they enter a culture in which the most immediately accessible features of adulthood are related to shopping. The baby's first excursions into the world beyond the family are likely to be to the supermarket; the most frequently observed interactions between parents and the wider society are likely to involve the consumption of goods or services; the 'high points' of family life are often associated with the purchase of major consumer durables; the rituals of gift-giving associated with birthdays, anniversaries, and Christmas are highly commodified.

The extent to which children's entry into social life has come to be synonymous with their entry into the market can be seen in the increasing commercialisation of 'rites of passage' over the course of this century. Consider birthdays, for example. Few people in their seventies and eighties would have had birthday parties and presents as children, for they grew up in large families under conditions of material scarcity, which precluded lavish spending to mark the passing of each year. Their children — whose childhood coincided with the postwar economic boom, and the technological advances that paved the way for mass production of cheap toys — were the first generation for whom birthday parties and presents became part of the taken-for-granted culture of childhood. Children's birthday parties in the 1950s and 1960s were modest affairs by today's standards, however. Food was either prepared at home or purchased from local bakers; entertainment consisted of games that cost little or nothing, and were organised by the children themselves. In contrast, children's birthdays in the 1980s and 1990s have become the focus of a substantial service industry. Food and entertainment franchises like McDonald's, Pizza Hut, Pancake Parlour, Zone 3, and Timezone — the commodification of Australian childhood is also its globalisation — offer special 'party packages', and 'specialist' children's party 'coordinators', caterers, clowns, and magicians can also be brought into the home, turning the children's party into an opportunity for what Thorstein Veblen (1953) called 'conspicuous consumption' — the competitive display of capacity to spend money on inessentials. Paradoxically, the 'packaged' party can also be seen as a response to scarcity (of time, rather than money) — a strategy adopted by harried parents to eliminate preparation and cleaning, and set limits to the duration of the event itself. Once commercially organised parties become the norm, home parties at which food and games are organised by parents become 'embarrassing', and the link between celebration and consumption comes to be taken for granted. So, too, with presents, which have become increasingly elaborate as the routine purchase of toys as 'treats' throughout the year (Langer 1989) raises the level of expectation surrounding 'special' occasions.

In the same way that rites of passage have become consumer events, the transition from childhood to adolescence and adulthood is now marked by increased access to consumption, first in the form of plastic cards allowing instant access to bank accounts, then in the right to negotiate loans without parental permission. In other words, a status transition, once effected by *earning* money, is now achieved by *borrowing* money. For example, children encouraged to develop the habit of saving by opening a Commonwealth Bank 'Dollarmites' account when they start primary school are automatically transferred to 'Club Australia' — which emphasises the pleasures of spending more than the satisfaction of saving — as they approach their twelfth birthday. They receive the following letter, whose adult mode of address (surname rather than first name) and offer of an electronic transfer card prompted the comment 'I feel so important' from one of my own children: 'When you opened your Dollarmite bank account you were probably in Kindergarten or Year 1. Now you're ready for a different kind of banking, and that's why your account has now been upgraded to Club Australia'.

Direct experience is not the only source of children's information about the social world. Australian households watch on average more than thirty hours of television each week (Cupit 1994, p. 161), which means that the interactive process through which the self is socially constructed cannot be conceptualised as one that necessarily involves face-to-face relations with 'actual' people. Characters in regularly watched programs become 'significant others' in the sense that their *imagined* response is incorporated into the child's definition of a situation; television is one of the major sources of information about the social world beyond the family through which children formulate a conception of the 'generalised other'. This serves to reinforce the sense that human existence revolves around shopping, for commercial television's 'product' is not entertainment but audiences, whose attention is sold to advertisers by the minute. In this sense, it is less a 'window on the world' than a 'window on consumer options', and a regular viewer may well come to the conclusion that consumption sits at the centre of social life. The 'generalised other', as mediated by television, is a satisfied consumer whose happiness resides in choosing the 'right' brand of margarine, the best deal in housing loans, the cola with the highest 'fun factor', and the most enviable holiday location. Rarely, if ever, is the production of goods represented. Things are not 'made' in television commercials, just consumed.

Children's minimal access to the sphere of production gives them little opportunity to 'act out' adult work roles in what George Herbert Mead (1934) refers to as the 'game stage'. 'Anticipatory socialisation' for shopping, on the other hand, is readily available. Stores like Toys "R" Us and KMart provide miniature trolleys so that children can 'pretend' to shop, and many of the toys and games currently marketed to children place them in consuming roles. Take, for example, Mattel's 'Barbie', which reconstructs 'playing with dolls' as socialisation for consumption rather than nurture. Described as 'Fun-to-Dress', Barbie's existence as an object of play revolves around having the right clothes for the leisure activities in her repertoire, some of which are illustrated on the back of each basic Barbie package. ('Hangin' out! Shopping! Glamorous party! Great date!') To purchase a Barbie is thus to embark on an infinite series of further purchases of clothing and 'lifestyle' props, and it does not take a great deal of 'sociological imagination' to see that playing with Barbie serves to socialise girls into a version of femininity organised around consumption and display. Boys, too, are socialised for consumption via 'commoditoys' (Langer 1989, 1994) like Transformers, DinoRiders, Teenage Mutant Ninja Turtles, and Power Rangers, all of which entail an extended series of interlocking purchases, with the packaging of each toy serving as an advertisement for others, without which it will be 'incomplete'. Even role-playing games like Dungeons and Dragons are imbued with consumer logic: they are 'commodified fantasies' that begin with transactions of exchange to equip each character with weapons and 'purchase' certain levels of strength, intelligence, and magical power.

Common to many of the toys and games marketed to children is the idea that the self can be made and remade through consumption — an idea central to the cultural logic of consumer capitalism. Take, for example, the extent to which personal transformation is presented as a matter of consumer choice: something to be purchased in the form of exercise programs, diet regimes, self-improvement courses, meditation classes, mood-altering drugs, psychotherapy, and cosmetic surgery. The newsagents of the nation are filled with magazines promoting various ways of 'consuming' health, fitness, beauty, relaxation, and improved relationships.

Bodies, in particular, are big business — not just women's bodies, as was once the case, but men's also. The American magazine *Men's Health*, for example, is indistinguishable in form, if not content, from the women's magazines that, according to feminist critics, 'commodify' women's bodies (Root 1984, pp. 51–68). The February 1995 issue has a special section entitled 'Lose That Gut!', featuring a series of zone-specific exercises ('Sculpt rippling abdominals — without doing a single sit-up') a diet plan ('A realistic plan for dropping weight and keeping it off from a man who went the distance, lost 30 pounds, and, more important, hasn't gained it back'), and advice on how to dress 'thin' ('Strategic style — or how to skilfully use the right clothes to minimise your weak points and emphasise your strong ones'). Facing the contents page is an advertisement of a type familiar to female readers. Promoting a skin moisturiser called Lift Off! from Aramis Research Labs ('For Younger-Looking Skin'), it begins with the anxiety-inducing question, 'Do I look my age?', printed in large bold letters. Similarly, the specialist magazine *Running* urges its readers to 'Burn Fat Faster with PR Bar', making the paradoxical promise, familiar to generations of female dieters, that consumption holds the key to weight loss. Marx's comment that, under capitalism, 'all that is solid melts into air' takes on particular poignancy in relation to the continuously reconstructed 'consuming self' of the late twentieth century.

Conclusion

When Margaret Mead (1981) set out for the Admiralty Islands north of New Guinea in 1928 to study child-rearing practices in the Manus village of Peri, she set herself the task of documenting the way in which the Manus 'prepare[d] their children for life'. The context of Mead's study — a monocultural community of 210 people in a fishing village built in a lagoon — made the question of what 'must' be learnt easy to specify, for the connection between survival and water safety was obvious. The question of what children 'have to' learn to become adults in Australian society at the end of the twentieth century is, at first sight, more complex, given the cultural diversity of a population drawn from over one hundred countries of birth, and the occupational diversity of an advanced capitalist economy. If we keep the experience of contemporary Australian children in mind as we read Mead's account of how Manus children learnt to negotiate their watery world, however, a striking parallel emerges. Just as Manus children were 'accustomed to water' from the first years of life, Australian children grow up in a world shaped, to a large degree, by shopping. Just as the boat was central to the production of material life in Manus culture, the shopping trolley is central to our own. Manus children had to learn not to fall out of the canoe. Australian children in the last quarter of the twentieth century have to learn not to fall out of the shopping trolley, and to accept the restrictive harness of the car seat in which they are transported to the supermarket. They also have to learn how to want — to live within the circle of desire and satisfaction on which consumer capitalism depends. In other words, just as children in hunter-gatherer societies must learn to hunt and gather, children in peasant societies to till the soil and care for animals, and children in industrial societies to take on a sense of self as 'worker', children in consumer society must learn to shop.

Discussion questions

1   Find out as much as you can about what it was like to be a child in your parents' and grandparents' generation by asking older relatives and friends to recall their toys, games, clothes, pocket money, and how they spent their time. How do their accounts compare with (a) your own recollections of childhood and (b) your observations of the culture of contemporary childhood? To what extent does this brief excursion into oral history support Ewen's thesis of a shift in self from 'producer' to 'consumer'? Mature-age students might better answer these questions by recollecting their own childhoods and comparing them with those of their children and/or grandchildren.

2   Is it over-stating the case to say that the interactive relationships through which we develop our sense of self are either (a) market relationships or (b) inextricably tied to market relationships? In other words, is the market

'universal', as Braverman argues, or are there aspects of the self and the social that are not 'commodified'.

3   What part does consumption play in the construction and expression of gender identity?

4   It is often argued that there are no classes in consumer capitalism, just market categories. Is this the case, or do we 'consume' class identity?

5   Does consumer capitalism *increase* 'exploitation' and 'oppression' by subjecting leisure and pleasure to the 'needs' of capital, or does the expansion of consumer choice contribute to greater freedom? (One way of approaching this question would be through a comparison of the chapter on shopping in Fiske, Hodge, and Turner, *Myths of Oz*, with the position argued by Ewen or Seabrook.)

Recommended reading

- Berger, J. 1972, *Ways of Seeing*, Harmondsworth, Penguin Books.

Chapters 4 and 7 are essential reading. Chapter 4 is one of the most lucid accounts of the connection between women's subordination and their status as 'objects' of the male gaze. Given that women's sense of themselves as 'sights' is inseparable from their sense of themselves as 'sites' of consumption, this is a good place to begin your reading on 'consuming' gender identity. Chapter 7 provides an accessible (and brief) critical analysis of publicity.

- Braverman, H. 1974, *Labor and Monopoly Capital*, Monthly Review Press, New York.

Chapter 13 (pp. 271–83) is essential reading on 'how capitalism transformed all of society into a gigantic marketplace'.

- Engelhart, T. 1987, 'The Shortcake Strategy', in T. Gitlin (ed.), *Watching Television*, Pantheon Books, New York, pp. 68–110.
- Ewen, S. 1976, *Captains of Consciousness: Advertising and the Social Roots of Consumer Culture*, McGraw-Hill, New York; and Ewen, S. and Ewen, E. 1982, 'Consumption as a Way of Life', part 2 of *Channels of Desire*, McGraw-Hill, New York, pp. 41–77.

The latter is a succinct and interesting summary statement of Ewen's thesis. Both *Captains of Consciousness* and *Channels of Desire* are very readable in their entirety, but if you have to be selective, read this section, or the sections headed 'Mobilizing the Instincts' and 'Advertising: Civilizing the Self' in *Captains of Consciousness*, pp. 31–48.

- Fiske, J., Hodge, B., and Turner, G. 1987, *Myths of Oz*, Allen & Unwin, Sydney, ch. 5.
- Kline, S. 1989, Limits to the Imagination: Marketing and Children's Culture', in I. Angus and S. Jhally (eds), *Cultural Politics in Contemporary America*, Routledge, New York, pp. 299–316; see also Kline, S. 1994, *Out of the Garden: Toys and Children's Culture in the Age of TV Marketing*, Routledge, London.
- Seabrook, J. 1985, *Landscapes of Poverty*, Basil Blackwell, Oxford.
- Sennett, R. and Cobb, J. 1973, *The Hidden Injuries of Class*, Vintage Books, New York.

The section on 'Destructive Replacement' (pp. 160–9) is particularly recommended.

- Williams, R. 1976, 'consumer', in *Keywords: A Vocabulary of Culture and Society*, Fontana, Glasgow, pp. 68–70.

Brief and essential reading.

- Willis, S. 1991, *A Primer for Daily Life*, Routledge, London.

See, especially, chapter 2, 'Gender as Commodity', and chapter 4, 'Work(ing) Out'.

Chapter 7

The Social Self: Experiences and Explanations

Allan Kellehear

Have you ever heard about 'near-death experiences'? These sometimes occur to people who have heart attacks and fall unconscious. When they regain consciousness, these people will sometimes tell other people rather remarkable stories. They may describe how they became 'out of body', and were able to watch people attempting to resuscitate them, as if onlookers to the event. Later they may describe being drawn through a long dark tunnel, experiencing feelings of great peace and happiness, and encountering a friendly being of pure light. Often they experience a review of their lives, and later meet friends or relatives who have died many years before. At sometime during these extraordinary events, they are 'told' to return to their former life; they are informed that 'it is not their time yet', and then they suddenly find themselves regaining consciousness. Surely here, in this ostensibly mystical or hallucinatory experience, the sociological understandings of self are elbowed aside by the seemingly more relevant psychological or biological models of self? Or are they?

Sociological ideas about the self provide us with several important insights into how we can understand our private experiences. The first insight can be described as the lesson of socialisation. In examining the different sources of social influence on our selves, we are able to assess the role of these influences in providing a specific and practical shape to this thing we call 'me'.

'Me' is a man or a woman, of a certain age, occupying a certain place and time, with a certain social class and ethnic inheritance. I am also more than these things. I am not simply a collection, a sum, of all these things. Nevertheless, these are the para-meters and the starting points of my social being and experience. I cannot readily transcend these points without first having to gain much experience. This experience takes me beyond those parameters and is gained by 'travelling', not necessarily by trains, planes, and automobiles, but through encounters with foreign people, circum-stances, and ideas anywhere in life.

That lesson of socialisation has been the principle insight of the previous chap-ters on the social self, although Finlayson and Anderson also discuss how racist con-cepts of self can be used with dire consequences for those with little power to resist them. In this chapter, however, I want to demonstrate two further insights that the idea of the social self has to offer the student of sociology.

First, I want to elaborate on the idea that the social self is more than an idea that tells us about the 'background factors' to the initial formation of the self. The social self is the most important way we have of understanding another person; it is a thing of ongoing substance and importance. When we slip too easily into 'psychologisms', seeing others entirely as a collection of personality traits, we risk restricting, rather than deepening, our view of others.

Second, and flowing from this first idea, I will argue that few perspectives on the individual self — psychological, biological or sociological — make sense as single explanations. Most scholars would agree with that statement, but would then add that it is important to identify which models are the most pertinent for the case under discussion. But as we shall see when I return to the earlier case of the near-death experience, it is not always clear which models of self are pertinent in each case. This is because the *process of deciding* which professional explanations 'fit' is itself determined by social forces.

Let me, by way of introduction, begin by building on the insights about the social self that the previous authors have offered. I will then describe two experiences of self that show how overlooking the social self can lead to significant barriers to understanding. Finally, I will discuss the near-death experience to show how social influences are at work in professional decision-making concerning which models of self are important in explaining consciousness.

Theories of the self: stories from biology, psychology and sociology

In preceding chapters, both Fiona Mackie and Kerreen Reiger have alluded to the long history in psychology and biology of attempting to find principles of self that hold true, irrespective of time and place. This has been particularly true of psychology in its behavioural, neurobiological, and experimental forms, rather than within social psychology itself. Sociology and anthropology, together with social psychology, on the other hand, have been more interested to show how time and place rule the self — a difficult task when the modern popular emphasis is placed on our differences, rather than our similarities, with other people.

Nevertheless, while both activities have been valuable and complementary, the popular obsession with individual differences has led many to think that, at the end of the day, it is psychology and biology that explain the substance of self, and sociology and anthropology that explain the broad shape of its expression. But this is not true. Let me explain how pivotal social factors and processes are in the work of explaining the self.

There are two broad approaches within psychology: the psychodynamic and the behavioural. In psychodynamic traditions, the inner workings of the 'mind' or 'personality' are emphasised. The presence of emotions such as sadness, fear, or anger is argued to be universal, and the triggers to their release context-dependent. In other words, emotions are emotions about *some thing*. Events trigger emotions. However, events live inside our minds long after they happen, sometimes remembered, sometimes not. The fact that they are sometimes not remembered does not necessarily mean that they are not still guiding or ruling our emotions nevertheless. So, for the most part, social experiences, either in fact or 'in the mind', shape the inner life of individuals on a daily, moment-to-moment basis.

And emotions are not just subjective feelings either. They are usually physiological events, even though we rarely think of them in that way. When you smile or are anxious, neurophysiological activities are occurring to make the smile appear on your face, or to create the sensation of 'butterflies in the tummy'. Those responses hold much interest for behavioural psychologists. They believe that the initial physical responses to events, whether it be pleasure or discomfort, can determine future responses, irrespective of rational thoughts that a person might have. In other words, the self as organism may overrule the self as rational thinker.

Another model of self underlying these 'reactional' models is the biological idea that the self is born with certain innate qualities — that genetic inheritance 'gives' people certain characteristics. Just as people are born with brown eyes or red hair, so too some people are 'naturally' intelligent or hot-tempered. However, most people do understand that genetic qualities, including those that are often thought to relate to personality, can be radically modified or accentuated by cultural circumstances.

As Katy Richmond earlier remarked, these influences can vary significantly even in the same family, so that it is no easy task to say which features of a person are genetic and which social. Debate and research continues on this front. Those who consistently favour biological or psychological explanations of self embrace what in earlier chapters, such as those by Richmond, and Finlayson and Anderson, have been called 'essentialist' concepts about the self. However, the nature of self is not easily accommodated by theories that turn away from social complexities. The discussions of self in the preceding pages represent several differing sociological traditions that underline this insight.

Fiona Mackie, in her discussion of the ethnic self, for example, draws on what some people call a 'phenomenological' perspective of the self (see Schutz 1970). In phenomenological accounts of the self, it is social meanings that are central to the structure of the self — that is, the make-up of a person's thoughts and emotions.

These meanings are not simply invented in some kind of private space inside the mind. Rather, these meanings always have social origins. Meanings reside *between* people, and then are attended to by them. The thought patterns of one's group, combined with the ability to reflect on these meanings in highly individual ways, make the experience of self what it is, to oneself and to others.

Other sociological ideas of the self used by the contributors in this section are closer to social psychology. These ideas may be described more accurately as 'symbolic interactionist' because they emphasise social contexts more than individual traits and attitudes. Katy Richmond and Beryl Langer are influenced by the insights of theorists such as George Herbert Mead (1934), Irving Goffman (1969), or

Thomas Scheff (1974). From this perspective, social life is a guessing game. We are given a basic map of our self and the world by our early childhood experiences, but then we must revise and change that map as we move through different social and cultural spheres of life.

We come to learn that there is public behaviour and private behaviour, and what you see is not always the way it is, whether it be federal politics or the more modest 'politics' of the home or workplace. Meanings are ambiguous and changing. If they are shared at all, they may be shared for reasons of convenience as much as from genuine consensus. To attempt to stabilise this seeming chaos of social affairs, we frequently attach fixed and simple meanings to events, experiences, or people: we stereotype. When this kind of labelling is emphasised in a sociological explanation, the perspective is often called 'labelling theory'. According to this theory, the self is shaped by meanings imposed and controlled by others. Labelling through language (for example, boy/girl, mad/bad, or intelligent/stupid) creates, with the collaborative help of important and powerful people, the self-images and ideas that we all embrace about ourselves. When the hypnotic and taken-for-granted power of language is stressed in an explanation of self, this is commonly called 'social constructionist theory' (Berger and Luckmann 1966).

The power of language, and of social sanctions such as labelling, helps reinforce those categories, helps make them 'true' and convincing for individuals. In turn, these experiences come to appear 'natural' and 'objective' to everyone participating in them. Because the social context that might reveal these processes is often obscure, or difficult for the participants to see, psychological ideas about others will tend to predominate.

This can lead to what some people have called 'blaming the victim', the idea that the responsible social forces that might explain individual behaviour are ignored. Instead, explanations that locate the responsible mechanisms within the individual are preferred or are inadvertently chosen. I will provide two experiences of self that illustrate and highlight these problems.

The ongoing importance of the social self: two case studies

Denial in the face of death

Consider the case of Mrs B, a fifty-year-old housewife with an advanced, malignant cancer of the breast. The diagnosis was arrived at some seventeen years earlier, and various treatment options employed by the hospital, combined with an apparently responsive tumour, have kept this woman alive and reasonably well for that time. Recently, however, she has been informed that all treatment options have been exhausted and that any subsequent treatment received will be to protect her as much as possible from the uncomfortable consequences of her deteriorating condition. She is dying. (For a full discussion of this case, see Kellehear and Fook 1989.)

When informed of this situation, Mrs B replied cheerfully that she is hopeful for a cure nevertheless. This response surprised the health team gathered and most present concluded that Mrs B was simply in a state of emotional denial. Denial is a defence mechanism originally formulated by Anna Freud. It is a psychological strategy designed to ward off any severe threat that may upset the emotional control and stability of the psyche. As a temporary response to crisis, it is considered a 'normal' response. As a continuing reaction, it is considered by psychiatrists as maladaptive, or 'abnormal'.

And what of the hapless Mrs B? It is now some seventeen years since she was diagnosed as terminal. As anyone can testify who has lived at least that long, many medical discoveries can be made in that time. The hope that the tide will turn against breast cancer soon is not an unreasonable one given the 'medical miracle' stories that we are bombarded with daily in the print and television media. At the very least, care and cure are expectations that might understandably blur in the minds of people such as Mrs B.

Second, Mrs B was feeling good when she was informed of her poor outlook. People's expectations about career, health, or relationships are always context-dependent. When feeling low or unwell, people will nearly always underestimate or take a less optimistic view of their prospects. Conversely, when people feel well, they are more optimistic about their future.

Finally, professional assessment of a person's illness is based on what is known about the usual and 'normal' course of a disease. Patients' assessments, particularly those of patients with little medical knowledge, are only partly based on what their doctors tell them. Patients' assessments of how they are feeling and of how others are reacting to them are important indicators of how they might view their prospects. This discrepancy between professional and lay understandings of dying can lead to entirely different expectations of what constitutes 'realistic' comments about the illness.

In this rather complicated context, denial serves as a professional label that (a) obscures the social forces responsible for the initial patient response, (b) interferes with the ability of professional people to learn more about the person they are labelling, and (c) stigmatises a person by mistaking a normal social response for a maladaptive psychological one.

Two observations are worth making about these comments. First, an impetuous preference for psychological explanations over social ones can lead to a significant misunderstanding about the nature of self — one's own and other people's. Second, essentialist ideas about self that ignore social context can lead to disturbing stereotyping of others. Finlayson and Anderson's discussion of racism demonstrates this problem well.

The tendency of people to always explain behaviour in purely psychological terms (such as defence mechanisms or personality traits) is a major impediment to understanding the social self in everyday life. Many people continue to see their selves as 'minds', and the major contents of this self as simple emotions and thoughts. All this sits inside the top 10 per cent or so of a coloured watermelon we call 'the body'. Few people appreciate that this particular idea of self as 'mind' is itself a cultural model, not a 'natural fact', and certainly not a model of self necessarily shared by everyone. The following case study demonstrates this insight.

Soul loss in a Hmong woman

Mai is a thirty-four-year-old Hmong woman, living in Melbourne. The Hmong are indigenous to Laos, in South-East Asia. Since giving birth to her latest child by Caesarean section, Mai has been complaining of feeling unwell and of experiencing some pain. She had seen several specialists, but all of these medical practitioners were unable to find anything wrong. (For a full discussion of this case, see Rice, Ly, and Lumley 1994.)

Mai's situation came to light when she was visited by an anthropological researcher from a local university research centre studying mother's and children's health. At the time of the visit, Mai explained to the researcher (after some prompting) what she believed to be the 'problem'. Pranee Liamputtong Rice (Rice, Ly, and Lumley 1994, p. 577), the senior researcher, explains: 'The Hmong believe that each person has three souls. One looks after the body during life and, upon death, travels to other worlds to await the opportunity for rebirth. A second soul tends the grave and the third soul lives with the person's ancestors in the other world'. If these three souls stay together in life, the person stays well. If, however, through illness or misadventure, the soul is frightened away, the person may fail to thrive. In these cases, a shaman may need to be called upon to conduct a ceremony to recall the soul back to its owner. Mai believed that she had lost one of her souls when she underwent general anaesthesia during her Caesarean section.

In an effort to assist Mai, Dr Liamputtong Rice contacted the hospital where Mai had given birth to her last child and explained the situation. The hospital readily agreed to the necessary ceremony. Mai returned to the exact place where she had undergone her procedures, but this time with her local shaman. A ritual lasting some thirty minutes was performed in these areas. Gradually, over the following days and weeks, Mai began to feel herself gain strength and health again.

Mai's case highlights several important sociological issues. First, ideas about the self vary, not only around the world but also around Australia. This is because, of course, representatives of much of the world's citizenry can be found in Australia. We are, as we shall see in Sue Harvey's chapter in the next section, one of the great migrant countries of the world.

Second, ideas about the self are not simply abstract beliefs about the workings of the 'mind', or how one should behave towards others. Ideas about the self are more than this. People's ideas about themselves are fully embodied — that is, they affect their very physical well-being — ask any woman recovering from anorexia, or any sedentary, overweight, and overworked man recovering from a heart attack.

Finally, Mai's ideas about the 'components' of her self may seem strange. The idea that one can have *three* bits of '*one*self' pulling in different directions may at first seem unfamiliar to many of us. However, even in Anglo-European culture, this is a common idea. We need only remind ourselves of Sigmund Freud's (1973) psychoanalytical ideas about the constituents of the self: the superego, the one who reminds us about the rights and wrongs taught to us by our family and society at large; the ego, the one who keeps a steady eye on reality; and the id, that unpredictable self of desire, who craves physical indulgence and is the source of aggression when blocked or thwarted by the demands of the other two 'selves'.

Are not these 'selves' like Mai's three souls, but with different duties? And how much 'scientific evidence' is there, after all, for any of this? Yet millions of people every year, in half the countries of the world, place themselves under the influence of these types of 'maps' of the self. Mai's case is a sure and steady reminder that, as Fiona Mackie argues in her chapter, we are many selves.

The near-death experience and explanatory models of the self

The pursuit of knowledge is not a neutral social activity. All researchers are influenced by the habits of their trade, and the ideas of their time and place. What is 'true' about the world is a thing rediscovered with the renewed gaze of each generation of people over time. What was self-evident to Galileo was not for Newton or for Einstein. Often, however, it is not information that changes over time, but rather the way we see that information, the way we view the relationships between bits of information. Knowledge, then, is often about *ways of seeing*.

The most common way of seeing appears to be the habit of comparing strange experiences with familiar ones: 'That event is like this one that we know', or 'That experience is similar to another we have encountered'. We are always comparing the new with the old, to find ways of understanding the new. It is the same in research circles.

When near-death experiences occurred in the Middle Ages in Europe, they were understood as visits to the afterlife, the place where God and His angels were to be found (Zaleski 1987). Today, religious explanations are generally scorned in educated circles, objects of suspicion. This is partly a result of the dominant materialist view of the self, made popular by psychology and medicine. This view of the self recognises no 'soul', nor does it recognise any part of the self that is not amenable to physical probing or logical systems of thought.

So when people report near-death experiences today, most medical and psychological opinion suggests that they are hallucinating (Blackmore 1993). This means that when people report that they are 'seeing' tunnels and experiencing life review, doctors and psychologists will argue that this is only the brain playing tricks on them because it is dying. As we have noted earlier, psychology and biology have been interested in developing principles that are universal, principles that stay 'true' in all conditions.

So with the near-death experience, they have been quick to show how tunnel sensations and life review are brought about by a malfunctioning central nervous system — how any or all the features of the near-death experience are the side effects of dying, of the brain responding to being depleted of oxygen. The old models on which these theorists rely for their new theories of the near-death experience are the hallucination and the symptoms of temporal lobe seizure activity. Unlike sociology or anthropology, the proponents of biopsychological models fail to consider, once again, the social self.

We know, if only from the previous discussion of the ongoing importance of the social self, that sociology views the social self as context-dependent. Meaning and experiences are symbolic structures that give thought and emotion their personal sense and direction. In this context, it is one thing to say that anger is a universal emotion, but less convincing to suggest that there are universal symbols of thought produced by physical processes. Near-death experiences are a good example of this problem (see Kellehear 1996).

Tunnel sensation appears to be how *travelling through darkness* is sometimes described by mainly Western experiencers. Chinese experiencers may describe it as emerging from the throat of a flower. An Australian Aborigine may describe it as an experience of night. Because tunnels are common symbols in the West, this word is often chosen as a descriptor. In other words, no experience can be understood separate from the language that describes it. There is no tunnel. There *is* a sensation of darkness, and this is described in different cultural ways. Western psychologists have tried to develop theories about a tunnel *before* checking the cultural information.

There are similar problems with attempting to develop psychological theories of life review based on only one form or model of the self. Life review appears absent in the near-death experiences of people from hunter-gatherer societies. This is perhaps because few of these people see their identity, their selves, as independent from the tribe. A personal review of their individual biography will have little meaning to them.

Finally, when the various features of near-death experiences are examined more closely by sociologists and anthropologists, we are able to show that many of the experiences that people have near death also occur to those who are conscious and healthy. Sociology, looking to areas familiar to its own research agenda, is able to identify experiences similar to those occurring near death: the experiences of castaways at sea, people lost in the wilderness, and trapped miners, and experiences of religious conversion, shamanic initiation, and bereavement.

All of these encounters are known to produce out-of-body experiences, life reviews, experiences of light and darkness, meetings with deceased or supernatural beings, and other personal experiences commonly thought to be associated only with near-death experiences. Perhaps, then, the key to understanding personal experiences near death is to examine how those situations are socially similar to other crisis experiences. Maybe, but who is right?

Conclusion

In the context of the historical development of ideas, the eventual answer may actually be 'no one'. A better question to ask is 'Which theory or model of self now appears more useful, in terms of coping with the obvious complexities of this intriguing experience?'. Clearly the biopsychological model of self, in concentrating on detailed features of near-death experiences, loses sight of the larger picture and significance of the social self.

On the other hand, sociology is not biology, and clearly there are biological experiences that accompany these social and psychological experiences of self. Nevertheless, it seems that biology may not 'cause' near-death experiences any more than ovens 'cause' dinner, or automobiles 'cause' driving.

The important sociological lesson to draw from this reflection on near-death experiences, in terms of competing explanations from different disciplines, is that no model has been shown to perfectly account for this thing we call 'self'. What we do know is that when past models have ignored the social life within and without ourselves, they have contributed to oversimplifying the human self. On occasion, as we have seen in earlier chapters, this has led to dangerous forms of stereotyping, either of races or genders, or of human consciousness itself.

Discussion questions

1   How do *you* present your*self* in everyday interactions — for example, when you attend and participate in class? Who or what is the 'you' and who or what is the 'self' in that previous sentence?
2   Describe an event or experience in which you were very frightened. Now recount the biological, psychological, and social ways in which your self performed under those circumstances.
3   What general lessons about the self can be learnt by viewing identity in social terms?
4   What theoretical perspectives (for example, labelling theory, phenomenology, symbolic interactionism, or social constructionism) seem to help explain the experience of self in the cases of Mrs B and Mai?
5   How are the competing explanations of the near-death experience derived from the social and political assumptions of researchers?

Recommended reading

Further interesting, yet simple, examples of how the social self makes its presence felt in our daily lives can be seen in the following readings:

- Eades, D. 1985, 'You Gotta Know How to Talk … Information Seeking in South-East Queensland Aboriginal Society', in J. B. Pride (ed.), *Cross-Cultural Encounters*, River Seine, Melbourne, pp. 91–109.
- Holmes, J. 1985, 'Sex Differences and Miscommunication — Some Data from New Zealand', in J. B. Pride (ed.), *Cross-Cultural Encounters*, River Seine, Melbourne, pp. 24–43.

Some original writing that introduces leading ideas of some key theorists in this area can be examined in the following readings:

- Berger, P. and Luckmann, T. 1966, *The Social Construction of Reality*, Penguin Books, Harmondsworth, pp. 194–200.

- Goffman, E. 1967, *Interactional Ritual: Essays in Face to Face Behaviour*, Penguin Books, Harmondsworth, pp. 5–46.
- Goffman, E. 1969, *The Presentation of Self in Everyday Life*, Allen Lane, London, pp. 15–66.
- Mead, G. H. 1934, *Mind, Self and Society*, ed. W. Morris, University of Chicago Press, Chicago, pp. 135–44, and also pp. 173–8.

Although a little more difficult to read, the following references are excellent overviews on contemporary research and debates in this area (Gecas and Demo should be read one after the other):

- Adler, P. A., Adler, P., and Fontana, A. 1987, 'Everyday Life Sociology', *Annual Review of Sociology*, vol. 13, pp. 217–35.
- Demo, D. H. 1992, 'The Self Concept over Time: Research Issues and Directions', *Annual Review of Sociology*, vol. 18, pp. 303–26.
- Gecas, V. 1982, 'The Self Concept', *Annual Review of Sociology*, vol. 8, pp. 1–33.

Community

Intellectuals are inclined to be dismissive of the quality of 'community' to be found among those who seek fellowship at the local shopping mall, family restaurant, or sports stadium. Then again, their ancestors were no less snooty about carryings-on around provincial parish pumps, on slum streets, and in music halls. Their criticisms, though, are not motivated merely by snobbery; often they are all too acutely aware that people have been sold short. And sadly, the measure of this is the extent to which the great mass of the population can be persuaded to settle for less.

Chris Eipper, Chapter 8

Chapter 8

Suburbia: The Threat and the Promise

Chris Eipper

'No, no! Anything but that! Anything!'

'Anything?' The judge stared at the prisoner in the dock. Until now he had given every impression of being as tough as they come — a real cool kid — but finally he had cracked. It might be wise, the judge thought to herself, for me to consider amending the sentence — for the sake of society, if not the youth himself. She motioned to the social worker and suggested that he accompany her to her chambers. 'I'm considering changing the punishment I said I'd impose. Just to be quite sure, I'd like to run through the background to the case one last time. I'm hoping you might be able to suggest something more appropriate, something that won't panic him quite so severely.'

The social worker opened the voluminous file. Where to begin? The boy's grandparents? His mother's father had migrated to Melbourne from the back of Bourke; his mother's mother had grown up in Collingwood back in the days when the old team was still capable of winning a Grand Final. The father's parents were bushies who'd stayed put, eventually perishing in a drought, fire, or flood — no one seemed to be quite sure which. The boy from beyond the Black Stump and the girl who barracked for the 'pies married, bought an FJ Holden, moved to Moonee Ponds, and started a family.

As a result, the youth grew up in a three-bedroom brick veneer on a quarter-acre block — just down the road, in fact, from a certain Mrs Everage, who even then was well known as a colourful local identity. The family subsequently moved to Sydney when the youth's father got a work transfer. The family initially rented in Parramatta before moving to Cabramatta, but got out of there quick smart (the neighbours weren't really their kind of people), finally settling in Watsitmatta, an up-and-coming suburb surrounded by open paddocks but featuring a kilometre-square, high-tech shopping complex, just off the Sydney–Canberra Freeway.

A late child, the prisoner found himself friendless. Without a car of his own and with no public transport — stranded, resentful, and rebellious — he ventured into petty crime, beginning as a graffiti artist. Arrested for defacing private property by spraying 'MuckDonald's fart-food family restaurant' at the local outlet, he graduated to car theft, which led to various high-speed police pursuits along the expressway, and eventual arrest when the four-wheel drive he had purloined bounced off a back-street speed bump, entered a pedestrian mall, and hurtled through the plate-glass window of the local video rental parlour. Taken into custody, the accused not only claimed to be Ferris Bueller; he also insisted he was adopted and that his parents were Mr and Mrs Simpson of Springfield, USA. The police were not amused.

'If', said the judge, 'I go ahead with this community service order and insist that he does a thousand hours as a volunteer with the Suburban Salvation Project, I'm afraid he'll —'

'Go berserk! It'll be living death for him, your Honour. If we're not careful, we could have another Freddy Kreuger on our hands.'

'So what would you suggest?'

'It's a tough one. But I've been thinking, you could do a lot worse than Sociology at Eureka University.'

'You've got to be kidding! From what I've been told —'

'It's not as bad as they like to make out.'

'But can you assure me that he'd learn something there that'd be of any use to him?'

'Let's just see, shall we?'

What might Sociology at Eureka University have to teach a Bart Bueller (not to mention his kid sister, Lisa — an authentic intellectual if ever there was one) about suburbia and the world he learnt to loathe so early in life?

We can begin by taking another look at the various social currents to which Bart was subject as a suburban boy (bearing in mind that his sister may often have been affected differently). We can then ask how things got to be this way. After a discussion of the rise of cities and the transformations wrought by (and upon) urban life, we will be in a better position to discuss contemporary trends. How is suburbia situated from a sociological point of view? How are locality-based relationships organised and experienced? How does this differ from the past, and how is it altering our futures? In an introductory chapter we cannot possibly consider everything of importance. To simplify things, it may be best if we focus on a couple of key topics. The ones I have chosen are patterns of differentiation and horizons of community. In addressing these topics, I will be exploring the connections between social boundaries in people's lives and the problem of belonging. I will also be asking you to ask yourselves why it is that, for some, suburbia promises paradise, while for others it feels like purgatory.

Our boy Bart and the sociology of suburbia

Bart's family background is fairly typical of many of his generation. His father's people are indicative of that declining minority of Australians: farming people, proud of the smell of the gum leaves on them and scornful of 'city slickers'. I know the type: I grew up among them. But like Bart's father, I moved to the city. After growing up in the bush, I find myself growing old in the suburbs — yet I will never reconcile myself to it. Sociologists speak of push/pull factors influencing the migration of people from rural areas to urban centres. On the one hand, such people find themselves pushed out of the country — either because established sources of employment have disappeared (due to farm mechanisation, for example), or because they feel trapped (there's got to be more to life than this), they are at war with those who will never leave (fathers and mothers usually), or they have brought scandal upon themselves. On the other hand, they feel pulled. Lured by big bucks and bright lights, they strike out after employment and excitement in the city (and sometimes, as in my case, a university education also).

Bart's maternal grandfather also made the move to the city; like me, he met and married a working-class girl (relax, this isn't a kiss and tell story — I've just about had enough of this autobiographical stuff myself). Deriving as she did from Collingwood, Bart's maternal grandmother was an Irish Catholic from a close-knit, kin-centred community that prided itself on the prowess of its giants on the footy field, the probity of its priests, and the virtue of its virgins. In key respects, the pattern of social control in Collingwood more closely resembled that of an Irish village than the Melbourne that was then emerging.

The new Melbourne was less inclined to pit English Protestants against Irish Catholics, as ancient sources of sectarianism were superseded by fresh prejudices once an unprecedented tidal wave of immigrants washed up in Australian cities, lured here by promises of jobs for all and a roof over everyone's head. Racial and ethnic tensions were not, of course, restricted to the English and Irish — ask any Aborigine, whose ancestors were not only dispossessed by the European invasion, but were also quickly reduced to slum-dwellers in the crude convict settlements, townships, and colonial cities that followed upon that first tent being pitched on the shores of Sydney Cove in 1788.

The Melbourne of the long postwar boom was a city that saw ordinary working people dreaming of buying not only a car, but even a home of their own. The newly married couple started a family on the assumption that the man of the house would be permanently employed, and his wife would cook, care, and clean for the children in a house equipped with an electric fridge, a vacuum cleaner, a washing machine, and, last but not least, a telephone. They started out accepting that it was entirely natural for him to enjoy a well-deserved beer at the pub with the 'boys' after work, even if she resorted to the occasional Valium washed down with a strictly medicinal dose of hospital brandy — but we won't dwell too much on that sort of thing, if only because everything else was on the up-and-up.

Impressed by their ability to rise in the world (as they saw it), people like Bart's parents were only too willing to move cities if opportunities arose. But the Sydney they moved to was a markedly different place from Mrs Everage's Moonee Ponds (why even dear old Edna was moving with the times — not only did she often pop up to Sydney herself, but she'd actually turned into a TV celebrity). Sydney, it had to be said — Mrs Bueller was to confide to Dame E. — Sydney was simply overflowing with Asians. It was like the Chinese on the Goldfields all over again, according to Mr B., except that this time it was the Vietnamese (as if the Italians, Greeks, Yugoslavs, Turks, and Lebanese hadn't been bad enough). Watsitmatta might have been bare and barren, but it was a little bit of old Australia, even if it did lack a Chinese caf.

Nothing better, as they say, than a spot of sweet and sour washed down with a ... a nice dry white — drinking wine and dining out was getting to be the done thing, like swearing in front of women and sneering at Germaine Greer.

Women! They would never be quite the same again. The pill had meant more sex but fewer children. Then, all of a sudden, wives were going out to work, which might have had something to do with why Bart had turned bad, except that his mother wouldn't have been able to fit a job in even if she'd wanted to — her time was too taken up with volunteer work for the school and church. Whatever the cause, in the eyes of the rest of the family, the boy had developed into a lazy, lonely, spoilt brat, destined to turn his back on his Mum and Dad's love while holding his hand out for more money. His parents asked themselves where they had gone wrong. Meanwhile Bart watched *Rebel Without A Cause* on late night television, *Ferris Bueller's Day Off* on school days, and played computer games at Timezone all weekend. His father had sold his soul and the last vestiges of family life to the company, his mother cried when 'Is This All There Is?' was played on 'The Midday Show', and his sister ... Bart had almost forgotten he had a sister. But then one night he dreamt that he bumped into her at the supermarket. A straight-A student, she'd nevertheless dropped out of school to become a checkout chick. She looked like she was doing drugs. 'That's this place for you', he slouched off muttering to himself, 'Watsitmatta!'.

In recapitulating Bart's beginnings, I have, of course, once again descended into satire. But then again, satire of this sort is itself a form of cultural critique and, as such, a species of social analysis also. That said, the picture I have presented is clearly a caricature. But it does serve to direct attention to the way the changing nature of suburbia helped shape, and was shaped by, a variety of other intersecting social forces. Among these, let me emphasise ethnic, gender, and generational dynamics and divisions; the phenomenal spurt and spread of prosperity in an era of great capital growth and full employment; the rising expectations associated with the acquisition of a home, car, and other consumer goods; and, last but not least, the invention and dissemination of an electronically transmitted mass culture (which began with radio, broke new bounds with television, and, with the advent of the home computer, appears set to take the impact of technology upon the home into a new dimension).

At this point, it would seem appropriate to put developments in this century into perspective by comparing them with preceding centuries and millennia.

Cities and suburbia in historical perspective

As far as is known from archaeological and other evidence, some 5000 years ago key human settlements evolved into what we are today inclined to call cities. Initially these walled settlements derived their wealth from the surrounding countryside and were associated, among other things, with the cultivation of crops, a developing division of labour, an expansion of craft skills, a growth in quantities and kinds of trade, and so on. Without a viable rural base, a city could not survive. But the relationship was a symbiotic one. As a result of the invention of new technologies of production, modes of exchange, patterns of distribution, and styles of consumption, urban innovations began to impact upon rural hinterlands, fostering agricultural expansion and development. The growth of cities thus contributed to the transformation of the countryside. It could therefore be said that (despite what country folk themselves are inclined to maintain) the country *needs* the city and has always done so (compare with Ward 1974, pp. 56–62).

Meanwhile, cities began to encroach upon, and overwhelm, the rural areas upon which they depended and from which they originally derived their identity. With the advent of industrial capitalism, the process acquired a seemingly runaway dynamic; it might even be said that cities began to *cannibalise* the countryside that first nurtured them. The figures are phenomenal. In 1800 the leading cities of Europe could still be traversed on foot in little more than an hour, being no more than about 10 kilometres in diameter; a century or so later a city like London had more than tripled in size and scope, doubling again in the next half century. In 1850 only four cities in the world contained more than one million people; by 1950 there were about 300. By the year 2000 there will be around 1000 cities of this size (Ward 1974, pp. 64–5). The most populous cities number many millions. But official boundaries tend, demographically speaking, to be nonsensical: mere administrative divisions, they tell us little about the actual size and spread of urban populations. Sydney, as we know it, for example, actually takes in the 'cities' of Parramatta and Liverpool; indeed, the geographical centre of 'Sydney' is now to be found within the boundaries of one of these supposedly autonomous entities. The metropolis has spread its tentacles to become a megalopolis. The trend is most pronounced in the USA, where the 'urban net' crosses the national border in the Great Lakes area to take in parts of Canada. But it can even be seen in Australia, for Sydney is really only the central node of an enormous, raggedy string formation, stretching from Newcastle in the north to Wollongong in the south. At the moment it remains a loose weave of industrial and manufacturing centres, commuter and dormitory suburbs, retirement villages and holiday resorts, national parks and rural enclaves. But as more and more of the vacant spaces along the coastal plain are occupied and put to intensified human use, as the texture becomes more grid-like, the result will be a single giant conglomerate. An image springs to mind of the city as a monstrous crustacean polluting the sea from which it came — having been imported here, as it were, in the belly of tiny sailing ships a mere two centuries or so ago.

Patterns of differentiation

Cities are highly condensed social spaces, which dramatically differentiate people from one another. What is going on within them? How do they differ from what went before? Are they as significant as they seem and, if so, where do they fit in the sociological scheme of things? For a long time debates about such things were profoundly shaped by the 'Chicago school' and its successors. Robert Park's so-called 'ecological approach' used organic metaphors in an attempt to understand processes of urbanisation. The emphasis was on evolutionary trends, competitive pressures, and mechanisms of adaptation. In his view, cities 'naturally' developed distinctive 'zones' — that is, characteristic patterns of internal differentiation (central business districts surrounded by decaying neighbourhoods, for example, beyond which stable class-differentiated areas formed, with the industrial poor nearer to the inner city than their more affluent 'suburban' counterparts). The city person lived in one place, worked in another, sought entertainment elsewhere, and travelled between zones, performing distinctive social roles in each — roles that were increasingly individualistic in purpose and perception. Consistent with this, according to Louis Wirth, cities were distinguished not only by their size and density, but also by the heterogeneity of their populations. In cities, crowds of people lived in close proximity to one another, with most not knowing each other personally. A significant percentage of social contacts were fleeting, fragmentary, and instrumental — means to ends rather than ends in themselves. Human connectedness and communal sentiment now had to answer to anonymity and indifference. Along with diversification, specialisation, and differentiation of function came the triumph of routine and impersonally administered rules of behaviour.

No less influential was the work of Robert Redfield. His interests centred on what came to be known as the folk/urban continuum. Debate about this topic revolved around the contrast between 'folk', peasant, or rural 'community' — defined by small, parochial, stable, face-to-face relationships that were customary in character, traditional in orientation, religiously devout, and underpinned by ties of kinship and marriage — and 'society', which was more or less the opposite of all that. Redfield's work, it needs to be said, was severely criticised in its own time, especially by Oscar Lewis. But it is in a tradition whose most notable exponent was Ferdinand Tönnies, a German thinker who earlier distinguished between *Gemeinschaft* (community) and *Gesellschaft* (association). Although it is no longer accepted that such a distinction can be applied in the way either Tönnies or his successors supposed, it remains an important reference point in the history of sociology, and one that is remarkably similar to many simplistic, everyday stereotypes of the 'big bad city' versus the idyllic, rustic life to be found in some distant, happy valley. (For good, brief introductory discussions of these writers' contributions, as well as what is wrong with their accounts, see Bell and Newby 1971, pp. 21–7, 42–8, 91–101; Giddens 1982, pp. 100–7; and Cohen 1988, pp. 21–38.)

Many other writers have made equally important contributions to urban analysis, including Lloyd Warner, who is famous for (among other things) his Yankee City project. In more recent decades, though, under the influence of Karl Marx and Max Weber, a key focus became the issue of capitalism. Prior to the modern era, cities were important as trading centres (as well as being crucial to processes of state-formation, civilisational dynamics, and even imperial ambitions). But with the rapid social explosion associated with the rise of industrial capitalism, the city and its role in society was never going to be the same again — particularly since, hand in (bloody) hand with these developments, came struggles that resulted in the expansion of democracy and citizenship rights.

The capitalist city is a marvel of commodification. Almost everything associated with it has been turned into a commodity — is available to be bought and sold for a profit on the market — from the natural environment itself to the buildings, roads, railways, canals, seaports, and airports dominating it; from the goods and services, and masses of information moving about within it to the labour of its citizens, which makes all this happen. The end result is a highly stratified, merchandise machine. It is a machine that distinguishes between people and divides them from one another. In large measure it does so according to their access to markets that determine their life chances: the labour market especially, but not it alone; housing, education, and information markets may also be decisive.

People are also divided by whether or not they live near to or far from one another. In Australia we are familiar with the 'tyranny of distance' and the way it imposes serious constraints upon the life chances of people confined to the outback. But the distance between people cannot be understood simply in a spatial sense; it may be measured as readily in terms of the distribution of wealth, privilege, and prestige — within and between suburbs, for example.

Indeed, today's cities perpetuate what might be called a porous social 'apartheid'. This has a racial and ethnic dimension, which is often tied to class. But certain areas are also stratified along age and generational lines: new suburbs are typically designed to cater to young married couples, many of whom move on as the family grows and finances permit; retirement villages and resorts separate and sequester the old. It is even possible to identify sex and gender zones in the city, though these are now somewhat less distinct than they were in the days when central business districts and industrial areas were male preserves, with homes and shops during business hours largely being abandoned to women and children. Although it may seem exaggerated, the term *apartheid* is actually appropriate, so long as we acknowledge that the system is porous and policed more by the market than the State. For it is a world in which people are set apart according to criteria over which they have little or no control; as part of the process, fate and fortune then allocate them separate social areas in which they are obliged to live out different parts of their lives. One of the consequences of this state of affairs is that, as citizens of the city, people come to feel alienated not only from one another, but even from themselves.

Horizons of community

This sense of alienation goes along with, and aggravates, the problem of belonging that plagues many people. They are never quite themselves, wherever they are; something is missing. They have surrendered community, or so they imagine, and seek it everywhere — at work, at home, in play, in love. If the city was once seen as signalling the end of community, suburbia today provides the point of departure for all those in search of it — sociologists included.

Intellectuals are inclined to be dismissive of the quality of 'community' to be found among those who seek fellowship at the local shopping centre, family restaurant, or sports stadium. Then again, their ancestors were no less snooty about carryings-on around provincial parish pumps, on slum streets, and in music halls. Their criticisms, though, are not motivated merely by snobbery; often they are all too acutely aware that people have been sold short. And sadly, the measure of this is the extent to which the great mass of the population can be persuaded to settle for less — limiting their horizons, resigning themselves, if I may put it this way, to discounted sunsets.

If *authentic* community is the elusive ideal, then actual communities nevertheless constitute some all-too-human approximation of it — flawed, fragile, contested, and compromised as they inevitably are. Whatever city folk may mean by this word *community* (and we can be sure that, like intellectuals and ideologues of every persuasion before them, once they try to define it, they will run into no end of trouble), the notion is symbolically significant in terms of what they share with those among whom they belong, and of what distinguishes them from others. (For an excellent discussion of 'the symbolic construction of community', see Cohen 1988.)

As an example of how things actually work out in practice, let us take a brief look at those immigrants against whom Bart Bueller's parents were so prejudiced. They arrived in Australia, many of them hoping to return home the moment they had the money. The longer they were forced to stay, the more they were inclined to become nostalgic, to pine for the place (and that part of themselves) they had left behind, to romanticise it. Often convinced that they were living in a lesser country, possessing an inferior civilisation, in cities that lacked minimal amenities as far as they were concerned, they tolerated the prejudice and discrimination directed against them, confident that they would one day escape it. But then ...

But then they returned 'home', only to be treated as 'Australians', and to discover that they were no longer what they had once been and still imagined themselves to be. Nor were the places to which they returned what they once were; they too had changed. Often it was all too confusing — no doubt doubly so for their children. (How many of you reading this does that include?) How could arriving back in Australia have that feeling of coming home? Spurred on to succeed rather like Bart's parents, the people caught in this predicament made every effort to move out of the inner city, to display their success by conspicuous consumption — by building domestic palaces in the outer suburbs. In so doing, they once again surrendered one kind of community — alleys and lanes, crowded with kids and camaraderie, as well as adversity — for another: the community of those for whom things have come good. Sadly, though, the streets of success often echo emptily.

The boundaries to belonging are many and varied, and nowhere more so than in suburbia. Some are self-constructed, but even these are socially shaped, not merely by the city, but also (among other things) by the capitalist dynamic that promises ever more advanced technological reconstructions of the world. In the developed West, if not elsewhere, the grit and grime, smut and smog, of the industrial city is being gradually rendered obsolete by the postmodernist promise of an electronic age in which we can not only work and shop from home, but find our friends on the internet. Utopia as a virtual community.

On the basis of past experiences, there is good reason to be sceptical about such prophecies. The road ahead will have more than its share of roundabouts and speed bumps. Things are difficult enough to deal with as they are. So let us pause and reflect for a moment upon some of what I have been saying.

I have sought to suggest that suburbia confronts us with a social paradox: in both imagination and practice, it simultaneously presents us with a threat and a promise. Bart Simpson's paradise is Bart Bueller's purgatory — whereas for Ferris Bueller it offers both treats and traps. In this at least, we might all be said to be a little like him: we remain profoundly ambivalent about suburbia. It offers us the best of things and the worst of things. Even though it allows us to purchase a generous portion of personal space for ourselves, it fences us off from our neighbours. While it may be rich in commodities, it seems poor in spirit. Though it may be close to everything, it appears isolated and isolating. It is comfortable, yes, but boringly so; secure and insecure at the same time — both too safe and yet not safe enough; so normal it's abnormal. Could it be that we cannot accept that we have inherited too much of a good thing? Or might it rather be that, whatever its merits, suburbia by no means provides the ultimate answer to Tolstoy's enduring question: 'What should we do and how should we live'?

Postscript

After his success at Eureka University, Bart Bueller was appointed Convenor of the Dame Edna Centre for the Study of Australian Culture and shortly thereafter Mickey Mouse Professor of Cultural Studies, Hollywood, Japan. Asked to comment upon his phenomenal rise to prominence, Professor Bueller remarked that he owed it all to what he had learnt in first-year sociology, to the fact that his teaching video, *The Burbs for Beginners*, had cornered the Asian market, and to his use of high-speed participant-observation research techniques: 'I've said it once, I'll say it again: life moves pretty fast; if you don't stop and look around, you could miss it'.

Discussion questions

1   What has been your own experience of suburbia? What, sociologically speaking, have you learnt from it?
2   As a sophisticated, self-aware product of contemporary social conditions, what can 'The Simpsons' tell us about suburban popular culture?
3   To what extent is today's youth culture, as represented in popular teen pics (including *Ferris Bueller's Day Off*) distinctly suburban in character?
4   Australia has often been described as the most urbanised country in the world. What are we to make of this, given the role of the bush in our national mythology?
5   What aspects of suburban and city life have been neglected by this chapter, and why are they important?

Recommended reading

- Berman, M. 1988, *All That Is Solid Melts Into Air*, London, Verso.
A passionate, personal exploration of the urban landscape of modernity.
- Carey, G. and Lette, K. 1979, *Puberty Blues*, McPhee Gribble, Melbourne,
A fictive memoir, this book became famous as an account of urban youth, beach culture.
- Carver, R. 1985, *The Stories of Raymond Carver*, Picador, London.
Laconic fiction from the bleak master of urban anomie; see also the film adaptation, *Short Cuts*.
- Dickens, C. 1983, *Hard Times*, Penguin Books, Harmondsworth.
The incomparable fictional portrait of an industrial mill town.
- Guinness, P. 1986, *Harmony and Hierarchy in a Javanese Kampung*, Oxford University Press, Singapore.
A sensitive and sophisticated ethnographic study of an urban community to our near north.
- Harvey, D. 1973, *Social Justice and the City*, Edward Arnold, London.
An influential study reflecting changes in critical sociological thinking dating from the 1960s.
- Johnston, G. 1990, *My Brother Jack*, Angus & Robertson, Sydney.
The landmark Australian novel about suburbia, the family, war, and so much else.
- Pearson, D. 1980, *Johnsonville: Continuity and Change in a New Zealand Township*, Allen & Unwin, Sydney.
An influential community study of a suburb just across the Tasman.
- Whyte, W. F. 1955, *Street Corner Society*, University of Chicago Press, Chicago.
A classic of urban sociology; as a study of urban youth culture, it reads like a novel.
- Young, M. and Willmott, P. 1957, *Family and Kinship in East London*, Routledge & Kegan Paul, London.
A keynote study in its day of a working-class community.

Film and television

Ferris Bueller's Day Off.
The best of the teen pics: cooler than cool!
'The Simpsons'.
Suburbanites as cartoon characters: analytical television at its best.
'The Sullivans'.
The classic Australian television serial; view it and compare it with your reading of *My Brother Jack*.
'Neighbours'.
Perhaps our most influential export; suburbia as a strife-torn, but relatively utopian, community.

Chapter 9

Religious Community

David de Vaus

Before you read any of this chapter, write down what you think the answers to the following questions might be:
1   What percentage of Australians are Jewish?
2   What percentage of Australians are Catholic (that is, Roman Catholic)?
3   What percentage of Australians attend church at least once a month?
4   'These days Protestants and Catholics are not very different from one another.' True or false?

In recent years we have seen an upsurge in the importance of religion in many societies throughout the world — a trend that goes against all the predictions of the early sociologists, who believed that religion would have little place in the modern world. In the USA, the influence of the religious Right has been keenly felt through groups such as the Moral Majority; in Iran, militant Islam has transformed society; in Algeria and Egypt, fundamentalist Muslims are challenging the secular State. Throughout Eastern Europe and in the republics that made up the former USSR, religion (Catholicism, Orthodox Christianity, Islam) is crucially linked with the various nationalist movements.

By comparison, religion in Australia is more marginal. The State is avowedly secular; religion and the Church do not play a leading role in public debates; and people appear more concerned about their material well-being than their spiritual well-being. However, most people identify with a religious group and accept core religious beliefs, and the Church has a far higher level of participation than any other voluntary organisation.

Australia is a religiously diverse society. Not only is there a wide variety of religious groups, but the nature of those religious groups or religious communities also varies markedly. In this chapter I provide a brief picture of religious groups and communities in Australia, and ask whether there has been a loss of religious community in Australia.

Religious groups in Australia

Despite the religious diversity of Australian society, about three-quarters of Australians identify with Christian groups. Most of the remainder (23 per cent) say they have no religion or will not state their religion. Only a tiny proportion (2.6 per cent) of Australians identify with non-Christian religions. (See Table 9.1.)

Table 9.1 Main religious groups in Australia (1991 Census)

Religious group	Percentage of Australians
Christian	
Anglican	23.9
Baptist	1.7
Brethren	0.1
Catholic	27.4
Church of Christ	0.5
Jehovah's Witness	0.4
Mormon	0.2
Lutheran	1.5
Oriental Christian	0.1
Greek Orthodox	2.1
Other Orthodox	0.7
Pentecostal	0.9
Presbyterian	4.4
Salvation Army	0.4
Seventh Day Adventist	0.3
Uniting	8.3
Other	1.2
Total Christian	**74.2**
Non-Christian	
Buddhist	0.8
Hindu	0.3
Islam	0.9
Jewish	0.4
Other	0.2
Total non-Christian	**2.6**
None	
No religion	13.0
Not stated	10.2
Total none	**23.2**

Source: Australian Bureau of Statistics

By far the largest religious groups in Australia are Catholics and Anglicans, who each account for about one-quarter of the Australian population. The next biggest groups are the Uniting Church, with 8.3 per cent, and the Presbyterian Church, with 4.4 per cent. Non-Christian groups are very small. There are only 140 000 Buddhists (0.8 per cent) 74 000 Jews (0.4 per cent), and 150 000 Muslims (0.9 per cent).

Since the Second World War there have been very marked changes in the religious make-up of Australian society. While the overwhelming number of Australians

Table 9.2 Trends in religious identification in Australia (selected figures 1947–91)

Religious group	Percentage of Australians						
	1947	1966	1971	1976	1981	1986	1991
Christian							
Anglican	39.0	33.5	31.0	27.7	26.1	23.9	23.9
Baptist	1.5	1.4	1.4	1.3	1.3	1.3	1.7
Catholic	20.7	26.2	27.0	25.7	26.0	26.1	27.4
Church of Christ	1.0	0.9	0.8	0.6	0.6	0.6	0.5
Jehovah's Witness	na	na	0.3	0.3	0.4	0.4	0.4
Lutheran	0.9	1.6	1.5	1.4	1.4	1.3	1.5
Orthodox	0.2	2.2	2.7	2.8	3.0	2.7	2.8
Pentecostal	na	na	na	0.3	0.5	0.8	0.9
Presbyterian, Methodist, Uniting	20.3	18.7	16.7	13.9	12.7	11.2	12.7
Non-Christian							
Buddhist	na	na	na	na	0.2	0.5	0.8
Jewish	0.4	0.5	0.5	0.4	0.4	0.4	0.4
Muslim	na	na	0.2	0.3	0.5	0.7	0.9
None							
No religion	0.3	0.8	6.7	8.3	10.8	12.7	13.0
Not stated	10.9	10.0	6.1	11.8	10.9	11.9	10.2

Source: Australian Bureau of Statistics

still identify with Christian groups, the particular groups with which they identify have changed. Mainstream Protestant groups, in particular, have shown a general decline, and the number of people without any religious identification has grown sharply.

Associational and communal aspects of religious groups

The above figures reflect the religious labels that people apply to themselves, but these tell us little about the involvement of people in these religious groups or communities. In his influential book *The Religious Factor*, Gerhard Lenski (1963) identified two ways in which we are part of religious communities: associational and communal.

Associational involvement

Associational involvement refers to involvement in the more formal activities of the group or organisation: attending church, involvement in church organisations, and the like. In this respect, religious communities are not very strong in Australia. By the early 1990s only 23 per cent of Australians claimed to attend church at least once a month; only 13 per cent of Australians are involved in church activities at least once a month. This low level of even irregular involvement in the formal

Table 9.3 Involvement in the associational activities of denominations

| | Percentage of denomination involved in church activities | | | | |
	Catholic	Anglicans	Uniting/Meth./ Presbyterian	Other Protestant	Non-Christian
Attend church at least monthly	45	18	28	50	26
Involved in other church activities at least monthly	17	12	20	36	17
Totals (N)	440	495	327	176	23

Source: National Social Science Survey 1992. See Kelley et al. 1992.

activities of religious communities reflects the current weakness of associational religious community.

Some religious communities and groups are stronger than others in the associational sense. About half the Catholics, and half the Protestants involved in the smaller Protestant groups (for example, Baptists, Salvation Army), attend church at least once a month, but only about one-quarter of other religious groups attend church at least once a month. Given that church services typically last from one to two hours, this is not a high level of involvement, and hardly the basis for a close or intimate community. As far as involvements other than religious services go, the level of associational involvement is even less. For most groups (except 'other Protestant') less than one in five people are involved in the activities of their religious group at least once a month. In other words, the everyday life of members of religious groups does not generally revolve around the organised activities of the religious group. In this sense, these religious denominations do not form close religious communities. The 'other Protestant' groups are the most active in this regard, followed by Catholics, who are relatively frequent attenders but are not very involved in other church activities. The mainstream Protestant denominations (Anglican, Uniting Church, Methodist, Presbyterian) are fairly weak in both respects.

There has been a substantial weakening of associational involvement over the last forty years. In 1950 almost half (47 per cent) of the Australian population claimed to attend church at least once a month. This level has declined steadily since then to its present level of 23 per cent. Most denominations have experienced this decline. In the early 1950s 61 per cent of Catholics attended church *weekly*. By 1992 this had halved to 30 per cent. The same drop has occurred in the Anglican Church, where weekly attendance has halved from 16 per cent in the 1950s to 8 per cent in 1992. Methodists and Presbyterians have dropped from about 23 per cent in the early 1950s to 12 per cent in 1992. The Uniting Church, which was formed in 1977, has dropped in just fifteen years from 34 per cent to 23 per cent in 1992. The main church to have shown any increase has been the Baptist Church, where weekly attendance has grown from 41 per cent in 1952 to 48 per cent in 1992.

Over the same period there has been a marked growth in the number of people saying they have no religion. This has grown from 0.3 per cent of people saying in the 1947 census that they had no religion to 13.0 per cent saying the same thing in the 1991 census. If those professing no religion and those who did not indicate a religion are combined, we see that in 1947 about 11 per cent did not give a religion. By 1991 this had more than doubled to almost one-quarter of the Australian population.

The general picture that emerges is this: the associational aspect of religious community is relatively weak in Australia and has been steadily declining over the last forty years. The bulk of people who identify with the various religious groups are largely nominal members who rarely get involved in the organised side of their religious group.

Communal involvement

Communal involvement is participation in the life of a religious subculture. It refers to the extent to which *primary-group* involvements and day-to-day activities revolve around people from the same religious subgroup. It refers to the extent to which people who belong to a religious subgroup develop ways of thinking, or a *world-view,* that reflect their involvement in the religious subculture. For example, do Catholics mainly mix with Catholics? Do they mainly marry Catholics? Do Catholics have a distinctive set of values that we might call 'Catholic values'? Are Catholics and Protestants separate or distinguishable in this sense. Do they form recognisable religious sub-communities? Are Catholics and Protestants socially different? Do they belong to different social 'classes'?

One of the big religious divisions in Australia in the past has been the split between Protestants and Catholics. They have represented two different religious communities or subcultures. In the past there has been a distinctively Catholic view of the world and a Protestant view of the world. There was a great degree of segregation, whereby Protestants and Catholics avoided mixing and certainly avoided marrying. Catholic schools kept Catholics apart from Protestants. Certain occupations were widely known to be reserved for Protestants, while others were reserved for Catholics. Catholics were seen to differ politically from Protestants. The Liberal Party was seen as a Protestant party, while the Australian Labor Party (ALP) and the Democratic Labor Party (DLP) were seen to be much more Catholic.

What evidence is there that Protestants and Catholics still form different religious communities in this sense? How different are they from one another? I will answer this by asking five questions.

Do Protestants and Catholics marry within their own community?

Protestants and Catholics predominantly marry within their own religious group. Seventy per cent of Catholics marry another Catholic, and 84 per cent of Protestants marry another Protestant. Only 11 per cent of Protestants marry Catholics. Very few Protestants or Catholics marry people with no religion at all (about 6 per cent). While there was even less intermarriage in the past, this is still a remarkable degree of segregation in marital terms between Protestants and Catholics. In this regard they form separate and strong religious communities.

However, religious similarity is becoming far less important in selecting marriage partners. People over forty years of age are far more likely to marry within their religious group than those under forty. For example, 78 per cent of married Catholics over forty have married another Catholic, compared with only 54 per cent of those younger than forty years old. Similarly, 87 per cent of older Protestants marry another Protestant, compared with 74 per cent of younger Protestants. In this regard, the Protestant and Catholic communities are breaking down.

Do Protestants and Catholics have a different social make-up?

The social differences among Protestants and Catholics are not as substantial as people often believe. Protestants are, on average, a little older than Catholics and are slightly more likely than Catholics to be female. The popular notion that Catholics form a solid working-class community, while Protestants are the heart of middle-class Australia, simply does not fit the facts. Marginally more Catholics (42 per cent) than Protestants (38 per cent) think of themselves as working-class, but the differences are hardly startling. Catholics on the whole are slightly better educated than Protestants. On average, Catholics have 10.8 years of education, compared with 10.5 years for Protestants. More Catholics (16 per cent) than Protestants (11 per cent) have university qualifications. As far as income is concerned, Protestants and Catholics are indistinguishable.

Do Protestants and Catholics hold different religious views?

We know that Catholics attend church services more than Protestants, but do they differ when it comes to basic religious beliefs? As far as religious beliefs go, Protestants and Catholics are quite distinct. Catholics are far more likely to believe in God, life after death, the Devil, Heaven and Hell, and miracles. As a group, Catholics are more religiously conventional than Protestants. In this regard, they set themselves apart from Protestants and do form a distinct religious community.

However, the gaps in religious belief are breaking down. On most religious beliefs, the gap between older Catholics and Protestants is far greater than among younger Catholics and Protestants. For example, among those over forty years old, 21 per cent more Catholics than Protestants believe in God without doubt, compared with only 13 per cent more among the under-forties. Among the over-forties, 20 per cent more Catholics than Protestants believe in the Devil, compared with only 3 per cent more among younger people. Among the over-forties, 26 per cent more Catholics than Protestants attend church at least once a month, compared with only 6 per cent more among younger Catholics and Protestants.

Do Protestants and Catholics differ in their political and social views?

Here the picture is somewhat mixed, and it depends on the particular aspect we look at. Catholics are more likely than Protestants to vote for the ALP (51 per cent

Table 9.4 Protestant and Catholic differences in social characteristics, and in social, political and religious beliefs

	Catholics	Protestants
Social characteristics		
Average family income (A$)	42 564	42 992
Average personal income (A$)	22 880	22 706
Percentage with university qualifications	16	11
Average years of education	10.8	10.5
Percentage working class (subjective)	42	38
Average age (years)	47.5	52.7
Percentage female	47	50
Religious beliefs (percentage)		
Attend church at least monthly	45	27
Believe in God without doubts	51	33
Feel close to God	74	55
Describe self as religious	71	54
Believe in life after death	73	56
Believe in Devil	50	34
Believe in Heaven	77	60
Believe in Hell	53	34
Believe in religious miracles	66	43
Social and political views (percentage)		
Vote ALP	51	40
Believe government should reduce rich–poor gap	56	47
Believe sex before marriage is OK	71	71
Believe homosexuality is OK	28	21
Believe husband should earn money while wife should care for family	28	32
Believe abortion OK (deformed baby)	65	79
Believe abortion OK (can't afford)	42	64
Believe government should punish criminals more	88	86
Believe Church should keep out of politics	64	64

Source: National Social Science Survey 1992. See Kelley et al. 1992.

compared with 40 per cent) and are more inclined to think that the government should reduce the gaps between the rich and the poor. Catholics are also a little less supportive of the traditional sex-role division of labour, whereby men earn the money while women look after the home. Catholics are less opposed than Protestants to homosexuality. On other matters, however, Catholics and Protestants are indistinguishable with regard to their social attitudes. Catholics are just as likely as Protestants to approve of sex before marriage, think that the Church should keep out of politics, and think that criminals should be punished more severely. Not surprisingly, Catholics were more opposed to abortion than were Protestants.

As in other areas, the gaps between Protestants and Catholics appear to be declining. The question of abortion has divided Protestants and Catholics for many years, but these differences are far more pronounced among older Catholics and Protestants than among younger ones. For example, among older people, 19 per cent more Catholics than Protestants opposed abortion of a baby with a serious birth defect. Among younger Catholics and Protestants, this gap has dropped to only 8 per cent.

Types of religious communities and groups

When we talk about religious communities, we need to distinguish between the different forms they can take. Ernst Troeltsch, an early sociologist of religion, distinguished between religious communities according to their *structure* and *the way they relate to society at large* (Troeltsch 1931). He distinguished between *Church* type and *sect* type religious communities. These two types of religious groups represent two ends of a continuum on which a Church is an example of a religious community that is mature and firmly established, while a sect is more dynamic and reflects a newer, less mature religious movement.

The Church

What are some of the main sociological features of a Church? The first is its universality. It is *the* Church of a nation or set of nations. The thirteenth century Catholic Church, before the Reformation, was an international Church that would tolerate no other religion. It was the 'universal Church'. The established Churches of England and Germany, although not the only religious groups in their countries, are the main Churches and are integrated closely into the social structure. With the Church, anyone who is born in the country of that Church is automatically a member of the Church. Typically, therefore, Churches have large memberships and are either nationally or internationally based.

Churches are hierarchical rather than democratically organised. Authority is centralised rather than diffused and shared. Leaders in the Church and in its local congregations gain their authority by virtue of their place in the hierarchy, and are sanctioned by the hierarchy. Their authority flows from the *positions* they occupy in the hierarchy rather than from their personalities, their 'charisma' or even their capacity to do their jobs well. Leaders in the Church are 'priests' rather than 'prophets'. That is, they fit into an established place in the institutional order and, rather than challenging existing patterns and acting as a new and innovating force, they reinforce established structures. Priestly leaders administer sacraments and rituals, and their role is defined as *crucial* (the members *must* have the sacraments) and *exclusive* (no one else can administer the sacraments). By so defining the role of leaders, their position is reinforced.

Churches are very much part of the world around them. They are part of the wider institutional order, and sanction the wider institutional arrangements (for example, coronations in England, prayers in Parliament, laws regarding Sundays and religious holidays). Churches therefore do not withdraw from the wider society or fight against it; they are part of it. There are close links between Church and government (for example, the Ayatollahs in Iran; the Queen as both the head of the Church of England and the head of State). The Church is influential in wider society: it dominates the society but is in turn dominated by it.

Sects

Sects are typically small and exclusive. Rather than membership being automatically conferred by birth, members typically join voluntarily as adults. Over time, with the birth of children, and as the children become socialised into the religious community of the sect, membership begins to become automatic, and the community can begin to lose some of its sect-like characteristics and become more Church-like.

Authority in sects is based on personal charisma rather than on position. Leaders win their authority by force of personality, rather than because the hierarchy bestows power and authority. While bishops in the Church have authority because they are bishops, the leaders of sects have authority because of the sorts of people they are. If the charismatic leader dies, then they cannot simply be replaced. Their authority is personal rather than bureaucratic or positional. Since authority is charismatic, rather than 'rational' or bureaucratic, then anyone, in theory, can be a leader. In this respect sects are more democratic, even though in practice they may appear authoritarian. Usually men, leaders in sects are prophets rather than priests. They lead because of their message rather than because of the functions they perform. Their authority is based not on the sacraments they perform (sects are frequently non-sacramental — the Salvation Army, for example, has no formal sacraments, and the sectarian versions of Methodism gave a relatively minor role to sacraments such as 'the Lord's Supper' and baptism) but on the message they deliver. Even where sectarian groups have sacraments, they are more democratic. Other people can deliver the sacraments; they are not the exclusive preserve of the pastor or minister. Typically sects reject the very idea of priests; they place a very heavy emphasis on lay participation, and insist that anyone can deliver the sacraments and preach.

Compared with Churches, sects are hostile to the wider, secular society. While Churches try to establish close links with the wider society and with government, sects reject the society around them. They reject its values, and may be hostile to many of its institutions (for example, schools, politics, churches, the particular family form). Because sects are hostile to the world and have a 'them and us' mentality, they find it important to have clear markers to define 'them' and 'us'. They need to know who is 'in' and who is 'out', and typically there are clear and strict behavioural expectations, which act as signifiers of belonging and commitment. Sects will have *clear boundaries* between themselves and the secular world, and they enforce these boundaries to give the group a clear identity and to make membership especially meaningful. Frequently, therefore, sects will monitor behaviour and values carefully, and be intolerant of deviations. Sect members will feel strong pressures towards behavioural conformity. Discipline is rigorous and based on mutual scrutiny of members: members who break the rules or do not live up to moral expectations will often be expelled (unless they confess and conform). There is a clear 'in' and a clear 'out'.

While sects are almost always hostile to the outside world, they all differ in how this hostility is expressed. There are two varieties of sect: *withdrawing* sects and *militant* sects. Both types are world-rejecting, stress the distinction between themselves and the world, and create a 'them and us' mentality, whereby people who are not part of the sect are 'them' and are to be rejected. Members of other religious groups — whether they be Churches, denominations, or other sects — are part of the 'them' and are rejected. Both types see society and its institutions as evil.

However the two types of sect differ in how they deal with the evil outside world. The withdrawing sect sees the society as beyond reform, and it keeps apart from the world without trying to change it. It creates its own world that is insulated from the world outside. It distinguishes itself by the dress and modes of behaviour of its members (for example, Amish, Closed Brethren, and monastic orders in the Catholic Church). Withdrawing sects create religious 'ghettoes' using devices such as ensuring that friendships and social activities revolve around the group, and establishing religious schools to prevent children being corrupted by the secular world. The militant sect is equally rejecting of the outside world but tries to change it. It actively recruits and tries to change society. Anabaptists, Jehovah's Witnesses, the early Salvation Army, and the early Methodists all provide examples of this type of sect.

Denominations

A third type of religious community, which represents a point somewhere between sects and Churches, is the denomination. There are two main types of denomination: the ex-sect and the ex-Church. Denominations such as Methodists, Baptists, and the Salvation Army are examples of sects that have been tamed and have made their peace with the secular world. In Australia the Anglican, Lutheran, and Orthodox churches, because they have been transplanted from countries where they were national Churches, have become just one religious group among many, and have therefore had to accept denominational status.

Normally denominations are larger than sects, and they will be organisationally more complex — typically with a set of local branches and a national organisation. The authority structure in denominations varies: in some denominations (more often the ex-Churches) it is very hierarchical and centralised (for example, Anglican, Orthodox, and Presbyterian churches), while in others (mainly the ex-sects) it is based far more on the authority of the local congregation (for example, Baptists, Congregationalists, and Methodists).

Denominations are more established and stable than sects, and they rely less on the charismatic authority of an individual, and more on structures, rules, and established procedures. In denominations that evolved from sects, the spontaneity of the sect has given way to the established routines of the larger organisation — a process that is given the label *routinisation*. Leaders can no longer rely on their character, personality, and style, but must rely on the roles they occupy. Their authority springs from *what* they are (position) rather than *who* they are (charisma). Priests and pastors (both modes can be found in denominations, the particular type depending on the origin or type of denomination) will typically be oriented towards the welfare of their congregation and be less concerned about winning new members — their evangelical zeal is more tempered than it is among the pastors of the sect. Leadership in the denomination becomes professionalised. Training (frequently with a significant degree of secular training) becomes important. More and more tasks and responsibilities are left for the 'minister', and the laity becomes less active.

Denominations strive for, and normally achieve, respectability. Instead of being world-rejecting, they cooperate with the secular world, but they are not in the same position as Churches to control or dominate the secular world. Denominations do not lay the same stress on 'us and them' as sects do — indeed, because they seek acceptance in the secular world, they break down the distinction between themselves and the world. The 'black-and-white' rules of the sect become 'grey', and there is much more room in the denomination for individuals to make their own decisions (regarding drinking, gambling, dress, or jobs, for example). The denomination appears much more worldly, and is more tolerant of certain behaviours, than is the sect. Discipline is less exacting and less fervid. Even definitions of membership become fuzzy, and the requirements of membership become less demanding (regarding, for example, frequency of attendance, tithing, and expectations regarding attendance at prayer meetings). In denominations it is less clear who is 'in' and who is 'out'.

The move from sect to denomination: Gemeinschaft to Gesellschaft

Sect, denomination, and Church can be thought of as existing on a continuum. Religious communities frequently evolve from sect to denomination, and sometimes to Church. Today's Churches were originally sects. Christianity was once a sect within Judaism and developed into a Church. Lutheranism initially had the characteristics of a sect and became a Church, as did John Calvin's Protestantism, which developed into State religion. John Wesley's revolt against Anglicanism, which led to the founding of Methodism, was very much a sectarian revolt against the inadequacies of the established Church. Although the Methodists never became a Church in the sense described above, they evolved into a mainstream denomination.

This process of evolution can be compared to a process of evolution that has often been observed in wider society, in which societies are seen to move from the communal *Gemeinschaft* mode, typical of small scale groups, to the anonymous, individualistic, *Gesellschaft* mode of modern mass society. Sects are akin to the *Gemeinschaft* mode, while denominations, and certainly Churches, are similar to the *Gesellschaft* mode. In other words, the move from sect to denomination to Church has much in common with the wider social transformation of community into society.

This is a transformation in which the spontaneity of sects gives way to the routines and regularised rituals of established denominations and Churches. The charismatic leadership of people like Martin Luther, Calvin, and Wesley gives way to officialdom and technocracy. Sects become bigger and are transformed into large, complex, bureaucratic organisations. Leadership and authority become routinised, bounded, and controlled by the regulations and procedures of these organisations. The enthusiasm, fervour, and zeal of sects are replaced by order, routine, and protocol. Discipline and scrutiny of individual behaviour, and group pressures to conform, give way to the greater tolerance that results from the anonymity of larger groups. The division between 'them' and 'us' fades, and denominations accommodate, rather than reject, the secular world. As sects become denominations, they become integrated and respectable. They embrace ecumenism in the same way that mass society embraces multiculturalism.

The move from sect to denomination, and from denomination to Church, can produce a reaction. Denominational organisation and culture, and the desire within the denomination for social respectability can produce conflict between the realists or pragmatists, who run the religious denomination or Church, and the idealists, who try to put its teachings into practice (Lenski 1963, p. 341). The idealists press for a return to the basics — for a return to the era when people were spontaneous, when there was enthusiasm and fervour, and when leaders were influential for *who they were and what they said*, rather than because of the *official positions* they held. The idealists want a religious community in which faith and ideals are more important than practical necessities and bureaucratic imperatives. Frequently the tensions between idealists and realists result in a split — a *schism* — the emergence of a new sect, and some reform and adaptation of the old group to prevent further splits (see Lenski 1963, p. 341).

The Pentecostal revival movements in the 1970s and 1980s provide a contemporary example of this. In some denominations the Pentecostal movement has led to divisions and the establishment of small, local, sectarian groups, in which members regain a sense of oneness and of *Gemeinschaft*-style community. In some Churches, the Pentecostal (or charismatic) movement has been accommodated. The Catholic Church, for example, has accommodated this by accepting the thread of charismatic renewal in the Church. By tolerating the charismatic renewal group, the Catholic Church has provided for a group that thrives on a sense of community and closeness, and that has many sectarian characteristics.

The capacity of the Catholic Church to provide for a *Gemeinschaft* group within a larger, more *Gesellschaft*-type group highlights an important point. The classic distinction between communal, *Gemeinschaft* groups and anonymous *Gesellschaft* society is not as simple or as linear as it sounds. Nor is the process always as linear as it is portrayed to be. There is ample evidence that small, communal *Gemeinschaft* groups can coexist within large bureaucratic organisations or in mass urban society. The feelings of alienation and aloneness experienced as a result of the anonymity of modern mass society, or as a result of being part of large bureaucratic organisations, can create reactions whereby smaller, more intimate subgroups develop, which provide for a sense of belonging and intimacy within the larger, anonymous whole.

Religious community and secularisation

The idea of religious community does not need to be restricted to the sorts of religious organisations or groups that I have mentioned so far. We can think of a whole community or society as being religious. This does not mean that each person is religious, but the whole *structure* of the society is based around religious institutions, and is legitimated by religious presuppositions and religious ways of thinking.

What does all this mean? One way of explaining what is meant by *religious community* in this sense is to contrast it with the notion of *secular society*. This contrast is based on the idea, put forward by influential sociologists such as Ferdinand Tönnies, Émile Durkheim, and Max Weber, that there has been a shift in the form of society over the last two hundred years. They draw attention to the historical shift from small local communities to the modern, mass, impersonal society. They describe a shift in which society has become larger and more complex, and in which people have lost their attachment to their local community. Tönnies described this as the change from *Gemeinschaft*-type communities to *Gesellschaft* society (Tönnies 1955).

Durkheim (1947) described this shift as a shift from societies that are based on *mechanical solidarity* to the modern society, which is based on *organic solidarity*. In societies based on mechanical solidarity, cohesion derives from uniformity. The society holds together because people are the same, and have the same values and beliefs. Uniformity is possible because these communities are small, and this enables people to monitor each other's behaviour and enforce conformity. These are traditional communities, in which individualism is absent and the individual is subordinated to the collective whole. Durkheim contrasts these societies with modern societies, which he sees as being based on organic solidarity. These are societies that hold together because of differences between people. In modern society, people are specialists who cannot survive on their own. It is like a body in which each part needs the other parts for the whole to function. The division of labour and narrow specialisation of skills mean that modern society is bound together by interdependence. It is the complementary nature of our roles and skills that makes us need each other, and this, rather than uniformity, creates social cohesion in modern mass society.

The changes to which these theorists refer involve a move from community to society. This move is not simply a move from small to large: it involves changes in ways of thinking, and in ways of relating to one another and to new styles of social organisation. The move to modern mass society is often described as the process of *rationalisation* of social relationships and modes of thinking. Compared to the communities of old, modern society is seen as impersonal, bureaucratic, instrumental, and technical. Instead of being based on feelings of loyalty, trust, obligation, belonging, and the ties of friendship and kinship, society is held together by the formal rules, laws, and regulations that govern our behaviour and relationships.

In certain ways, the old community-based society was fundamentally religious. Magic, mystery, and the supernatural were part of the fabric of everyday life in these communities. The way people thought, the way they explained things, and their justifications for the social order were fundamentally religious. As society has been transformed from small community-type groups into modern mass society, there has been a corresponding marginalisation of religion. Religious ways of thinking have been replaced, and religion has moved from the centre to the margins of social life.

The process of moving from a society based on fundamentally religious communities to a modern and secular mass society is called *secularisation*. Bryan Wilson, a prominent sociologist of religion, describes secularisation as 'the process by which religious institutions, actions and consciousness, lose their social significance' (Wilson 1982, p. 149). It does not mean that everyone abandons their religious beliefs and are no longer involved in any religious activities, or that religion ceases to be *personally* important to people. What it means is that religion becomes unimportant with regard to the way the social system works. Rather than being part of the texture of social life, as it was in communities, religion in modern society (it is argued) occupies the chinks and crevices of the system (Wilson 1982, p. 155).

How is community religious?

In what sense can communities be thought of as being fundamentally religious? Wilson argues that in communities there is a clear *moral order*, which means that decisions are made (or at least they are claimed to be made) on the basis of a set of moral values. People behave according to what these values determine to be *right* or *wrong*. Moral decision-making can be contrasted with purely *instrumental* decision-making. Instrumental decision-making is that in which decisions and behaviour are based on calculations of the outcome in terms of profit or loss, costs and benefits.

According to Wilson, the moral order within communities is ultimately religious in that it relies on some non-empirical authority to decree what is right or wrong. Ultimately, something is right or wrong because it is what the gods have decreed. The ten commandments are just such an example. These provide the basis of a moral order in which decisions are made and behaviour determined with reference to these moral imperatives. They gain their authority not so much because they make sense or are useful, but ultimately because they are given by God.

The social order of a community is based on a set of values, and these values gain their authority or legitimacy because they are seen to be given by a god. The community is, therefore, religious.

As well as acting as the source of moral order, religion also provides the basis for the political and social order of the community. The 'will of the gods' is used to legitimate the power of those who rule, and the social hierarchy is justified in religious terms. Respect for the elderly, obedience of the young, subordination of women, and separation of roles are justified in religious terms. Wealth and poverty are given religious justifications and are seen as reflecting God's will. People learn to accept that their position in the hierarchy is right because this is the way the gods have ordained it. Wilson states, 'By reference to religion men were secured in power, secured in their status, justified in their wealth and consoled in their poverty' (1982, p. 159).

In summary, Wilson argues that, in communities, religion regulates daily life and helps people make sense of their day-to-day experiences. It is used as a source of authority, and to legitimate the hierarchy of the community and provide the basis for morality, behaviour, and social relationships.

Secular society

In what sense is modern society secular? Most people identify with religious denominations; many people still attend religious services; most say they believe in God. People subscribe to a whole range of religious beliefs. However, when people like Wilson argue that modern society is secular, they are not referring to these things. They are saying that, in modern society, religion has become marginalised in that it no longer forms the basis of social order. Religion is not used to control people, to explain or justify the social hierarchy, or to legitimate those who hold power. In modern secular society religion is not the source of morality or decision-making. Wilson puts it this way: 'The large scale social system does not rely, or seek to rely, on a moral order, but rather wherever possible on a technical order ... [the] societal system relies less on people being good ... and more on them being calculable' (1982, p. 161). That is, in modern secular society people are controlled and motivated by material rewards or deprivations. In this sense their behaviour is instrumental and rational rather than moral. They think, 'If I do this, then I will get this much more' or 'I will not do this because it's not worth it'. The moral rights and wrongs become less important than a cost–benefit analysis of the action.

Why does religion become marginal in modern mass society? Wilson and others argue that modern society is secular because it no longer needs religion to hold it together:

> All [the] one time functions of religion have declined in significance as human involvements have ceased to be primarily local, and as human associations have ceased to be communal. Industrial society needs no local gods, or local saints; no local nostrums, remedies or points of reference. The means of sustenance are not local. Personal gain is the common sense of modern life, needing no further legitimation, whilst material provision, not spiritual solace, is what society now offers the poor ... Public recognition and identification are impossible for the vast majority and men enjoy their anonymity; ... local life now needs no celebration: what is there to celebrate when the community that sleeps together is not the community that works together or plays together?
>
> 1982, pp. 159–60

In summary, Wilson argues that community is ultimately religious. It is governed by a moral order in which the notions of right and wrong are justified by reference to the supernatural. Furthermore, explanations of the way society works and justifications for the social hierarchy are based in religion. In modern society, religious justifications have given way to a rational, technical one, according to which actions are judged by material profit and loss, rather than by what is right and wrong. It is a society regulated by laws rather than morality. These laws are based on the principles of rational consistency, rather than on moral considerations of right and wrong. The move from community to society, then, is a move from religious community to rational, secular society. The loss of community leads to the loss of religion's central role in structuring social life: it leads to secularisation.

Discussion questions

1 Examine Table 9.2 and describe the main changes in the religious make-up of Australian society between 1947 and 1991. What factors might have caused these changes?
2 What are the main criteria according to which denomination, sect, and Church can be compared?
3 Describe the concept of routinisation and explain how it relates to the sect–denomination–Church continuum.
4 Is our modern society purely based on rational cost–benefit analysis? Does morality (the notion of right and wrong) influence our behaviour? List some examples and discuss whether these are instances of rational or moral behaviour.
5 What is the evidence that there has been a loss of religious community in Australia? What evidence is there that religion continues to play an important role in our community? The concept of 'religious community' has been used in a variety of ways in this chapter. Outline what these are.

Recommended reading

To learn more about the characteristics of religion in Australia, see:
• Bouma, G. 1992, *Religion: Meaning, Transcendence and Community in Australia*, Longman Cheshire, Melbourne, especially chs 5 and 6.
For a classic discussion of the idea that different religious groups constitute religious communities, see:
• Herberg, W. 1960, *Protestant, Catholic, Jew*, Anchor, New York.
An insightful look at religion in rural Australian communities and the process of secularisation can be found in:
• Dempsey, K. 1983, 'Country Town Religion', in A. Black and P. Glasner (eds), *Practice and Belief*, Allen & Unwin, Sydney, pp. 25–42.
• Dempsey, K. 1983, *Conflict and Decline: Ministers and Laymen in an Australian Country Town*, Methuen, Sydney.
For an excellent and accessible discussion of the literature on secularisation, see:
• Ireland, R. 1988, *The Challenge of Secularisation*, Collins Dove, Melbourne.

Two excellent articles that document the loss of religious community as sects are transformed into denominations are:

- Chamberlayne, J. 1964, 'From Sect to Church in British Methodism', *British Journal of Sociology*, vol. 15, no. 2, pp. 139–49.
- Howe, R. 1967, 'The Social Composition of the Wesleyan Church in Victoria in the Nineteenth Century', *Journal of Religious History*, vol. 4, no. 3, pp. 206–17.

For an insight into the nature of sects and their communitarian characteristics, you should read:

- O'Brien, L. 1983, 'A Case Study of the Hare Krishna Movement', in A. Black and P. Glasner (eds), *Practice and Belief*, Allen & Unwin, Sydney, pp. 134–53.
- Millikan, D. 1991, *Imperfect Company: Power and Control in an Australian Christian Cult*, Heinemann, Melbourne.

Chapter 10

Work and Community

Doug Ezzy

The Egyptians built enormous pyramids as tombs for their Pharaohs, whom they considered to be gods. In the Middle Ages the biggest buildings were the cathedrals, the building of which would often take three generations to complete. Imagine beginning to build something that would only be finished when you were dead and your unborn grandchildren were adults. These monuments from the past point to central aspects of the societies that created them. The enormousness of the pyramids is symbolic of the Pharaoh's god status and centrality to an elaborate religious system that permeated Egyptian life. The cathedrals are also symbolic of the centrality of Christianity to the lives of medieval Europeans.

I am always struck, when I look at the skylines of modern Australian cities such as Sydney and Melbourne, by the dominance of the skyscrapers that house the offices of big business. The size and centrality of these buildings say something very important about society. An obsession with big business and making money dominates society in a similar way to Pharaoh-worship in ancient Egypt and Christianity in the Middle Ages. Two other large buildings common in modern cities are factories and shopping centres, both of which also point to the centrality of work. Modern communal and social life revolves around working and consuming.

Henry Ford, one of the most influential individuals in the development of modern forms of work, concludes his book, *My Life and Work*, with a quote from the Bible: 'Everything is possible ... "faith is the substance of things hoped for, the evidence of things not seen"' (Ford 1923, p. 281). Ford, however, is not referring to heaven or eternal life, but to his faith in the promise of modern industry and business. Ford had a religion-like faith in business, which he believed would solve the problems of the world. Big business and assembly lines would eliminate dangerous jobs, poverty, environmental degradation, and crime. The modern religion-like devotion to work, with leaders of big business as priests, is in many ways the centre of contemporary community life. However, as the rest of this chapter will demonstrate, big business has not solved these problems; in fact, it might have created as many, if not more, problems than it has solved.

This chapter examines the relationship between work and community from three perspectives. After introducing the basic concepts, I discuss the transition from school to work. School leavers' experience of finding their first job highlights just how important work is in making a person a community member. Second, I outline Henry Ford's assembly-line production methods and his obsession with efficiency, control, and predicability. Third, I compare experiences of unemployment in the 1930s and 1980s to explore the changing ways in which working makes one a community member. I argue for an ambivalent attitude towards the effects of the obsession with efficiency in modern work.

Work and community defined

'Work' has been defined as 'an exertion of mind or body undergone partly or wholly with a view to some good other than the pleasure derived directly from work' (Marshal, in Jahoda 1981, p. 187). In this sense, work is almost the very essence of being alive. However, such a definition does have the advantage of including tasks that are typically not thought of as work, such as child care, doing dishes, and caring for the elderly. Belinda Probert (1989, p. 89) points out that women do nearly all such domestic labour, and that this has been the case for some time and has not changed significantly in recent years. Although domestic labour clearly is work, it is not traditionally thought of as 'real' work because it is both unpaid and done in the home. The devaluing of domestic labour can be understood both as part of the patriarchal oppression of women, and as a consequence of modern society's obsession with making money through big business. The latter point is taken up in this chapter's focus on factory work and unemployment.

'Community' is used throughout this chapter to refer to the group of people that a person feels or understands to be their community (Cohen 1985, p. 20). I describe community from the perspective of the person experiencing it. Further, community is not only something that is 'out there' and that a person must fit into; community is also 'in here' — it is formed and constructed by people in, and through, their understandings, thoughts, and actions. In technical terms, this is a 'phenomenological' approach to community.

Schooling for work

Bruce Wilson and Johanna Wyn (1987) describe Australian young people's experience of work as the struggle to find a 'livelihood'. The concept of a 'livelihood' points to the importance of earning money from employment, while also indicating the less obvious, but no less important, aspects of friendship, independence, skill-use, and sense of achievement and community contribution. One of the most significant experiences for many young school-leavers is their first experience of working for an adult wage: 'Having a job comes to signify, through the wage at least, one's independence as an adult, a means of establishing some control over one's own life as an accepted member of the society' (Wilson and Wyn 1978, p. 5). 'Having a job' means becoming an accepted member of adult society, which affirms a new understanding of the self and the person's place in society.

Wilson and Wyn (1978, p. 3) argue that, during the 1950s and 1960s, Australia's growth and prosperity concealed deeper social divisions. The promise of policymakers and others was that continued economic growth would provide all Australians with good work and a high standard of living. The emptiness of this promise has become increasingly evident through the 1980s and early 1990s, as economic recession has made it more difficult for young people struggling to find a livelihood. One effect of Australia's high level of unemployment brought about by the recession is that the average number of years people attend school has been lengthening. This has extended the period of childhood or adolescent dependence on parents by several years. Also, it has deepened the disadvantage experienced by young people whose family backgrounds already make it difficult for them to succeed.

Longer periods at school and high unemployment rates have had different effects on males and females. Working for money has traditionally been a male task, while females could legitimately stay at home as a mother. Men leaving school still feel a responsibility to earn a wage, especially if they marry and have children (Wilson and Wyn 1978, p. 35). Being unable to find work represents a serious obstacle for male school leavers. In contrast, Bob Connell reports that, for the majority of women in the Australian working-class schools he studied, 'the future looks rather more familiar: early leaving, a job, early marriage, and full-time motherhood' (Connell et al. 1982, p. 99). While being a mother promises to protect women from some of the threat of unemployment, it 'does not constitute a satisfactory means of livelihood for young women' (Wilson and Wyn 1978, p. 40). Young unemployed women can feel as humiliated and powerless as unemployed men. In part, this is because women are experiencing increasing pressures to stay at work. Perhaps one of the newest life-transitions is the return to work of married women when their children all attend school (Connell et al. 1982, p. 177).

It is clear that the relationship between schooling and work is undergoing a significant transition. These changes are only part of a broader change occurring in the relationship between working and being a member of a community. The next two sections of this chapter discuss the way experiences of work and unemployment have changed during this century.

Working for Ford

Henry Ford founded the Ford Motor Company in 1903, when he was forty years old. Ford led the way in transforming the manufacture of cars, and in manufacturing more generally. His contribution was so important that a new term — *Fordism* — has been coined to refer to the style of manufacturing that is dominant throughout the world in this century. What did Ford do that was so revolutionary? At its core, his innovation was a new way of organising working: the assembly line.

When Ford initially began making cars, the work was done by skilled mechanics who would move around the cars, each doing a variety of tasks as the cars came together. The cars remained in one place while workers, parts, and tools all revolved around them. Ford argued that this arrangement wasted time and therefore began experimenting with various ways of moving the cars while the workers and tools stayed in one place. Skilled mechanics also had to be paid high wages, and Ford wanted to reduce his costs. The assembly line achieved two things: first, energy was saved because cars and parts came to the worker, and second, Ford simplified the tasks required of each worker to the extent that anyone could do it. For example, Ford describes one of his workers who 'all day long did little but step on a treadle release ... going through the same motions daily for eight hours' (Ford 1934, p. 105). This meant Ford could pay his workers much less for their unskilled labour.

Ford's assembly-line method of production was amazingly successful, bringing about increases in sales from 1700 cars in 1903 to one million cars a year in 1919 (Ford 1934, p. 54; Beynon 1973, p. 17). These sales brought large profits to Ford, and he soon became very wealthy. Why was the assembly line so successful? Clearly, Ford could pay his workers less, and therefore sell the cars for less. Also, it actually took much less time to make a car. Why did it take less time? Ford claimed that he was saving time by moving the cars and parts instead of the workers having to do the moving. However, Probert (1989, p. 29) argues that 'The main benefit of the moving assembly line was that it determined the pace at which Ford's employees worked'. The assembly line also meant that management controlled how hard people worked. Workers on an assembly line worked hard and fast all day, every day.

The positive impact of assembly-line production should not be ignored. It enabled many more people to afford cars, washing machines, telephones, and other pieces of technology that have changed modern life. Also, because Ford initially paid high wages for unskilled labour (although still much less than skilled mechanics received), people were able to live relatively free from concern about starvation, and to purchase more material possessions. Ford certainly believed his new form of production had the potential to solve the problems of the world. However, assembly-line production has also created many problems.

As Ford began to produce cars more rapidly and cheaply, other car companies had to follow suit in order to keep up. The assembly-line method of production, and the general ideas behind it, began to spread, so that the making of washing machines, telephones, and hamburgers, growing vegetables, and cleaning chickens, for example, all began to use similar principles. Whether the workers and managers wanted to or not, they were forced to introduce faster and more efficient means of production. If they did not, they would go out of business because someone else would do it and sell their product more cheaply.

Central to all this is an obsession with *efficiency*. Ford invented a faster way of making cars, which used less time and energy. McDonald's, to use a contemporary example, offers us the quickest, cheapest way of making a large number of hamburgers. Everything is calculated and controlled to produce a predictable product, which the consumer can expect to do what it says it will do. This obsession with efficiency was described by Max Weber (1976) as *calculative rationality*. While it means that cars and hamburgers are made quickly and cheaply, it also has some undesirable consequences, particularly for the workers.

Ford began work on an assembly-line plant in Australia at Geelong in 1924, and by the end of 1925 they were assembling cars (Darwin 1986, p. 42). A Melbourne man, born in 1906, remembers what it was like to work during the 1930s on an assembly line: 'When you ask about how I felt about my employers, I felt very bitter.

Why? Because of the way they treated me — you couldn't go fast enough. They treated you more like an animal' (Potts 1988, p. 24). George Growdowski (in Kriegler and Stendal 1984) describes his more recent experience as an assembly-line worker in a large car manufacturing plant in Melbourne. The theme in his account of his work experience is the inhumanity of the assembly line: the monotonous rhythm that does not stop, and the terror and panic when you cannot meet the completely unvarying demands of the line. Two hundred times a day he mounts a door on the car, doing it at the same maximum speed every time:

> When I first came to work here, I wasn't prepared for the soul-destroying monotony of the line. I had just come out of university with an Arts degree, and after being on the dole for a while you tend to forget that some factory jobs are bloody awful. And you are pleased to get a job, no matter how mundane. But I can't see myself lasting at it for very much longer really.
>
> Kriegler and Stendal 1984, p. 32

Similarly, Ern Reeders (1988, p. 148) reports the experience of a McDonald's worker:

> You actually had a bench, with all your condiments, your pickles, whatever you had, lined up. And you had a sequence in which you actually arranged everything. Just like a conveyor belt. An' you'd get your buns out which'd been toasted by someone else. An' someone else's responsible for dressing the buns. An' you'd spend eight hours, or your whole shift doing that. Oh it used to alternate sometimes.

Speed in performing predetermined actions is the skill required. Buzzers tell the workers when a bun or a burger is cooked, and the number of slices of pickle per hamburger is clearly specified.

These principles of work organisation have permeated many more areas than just car manufacture and the fast-food industry. Most factories are arranged along these lines, as well as banks, insurance companies, airlines, engineering firms, and medical services, to name a few. Modern society is increasingly obsessed with doing things efficiently in a controlled and calculated manner. The strange thing about this obsession is that it focuses on the *way* things are done, not on the *results* or consequences of what is done. This is perhaps most clearly demonstrated in the driving desire to obtain more money. Money is nothing in, and of, itself; it is only a means to an end. However, 'man [sic] is dominated by the making of money, by the acquisition as the ultimate purpose in his life' (Weber 1976, p. 53). Money has become an end in itself. The possession of money has become more important than what is done with it. Efficient assembly lines, banks, and fast-food chains are more important in modern society than ensuring that people have the opportunity to live a life with meaning and purpose. Weber called this the 'iron cage of modern calculative rationality'. In other words, the modern obsession with efficiency, calculation, and control is like a cage: it locks people into a world that is often extremely restricting and prison-like; humans are dehumanised and treated like animals.

Karl Marx (1975), particularly in his early writings, tried to understand the relationship between work and what it means to be human. One suspects that Marx would have angrily opposed Henry Ford. Ford seemed to believe that most people would be happy doing boring, meaningless work, so long as they were paid well and had plenty of possessions. Marx, on the other hand, argued that to be human was to be able to think and to creatively labour to make things. The difference, for Marx, between people and animals is people's ability to think about and plan activities. Assembly-line work requires almost no thought or planning and therefore denies our humanity. The work Ford thinks appropriate for those of 'lesser ability' is inappropriate, degrading, and *alienating* according to Marx's argument. Factory work is alienating because whatever the worker is making becomes alien: it does not belong to the worker, and the worker has no control over how it is made. Most important, in the present context, is Marx's argument that work should be the foundation of people's relationships. Working should provide people with a sense of community. However, in some factories, people are not even permitted to talk to each other. Factory production alienates and separates people from each other. Not only are workers separated from each other, but owners also often never see their workers, which means that some owners never have their perception of workers as stupid animals challenged.

Marx's and Ford's understandings of factory work represent different ends of the spectrum. Although, it should be pointed out that Marx thought that industry and factories were an improvement on what had existed before. More recent thinkers have argued that some industrial workers do not mind their work being boring, preferring to find meaning and community in leisure activities (Goldthorpe et al. 1968; Bodrow 1977). This is described as an instrumental attitude to work and is linked to the growing importance of consumerism discussed in the next section.

Unemployment in the 1930s and 1980s

Jeremy Seabrook reports a conversation with a shipyard worker who was unemployed in the 1930s. The worker remembers there being a sense of sympathy and compassion within the community in the 1930s, evidenced in street marches by, and for, the unemployed, and in the fact that 'Nobody ever called us scroungers'. He also remembers a sense of hope in the 1930s. There was hope that work would pick up, and that workers' skills and labour would be in demand again. There was also a more general political hope in socialism and the future of the Australian Labor Party. In contrast, the worker points out that now the young have no such hope: 'Their only hopes are centred on individual salvation — the dream of the pools, the big win, the stroke of good fortune. We hoped for the whole working class, not just for ourselves' (Seabrook 1982, p. 5).

Seabrook captures a revealing image of poverty in the 1980s in his description of a family whose young child falls and cuts her forehead. It is not simply that they have no car or easy access to public transport to take the child to the hospital — a trip that may or may not have been necessary. It is that they have no bandages with which to bandage the child's head and so use torn strips of sheet instead. A visiting relative looking at the bandage asks, 'Is that the best you can do?'. To which the husband angrily replies, 'Do you think I want my kid to wear a bit of sheet round her because we can't buy bandage?' (Seabrook 1982, p. 23). While a torn clean sheet is probably just as good medically, a bought bandage seems better simply because it is bought. The people Seabrook describes felt their lifestyle to be inadequate and inferior because they could not afford to *buy* a bandage. This is the source of their poverty: an attitude deriving from the unreal, almost surreal, images of lawn-mowers, cars, American Express cards, and holidays that they watch every day on televisions that scream that you must buy things in order to be normal. It is no wonder that Anthony Winefield and his associates (1993), relying on a sample of South Australian school leavers during the 1980s, report that, the more television an unemployed person watches, the more likely it is that he or she will be depressed and psychologically distressed.

There is, of course, a danger here of romanticising the past through images of 'the good old days'. This is not what Seabrook is doing. He recognises that both working and being unemployed in the 1930s was very difficult, dangerous, and often unpleasant. Rather, he is trying to identify not simply what we have been gained, but also what we have lost, as we move into the future. Too often it is assumed, as in the writings of Henry Ford, that the effects of modernised forms of work will lead to a new future in which everyone will be satisfied. Clearly, things are not so simple. One of the costliest consequences of modern patterns of production and consumption is to be seen in changing community relationships. Studies of the Great Depression in Australia portray a similar picture to Seabrook's account of the United Kingdom. Some things were much worse in the 1930s than in the 1980s: families lived in tent cities, and more people slept out on streets and in parks. However, there was a much stronger sense of community and resistance, and shared values of trust, endurance, and hope for a better future.

During the Great Depression, the unemployed in Australia were not quiet and compliant (Wheatley 1981). Many participated in marches, meetings, rallies, and deputations to various federal and state ministers in an effort to obtain full-time work at award wages, or a basic-wage dole to enable them to survive. There were hundreds of such gatherings, many attended by thousands of unemployed workers. Some of their more provocative actions included a dole boycott and picketing. Although the boycott was dangerous for the obvious reason that the unemployed were those who suffered, it was for this very reason that it had an impact: it could potentially result in starvation. When the unemployed had time and local support from workers and union leaders on their side, these tactics could be very effective. Picketing was most successful in preventing people from being evicted from housing because they were unable pay rent. These examples demonstrate a sense of community, militancy, and concern for others that is largely absent from responses to more recent Australian experiences of unemployment.

In contrast, in Australia in the late 1970s, almost no one identified with the plight of their fellow victims of unemployment (Brewer 1980, p. 77). Almost everyone interviewed by Graeme Brewer tended to blame other unemployed people for their jobless state, suggesting that they were not looking hard enough and were probably 'bludging', while the interviewees vigorously denied that they themselves were 'bludgers'. Brewer also documents the way in which *not* having money has become central to the experience of unemployment, not because of an inability to pay for accommodation, food, or other essentials for survival, but because, without money, it is almost impossible to participate in most social activities: 'I feel awkward with my friends who are working because they've got money and I haven't … I don't go out much because they might think I'm using them' ('Paul', in Brewer 1980, p. 72).

This discussion of unemployment is intended to demonstrate that the way in which work integrates a person into community life has changed and is continuing to change. The experiences of the 1930s suggest that people felt a part of a community by birth, history, and shared work. Neighbours knew and helped each other out through the difficult times. The unemployed banded together and demanded a better solution to their situation. Again, I do not suggest that everything was wonderful. The Great Depression resulted in malnutrition and high rates of disease, which we have largely been spared in Australia in the 1980s and 1990s. However, for all the gains in material prosperity, something has been lost on the level of social relationships that is much harder to measure. This loss is indicated by the greater social isolation of the modern unemployed, and their dreams of winning Tattslotto or the races. Why is it that unemployment is still a terribly painful experience in the 1980s and 1990s, when, in Australia at least, we are experiencing much greater wealth and prosperity than ever before? In part, it is precisely because of this prosperity. Consumerism, the act of buying and selling, is more and more at the centre of communal life, and unemployed people are increasingly excluded from this consumerist culture and, therefore, from participation in community.

Conclusion

Work has become both more and less important in modern society. Without work it is difficult to participate in community life, and this is reflected in women's increasing participation in work as an explicit response to their marginalisation in modern society. Similarly, Jocelyn Pixley (1993) has argued that any solution to the problems of high unemployment can only come through the provision of work. To deny a person work is, in many ways, to deny them their citizenship. On the other hand, work is increasingly simply a means to an end — a way of making money — and thus work is becoming less important. Work is only needed in so far as it allows a person to be a consumer, and in consuming, a person sees themselves as a member of the community.

Henry Ford dreamt that his more efficient assembly-line method of production would solve the problems of poverty and inequality in the modern world. In Australia, as in other countries, more efficient factories have increased material wealth, but have also been accompanied by the rise of a new kind of culture and a new kind of poverty. Modern society is increasingly individualistic, selfish, and consumerist. These cultural characteristics are the flip side of the obsession with efficiency, control, and predicability that characterises modern forms of work.

Discussion questions

1   How have the high levels of unemployment in the 1990s changed men's and women's experiences of leaving school compared with the 1960s?
2   If the workers felt alienated, why was Henry Ford's assembly line so successful?
3   What are the benefits and costs of McDonald's efficient, predictable way of making hamburgers?
4   What are some of the effects consumerism has had on the relationship between working and being a member of a community?
5   Is being unemployed easier in the 1990s than it was in the 1930s?

Recommended reading

For a general introduction to working life and the assembly line:
• Probert, B. 1989, *Working Life*, McPhee Gribble, Melbourne, chs 1 and 2.
For a discussion of the transition between school and work:
• Wilson, B. and Wyn, J. 1987, 'The Struggle for Livelihood', in *Shaping Futures*, Allen & Unwin, Sydney, ch. 6.
• Connell, R., Ashenden, D., Kessler, S., and Dowsett, G. 1982, *Making the Difference*, Allen & Unwin, Sydney, chs 3 and 4.
Some detailed examples of assembly-line production are provided in:
• Beynon, H. 1973, *Working for Ford*, Penguin Books, Harmondsworth, chs 1, 5, and 6.
• Kriegler, R. 1980, 'Work and Control', in *Working for the Company*, Oxford University Press, Melbourne, ch. 6.
The following provide introductions to Weber's and Marx's theories of work:
• Ritzer, G. 1993, *The McDonaldization of Society*, Sage, Thousand Oaks, Calif., ch. 1.
• Grint, K. 1991, *The Sociology of Work*, Polity Press, Cambridge, ch. 3.
• McLellan, D. 1971, 'Alienation', in *The Thought of Karl Marx*, Macmillan, London, pp. 105–21.
Two excellent accounts of people's experiences of unemployment can be found in:
• Seabrook, J. 1982, *Unemployment*, Quartet Books, London, chs 1 and 11.
• Brewer, G. 1980, *Out of Work, Out of Sight*, Brotherhood of St Laurence, Melbourne, chs 1, 4, and 8.

Chapter 11

Ethnic Communities

Susan Harvey

[T]he effective stimulus to group organisation ... comes, for one thing, from the positive value attached to the opportunities of self expression, gaining recognition and exercising influence provided by ethnic associations and the role of the informal networks in channelling resources from the wider society to the individual immigrant. Above all, this stimulus represents the positive concern to maintain group — and hence individual — identity, to keep alive 'long and profound' traditions or, less self-consciously, to preserve continuity between past and present, and safeguard the individual's sense of personal location in time.

Martin 1972, p. 133

Most Australians know that they are a nation of immigrants with a great diversity of peoples; Australia is a 'multicultural' society. You can see it in the big capital cities and many of the industrial towns, by the faces in the street and the signs on the shops; you can hear it in the football commentaries, whichever code you follow. By 1991 we numbered more than seventeen million, and about two-fifths of us were born overseas or were the children of at least one parent born overseas. Moreover, around one-half of those born overseas came from a country where English was not the 'mother tongue'. Among the so-called 'settler' countries, like the USA, Canada, and Argentina, Australia has the second highest proportion of immigrants (Israel has the highest). Whenever immigrants have settled in Australia, there has been the possibility of forming ethnic communities. The aim of this chapter is to explore the history of post-1788 immigration to, and settlement in, Australia, and to look at the ideas and realities of 'ethnic community' among settlers. (The history of the Aborigines, and their relations with White settlers, is dealt with in Chapter 17.)

The chapter is organised into:
- a brief social history of convict and voluntary settlement in Australia up to the Second World War (1939–45)
- a description of postwar migration, both voluntary and assisted, as well as refugee movement
- an exploration of concepts of community, and some of the realities of ethnic communities and their organisations in Australia
- a brief survey of current settlement in Australia, following the end of large-scale 'economic' voluntary migration, with some reference to communities and multiculturalism.

A brief social history

There is a widespread misconception that there has only been diversity within Australian immigration since 1945 — that, until then, we were wholly Anglo-Saxon (or perhaps Anglo-Celtic) and English-oriented in culture. Historically, the European settlement of Australia was British in origin. But British is not English: the Scots, the Cornish, the Welsh, and the Irish cannot be categorised, historically, ethnically, or linguistically, as Anglo-Saxon. *Celtic* is not an adequate term for such mixed groups either: history, religion, and language separated the non-English Britons, and those divisions are still visible today in group organisations and churches. Irish names predominate in the Australian Roman Catholic hierarchy; old Scottish families still attend the Presbyterian or the Uniting Church.

Moreover, it was not only the British who came to Australia in the nineteenth century; in fact, there were also some English Jews recorded among the original British convicts. Later, among 'free' settlers, there were Americans, French, and Russians. A group of Silesian Germans came to the Barossa Valley with their pastor in 1838, seeking a country where they could use the prayers they wanted, rather than the new versions prescribed by the King of Prussia. They planted vines, and by 1851, there were already three family wine firms. They had churches and schools — there was a complete German-speaking settlement.

Other Germans were explorers and prospectors; the best known of the former was Leichhardt, and of the latter, Rasp, who discovered the rich mineral deposits of Broken Hill in 1883. Scandinavian sailors and 'Russians' (frequently from Finland and the other Baltic countries then under Russian domination) often jumped ship or missed their sailing, and settled. By 1868, when transportation of convicts ceased in Australia (about 165 000 convicts were transported overall), there were many diverse immigrant groups, including Chinese shepherds. Although many convicts returned to Britain, many stayed on as emancipists and took up grants of land.

The 'gold discoveries' of 1851 followed the decline of the 1849 gold-rush in California, and attracted people from all over Europe, North America, the British Empire, and China. The population of Australia trebled in the decade from 1851 to 1861. The new colony of Victoria had 76 000 people in 1850 (and six million sheep), and 500 000 people in 1860, including 200 000 from Britain and 25 000 Chinese. Despite friction between Chinese and European diggers, and later racist exclusionary policies, there are many thousands of Chinese Australians in Victoria and the rest of eastern Australia today who are descended from some of those original Chinese gold-diggers. At one time, one in ten Victorian workers was Chinese.

The First World War (1914–18) severely tested Australian tolerance of difference. Anti-German sentiment during the war was extreme, and forty-two German town names were changed — for example, 'Germantown' became Holbrook. The Commonwealth had been formed at least partially in response to a wave of racist, nationalist sentiment aroused by a perceived threat of an Asian immigrant invasion. 'Australia for the White Man' was a *Bulletin* masthead, and government policies severely restricted Chinese and Kanaka immigration and settlement. Curiously, despite the entrenched belief in the existence of a 'White Australia' policy, there was never complete exclusion. Chinese Australians could bring in their wives and families from China, and did so. Dixon Street in Sydney and Little Bourke Street in Melbourne have been centres of Chinese settlement since the nineteenth century and are treasured 'Chinatowns' today. And Broome, that West Australian pearl-diving centre, has been home to a community of both Chinese and Japanese settlers since the last century.

Many believe that the First World War transformed Australia from a colony into a nation. Over 400 000 men enlisted; 330 000 served overseas; 60 000 were killed, with over 220 000 casualties. The gallantry of the Australians at Gallipoli became a source and symbol of national pride, contributing to the development of a distinctive Australian identity. The Australian Prime Minister, Billy Hughes, was able to take a full part in the peace settlement at Versailles, speaking for 'sixty thousand Australian dead'.

Restriction on international shipping during the war isolated Australia for some years. After the war there was some immigration from the United Kingdom, as returned soldiers took up land under an Empire Settlement scheme. Many had no farming expertise and, alongside Australian soldiers in similar circumstances, experienced dreadful hardship during the years of drought and recession in the 1920s and 1930s. In 1924 the USA severely restricted immigration, especially from southern Europe. Thousands of migrants from Italy and the Balkans changed direction and came to Australia instead.

Nonetheless, by the end of the 1930s — years of severe rural and urban economic depression — Australia's population was the most homogeneously British it had been since 1788. Less than 10 per cent of the population were born outside the country; of immigrants, 90 per cent were from Great Britain. In 1938 the Australian Government supported the immigration of 15 000 Jewish refugees from Hitler's Europe, but only 7000 reached Australia before the Second World War in Europe again stopped international civilian shipping and ended hopes of survival in Australia for the rest.

Postwar migration

After the Second World War (1939–45) there were again great changes. The lowered birth rate during the depression years, the perception that seven million people would face horrendous difficulties in defending such a huge land mass ('populate or perish' was a popular slogan at the time), the need for construction and reconstruction after the war years, and political changes in our relations with greater powers all combined to cause Australia to seek more immigrants, as workers and to build the population.

War-torn Britain and Europe had millions who needed homes and a fresh start, for themselves and their children. Once shipping could be obtained again, the government launched an ambitious program that aimed to bring in the equivalent of 1 per cent of the population each year as new settlers.

As Graeme Hugo says in his introduction to Wooden et al. (1994, p. 2), 'few questioned the importance of immigration as an engine for economic development and industrialisation'. Great constructions like the Snowy Mountains Hydro-Electric Scheme were built to provide power for population expansion. Houses, roads, and factories were built or expanded as the population also expanded. First came the Britons and some British war-time allies (Dutch, Poles, and Belgians); then came the large groups who had been existing in refugee camps in Europe— the 'displaced persons'. Forced labourers, dissidents, or prisoners of war, they were mainly from northeastern and eastern Europe, and they had been dispossessed of their countries: Latvians, Estonians, Lithuanians and Ukrainians, more Poles, and Jews fleeing terrible wartime experiences. Over the five years from 1947 to 1952 about 200 000 such refugees came to Australia.

Refugees

We had had 'refugees' or political exiles arrive in Australia before: exciting young radicals like Rafaello Carboni, who was so active in the defence of the rights of miners at Eureka in 1854. However, the greatest migrations from the Russian and Austro-Hungarian (Hapsburg) empires in the late nineteenth century had been chiefly to North America. Only a small number of Jewish refugees came to Australia in 1938–39. The existing Jewish community organised reception and care for them. There were some other Italian political refugees in the 1930s also, who found refuge among compatriots.

It was different for the displaced eastern Europeans. They had no fellows here, no places of worship; there were few who spoke their languages or knew where they came from, or why. Many of them were educated and had been part of the rising middle class — an intelligentsia under threat from both the German and Russian invaders of their new nation-states. Ukraine had only eighteen months' independence after the First World War, but Latvia, Lithuania, Estonia, and Poland had two decades of independent nationhood. Many of those who came to Australia had played active roles in building national institutions and identities: in their homelands they had organised national festivals, scout groups, agricultural and industrial co-operatives, national consciousness-raising discussion groups, little magazines, and poetry readings. During their sojourns in camps, they had tried to keep the flame alive, and had kept their own, and others', spirits up by organising as much as they could there.

Naturally, they tried to do the same here, and they were impressively successful. Forty years on, you can read about their creations still in the *Directory of Ethnic Community Organisations*. Of course there had been ethnic organisations and 'communities' before 1950. The first Greek Orthodox church was founded in the nineteenth century, and some Chinese associations have existed for more than one hundred years. The Swedish Church in Melbourne was founded in 1883 and remains active, but the first services were held on the goldfields in 1856. The first Jewish services were held in Sydney and Melbourne more than 150 years ago.

Whenever compatriots found each other in significant numbers, at least some joined together to socialise, pray, or further their interests and activities. A shared history and sense of place, a common language, and common values, beliefs, skills, and occupations helped to create social networks. Hostility, active discrimination, or lightly veiled contempt can unite peoples living in a foreign land. They group along ethnic or communal lines. Usually, perhaps, the majority group is the hostile party, but not always. Historically, small groups of colonial administrators, traders, settlers, and soldiers have been able to maintain dominant influence and outright power over subject peoples, even when the latter are from a 'civilised' nation — Europeans in Asia rarely saw their subjects as social equals. A common foe is a potent force for unity among those opposed; but it is as well to notice that division and differentiation, group boundaries, and shared interests are not confined to ethnic, religious, or linguistic groups — or, indeed, any particular group.

Concepts of community

Both ethnicity and community are complex, disputed concepts: 'It is commonplace to assume that ethnic communities exist, leaving researchers to describe ... the range of organisations each community has built up' (Holton 1994, p. 200). The term *community* is often used by the media, and others, simply as a category. All those originating from Latvia, for example, — along with their children, wherever born — comprise 'the Latvian ethnic community'. Most of us recognise, after a moment's reflection, that all the people in a particular country are unlikely to be very alike. A variety of religious, linguistic, and national backgrounds, rural, urban, regional, class, and status divisions, and ideological chasms create a complicated and cross-cutting set of cleavages.

The word *community* should never be used in a simple categorical sense; it refers to a group of individuals, regularly interacting on a basis of common interests and identification, who, when they act, take each other and the whole into account. Such communal groups develop institutions appropriate to the group circumstances (for example, unskilled rural workers in an industrial society, or refugee professionals in a mainly rural society), and according to group members' needs and aspirations. A community has a boundary: like any group, if you can get in or leave it easily, it is probably not really a community at all. Communities can be based on a common language, any common interest or goal, a particular territory, a common religion, or a common sense of ethnicity or peoplehood.

Ethnicity itself rests on (any combination of) a belief in common descent or 'blood', a shared history, a religion special to the group, shared culture and tradition, or a shared homeland, even if the people do not now, or never did, inhabit it. The traditions and the history can be, and often are, imaginary or invented. The sense of belonging together, and of shared fate, is more tangible.

The bonds between members of an ethnic group are assumed to be like those in a family: lacking ulterior motives. However, ethnic groups can lobby or act politically. Ethnic organisations grow up out of the needs of group members: clubs for games, for sociability; associations to meet welfare needs. Members set up organisations to further their own commercial and financial interests, as well as those of the community (travel agencies, for example). 'Ethnic' families need communal support to maintain their language and culture among young people. A variety of organisations and activities, as well as language schools, will help to ensure the survival of the culture, if parents and community can ensure the loyalty and enthusiasm of their young people. Who marries whom is important to the survival of the ethnic inheritance, as well as the survival of the community itself.

But community is constructed from the outside as well. In a democratic polity, all citizens, indeed all residents, have civil rights of access to health care and welfare, to work opportunities, and to social justice. The task of doing justice to individuals with widely disparate ways of communicating and means of understanding is too difficult even for official bureaucracy. But the ethnic organisations can communicate, and aid can be delivered through the mediating community. Grants can be channelled through financially responsible committees and associations. Organisational leaders can be seen by the government as the representatives of needy individuals. So for a government grant-in-aid to reach people in need, there must be an ethnic community through which aid can be channelled. Ethnic communities are thus in part defined, or created, by a bureaucratic need to deal with organisations.

However there is another conceptual difficulty here. How many of those whose birthplace and ethnicity connect them to a particular community actually ever use or contact any of that community's organisations? If they never do, does this mean that they are not part of the community? Unless they do contact the community organisations, they may, of course, miss out on the help provided by the grants-in-aid. But community organisers frequently lament the fact that so many of their potential members are never seen, or play no part in the organisational life of the community. Others worry that, through organisations, the communities become, in some sense, an arm of government.

In the 1970s, Jean Martin studied some refugee communities in Adelaide and noted that 'common ethnic origin is a source of network ties that operate very much like kinship networks . . .' and that, indeed, 'associations often appeared to have developed as a formalisation of network ties' (Martin 1972, p. 133). Like families, ethnic networks 'operate as a major mechanism for the distribution of information, services, positions, status and power' (Martin 1972, p. 131). Networks can be more comprehensive and resilient than organisations and communities. In addition to their usefulness in delivering various services to members, ethnic communities are an important arena for public service and for public careers among members. Entrepreneurs and professionals may find their customers and clients through communal activities; many communities have been greatly strengthened by financial endowments and personal service provided by members who have been successful in the wider society.

Again we cannot generalise about this: many people of ethnic origin find that communities based on their professional or business interests are more relevant than ethnic communities to their lives and social interaction. Or they may find community with their neighbours, or with those with whom they share leisure or sporting activities. Some potential community members may actively avoid ethnic communal ties and activities, not only because of other interests, but also because they wish to deny any identification with the perceived values, goals, and beliefs of particular ethnic communities in Australia.

Those who remain outside such group identities — their communities — sometimes argue that they want to be free of communal restraints, or that they are out of sympathy with the ethnic culture they find here. They may argue, like some philosophers and social scientists, that such allegiances and cultures are 'old fashioned', that modernity and globalisation will remove the need for community. Marxists would argue that class will override ethnic differences; philosophical and political liberals still argue that progress and education (or reason, or faith) will help humanity transcend tribal distinctiveness. In Australia over the past forty years, such arguments have often arisen in the 'debate' about multiculturalism (itself a particularly ambiguous concept, as discussed in Castles et al. 1990).

What is an ethnic community?

Communities are recognised public entities, with or without ideologies of ethnic difference. The 1992 *Directory of Ethnic Community Organisations in Australia* lists over ninety ethnic communities. Some of these 'communities' have only one or two organisations listed; some have over fifty; probably none are exhaustive. The types of organisation depend on various factors:

- the circumstances that brought the migrants to Australia
- when they came, and how long the group has been here
- the composition of the group (single, married, young families, aged dependants)
- their education, qualifications, and English-language skills.

Circumstances of immigration

Refugees have few or no possessions, and may have few compatriots in Australia. They often have no choice regarding where they are resettled and little time to prepare themselves for the new society. They receive some allowances and temporary hostel accommodation until they can find their own accommodation and income. They are helped with medical treatment, English-language courses, and assistance with finding employment.

This support is also available from the Federal Government, in association with each State, for people who arrive in Australia with assisted passages, or for those who are not technically refugees but come as 'humanitarian' immigrants. However, many 'economic' or voluntary immigrants are sponsored by families, or sometimes employers, and receive little or no governmental support.

The organisations of refugee ethnic communities, in addition to meeting the needs common to all immigrants, may have as a goal the restoration of the political, social, and cultural structures altered by the conflicts they have fled. Refugees from

Baltic countries, for example, preserved ethnic, cultural, and intellectual traditions that had been overthrown by the USSR, in the hope of reviving them once their nations were free.

Economic migrants often sponsor family, friends, or others, and may build up a network of friends from home; a particular form of this network-building is called 'chain migration', usually attributed to southern Europeans who are unskilled and often from rural areas. Although they often received no government assistance, the recreation of the 'communities' in which they had lived before seemed almost possible. Some villages in Sicily or Greece eventually had their populations decreased by more than half, as many of their inhabitants emigrated to Australia.

Time and context of immigration

Over time, variations in source countries and types of immigration, and changes in Australia itself have affected the nature of ethnic community organisations. The needs of the immediate postwar immigrants from 'Allied' countries, coming to work on reconstruction projects, were very different from the needs of Hong Kong Chinese business immigrants coming to Australia today. The Australia they come to is also very different.

Immigrants who share ethnicity with established communities in Australia may or may not join those communities. German immigrants in the 1950s seldom tried to live in the Barossa Valley, but Jewish refugees were very often incorporated in established Jewish communities.

Composition of immigrant groups

The goals and structure of an ethnic organisation are influenced by the composition of the immigrant group served by the organisation. Unmarried immigrants are in need of organisations that put them in contact with others and that provide social networks. Family groups may have special needs to do with health, education, and child care. If English is not their first language, some immigrants may need help with language maintenance.

Qualifications and skills of immigrants

Immigrants who are highly educated, literate, skilled, and perhaps wealthy may find more in common with other people of similar education and social status than with their ethnic community as a whole. For these people, ethnic community organisations may provide the opportunity to be of service, rather than meet specific needs. Or they may form organisations simply to preserve cultural traditions, such as Scottish sword-dancing.

Intake of immigrants and their settlement

The immediate postwar intake of refugees and economic immigrants from the United Kingdom and western Europe fuelled Australia's growing manufacturing industries, which were chronically short of factory workers. The centres of employment moved from rural construction sites to the big cities, but considerable growth also occurred in smaller places. Port Kembla, Wollongong, Whyalla, and Elizabeth all attracted labour, mostly hard and heavy work in metal industries, very largely undertaken by immigrants. Factory recruitment grew through the 1950s and 1960s, but as Europe itself recovered, it too started recruiting temporary factory workers.

By the 1960s the southern Europeans — Yugoslavs, Italians, Greeks, Turks — emigrated more often to Germany than to Australia. Early in the 1970s, with the worldwide shock of the oil crisis, all the industrial countries that had been recruiting factory labour faced industrial recession and closed their doors to workers; but most still allowed family reunion. Australia stopped assisting passages to 'economic' immigrants. Since the 1970s Australia has still recruited some skilled labour; but in smaller numbers, and to more rigorous language and skills standards than in the past. In addition, relatives and dependants of those already here have, in most cases, been granted admission.

Among these, Filipinas have increased in number as Australian men have found brides in the Philippines. The late 1970s saw a rise in refugee settlement after the Vietnam war: over 100000 Vietnamese immigrants came to Australia in a decade. Crises in Cambodia, Laos, Chile, Lebanon, Afghanistan, Cyprus, Eritrea, China, and El Salvador all brought refugees to settle.

Refugee immigrants often arrive in a strange and unknown country, with few or no compatriots already there to welcome them, but many Europeans found familiar communal institutions on arrival in Australia. Even if they had no relatives, many had friends, former neighbours, or acquaintances here. By a process of chain migration, one or two pioneers have arrived, settled, and become a base for bringing families, relatives, fellow villagers, friends, and acquaintances in chains of sponsorship and assistance. These bonds lessened some of the hardships for new arrivals, and contributed to the ethnic group networks and, later, communities. Shops, restaurants, and travel agents created links with home. Housing and employment were arranged, and this very often meant that groups were geographically clustered. Those who came in chains often settled in inner suburbs of large cities (Leichhardt, Marrickville, Carlton, Coburg). Refugees, and others without relatives or friends already here, often settled near the hostels in which they first lived (Springvale, Maribyrnong).

Australian cities have different mixes. In 1986 one-half of the 137000 Greek-born immigrants and more than one-third of the 260000 Italian-born immigrants in Australia lived in Melbourne. Sydney had 30 per cent and 23 per cent respectively. But Sydney had 73 per cent of all Lebanese-born immigrants, and Melbourne only 20 per cent, so the two cities have different religious profiles (there are more mosques in Sydney). Even more important to community life for smaller ethnic groups, however, is the size of the pool of possible marriage partners. This is important for young immigrants and for the second generation of young people within an ethnic community if the community is to continue. Sydney and Melbourne pose no problems in this respect for Greeks and Italians. Melbourne is somewhat more restrictive for the Lebanese, and Perth would be really problematic — there are only 467

Lebanese-born there. Not all groups are concerned about the 'right' ethnic partners for their young people, but most parents have a preference for familiar in-laws for their children, and the continuity of traditions and familiar ways. They want to be able to talk to their grandchildren too.

There are other important demands made upon communities. When groups with strong language loyalties have young families, one of the most urgent needs is organisational help in maintaining the mother tongue. In a society with a massive majority of English-speakers, and with no common language among the other non-English-speakers, language maintenance is extremely difficult. Some groups have managed a school system from kindergarten through to matriculation, but most have to make do with Saturday schools. If there is a national church, much of the language teaching will be carried out under its aegis (for example, the Greek Orthodox Church often runs language classes).

Ethnic communities change with age, as do their members. Where schools were once necessary, support for the aged becomes a need: help at home, transport to clubs, and especially the provision of familiar meals. Many older immigrants have lost the English they learnt, and if they are too frail to live alone or with families, the care they need is more acceptable if provided in their mother tongue. The Italian community has an especially wide-ranging program of welfare groups serving the aged, as well as community hostels and nursing homes.

I have already described some of the ways in which, in the early postwar years of mass immigration, eastern European refugees put into practice, as it were, earlier experience in community formation and maintenance. The same methods can also be seen in more recent refugee groups to arrive in Australia — they were apparent, for instance, among some of the early Vietnamese Chinese who came here in the 1970s. They were well acquainted with bureaucracy and the virtues of social cooperation.

Immigrants from southern and central Europe, and western Asia that had been part of the multinational, multilingual, polyethnic empires of Czarist Russia, the Ottoman Turks, and the Austro-Hungarian Hapsburgs were often aware of the need for community defence. After those empires broke up in 1918, the south Slavs — Bosnians, Macedonians, Serbs, Croats, Slovenes, and Montenegrins — formed an uneasy national alliance, but remained loyal to their varied origins. (Recent history has shown the fragility of a 'Yugoslav' state, and the fierceness of its constituents in reasserting division.) Similarly, historical loyalties among Greeks manifest themselves in disputes over boundaries with the old Turkish oppressors (such as in Cyprus, for example) and with new neighbours (such as the 'Former Yugoslav Republic of Macedonia'). Lebanon, Syria, Iraq, Jordan, and, later, Israel developed national ideologies that grew out of consciousness of kind, as well as out of conflict with enemies. These histories of national and ethnic conflict sometimes form the basis of ethnic group loyalty among immigrants and have even led to conflict in Australia.

People who were bitterly divided in their homeland seldom want to unite into an ethnic community in Australia. Langer writes movingly of the futility and cruelty of linking together mistress and servant, tortured and torturer, *indigene* and *blanco* Salvadorean refugees — a mistake that can be both emotionally and practically devastating for those misrecognised (Langer 1990). Divisions of class or region often mean that the perception of some unified 'ethnic group' is nothing more than a chimera.

Because of the functions performed by an official ethnic community, however, even those united only by birthplace or language — but otherwise consisting of separate congeries, or relatively separated networks of kin and friends — often do make up an 'ethnic community'. Division and antipathy are not, of course, confined to recent migrants.

A general ignorance of history and fear of conflicts within in the wider Australian community may be expressed as hostility towards those ethnic communities that appear to threaten national cohesion. Such fears were widely expressed during the religious conflicts between Protestant and Catholic communities in the nineteenth and early twentieth centuries. The social fabric of Australia did not unravel as a result of these conflicts; perhaps it can withstand divisions among a variety of communities.

How long can ethnic communities survive? As the first generation leaders retire from their organisations, will the second generation step in? Community leaders often lament the fact that the second generation (their children) do not share their interests in community organisations. Even if these children marry inside the community (and many do not), they have been educated in Australia, and many of their interests and activities lie outside the community. A new wave of immigration can revitalise a community, but without that, as American experience suggests, ethnic communities dissipate, and the ethnicity that remains is symbolic only. A 'community' is no longer necessary.

As communication and travel have become easier and more accessible, the need for immigrants to keep in touch with their homelands and histories, cultures and relatives, can almost be met without ethnic community organisations. Although they still have social and welfare needs, the telephone, video, and relatively cheap travel mean that they are no longer so easily alienated and isolated. Directly keeping in touch also means that it is much easier to maintain language in the home, for example, especially if there are regular holidays in the homeland.

Conclusion

The diversity of Australian immigrants has brought about a diversity of communities based on the ethnic loyalties of their members. The usefulness of the 'ethnic community' as a concept is open to debate: as sociologists, we must be aware of how much is disguised by the term as well as the variety of uses to which it is put.

Tension between the idea of a multicultural society, with diverse interests, and social harmony in Australian society can be allayed by recognising that Australia has always accommodated a diversity of ethnic groups and communities. The absence of an enforced Australian conformity and identity has preserved tolerance and allowed diversity.

Discussion questions

1 How clearly can we define 'ethnic communities'? Why do so many people use the term?

2 Compare the likely characteristics of an ethnic community based upon an 'ethnic' religion with one consisting of refugees who share a birthplace.

3 If you and your family emigrated to Sweden, what do you think your collective needs would be? And to Kazakhstan?

4 What effect does the social class of immigrants, before or after migration, have on the foundation of an ethnic community?

5 Do ethnic communities threaten social harmony and cohesion in Australia?

Recommended reading

- Department of Immigration and Ethnic Affairs, *Directory of Ethnic Community Organisations in Australia* (published annually), AGPS, Canberra.
- Langer, B. 1990, 'The Continuing Trauma of Refugee Settlement — the Experience of El Salvadoreans', in P. S. J. Hosking 1990, *Hope After Horror: Helping Survivors of Torture and Trauma*, UNIYA, Jesuit Social Justice Centre, Sydney, pp. 69–85.
- Learmonth, A. T. A. and A. M. 1968, *Encyclopaedia of Australia*, Warne, London.
- Marrus M. R. 1985, *The Unwanted: European Refugees in the Twentieth Century*, Oxford University Press, New York.
- Martin, J. I. 1972, *Community and Identity: Refugee Groups in Adelaide*, ANU Press and the Academy of the Social Sciences in Australia, Canberra.
- Wooden, M., Holton, R., Hugo, G., and Sloan, J. 1994, *Australian Immigration: A Survey of the Issues*, AGPS, Canberra.

See G. Hugo's Introduction and his chapter, 'Demographic and spatial aspects of immigration', especially sections 2.6, 2.7, and 2.8 (pp. 82–110), and R. Holton's chapter, 'Social Aspects of Immigration' (pp. 158–217).

Chapter 12

Alternative Communities: Beyond the Fringe

Rosemary Wearing

When I am an old woman I shall wear purple
With a red hat which doesn't go, and doesn't suit me,
And I shall spend my pension on brandy and summer gloves
And satin sandals, and say we've no money for butter.
I shall sit down on the pavement when I'm tired
And gobble up samples in shops and press alarm bells
And run my stick along the public railings
And make up for the sobriety of my youth.
I shall go out in my slippers in the rain
And pick the flowers in other people's gardens
And learn to spit.
You can wear terrible shirts and grow more fat
And eat three pounds of sausages at a go
Or only bread and pickle for a week
And hoard pens and pencils and beermats and things in boxes.
But now we must have clothes that keep us dry
And pay our rent and not swear in the street
And set a good example for the children
We must have friends to dinner and read the papers.
But maybe I ought to practise a little now?
So people who know me are not too shocked and surprised
When suddenly I am old, and start to wear purple.

Joseph 1991

In order to understand the concept of 'community', we need to know what the dominant values and rules (or laws) within a community are, and we need to know the main forms of social control used to implement and promote conformity to these values and rules. We need to understand not only the paradoxical nature of community, but also how and when and why alternative or counter cultures have emerged within parent communities in reaction to these dominant features and their imposition on members.

We will explore some of these paradoxes by drawing upon some important traditional symbols of, or metaphors for, community. We will then take a closer look at some of the paradoxes of community before examining one such community: youth culture. We will then end with a summary of the sociological characteristics that feature prominently in these alternative communities.

The traditional idea of community

The sociological literature on community has emphasised its positive features, and it is difficult for the reader not to be enticed and entrapped by what Stan Cohen (1989) calls 'a profound sense of nostalgia' and, in particular, the symbols of 'village', 'pre-industrial', 'small', 'traditional', and '*Gemeinschaft*'. These concepts are dredged up constantly, giving many the impression that the ideal and ultimate form of community can only be found in the past. Do you remember those floating lands at the top of Enid Blyton's (1971) Magic Faraway Tree? As students of sociology, we must be careful to recognise that these renditions of community run the risk of appearing 'reactionary and conservative', as Cohen would warn us.

Symbols are powerful tools, and can be used effectively to control and influence our own beliefs and behaviours. We are constantly exposed to them in the form of legislation, the media, or ideologies. Not only are we, to some extent, coerced or forced into accepting the dominant symbols, but we also consent to them, and to those who have the authority and power to so coerce us. In this way, there is a fundamental tension between being a creative, innovative, independent, self-expressive, need-fulfilling individual and being a member of a community that demands or encourages solidarity, cohesion, conformity, social control, traditions, discipline, and 'belongingness'.

Our authorities, leaders, or implementers of policy must struggle with the simultaneous need to coerce, control, and punish, on the one hand, and to appear to be benign, caring, and concerned for individual welfare, privacy and property, on the other. A community has to be both a haven of autonomy and individual freedom and, at the same time, a social system that disciplines, sanctions, and even oppresses.

Symbols of community are best understood when they are studied with their opposites — for example, we can more clearly understand what is meant by 'peaceful' if we contrast it with 'violent'; 'freedom' with 'control'; 'rewards' with 'punishments'; 'order' with 'disorder'; 'hierarchy' with 'equality'; or 'urban' with 'rural'. Verity Burgmann (1993) says something similar in her account of the gay and lesbian movement in Australia: 'Our society has decreed that homosexuality constitutes sexual deviance: heterosexuality and heterosexual people are "normal", homosexuality and homosexual people are "abnormal"' (pp. 138–9).

Thus we will explore the concept of community with the symbols of 'alternative' community, or 'conformity' with 'deviance', and we will use a case study to assist us. Any discussion of alternative communities must appreciate that, over time, communities change in their nature, meanings, structures, and so on, and what may be seen as 'alternative' and 'deviant' in one culture can be quite acceptable in another place or time. For example, homosexuality is not perceived to be offensive or illegal in Australian Aboriginal culture, yet in Nazi Germany, homosexuals were stigmatised to the extreme by being sent to concentration camps, as were the Jews.

The processes of labelling and of social control (power relations) can actively create alternative communities by virtue of their ability to exclude and stigmatise.

Conversely, such counter-communities can choose to set up a different and separate world, with its own goals, traditions, and practices. In other words, these processes can be constructive as well as destructive; they can lead to reform and change for the better, rather than creating further violence and struggle. This is one way of indicating some of the paradoxes of 'community' as an idea.

The paradoxes of community

Public vs. private spaces

Community can refer to a space (some call it terrain; others may use the term *territory*), and another dominant paradoxical theme concerns the distinctions or boundaries that are drawn between public and private. For example, Irving Goffman (1967) refers to 'frontstage' and 'backstage', implying that when we are at frontstage we are *performing* to an audience, using various masks and other props to enhance our performance and to persuade our audience of our credibility and value. But in order to carry out our public performances effectively, we need a backstage, where we can drop the masks, privately rehearse, or just be the self we feel most relaxed being.

Other sociologists refer to public space as those institutions and places *outside* the family, including structures of the State. Although it is often difficult to determine where the public ends and the private begins, we have a legal system that claims to have the knowledge and authority to make such a determination. The paradoxical web of symbols that conveys the public-private dimension gives rise to a further paradox, which is that the private space, such as the family household, can have a boundary akin to a prison wall — impenetrable and concealing a great deal of hidden and private abuse and violence.

Because it is private, agents such as the police are sometimes reluctant to intervene as they see the family as a sanctuary — too personal. And the boundary between public and private space can have frightening ramifications for those people, such as some young people, who have to escape from violent homes and relocate themselves in the public spaces of the street, parks, beaches, and so on. It could be regarded as paradoxical that public space can ensure that one's visibility becomes one's vulnerability. It is difficult to justify 'doing nothing' in a public space: one is immediately suspect.

The tensions and conflicts surrounding the creation and maintenance of the boundary between public and private space were significant reasons for the emergence of counter-cultures in the 1960s. The members of these counter-cultures expressed both a fear and a resentment of the State (represented, for example, by the police, the laws, and professionals working in areas such as welfare, psychology, and medicine) which they saw as penetrating — some would say invading — the boundary between public and private, and increasingly monitoring family households. Indeed, a salient feature of most alternative communities is the desire of community members to escape the surveillance of the State, to create their own boundaries, to control both access to, and exit from, such private space, and to have the freedom to live and relate according to their own rules and goals.

Control vs. freedom

In all parts of society, whether they be public or private, upper class or lower class, Black or non-Black, people are variously distributed along what is sometimes referred to as a dimension or hierarchy of power. Two points can be made about this in relation to the idea of community.

The first point concerns a paradox inherent in our community: that those people to whom we turn for advice or protection, because they are 'agents of social control', are those who can usually be found at the top of the socio-economic and political hierarchy. They possess the power to create and enforce our laws, our regulations, and our institutions (especially legal institutions). These are the same people who look downwards and label those who are lower on the same ladder, and who are relatively powerless and propertyless, as 'deviant' or even 'dangerous', with implications that Jan Pettman (1991) identifies: 'Those in a position of power in a society can validate and impose their own definitions of normality, and define boundaries for the purpose of excluding, enclosing or exploiting others'.

Steven Box (1983) has suggested that the community's strategies for social control (even criminalisation) of such deviants have led to further paradoxes: those persons who are least powerful and least privileged are the most likely to be arrested, punished, and imprisoned; the people thought to be most dangerous to the community are those who are relatively poor, uneducated, morally inferior, and in the lower occupational positions; and those people who are at the top of the hierarchy (for example, judges, media magnates, corporation heads, and so on) are 'mystified', their behaviour and practices remaining well hidden and remote from the punishing arm of the law.

The second point is made by Cohen (1989), when he argues that, during the 1950s and 1960s (a period when so many so-called alternative communities emerged in many Western countries), there was a powerful global reform movement to dismantle and replace the dominant institutions and structures, along with their experts. This movement was primarily concerned with issues of law and order in our community (which include policing, punishing, treating, classifying, and so on).

Cohen and others refer to this global pattern of reform as 'de-institutionalisation', 'de-carceration', or 'de-professionalisation', all of which involve shifting the burden of control on to ordinary folk, and informal groups and networks in the community. This movement was beset by conflict and tensions. Paradoxically, the attempt to replace and remove the old structures of social control failed, in that these structures — prisons and psychiatric hospitals, for example — remained as strong as ever, and the social control 'net' (Cohen's metaphor) spread wider, with three consequential 'failures'.

First, there has been an increase in the numbers of persons detected, processed, and labelled as 'deviants' in need of treatment or punishment. One significant outcome of this is that more people than before are stigmatised and hence excluded from mainstream society. Second, the 'intensity' of the intervention of these social control agents has actually increased. Finally, the new, alternative community agencies were not replaced, but rather remained in the shadow of, or were attached to, the old traditional structures. Hence this paradox remains: by trying to limit the power of authorities and institutions over people's lives, we have simply extended and even heightened the intervention strategies of social control in the parent community. To quote Cohen (1989, pp. 41–2): our system of social control is like

> ... a gigantic fishing net. Strange and complex in its appearance and movements, the net is cast by an army of different fishermen and fisherwomen working all day and even into the night ... Society is the ocean — vast, troubled and full of unchartered currents, rocks and other hazards. Deviants are the fish. But unlike real fish ... deviants are not caught, sorted out, cleaned, packed, purchased, cooked and eaten ... deviants are in fact kept alive ... and processed (shall we say punished, treated, corrected?) in all sorts of quite extraordinary ways. Then those who are 'ready' are thrown back in the sea. Back in the ocean (and often with tags and labels which they may find quite difficult to shake off), the returned fish might swim around in a free state ... or more frequently they might be swept up into the net again.

Thus we may find alternative communities forming either as direct strategies to reform and de-institutionalise social controls, or as direct consequences of the increased intensity of processing, identification, and treatment. For example, Burgmann (1993) defines what are termed 'new social movements' as:

> political expressions of those tensions within our society, apart from class, that have impinged most clearly on our collective social awareness in the past two or three decades [p. 17] ... [They] provide a forum in which to criticise growth in all its aspects, its self-destructive consequences and the intrusion into personal life of material values; they constitute resistance to the tendencies towards increasing administration of all aspects of everyday life [p. 11].

Thus new social movements, as representative of alternative communities, range from being global in form, size, and goals, to smaller, self-interested, and localised groups. Burgmann discusses five examples: the Black movement, the 'second-wave' of the women's movement, the gay and lesbian movement, and the green and peace movements. In this chapter, though, I will briefly discuss what has been called 'youth culture' as an example of an alternative community.

Youth culture, with special reference to homeless youth

In the following brief discussion of youth culture, many of the variables and issues raised above are exemplified in the emergence and nature of youth subcultures.

Definitions

Mike Brake (1980) used youth subcultures (and, in particular, those of young working-class men) as the basis for his definition of a subculture: 'a subculture exists in the attempt to solve certain problems in the social structure, which are created by contradictions in the larger society'. Thus, although a subculture or alternative community must share some things in common with the parent society within which it is located, it is nonetheless distinctively focused upon its own activities, values, territory, language, and dress. Youth subcultures can also embrace the descriptions that exist in the literature about counter-cultures — Bernice Martin (1981) describes a counter-culture, for instance, as 'a single-minded, often fanatical onslaught on boundaries and structures, a crusade to release ... the infinite, expressive chaos into the everyday world ... it was an index to a whole new cultural style, a set of values, assumptions and ways of living'.

Youth subcultures have been heavily, if not fanatically, researched since the 1930s, both in the USA and, a little later, in the United Kingdom. Most attention has been paid to working-class male youth, since that has been the most visible, the most sensationalised by the press, and the most frequently and intensively labelled group in the wider community. Indeed, Box (1983) goes further than this and argues that the typical convicted criminals or deviants are 'young, uneducated males, who are often unemployed, live in a working-class impoverished neighbourhood, and frequently belong to an ethnic minority' (p. 2).

Mike Presdee (1989) has demonstrated, through an analysis of the tabloid press in Australia since White settlement, that male youth have been a constant target of punitive official policies and media labelling. Their visibility, as a result of poverty and economic crises, has resulted in constant police attention and consequent institutionalisation. Australian authorities have thus created a youth subculture of a negative kind, with the media employing language such as 'idleness', 'depravity', 'drunkenness', 'larrikins', or 'hooligans'. Youth are blamed for not having enough to do, for being unproductive, and adult citizens are warned that such youthful idleness breeds criminality.

Studies carried out in the United Kingdom, in particular, have argued that the distinctive youth culture that we know today really emerged after the war in the 1950s, with a new wave of adolescent consumerism and the emergence of rock music (B. Martin 1981).

Symbols of youth culture

Martin (1981) and Simon Frith (1981) suggest that the most distinctive feature of youth subcultures has been their expression of values, beliefs, and ritual through rock music. Frith believes that rock music has fulfilled at least four important functions for youth culture:

- It has shaped the self-definition of young people, giving them an identity and offering a haven with a very clear boundary, which is both inclusive and exclusive.
- It has offered young people a means of dealing with contradictory and paradoxical relationships, especially those that bring pain and trouble. The lyrics and symbols of rock music articulate what young people might well find difficult to express themselves, both publicly and privately.
- It has the capacity and power to link the past with the present, and to merge present and future into a web of timelessness, which enables young people to indulge in nostalgia, to bask in memories, and to help expunge daily anxieties and fears. Their music can define for them what youth and youthfulness means — in a sense, it emphasises their separateness, and represents their resistance and struggle (Pettman 1991, p. 190).
- It can offer the consumer and user something that can be owned, possessed — not only the song but also, in a sense, the performer — such that the music becomes a part of the young person's identity.

I suggested above that subcultures can also contain and express contradictions and differences within their own group. As Angela McRobbie (1991, pp. 16–28) has pointed out, those youth subcultures that have been visible and studied have defined females as invisible and irrelevant. Indeed, she argues that the male working-class youth subcultures are explicitly and violently masculine, to the point of being ugly, brutal, and degrading in their dealings with women.

Youth homelessness

Researchers have demonstrated the strong link between violence in the private space of the family household and youth homelessness, across all class groupings. At the same time, the very existence of homeless youth threatens the values and institutions that are so revered in mainstream culture, such as the family.

The marginal and alternative existence of homeless youth is threatening for at least four reasons:

- They are detached from that sacred institution and icon of private space: the family.
- Most of these youth are outside the influence and tutelage of the school, and hence pose a moral threat to other young people.
- They frequently engage in breaking rules and the law, as documented by constant police surveillance and interventions.
- They have exposed themselves to continual violence and harassment, and perhaps of greatest concern is the fact that females are more likely to be the target of such abuse and violence (see Alder and Sandor 1989; Alder 1991; and Human Rights and Equal Opportunity Commission 1989).

The 1989 Burdekin Report indicated that 50 per cent of homeless female youth left home because of sexual abuse, and the physical and verbal abuse continued in the public domain, with 47 per cent of homeless females stating that they had been physically abused by police, and even more having been abused by peers. It is disturbing to place this finding against the statistic, cited by Riaz Hassan (1991), that suicide rates among adolescent girls in Australia have doubled. According to Nanette Davis (1993), homeless female youth is a phrase that is synonymous with powerlessness and oppression. They are victims of inequality.

Key features of alternative communities

Let me now summarise the key features of alternative communities as they have emerged in the context of our general discussion and case study. Within the parent culture, we find smaller, 'minority' subcultures — youth cultures, for example — which vary in their degree of alternativeness or deviance.

We have examined the concept of 'alternative community' from a particular perspective: one that views 'alternative' as 'deviant' in the broad sense of breaking social rules. If members of a group break the important rules, or violate the dominant values, of the parent culture, these violators can find themselves reacted to with various degrees of sanctions, discipline, stigma, and exclusion. Indeed, in this chapter I suggest that 'alternative' subcultures can be placed along a continuum that represents degrees of 'deviance' or 'deviation' from what are accepted as the mainstream or dominant beliefs, norms, laws, traditions, practices, and behaviours.

In this way alternative communities will have many, but not necessarily all, of the following characteristics. They will feature:

i   anti-structural tendencies — expressed through opposition to secrecy, the wish to expose power relations, opposition to mainstream authorities' lack of accountability, and concern about the increasing gap between officially stated goals and intentions (rhetoric), on the one hand, and practice, on the other

ii   a search for a distinctive *style* — in the form of symbols, language, dress, music, values, vision, and strategies

iii   a quest for members to gain control over their own destinies, bodies, identities, and environment. The issues of autonomy and self-determination evident in the Black Land Rights movement, or in youth cultures, is a good example

iv   a desire to escape an oppressive and destructive parent culture

v   plans for, and dreams of, a world that is based on happiness and fulfilment, not order and discipline

vi   resistance to, and replacement of, the dominant ideas about punishment, institutional intervention, and psychiatric processing

vii   an attempt to discover and eliminate the major causes of violence, crime, and oppression

viii   the attempt to create a classless society that removes the destructive imposition of differences based on class, race, gender, religion, and so on

ix a tendency to possess a fundamental pessimism, cynicism, realism, and/or fatalism

x the devising of strategies for survival, resistance, defensive action, subversion, negotiation, mediation, reform, or compromise

xi promotion of the importance of rights, including civil rights, victim rights, land rights, and human rights

xii a feminist agenda, which includes bringing personal experiences into political/public issues debates and policy.

The notion of deviance helps us to understand the ways in which alternative communities emerge and how they continue to survive. Alternative or deviant behaviour is simply behaviour that is rule-breaking and different from what is 'normal'. This means that we need to look at the kinds of rules that exist, who constructs them, how they are implemented and enforced, who enforces them, and who imposes the relevant punishments. To quote the famous sociologist Howard Becker (1963, p. 9):

> Social groups create deviance by making the rules whose infraction constitutes deviance, and by applying those rules to particular people and labelling them as outsiders ... deviance is not a quality of the act the person commits, but rather a consequence of the application by others of rules and sanctions to an 'offender'. The deviant is one to whom that label has successfully been applied; deviant behavior is behavior that people so label.

It is important, therefore, that, in the above description of an alternative community, we understand not only the dominant rules and values or norms of the mainstream culture, but also how these are imposed and controlled, and how subcultures emerge in response, or reaction, to these social controls. In studying various alternative communities, we need to be cognisant of the significance of aspects (sociologists call them 'variables') such as age, gender, sexuality, ethnicity, and race.

And finally, we also need to recognise that members of the reacting subcultures (also referred to as counter-cultures or new social movements) are not merely passive recipients of such controls and labels. Jan Pettman (1991) has cautioned that subordinate groups are not only victims:

> They resist, subvert, use, and collude in their own interests. They may 'seize the category', claim it for their own and invert it, attaching positive value where before it was negative. They seek to use the common experiences of those so labelled to organise, mobilise and claim against dominant groups and [their] state ... Subordinate groups ... may use difference to mystify, deny knowledge of themselves to the dominant groups and to confuse and neutralise those who attempt to control or 'help' them. They may use their difference to stress their own separateness and to authorise their own representations. They may seek to legitimise their definitions of cultural differences, including those against others within their own collectivity (p. 190).

Conclusion

To assist us in this brief analysis of alternative communities, we have used the concept of deviance to understand the ways in which rule-breaking results in the parent or mainstream culture reacting with its strategies of discipline and control. This way of seeing things has allowed us to view alternative communities as being *outside* the normal and acceptable practices and belief systems.

As Pettman observed, those persons in positions of power can impose their own definitions about what can be tolerated and where the boundaries exist, which determine who gets excluded, who gets entrapped, and who is exploited. It would seem that alternative communities, as a form of deviant behaviour, feed on the parent culture's systems of control, intervention, and punishment, and this unhealthy relationship is promoted by the sensationalising and stigmatising tactics of the media. But Jenny Joseph, in the poem that opened this chapter, reminds us that, despite these constraints, reactions to mainstream society and attempts to be different (or alternative) can, in a paradoxical fashion, be positive, even if they only remain quests for community and dreams of what 'might be'.

Discussion questions

1 If you were to apply some of the ideas in this chapter to the homosexual community, which issues and ideas would you regard as most relevant in your analysis? Why?

2 This chapter has not gone into detailed discussion about the relative significance of different factors such as ethnicity, age, religion, gender, and sexual preference. Could you select two or more of these factors and discuss what you consider to be their role and influence in alternative communities of your choosing?

3 Could you attempt to predict the kinds and shapes (goals, strategies, ideas, dress, and son on) of alternative communities that might arise and become dominant in the decade to come? Would you distinguish between Australia, on the one hand, and the USA, on the other, for example?

4 Discuss the role and impact of the media on popular images of alternative communities. Distinguish between different forms of the media, and apply your discussion to a comparison of the 1960s/1970s and the mid to late 1990s.

5 Have you had any personal involvement or contact with what you would define as an alternative movement? If so, please identify which of the issues discussed in this chapter apply most readily and appropriately to your experiences. If not, why do you think that you have had no contact with an alternative community?

Recommended reading

To help gain a broader sociological understanding of communities or subcultures that can be viewed as different or deviant, I suggest the following:

- Pettman, J. 1991, 'Racism, Sexism and Sociology', in G. Bottomley, M. de Lepervanche, and J. Martin (eds), *Intersexions: Gender, Class, Culture, Ethnicity*, Allen & Unwin, Sydney.

For a theoretical and empirical exploration of the topics of deviance and social control, you should find the following references of value:

- Anleu, S. R. 1991, *Deviance, Conformity and Control*, Longman Cheshire, Melbourne.
- Box, S. 1981, *Deviance, Reality and Society*, 2nd edn, Holt, Rinehart & Winston, London.
- Cohen, S. 1989, *Visions of Social Control*, Polity Press, Cambridge, pp. 30–2, 41–2, 116–27.

Protest and alternative subculture movements provide a context for understanding youth homelessness. For a broader picture of youth culture, you may find these references informative:

- Burgmann, V. 1993, *Power and Protest: Movements for Change in Australian Society*, Allen & Unwin, Sydney, ch. 3.
- Frith, S. 1978, *The Sociology of Rock*, Constable, London.
- McRobbie, A. 1991, *Feminism and Youth Culture*, Macmillan Education, Hampshire, chs 1 and 2.

For more detailed analyses of youth homelessness in Australia, read the following:

- Alder, C. 1991, 'Victims of Violence: The Case of Homeless Youth', *Australian and New Zealand Journal of Criminology*, vol. 24, March, pp. 1–14.
- Davis, N. 1993, 'Systemic Gender Control and Victimisation among Homeless Female Youth', *Socio-legal Bulletin*, no. 8, Summer, pp. 22–31.
- Pettman, J. 1991, 'Racism, Sexism and Sociology', in G. Bottomley, M. de Lepervanche, and J. Martin (eds), *Intersexions: Gender, Class, Culture, Ethnicity*, Allen & Unwin, Sydney, pp. 187–202.
- Presdee, M. 1989, Youth and 'Law and Order' in Australia: Class and the Criminalisation of Culture, unpublished paper presented to the American Society of Criminology Conference, Chicago, November.

Chapter 13

Community: Experiences and Explanations

Ken Dempsey

Community has many meanings; it involves different sets of
experience for different groups of people, and indeed for the same
people at different times in their lives.

Crow and Allan 1994, p. 183

There is no slipperier concept in sociology than community. Although sociologists
have been using the term for well over two hundred years, they have not achieved
consensus concerning its meaning. Not only sociologists, but also politicians, journalists, current affairs broadcasters, and lay people use it in a bewildering variety of
ways. It is used to refer to such diverse groupings and collectivities as local villages,
towns, cities, nations, and even the whole human race. It is used to denote institutions with narrow purposes, such as prisons and mental asylums, and sometimes to
denote non-residential groups, such as the practitioners of a particular profession —
hence we speak of the medical community. Its multiple meanings make it a difficult
tool with which to work. These problems are magnified by the common practice of
using the concept of community evaluatively as well as descriptively — that is, in
such a way as to suggest that community is good for people and its absence bad:
'Below the surface of many community studies lurk value judgements, of varying
degrees of explicitness, about what is the good life' (Bell and Newby 1971, p. 16). Its
diverse and confusing usages have led some sociologists to suggest abandoning it
altogether (Stacey 1969). However, it is a concept that will not go away, because people cannot find a satisfactory substitute: 'Community is a concept that just will not lie
down' (Day and Murdoch 1993, p. 85, quoted in Crow and Allan 1994, pp. xiv–xv).

Several of the diverse ways in which sociologists use the term, and a number of
the connotations it has for some of them, are illustrated in the accounts of community and various facets of social life offered in the previous chapters in this section.
Rosemary Wearing and David de Vaus stress the historical association of community
with small settlements, such as rural villages and the special kind of social life they are
believed to generate. Doug Ezzy, David de Vaus, and Susan Harvey emphasise that
community occurs in places other than the settlements where people sleep. They
point out that special interest groups, such as ethnic associations, church congregations, and work organisations, may be contexts for the experience of community.
Doug Ezzy and Susan Harvey draw attention to the subjective meaning that is often
given to community. Ezzy says that community can occur inside the individual as well

as outside, and Harvey shows that community can give rise to a sense of belonging together. Rosemary Wearing and Chris Eipper emphasise several of the costs of community for those who do not fit in or who are shunned by other community members. Both of these authors convey the important message that individuals may be members of a community yet have no sense of belonging to it. In some of the writing, there is just a hint of the idea that community is qualitatively better than non-community, and in some accounts, it is suggested that we have lost, or are in the process of losing, community.

Problems of definition

In the light of the wide variety of meanings given to the term, it is not surprising that sociologists have failed to produce a definition of community that has won general acceptance. In a search for commonality, an American sociologist, George Hillery, analysed no fewer than ninety-four definitions of community reported either in widely used text books or highly respected scholarly journals (1955). He found that the only thing they had in common was a reference to humanity. Beyond that there was no basic agreement. For example, not all definitions mentioned geographical area, whereas some writers saw geographical area as the most important component of community. Notwithstanding the diversity in meanings, Hillery found that many writers subscribed to the view that a community is a group of people occupying a common territory, sharing a common life, whose members had one or more social ties in common. Frequently writers also stressed that a community was an autonomous grouping that is able to meet the needs of its people from its own resources.

Many other writers have subsequently attempted to codify the main usages of this elusive term (Warren 1966; Minar and Greer 1968; Bell and Newby 1976; Willmott 1986; Crow and Allan 1994). While there is considerable diversity in their accounts, there are several characteristics that are repeatedly cited as the distinguishing marks of community (Crow and Allen 1994, Introduction). Two of these concern us here. These characteristics are, first, having the kind of social ties in common that produce a high degree of social solidarity (a structural characteristic) and, second, the experience of belonging together (a subjective quality). Some authors emphasise one and not the other. Often, however, writers lump the structural and subjective characteristics together, inferring that community only occurs when both a high degree of social solidarity and a strong sense of belonging occur. This is a confusing practice, because it is possible for the objective (or structural) characteristics of community to be present and the subjective characteristics to be absent. People may be linked by social ties of interdependence and yet have no sense of belonging together. It is also possible for the opposite to be true: for people who do not know one another to have a sense of belonging together.

Community is a rubbery enough concept without the additional baggage that comes with combining objective and subjective features. I am therefore following the practice adopted by Colin Bell and Howard Newby of reserving the term *community* for the type of social structure that results in many, and probably most, people knowing one another personally, or at least knowing of one another. The occurrence of community, understood in this way, is not an all-or-nothing phenomenon, but always a matter of degree. I am also adopting their practice of using Herman Schmalenbach's term, *communion*, to refer to the subjective experience people may have of belonging together (1961). I argue that, whether or not community gives rise to communion, the social bonds it creates always constrain the behaviour of its members.

Community and sharing territory

Most of the writers who have conducted major reviews of the literature on community acknowledge that communities need not inhabit the same territory in order to be communities. They may have things in common that distinguish them from other groups. For example, many interest-based communities, such as those bonded by the tie of ethnicity, are dispersed geographically. These same writers also acknowledge that the view most commonly held is that which Hillery's work highlighted: communities are groups of people sharing a common locale. These are often referred to as communities of place. While community can occur among people who are dispersed geographically, I am going to concentrate in this account on communities of place, especially those that are relatively small in size. These are the communities with which I am more familiar, and these communities have been the focus of most of the community research conducted in this country (Oxley 1978; Wild 1974; James 1979; Poiner 1990; Dempsey 1992).

Perhaps only a minority of us live in such settlements. Yet, as Bell and Newby (1971) note, we all live somewhere, and wherever it is, we all participate in some social relationships, even if they are often of a highly segmented and cursory character: perhaps we play in a local basketball team, attend a conservation group, or join a drama club. For some, participation may not extend beyond chatting with neighbours, but for all of us, there are some social relationships associated with the place where we live. Their study can provide insight into their character and the factors influencing them.

Can there be community without autonomy?

Throughout much of the history of sociology, one of the most recurring ideas advanced by writers has been that communities are groups that are able to meet the daily needs of their members from the resources of their own area and their own people. The day-to-day relationships of members occur mainly among themselves, rather than with outsiders. Even in many of the definitions offered in recent years, there is still a strong suggestion of this traditional conceptualisation. For example, one well-known scholar incorporated this view in the definition of community he provided for a prestigious sociology dictionary. He defined community as 'a collectivity of actors sharing in a limited territorial area as the base for carrying out the greatest share of their daily activities' (Sjoberg 1965).

Despite the persistence of this viewpoint, the reality today is that no settlement in the Western world is economically, politically, or culturally autonomous. Nor do the inhabitants of any community have all, or even most, of their needs met within the boundaries of the community. It is also becoming increasingly unlikely that most of their significant social ties will be restricted by those boundaries. Today local settlements are increasingly dependent on regional and metropolitan centres, and on international organisations and entities, for many of the goods and services they use in the course of their daily lives, as well as for the disposal of the goods they produce. The decisions that have the greatest impact on the quality of their lives are made elsewhere.

The residual local autonomy settlements possess is rapidly diminishing. In many instances the community members may cease to control all of their key institutions. This is one of the manifestations of the globalisation of all societies, and of all sub-groupings within them, no matter how small. The less autonomy a local grouping has, the more the grouping and its members will depend on external sources for many of their local needs, and consequently, the members will have less local social ties with each other. In pursuing their economic or leisure interests, local people will form many relationships with people who reside outside the locally based group they call their community. The point may be reached at which most of their more important social ties are with people living outside their settlement.

While developments of the kind that have just been described will reduce the community character of a settlement, it will not eliminate its occurrence. There are, for instance, literally hundreds of small rural settlements in Australia in which there are a sufficient range of institutions, or local representations of wider institutions, to provide opportunities for people to engage in many of their daily activities in the neighbourhood where they live. In going about their daily activities, they interact with many other people who live locally. For example, I found, in the research of a Victorian rural community, which I called Smalltown, that, the longer the study went on, the more ultimate control of educational, legal, religious, economic, and even many of the leisure activities of the community shifted from Smalltown to centres such as Sydney, Melbourne, Canberra, Hong Kong, Tokyo, and New York. Nevertheless, at the time the research ended (1991), sufficient institutional activities still remained in the Smalltown settlement to facilitate a pattern of relationships that more than justify calling Smalltown a community. Although it only had a population of about 4000 people, Smalltown had a court house, churches, employment opportunities, a law-enforcement agency, local branches of a range of government authorities, and a wide range of sporting and other leisure facilities. Voluntary organisations, such as the fire brigade, and the Rotary and Lions Clubs, provided a range of services for local people.

While autonomy does not characterise modern settlements, the more institutions, organisations, and activities of the kinds I have been describing are present in the locality where people are housed, the more likely it is that social ties of the kind that distinguish community from non-community will occur (Stacey 1969, p. 21).

The distinguishing social characteristics of community

Bell and Newby stress that, to justify saying that community is occurring, the social ties prevailing among people must display two special characteristics: first, the ties are multi-stranded rather than single stranded; and second, those ties give rise to a series of overlapping close-knit, rather than loose-knit, networks among members (1976). In ordinary language, the term *multi-stranded ties* means that instead of, say, two people being linked by a single activity, such as membership of the same organisation or employment at the same place, they are linked by at least two, and possibly many, ties. This means, for instance, that, as well as being my neighbour, John also belongs to the same tennis club, serves on the church council with me, and his daughter and my son attend the same school.

The formation of multi-stranded social ties of this kind is more or less inevitable in Smalltown because there are few ways for residents to fulfil their daily needs other than by going to one of two schools, joining the only golf club, attending one of the handful of local churches, shopping in one of the two supermarkets, joining the only Rotary Club or branch of the Red Cross Society, and working locally. In such circumstances, more or less the same people keep coming across one another and find themselves in relationships of mutual interdependence.

The members of a settlement who display the level of social solidarity, and of personal knowledge of that solidarity, characteristic of community will have close-knit, rather than loose-knit, local social networks (Bell and Newby 1976). Wherever we live, we all have personal networks. These are comprised of friends, acquaintances, relatives, work associates, and so on. There may be hundreds of people in an individual's network. If my network is loose-knit, then it is one in which most of the persons with whom I have contact do not have anything to do with one another, and do not even know one another except through me. So, for example, I may work with Tom, play tennis with Bill, go to the pictures with Mary, and have Sunday dinner with my mother, who has never met Tom, Bill or Mary. A loose-knit network does not bear much resemblance to a group. If Tom, for instance, wants to apply pressure to me to think or behave in a certain way, he will have to do it single handed, because he is not in touch with the other people I know in order to organise them to apply pressure to me collectively. By contrast, a close-knit network does resemble a group, or at least part of it may take on the qualities of a group. The people in it not only know and interact with me, but also interact with each other. So, for example, Bill, with whom I play tennis, belongs to the same cricket club as Tom, with whom I work, and Mary, with whom I go to the pictures, also meets up with Tom at the photography club, and all of us go out on picnics and attend restaurants together. If I belong to a close-knit network, I am more likely to be subjected to collective pressure or given collective support. Close-knit networks of the kind I have just described are repeated many times over in places like Smalltown. The result is that virtually all of the locally based networks of residents overlap to at least some degree. These networks help produce the social solidarity that gives the settlement its community character.

Here everybody knows everybody else

In every rural town in which I have lived, including Smalltown, the members proudly boast that theirs is a community in which 'everybody knows everybody else'. Members see this as a quality that distinguishes their community from larger entities such as the city, with which they constantly compare their group. It is not literally the case that, in a community of Smalltown's size, everybody knows everybody else, but it is more, rather than less, true. In Smalltown, for instance, any strange face or motor vehicle will *always* stimulate questions by one 'local' or another: 'Do you know who she is? Is there a new family in town? I have not seen her around the place before'.

The validity of saying that most people know each other, or know of each other, is borne out at any meeting of the town council, or when a stranger seeks directions from an inhabitant. If, for example, a council officer is reporting to councillors on the need to mend a broken water pipe in Dawson Street, he will not say that the break is at 24 Dawson Street but that it is outside Trevor Snow's house. When he makes this statement, the councillors will indicate with a nod of their heads that they comprehend precisely at what point in the street the damage has occurred. If a 'local' is asked how to get to the property of somebody living in the surrounding farming district, then the directions are frequently given in the following way, even to a stranger: 'You go out along the Buckjump Road past Bill Smith's place, then when you get to Tom Brown's place, you turn to the left. You won't be able to miss it; it will be just on the right'.

People know more about one another than just their place of residence. They know what they do for a living, often what their parents did before them, what scrapes some of their family members have got themselves into, what successes or failures their children have had, what sport they play, certainly what car they drive, and usually who their closest kin are. It is this level of 'knowing' that Newby (1980), Robert Hall et al. (1983), and others say justifies calling a locally based group like Smalltown a community. It is more likely to happen in settlements that have small populations and where many of the institutions people participate in daily are located where they live. It is also fostered by most members residing in the community for sufficient periods of time to establish relationships.

The chances of most people knowing each other is also increased by a settlement being relatively isolated geographically. Isolation will encourage residents to pursue their interests locally, to enter into work and economic ties, and to pursue their leisure interests and find many of their friendships near where they live.

The ties that bind

The notion of 'everyone knowing everyone' is useful for suggesting something of the essential character of a locally based community. It is a mistake, however, to jump to the conclusion that, because everyone knows everyone else, community is a good thing and its absence a bad thing. We cannot, for instance, assume that community members have strong feelings of attachment to one another or are necessarily supportive of each other. In arguing that community exists when a sufficient number of people know one another, we focus on the form, and not the content or substance, of relationships. Fellow residents may, indeed, hate one another and be in a state of constant conflict but, nevertheless, constitute a community (Newby 1980, p. 13). Irrespective of their feelings for each other, residents are locked into reciprocal ties of mutual obligation.

For many commentators, the social bondedness of community is its distinguishing feature. The interdependence of members produces constraint, which is experienced as obligation by the individual (Crow and Allan 1994, p. 11). As long as one stays in that social situation, there may be no escaping community. It is, says Heller, a matter of necessity (1984, quoted in Crow and Allan 1994, p. 10).

The multi-stranded ties and the close-knit networks that produce the level of interpersonal knowledge characteristic of community may result in the giving and receiving of social, emotional, and material support among locals. However, they do not necessarily produce these outcomes. A social situation in which 'everybody knows everybody else' may help produce a sense of belonging among most community members. However, whether or not it achieves such ends, this level of knowing will certainly facilitate the exercise of social control, and even the ostracism of those who fail to play the game according to the rules, or who pose some kind of threat to the main local power-holders. Numerous studies have demonstrated that community ties are used repeatedly to control the individual. Gossip, ridicule, and explicit condemnation in the presence of other residents are used to ensure compliance with expectations. Those who fail to respond to such pressures, or whose breach of community values is viewed as outrageous may be shunned in the first instance, socially marginalised, or even permanently ostracised (Dempsey 1990, chs 3 and 4).

Usually, the 'locals' do not see themselves as behaving in such ways. They boast that their community is a very friendly place, where everybody is made welcome and looked after: 'People are easy to get along with here'; 'We're like one big happy family here. That's what is so different about our town'. Residents, especially newcomers, are, however, much more likely to experience their town in these ways if they think and behave like powerful 'locals'. It certainly is *not* the case that all residents of locally based communities are looked after and treated in a friendly manner. In several of the communities in which I have resided or conducted research, I have witnessed the use of close-knit networks for punishing and sidelining those who offended local sensibilities. For instance, a few days after the wife of a professional man arrived in one town, she asked the president of a local organisation if she could share a job that was already being carried out by another person. She was breaching the unwritten rule that newcomers wait to be asked. She was refused, and this and several other incidents led to local leaders claiming the woman was a social menace who was 'coming in and telling everybody how to run things they had run for years'. The word was put around: 'Don't have anything to do with her, she's murder'. Her subsequent attempts to join several other organisations were unsuccessful. She and her husband found living in the town unbearable, and the husband terminated his appointment prematurely. As a local professional man who had lived in a capital city for a number of years perceptively remarked:

If you dirty one of your nests in the city, no one but those immediately involved need know, and you can get on with the rest of your life as though nothing has happened. But in this community, if you dirty one nest, you have in effect dirtied them all. The local grapevines work so efficiently: the story of the *faux pas* is relayed with exaggerations and embellishments at the pub that night and within a day it has spread throughout the community. The offender has nowhere to turn and will face criticism and rejections from community leaders and ordinary members.

In small communities, being publicly stigmatised, criticised, and sometimes ostracised is often the fate of women who breach the local norms of respectability by having an affair, of newly arrived men who try to take over local organisations, of couples who fail to care properly for their properties or their children, and even of those who do not 'join in enough and keep to themselves'. However, the ties of interdependence, coupled with a fairly homogeneous value system, work to constrain the behaviour not only of such 'deviants', but also of the great majority of community members. Those who start to step out of line in some minor way — by, say, criticising a local leader — retreat once disapproval is voiced. They say something of this nature: 'I've learnt to keep my mouth shut. I want to go on living here. I want people to like me'.

Drawing the boundaries

Communities are often said to be distinguished by their members having something in common. It may be shared land, a shared outlook on life, similar values, and so forth (Crow and Allen 1994). The material introduced in the previous section illuminates a distinctive quality of communities. They are as much about *not* having things in common as they are about having them in common. Members are drawn into a system of interdependence by participation in the same activities and organisations, sharing the same territory, and holding similar values and beliefs. There are, however, antagonisms and competition between various segments of the community: business people and farmers, transient professionals and locally born members of the middle class, and Catholics and Protestants, for instance.

Members of many Australian communities claim that the egalitarianism of their community is one of its distinctive features. However, certain categories of people are inevitably more politically or socially peripheral than others. For example, locally born members of the community often gain acceptance socially and politically more readily than the non-locals. In Australia, non-locals are frequently referred to disparagingly by locally born people as 'two-bob blow-ins'. Frequently, the non-locals may spend years trying unsuccessfully to win the degree of acceptance they believe the locals gain as a birth right (Elias and Scotson 1965). They are likely to report that even partial acceptance depends on being a follower in any community activity, and certainly on not attempting to take over things. Middle-class men exercise more power than other sections of the community (Newby et al. 1978). Men are more at the centre of the community than women, and the young and middle-aged are more likely to exercise positions of influence and prestige than the elderly (James 1979; Dempsey 1990).

Many of these divisions and distinctions, however, are to put to one side, or even healed, in the face of what are perceived as threats to the community collectively — threats that arise from both outside and inside their own area (Cohen 1985, p. 16). Community ties are strengthened by members' opposition to values and lifestyles that occur in their own midst but that they perceive as different to their own or as a threat to their collective. They close ranks against those in their midst who flout their standards or refuse to play the parts allotted to them. The more powerful members of the community utilise close-knit, face-to-face relationships to marginalise these people. This process enhances the social solidarity of the community and the experience of communion (sense of belonging together, of a shared fate) of those who are included, while alienating those who are excluded.

Seeking and experiencing communion

Psychologically, communities of place are potentially important to their members because people need to feel a part of something. The desire for communion is a desire for acceptance, intimate relations, and a sense of identity beyond the individual's own household (Newby 1980). Such communities provide these emotional rewards for members who are at the centre of political and social life, and who hold leadership positions in the more prestigious organisations. The community's powerful organisations provide members with a stage on which they can enhance their public self-esteem. Often, these people speak of their community as the greatest place on earth, and stress how much they feel a part of the place. Their positive feelings about their community are understandable, given the significant rewards they receive. The community rewards them emotionally as well as politically, economically, and socially. It informs their sense of personal and public identity.

What is surprising is that many people who do not occupy any positions of power or prestige, and even some who have been the focus of sustained criticism or have been shunned, can still say they feel a part of the community. This, however, is not, as local leaders insist, as much a measure of the place's unique qualities as it is of the fact that most of the 'lesser lights' belong to their own local close-knit networks. The members of these personal networks, rather than the community as some collective entity, provide them with the sense of security that comes from the experience of belonging. The group-like quality of their networks provides many (but not all) of them with a sense of attachment, despite their being the objects of criticism, and sometimes of shunning, by substantial numbers of other community members. For these people, personal networks of friends, neighbours, and kin are their community.

Conclusion

Community is one of the most contested concepts in the social sciences. Yet sociologists persist in using it, because informal relationships beyond the household continue to play a significant part in people's daily lives, and they find the notion of community indispensable to talking about these experiences. It has many meanings. It has been impossible to consider them all here, so I have chosen to rely mainly on a structural perspective for discussing the nature and experience of community. I have tried to show that, from this perspective, community is distinguished by the character, rather than the content or quality, of the social relationships of those who participate. It is doubtful whether, in recent history, locally based communities of place have been autonomous groupings. They are certainly no longer so. However, there is often sufficient activities occurring in the neighbourhoods where people sleep to lead to the formation of community-type social ties.

I have focused mainly on smaller communities of place, but the distinctive characteristics of community can be found in a range of human associations and in large urban settlements, as well as small rural ones (Gans 1968; Newby 1980). The occurrence of community is always a matter of degree. The more aspects of participants' daily lives that are expressed through these relationships, the more the grouping concerned takes on the character of a community, and the greater the social solidarity among its members. I have argued that it is confusing and misleading to view community evaluatively — to conceive of its occurrence as good and its absence as bad. A community may produce the experience of communion for some, or most, of its members. It may be the source of emotional security and various forms of practical assistance. It may contribute significantly to the understanding members have of themselves — to their sense of identity. However, whether or not it does any of these things for particular members, they will, nevertheless, find themselves constrained, to at least some degree, by the reciprocal obligations inherent in community ties. Even those men and women who feel alienated, and who are not at the centre of things socially, will find that, as long as the neighbourhood or interest group remains one in which a substantial number of people know one another, their lives will be affected profoundly by the bonds of community. Sometimes they will be affected in ways that hurt them badly. Sooner or later most members learn that any gains community has to offer (and there may be significant gains) always come at considerable cost (Crow and Allan 1994).

Discussion questions

1   Many writers say that what distinguishes community from non-community is sharing territory. Do you disagree or agree with this viewpoint? Please provide reasons for your answer.
2   How would you distinguish community from communion? Can you have one without the other?
3   Do many people know one another in the street where you live? Are any social ties that exist mainly multi-stranded or single-stranded? Are there chains for communicating information and gossip? Are some residents more on the margins of any social interactions that occur? If they are, what distinguishes them from those who are actively involved in street or neighbourhood activities? How meaningful would it be to regard the street or neighbourhood as a community?

4   Plot your personal network. Do you have mainly single-stranded or multi-stranded ties with those in your network? Are there many cross-cutting ties among those in your network? Does the network as a whole, or segments of it, take on the character of a group? Does it provide you with a sense of belonging?

5   There is a long tradition among sociologists of regarding community as good for people and society, and its absence as a bad thing. In the light of your reading and personal experience, what position would you take on this issue? Please provide reasons for your answer.

Recommended reading

For an excellent introduction to the field of community studies, see:

* Crow G. and Allan, G. 1994, *Community Life: An Introduction to Local Social Relations*, Harvester Wheatsheaf, London.
* Newby, H. 1980, *Community*, Open University Press, Milton Keynes.
* Worsley, P. 1987 (ed.), *The New Introducing Sociology*, Penguin Books, Harmondsworth, ch. 7.

For a summary of Australian and overseas studies up to the end of the 1970s, you should find the following helpful:

* Wild, R. 1981, *Australian Community Studies and Beyond*, Allen & Unwin, Sydney.

The following studies should expand your knowledge of community research in Australia in the 1980s and 1990s. They all also examine the influence of gender on relationships:

* Bowman, M. 1980, *Beyond the City*, Longman Cheshire, Melbourne.
* Williams, C. 1981, *Open Cut: The Working Class in an Australian Mining Town*, Allen & Unwin, Sydney.
* Dempsey, K. 1990, *Smalltown: A Study of Social Inequality, Cohesion and Belonging*, Oxford University Press, Melbourne.
* Dempsey, K. 1992, *A Man's Town: Inequality between Women and Men in Rural Australia*, Oxford University Press, Melbourne.
* Poiner, G. 1990, *The Good Old Rule: Gender and Other Power Relationships in a Rural Community*, Sydney University Press, Melbourne.

The following references deal with the issue of whether differing settlement patterns influence the type of community that occurs:

* Gans, H. 1968, 'Urbanism and Suburbanism as Ways of Life', in R. Pahl (ed.), *Readings in Urban Sociology*, Pergamon Press, Oxford.
* Pahl, R. 1968, 'The Rural Urban Continuum', in R. Pahl (ed.), *Readings in Urban Sociology*, Pergamon Press, Oxford.

For a greater understanding of the subjective dimension of community, consult:

* Schmalenbach, H. 1961, 'The Sociological Category of Communion', in T. Parsons et al. (eds), *Theories of Society*, vol. 1, Free Press, Glencoe, Ill.
* Cohen, A. 1985, *The Symbolic Construction of Community*, Tavistock Publications, London.

Nation

Imagine Australia, if you can, into the
new century ...

Peter Beilharz, Chapter 18

Chapter 14

Class and Inequality

Brian Graetz

> ... Australia is the most egalitarian of countries, untroubled by
> obvious class distinctions, caste or communal domination, the
> tensions of racialism or the horrors of autocracy ... Australia has
> one of the highest per capita national incomes in the world; there
> are more cars and TV sets for its population than almost anywhere;
> there is the largest rate of home ownership in the world; there are
> more savings accounts than people ... Not only are very rich or
> very poor people rare; the average income is not a simple
> average, it is also close to the typical income.
>
> Horne 1971, pp. 17–19

In past years, it was not uncommon for people to describe Australia as a truly egalitarian nation, forged by hearty bonds of mateship and broad material equality. But
from the 1960s onwards, social scientists began to subject such views to closer
scrutiny. What they found was not simply that material inequality did exist on a
large scale, and had done so since European settlement, but also that views about
equality and egalitarianism formed part of wider stereotypes, myths, and sentiments
entrenched within Australian culture. At the same time, they began to draw upon a
range of theories, concepts, and hypotheses to help explain the origins, nature, and
persistence of inequalities.

In this chapter, issues of inequality and class in Australia are examined. The discussion begins with a brief outline of some of the key dimensions of inequality today,
then considers how problems of inequality have been approached by social scientists.
The aim is to identify some of the main theories and concepts of inequality, the
images of social structure they convey, and the ways in which they can help us understand inequality within our own society.

Inequality in Australia

Inequality may derive from a range of sources and exist in many different forms. In
this section, three main types of inequality are examined. First, we consider material
inequality, evident in disparities of income, property, and wealth. Second, we look at
inequality associated with employment and the labour market, and third, at inequality arising from education and schooling. Each section draws on publicly available
information about inequality, compiled and regularly updated by the Australian
Bureau of Statistics and available in most university libraries.

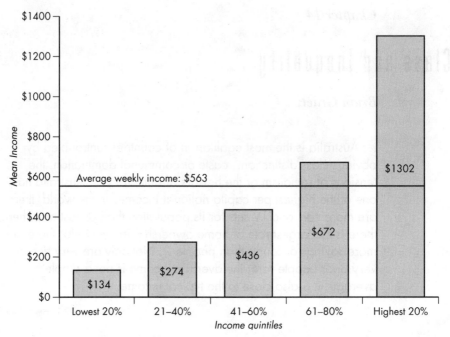

Figure 14.1   Average gross weekly income by income quintile groups, Australia 1990

Source: Australian Bureau of Statistics 1993b

Income, property, and wealth

Income and wealth are perhaps the most easily recognisable forms of inequality. Income, in particular, may be used to purchase a whole range of goods and services, from the necessities of everyday life, such as food, clothing, and accommodation, through to luxury items, such as expensive cars, video recorders, and holidays. Disparities of income and wealth are typically related to other forms of inequality and directly affect the way people live.

Information about the distribution of incomes in Australia can be obtained from the *1990 Survey of Income and Housing Costs and Amenities* (ABS 1993b; 1993c). It shows that the average gross income that year was $563 per week. However, there was considerable variation on this figure, as shown in Figure 14.1. For example, the average income for the bottom 20 per cent of earners was only $134 per week, well below the overall average. At the other extreme, the average income for the top 20 per cent of earners was $1302 per week, well above the overall average and almost ten times the income of the bottom 20 per cent.

There is also considerable variation in the main source of people's income. Out of all the income units in Australia (units being made up of individuals who earn their own income, or groups of people who live together and form single spending units, such as a families), just over one-half (58.3 per cent) derived most of their income from wages and salaries, and just over one-quarter (26.4 per cent) from government pensions and benefits. The remainder derived most of their income either from conducting their own business, trade, or profession (6.6 per cent), or from private income sources (8.5 per cent). However, among the top 20 per cent of income-earners, more than four out of five people (82.9 per cent) obtained their income from wages or salary, and a further one in ten (10.6 per cent) from their own business, trade, or profession. In stark contrast, almost three-quarters (72.3 per cent) of those in the lowest income group obtained most of their income from government pensions and welfare benefits, and only 12 per cent from wages and salaries. Overall, wage and salary earners received an average of $701 gross income per week, business owners $786 per week, and those on government pensions and benefits only $210 per week.

Information on income distributions is also provided in the 1991 census (ABS 1993a). Results show that in 1991 the average annual income for the lowest 20 per cent of income-earners was only $5700, and one-half of this group earned $2500 per annum, or less. In contrast, the average income for the highest 20 per cent of earners was more than $28 000 per annum, and one-half of them earned more than $36 500. These disparities are highlighted in Figure 14.2, which shows the slice of the overall income pie received by each income group. The highest 20 per cent of income-earners received nearly one-half (47.8 per cent) of all income, and the next highest received one-quarter of all income. In contrast, the lowest 20 per cent of income-earners received only 2.7 per cent of the total income pie.

While income refers to the regular receipt of money, whether from wages and salaries, business profits, pensions and benefits, or investments, another important criterion of material inequality is wealth. Wealth depends in part on immediate income, but also on the longer term accumulation of assets and financial resources.

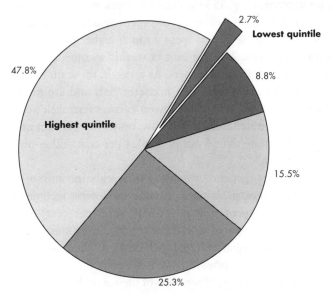

Figure 14.2 Share of gross annual income received by income quintile groups, Australia 1991
Source: Australian Bureau of Statistics 1993a

Wealth may take the form of savings and investments, shares in companies and corporations, or ownership of assets such as houses, business enterprises, or farms.

Unfortunately, there are no official statistics on the distribution of wealth in Australia. Instead, analysts have tried to estimate, from time to time, the distribution of wealth from sources such as income surveys or investment data. Recent analyses suggest that there are even greater disparities of wealth than income. For example, during the 1980s, it was estimated that there were more than 30 000 millionaires in Australia. At the other end of the scale, more than two million people lived below the poverty line — that is, with income less than that needed to sustain a basic existence. In addition, it was estimated that the wealthiest 1 per cent of the population controlled nearly 20 per cent of all personal wealth, and the wealthiest 10 per cent controlled more than one-half of all wealth, leaving the bottom half of the population with just 1.5 per cent of all personal wealth (Dilnot 1990). Overall, disparities of wealth and income in Australia are substantial. Those with the least wealth include people with disabilities or chronic illness, aged and invalid pensioners, sole parents supporting dependent children, people who cannot find regular employment, and others who, likewise, rely on government financial assistance to meet their daily needs.

One of the most fundamental uses to which wealth and income can be put is to obtain housing. Most people need at least some money either to pay landlords for rented accommodation, to pay family or relatives for shared accommodation, or to make mortgage repayments when purchasing a dwelling. Clearly, the level of income and wealth a person has will influence the type of housing obtained.

For example, Table 14.1 shows that in 1990 the lowest 20 per cent of income-earners spent, on average, only A$34 dollars per week on housing, compared with the highest 20 per cent of income-earners, who spent an average of A$137 per week. At the same time, low income-earners spent a much higher proportion of their limited income on housing costs: 25.3 per cent of weekly income, compared with only 10.5 per cent spent by high income-earners. As a result, those on lower incomes are less able to afford to purchase their own house or flat, and are more likely to be renters. For example, 39.1 per cent of the lowest earners rent their accommodation, and only 6.1 per cent are purchasers; in contrast, only 16.5 per cent of high income-earners are renters, and more than 4 out of 5 (81.1 per cent) either own or are purchasing their own housing.

Table 14.1 also shows that the proportion of weekly income spent on housing varies with the type of housing obtained. Among the lowest income-earners, those purchasing their dwelling spent nearly one-half (45.9 per cent) of their weekly income on housing costs, compared with those renting government accommodation, who spent only about one-quarter (26.1 per cent) of their income on housing. However, people renting from private landlords spent the highest proportion on housing — more than one-half (55.6 per cent) of their weekly income, on average. In contrast, the highest 20 per cent of earners spent on average only 16 per cent of their income to purchase dwellings, and even less if they were renting.

Table 14.1 Housing characteristics by income quintile group, Australia 1990

Housing characteristics	Gross weekly income quintile					
	Lowest 20%	21–40%	41–60%	61–80%	Highest 20%	Total
Mean weekly housing costs (dollars)	34	41	64	95	137	74
Housing costs as a proportion of income	25.3	14.7	14.6	14.0	10.5	13.1
Nature of housing occupancy	*Per cent*					
Owners	34.9	38.9	26.6	30.4	34.1	33.0
Purchasers	6.1	8.6	18.5	34.1	47.0	22.8
Renters	39.1	40.9	44.2	30.3	16.5	34.2
Rent-free	19.9	11.5	10.8	5.2	2.4	10.0
Total	**100.0**	**100.0**	**100.0**	**100.0**	**100.0**	**100.0**
Nature of housing occupancy	*Housing costs as a proportion of income*					
Purchasing	45.9	27.9	23.1	20.3	16.0	21.9
Renting government	26.1	20.2	19.6	19.0	13.4	17.4
Renting private	55.6	31.2	22.8	18.7	13.6	20.8

Source: Australaian Bureau of Statistics 1993c

Finally, the census also shows extreme variations in standards of accommodation. High income-earners, for example, are concentrated in particular residential areas. In Victoria, where 1.6 per cent of households have annual incomes exceeding $120 000, the highest proportions of such households can be found in prestigious areas of Melbourne, such as Kew (7.6 per cent of households), Brighton (7.5 per cent), Malvern (6.5 per cent), Camberwell (6.2 per cent), and Hawthorn (6.0 per cent). In New South Wales, where 2.3 per cent of households have incomes exceeding A$120 000, the highest proportions are found in Ku-ring-gai (15.0 per cent), Mosman (11.7 per cent), Woollahra (11.1 per cent), and Hunter's Hill (10.4 per cent) (ABS 1993a).

In contrast, many low income-earners are not so fortunate. For example, in 1991 more than 100 000 households (almost 200 000 people) were living in caravans or similar shelters. A further 9500 households (26 800 people) were living in improvised dwellings or camping out, among them many homeless people. Other homeless people were among the 6600 people who, on census night, were living in night shelters, refuges, or hostels for the homeless (ABS 1993a). A large number of Australians, therefore, live in housing that, at best, can only be described as inadequate.

In summary, disparities of income and wealth in Australia are substantial and directly affect the way people live. In general, low income-earners have less to spend on accommodation and less choice in the accommodation they obtain. As a result, many cannot afford to buy their own homes, and so pay rent for accommodation owned by others, or make do with inadequate or improvised housing. They also spend a much higher proportion of their income on housing and have much less money left over to spend on other necessities, such as food, clothing, electricity, gas, and transport.

Work and the labour market

While income and wealth are important measures of material inequality, the main source of income for most people is determined by their relationship to the labour market and the type of work they do. One of the most basic indicators of a person's relationship to the labour market is employment status. The employment status of the population in January 1995 is shown in Table 14.2. Just under nine million people were registered as part of the workforce. Six million, just over two-thirds of the total labour force, were employed in full-time jobs, and almost two million in part-time jobs. However, well over three-quarters of a million people were unemployed and looking for work, representing 9.7 per cent of the total labour force. Almost 700 000 of those without jobs were looking for full-time employment, and a further 154 000 for part-time work. Unemployed people do not have the same opportunity to obtain income and meet their daily needs as do those in full-time employment, and typically must rely on limited government assistance.

In addition, unemployment levels have been much higher in recent years than they once were. Figure 14.3, for example, shows that less than 2 per cent of the workforce was unemployed during the 1960s and early 1970s, a period of sustained economic growth, low inflation, and relative economic prosperity. However, unemployment rose rapidly during the 1970s and 1980s, and reached 11.6 per cent in 1991 (ABS 1993a). By early 1993, and again in early 1994, more than one million people were out of work (ABS 1995). Although the unemployment rate has dropped below 10 per cent since then, it is unlikely to ever return to the very low levels of the 1960s. This means that substantial numbers of people will continue to remain unemployed, and continue to experience disadvantages and inequalities.

Table 14.2 Employment status of the Australian labour force, January 1995

Emploment status	Males	Females	Number	%
Employed full-time	4 111 600	1 969 900	6 081 400	69.1
Employed part-time	484 200	1 387 800	1 872 000	21.3
Total employed	4 595 800	3 357 600	7 953 400	90.3
Looking for full-time work	454 800	244 900	699 700	7.9
Looking for part-time work	57 800	96 200	154 000	1.7
Total unemployed	512 600	341 100	853 700	9.7
Total labour force	5 108 400	341 100	853 700	9.7
Total labour force	**5 108 400**	**3 698 700**	**8 807 100**	**100.0**

Source: Australian Bureau of Statistics 1994c

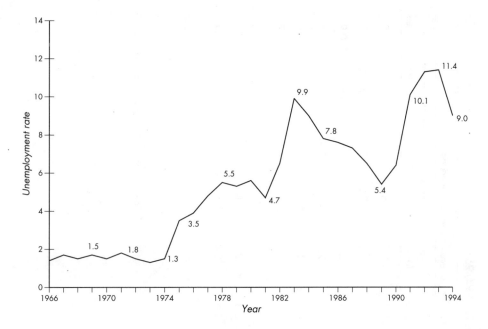

Figure 14.3 Unemployment rate, Australia 1966–94

Source: Australian Bureau of Statistics 1994b; 1995

One important feature of unemployment is that it occurs disproportionately among certain groups of people. Among young people, unemployment rates are particularly high. In late 1994, the overall rate for those aged 15–19 years was 21.8 per cent, and among 20–24 year olds, it was 12.1 per cent. Even among those aged in their thirties and forties, many of whom have a dependent partner or dependent children, 6 per cent were unemployed. Overall, 23.1 per cent of unemployed people had dependants, and 4.6 per cent were single parents with children under fifteen years of age (ABS 1994c). In addition, just over one-third (34.5 per cent) of all unemployed people were long-term unemployed, having been out of work for one year or longer.

The labour market is also important in influencing not just whether people find work or not, but also the type of work they do. Table 14.3 shows the different types of full-time jobs in which Australians work. Almost 1.2 million people (18.1 per cent of full-time workers) have clerical jobs, and a further 1.1 million (17.2 per cent) work in sales or personal service occupations, one of the fastest growing sectors of the economy. A further one million people (15.5 per cent) work as labourers or in other unskilled jobs. There are also nearly one million people (14.7 per cent) working in professional occupations, such as doctors, dentists, lawyers, and teachers.

The next column in Table 14.3, however, shows that average weekly earnings vary considerably across jobs. Overall, managers and administrators have the highest weekly earnings, followed closely by professionals. However, all other occupations have considerably lower earnings. Labourers, at the bottom of the income hierarchy,

Table 14.3 Occupations, average weekly earnings and selected work benefits, Australia 1994/95

				Percentage receiving selected work benefits						
Occupation	Number[1]	Percentage	Earnings[2]	Transport	Telephone	Housing	Low interest finance	Shares	Entertainment allowance	Club fees
Managers and administrators	480 900	7.4	822	45.9	29.5	9.5	5.6	9.8	8.7	6.8
Professionals	956 800	14.7	793	16.4	9.9	4.2	1.9	3.6	1.9	3.1
Para-professionals	423 200	6.5	681	12.0	6.9	3.1	1.0	1.6	0.6	0.9
Tradepersons	867 200	13.3	545	17.6	7.9	2.3	0.9	2.6	0.3	0.8
Clerks	1 183 700	18.1	530	8.8	6.6	1.6	5.6	4.3	0.8	1.0
Sales, personal service workers	1 125 100	17.2	524	13.7	4.6	1.4	3.4	4.7	1.9	1.7
Plant & machine operators, drivers	474 400	7.3	588	10.3	3.3	2.4	1.1	3.7	0.0	0.5
Labourers and related workers	1 014 500	15.5	472	6.5	2.6	2.4	0.5	2.2	0.2	0.4
Total	**6 525 800**	**100.0**								

1 Full-time and part-time employees
2 Average weekly earnings, full-time employees only

Source: Australian Bureau of Statistics 1994c; 1995

earn only three dollars for every five dollars earned by the average manager or professional. In addition, the lowest paid jobs often involve unattractive or unpleasant working conditions, and offer few of the fringe benefits attached to the best jobs. For example, while most employees these days receive some work benefits, usually in the form of superannuation or holiday pay, Table 14.3 also shows that managers and administrators are much more likely to receive additional benefits such as transport (usually cars), telephones, housing, low interest finance, shares, an entertainment allowance, or club fees (ABS 1995).

In summary, labour market experiences are directly related to inequality. A large number of people who wish to work are unable to find secure employment. As a consequence, many rely on government assistance to meet their daily needs. Even among those who do find employment, considerable variations occur in the amount of income they earn, with some jobs providing much more attractive salaries, benefits, and working conditions than others. Both employment and unemployment, then, contribute to the overall patterns of inequality in Australia.

Education, schooling, and qualifications

While disparities of income are related to labour market experiences, these experiences in turn are associated with schooling, level of education, and qualifications. The level of education completed, the skills acquired, and the qualifications obtained are all important in influencing not only whether people find work, but also the sorts of jobs obtained.

For example, Table 14.4 shows the relationship between employment status and educational attainment. The first column shows the number of people with qualifications and the second column the corresponding percentages. These figures indicate that the labour force is almost equally divided between those with and those without post-school qualifications. Many of those without qualifications are older people who attended school some years ago, while others are recent school-leavers who left school early or did not proceed to further study. Those with qualifications include 1.4 million with skilled vocational qualifications — from a TAFE college, for example — representing 16.8 per cent of the workforce. A further 13.9 per cent have university degrees at Bachelor level or higher.

The importance of education to labour market experiences can be gauged from the remaining columns in the table. These show, first, that levels of unemployment vary with educational attainment. For example, the unemployment rate among people without post-school qualifications (14.6 per cent) is almost twice that of those with qualifications (7.6 per cent), and even higher among those who did not complete the highest level of schooling. Even among those with qualifications, unemployment rates vary. For example, the unemployment rate among those with only a basic vocational qualification (11.4 per cent) is nearly twice the rate experienced by those with university degrees (4.8–6.2 per cent). In general, people with qualifications are more successful in obtaining work, and the higher their qualifications, the more successful they are.

Table 14.4 Employment status and educational attainment, persons aged 15–69 years, Australia 1994

Occupation	Number	Percentage	Unemployment Rate	Occupation (row percentage)							
				Managers	Professionals	Professionals	Trades	Clerks	Sales	Operatives, Drivers	Labourers
Without post-school qualifications	**4 402 600**	**51.9**	**14.6**	**11.4**	**3.1**	**2.9**	**10.2**	**20.4**	**19.0**	**10.8**	**22.1**
completed highest level of school	1 541 400	18.2	13.5	10.5	5.2	4.4	7.6	23.6	25.1	6.2	17.5
did not complete highest level	2 853 500	33.7	15.2	12.0	1.9	2.1	11.7	18.6	15.7	13.5	24.5
With post-school qualifications	**4 072 800**	**48.1**	**7.6**	**11.2**	**24.2**	**9.3**	**19.8**	**13.8**	**10.6**	**4.1**	**7.1**
higher degree	145 600	1.7	4.8	13.5	74.3	3.0	1.3	3.7	2.8	0.2	1.2
postgraduate diploma	180 600	2.1	4.8	11.6	70.1	5.5	1.2	6.6	3.5	0.0	1.6
bachelor degree	855 100	10.1	6.2	11.0	53.0	10.7	1.7	10.5	8.2	1.5	3.3
undergraduate diploma	295 000	3.5	5.3	9.5	34.6	27.9	2.2	9.9	10.1	1.6	4.2
associate diploma	589 600	7.0	8.1	13.6	16.7	12.0	15.0	18.6	13.2	3.0	7.8
skilled vocational qualification	1 420 300	16.8	7.7	11.6	4.2	5.6	46.8	6.6	7.8	7.6	9.6
basic vocational qualification	586 500	6.9	11.4	8.1	3.6	6.2	5.0	39.5	23.1	4.1	10.4
Total labour force[1]	**8 475 400**	**100.0**	**11.5**	**11.1**	**13.4**	**6.0**	**14.7**	**16.8**	**15.6**	**7.4**	**15.0**

1 Omits people still at school

Source: Australian Bureau of Statistics 1994a

Education also influences the jobs that people get. For example, almost two-thirds of people without post-school qualifications are employed as clerks, sales workers, or unskilled labourers, and very few enter jobs as professionals or para-professionals. In contrast, only 11.2 per cent of people with post-school qualifications work as labourers, operatives or drivers, and most people with university degrees work in professional jobs. In fact, almost three-quarters of those with higher degrees work in professional occupations, and a further 13.5 per cent in managerial positions. Similarly, almost two-thirds of those with undergraduate diplomas work in professional or para-professional occupations.

In summary, wealth, labour market experiences, and education are some of the key dimensions of inequality in Australia. The evidence suggests that inequalities are substantial, and that they directly influence how people live and their capacity to obtain the necessities of everyday life. In addition, some people are systematically disadvantaged in comparison with others, suggesting that disadvantage and inequality do not occur by chance, but are consistently related to the ways in which our society is organised. This systematic feature of inequality has interested sociologists for many years, and has prompted a number of attempts to account not only for the existence of inequality, but also for the emergence of typical patterns of social stratification — that is, ways in which inequality divides societies into groups, classes, or social strata. These approaches are considered in the following section.

Explanations of inequality

Three distinct traditions have emerged in studies of inequality and social stratification. One is associated with the writings of Karl Marx, and focuses on class-formation and class relations. Another is associated with the work of Max Weber, and focuses on class, status, and power. A third tradition focuses on socio-economic status, and processes of status-attainment and social mobility.

Marx and class theory

One of the most influential approaches to understanding inequality in capitalist societies was proposed by Karl Marx. He suggested that we need to look beyond simple material inequalities to understand why some people are better off than others. He argued that the main forms of inequality were associated with the formation of classes (Marx 1909; 1938). These were defined by their relationship to the means of production — that is, the way in which the economy and the production of goods are organised.

In capitalist societies, where the means of production were owned privately, Marx argued that there were two main classes. The most powerful was the capitalist class, which owned the means of production. The second class was the proletariat or working class. It consisted of those who did not own the means of production but, instead, were employed by capitalists to work in exchange for a wage. In Marx's view, capitalists and workers had opposing interests, and relations between them would be characterised by hostility and industrial conflict. Moreover, the working class was exploited by capitalists, and was destined to become increasingly impoverished and disadvantaged until the inevitable occurred: capitalism would be overthrown by working-class revolution and replaced by socialism.

Although some contend that Marx's approach is still useful for understanding inequality in Australia today (for example, Connell 1977; Connell and Irving 1980), others argue that processes of class-formation in modern capitalist societies are now more complex. A revised approach has been proposed by Erik Olin Wright (1985; 1989). He argues that the increasing importance of education in the twentieth century has seen the emergence of groups whose economic role is determined not by the work they do with their hands, but by their educational qualifications and expertise. In addition, the growing complexity of large corporations has led to rapid growth in the number of managerial and supervisory positions, in which people who are not capitalists themselves manage and direct business activities, and exercise control over other workers. In this view, people with managerial and supervisory responsibilities, and people whose work depends on skills and professional expertise, are neither capitalists nor workers, and occupy what are described as contradictory class locations. Wright also contends that the class experiences of capitalists who own large corporations and employ others are distinct from the experiences of those who own small businesses and do not employ others.

In viewing Australian society from this perspective, it is argued that inequality is still best seen in terms of differences between classes (Emmison 1991; M. Western 1991). In addition, it is estimated that the working class remains the largest single class today, representing about 32 per cent of the workforce (J. Western 1991). A further 12 per cent occupy skilled manual positions. The capitalist class is considerably smaller: only around 5 per cent are employers, and 9 per cent are self-employed. The remaining 42 per cent of the workforce is distributed between contradictory class locations that are neither capitalist nor working-class. Although the working class is considered to be the largest single class, an even larger group — nearly half the workforce — is located between capitalists and workers in what some might refer to as a broad middle class.

Weber: class, status, and power

The second core perspective on inequality in modern societies derives from the work of Max Weber. Like Marx, Weber (1968) associated one of the main forms of inequality with social classes. The main determinants of class position included not just ownership of productive property, but also possession of marketable skills, qualifications, and credentials. These contributed to a person's market capacity, and could be used to enhance life chances, financial rewards, and social privileges. For example, owners of productive property are able to determine how that property is used and derive profits from their enterprise; those with sought-after skills have an advantage in competing for jobs and can demand higher salaries. Those who own no property and have few marketable skills are at a disadvantage in competing for jobs and wages.

A second important concept in Weber's writings is that of status. Whereas class position is determined by objective economic characteristics, status depends upon subjective perceptions and evaluations of social honour or prestige. Some groups, such as royalty, sporting personalities, or High Court Judges, may enjoy privileges and advantages that enhance their life chances because they are held in high regard by others. Those who do not attract the same degree of esteem may not enjoy such advantages.

A third dimension of stratification in Weber's analysis is associated with the use of power. Groups with privileged access to material resources may exercise economic power on behalf of classes, while those with high prestige or esteem may exercise social power on behalf of status groups. In addition, groups that act through the agency of the State may exercise political power on behalf of organised parties or interest groups.

Weber also recognised that attributes, such as age, gender, race, or ethnicity, may further distinguish people. As a result, class and status are not always consistent, and people in the same class situation may not enjoy the same status. Solicitors from non-English-speaking backgrounds, for example, may not be as highly regarded as their Anglo-Saxon counterparts; or a male nurse may have less status than a female nurse. In the Weberian view, then, modern societies are more complex than class theory portrays them to be, and may be stratified in diverse ways and along a number of distinct dimensions.

A number of attempts have been made to analyse Australian society from a Weberian perspective, although, as Diane Austin (1984, p. 141) points out, a thorough analysis has yet to be conducted. One approach is provided by Sol Encel (1970), who identified a number of different social strata based on distinctions of class, status, and power. He suggested there is an upper class, which consists of the higher professions, old established pastoral families, old established business families, politicians, and senior public servants. The upper-middle class consists mainly of people with professional and managerial occupations, while the lower-middle class is represented by other white-collar occupations. The working class, divided into upper and lower sections according to skill, embraces people with manual occupations.

Ron Wild (1978) argues that the three main determinants of social position in Australia are income-generating property, qualifications, and labour. These give rise to three main classes. The upper class consists of property-owners and business entrepreneurs. The middle class consists of propertyless workers whose market capacity and social position are determined by technical and professional qualifications. The working class, also thought to be the largest, consists of propertyless workers whose market capacity is derived from exchanging their labour in the market-place for wages. Wild concludes that status evaluation and class organisation remain important features of social life, and continue to generate inequality and disadvantage.

More recently, Ken Dempsey (1990) examined inequality and social position in a country town. He shows how social location, privilege, and disadvantage are determined by a variety of influences associated with class, status, and power, and highlights the impact of gender inequalities and the marginal position of the elderly.

Weber's perspective is also reflected in studies of occupational prestige that attempt to map the hierarchy of social status in Australia by measuring the social desirability of occupations. A. Daniel (1983), for example, asked people to rank a total of 160 occupations on a scale from 1 point (representing high status) to 7 points (representing low status). After calculating the average rating given to each occupation, she found that the most prestigious jobs were held by judges (an average rating of 1.2 points on the 7-point scale), cabinet ministers and medical specialists (1.5 points). White-collar jobs, such as computer programmer (3.4), social worker (3.5), and librarian (3.8), were ranked around the middle of the scale. Manual jobs, such as motor mechanic (4.7), bricklayer (5.2), and farm labourer (6.3), were ranked lower down. Garbage collectors, road sweepers (both 6.7), and prostitutes (6.9) were ranked at the bottom of the prestige scale. These results reveal considerable diversity in the social status attached to jobs, and illustrate how class, status and authority contribute to social inequality.

Status-attainment

The status-attainment approach is related to the work of writers such as Émile Durkheim (1933), Talcott Parsons (1954), and Kingsley Davis and Wilbert Moore (1945), and is exemplified in studies by Peter Blau and Otis Duncan (1967), and Duncan et al. (1972). This approach portrays inequality not as a division between discrete classes or groups, but as a gradation of many different layers or social strata. The composition of each layer is determined by a combination of social and economic forces that, collectively, contribute to an individual's socio-economic status. The key indicators of socio-economic status are education, labour market experiences, and income. Occupations are particularly important, in part because they are associated with subjective evaluations of prestige, or social status, and in part because they provide rewards in the form of remuneration and earnings, or economic status.

The main processes that determine social position are social mobility and status-attainment. Status-attainment refers to the processes by which individuals attain their education, occupation, and income. These processes may be influenced by ascribed attributes associated with family origins and the inheritance of social position between generations, or by the achievements that individuals accomplish themselves. Social mobility refers to changes that may occur in levels of individual attainment, either from one generation to the next, or during the course of an individual's career. In an open society characterised by a high level of social mobility, social position is neither fixed by social origins nor prescribed by a person's own starting point in life. By contrast, in a closed society, privilege and deprivation are much more entrenched and more likely to be transmitted across generations. In this view, inequality and social location are influenced by social processes that link family background, schooling, labour market experiences, and wealth within a socio-economic life cycle.

In Australia, a number of studies in this tradition have been conducted. In one study, Leonard Broom and Frank Jones (1976) compiled status profiles for individuals according to their education, occupation, and income, and identified ten reasonably consistent social strata, ranging from upper-middle-class to working-class locations. More recent research has concentrated on the status-attainment process itself. It shows that social background has an important influence on educational attainments, but much less effect at later stages of the socio-economic life cycle. In turn, education influences career beginnings and occupational attainments, and these, in turn, determine the income people earn (Broom et al. 1980; Jones and Davis 1986; Williams et al. 1993).

Other studies suggest there is a high level of social mobility in Australia, although much of that mobility takes place between adjacent positions around the middle of the occupational structure (Broom et al. 1980; Graetz and McAllister 1994). In addition, educational achievements have increasingly had an impact upon occupational attainments in comparison with ascriptive processes, although the degree of status-inheritance for women has changed little in the postwar period (Hayes 1990; Marks 1992). These results show how inequalities in social background and in early achievement affect later job status and earnings, and contribute to socio-economic inequality.

Conclusions

The evidence presented in this chapter shows that inequality is a fundamental and pervasive feature of our society. There are considerable disparities of income, wealth, and property ownership, and these are linked to inequalities in the labour market and educational attainments.

In trying to understand and account for inequalities, social scientists have drawn on a number of different perspectives. These provide alternative explanations for the existence of inequality and the nature of social divisions. One approach focuses on inequalities arising from private ownership of economic resources, class-formation, and relations between classes. One regards class, social status, and power as fundamental and potentially separate dimensions of social stratification. Another views inequality in terms of socio-economic status, and focuses on processes of social mobility and status-attainment.

Although sociologists, at times, have argued at length about which of these perspectives is 'correct' (see, for example, Austin 1984; Waters 1990), all three contribute something useful to our understanding of inequality, stratification, and class-formation in Australia today. For social scientists, the most important tasks are to identify clearly the dimensions of inequality, provide theory and concepts that help to explain why it exists, and apply these so that viable and meaningful strategies can be devised to help reduce inequality and the problems associated with it.

Discussion questions

1   What are some of the main ways in which you can identify inequality that exists in the area where you live?

2   How much do you think the following attributes contribute to inequality in Australia: family background? ethnic background? age? level of education and qualifications? type of school attended (government, private)? unemployment? occupation? owning your own business? income? accumulated assets and wealth? What other characteristics might you add to this list?

3   From the attributes listed above, which do you think are most important and least important respectively in shaping inequalities in Australia today?

4   Do classes exist in Australia today? If so, what are they? Is there a middle class? What information would you use to work out which class someone belonged to?

5   How important, respectively, are economic power, social power, and political power in Australia today? To what extent are they consistent? For example, do people with economic power also have social and political power? Try to think of specific examples and exceptions.

Recommended reading

For overviews of class and stratification theory, see:

* Saunders, P. 1989, *Social Class and Stratification*, Routledge, London.
* Waters, M. 1990, *Class and Stratification: Arrangements for Socioeconomic Inequality under Capitalism*, Longman Cheshire, Melbourne.

Evidence about inequality in Australia can be found in:

* Jamrozik, A. 1991, *Class, Inequality and the State: Social Change, Social Policy and the New Middle Class*, Macmillan, Melbourne.
* Western. J. 1983, *Social Inequality in Australian Society*, Macmillan, Melbourne.
* Graetz, B. and McAllister, I. 1994, *Dimensions of Australian Society*, 2nd edn, Macmillan, Melbourne.

Analyses of Australian society from particular theoretical perspectives also make valuable reading. For a Marxist analysis, see:

* Connell, W. 1977, *Ruling Class, Ruling Culture*, Cambridge University Press, Melbourne.

A neo-Marxist approach based on Wright's class model is presented in:

* Baxter, J., Emmison, M., and Western, J. (eds) 1991, *Class Analysis and Contemporary Australia*, Macmillan, Melbourne.

Examples of the Weberian approach can be found in:

* Encel, S. 1970, *Equality and Authority: A Study of Class, Status and Power in Australia*, Cheshire, Melbourne.
* Dempsey, K. 1990, *Smalltown: A Study of Social Inequality, Cohesion and Belonging*, Oxford University Press, Melbourne.

The status-attainment approach is adopted in both:

* Broom, L. and Jones, F. L. 1976, *Opportunity and Attainment in Australia*, Australian National University Press, Canberra.
* Broom, L., Jones, F. L., McDonnell, P., and Williams, T. 1980, *The Inheritance of Inequality*, Routledge & Kegan Paul, London.

Chapter 15

Understanding the Welfare State

Kerreen Reiger

> I think the Government should give up their posh jobs and live one
> week like a pensioner. I'm living on $125 a week with four kids. I
> spend $70 a week on food, and that's basic, no luxuries.
> Pensioners are on their own. No one cares how they live. Often
> the Commission rent increase is more than the pension increase,
> so pensioners are going backwards ... Some of the Welfare
> people are alright but some of them make you feel awful — you
> would think the money came out of their own pocket.
>
> McCaughey 1987, pp. 66–7

The experience of this woman, recounted in a study of people on low incomes, raises many questions concerning 'just surviving' in contemporary Australia, and what we do about it as a nation.

In the decades following the Second World War many Australians believed that poverty was either a thing of the past, especially of the Great Depression, or something only to be found in developing nations. Since the 1970s, however, public inquiries, the media, the churches, and those working in social welfare have disputed this view. They have provided ample evidence that significant economic and social inequality continues to exist (Wiseman 1991, pp. 76–7; Watts 1988, p. 85). At its worst, poverty is concentrated among Black Australians, recent immigrants, the unemployed (particularly youth without jobs), and among some groups of women, such as the aged, and single mothers.

This finding seems curious in the light of the amount of government finance going in income support, now in the order of $35 billion. In this chapter we will explore this conundrum. How is it that, in spite of the so-called 'welfare state' — a system of services and direct income provision — the problems of poverty and inequality remain? The history and experience of 'welfare' can only be understood in context. We will also consider some of the concepts of and debates about what the welfare state really means, and how we could go about assessing its role.

During the last one hundred years the question of just 'what should be done' to alleviate poverty has reared its head in many ways, with Australia largely following in British footsteps. The idea of going one step further and trying to *remove* social inequalities, however, has received far less attention. Here we will trace one outcome of concerns about poverty, the development of government-supported schemes, or the idea of a welfare state. Leaving aside for the present the issue of whether *welfare* is an accurate term, we can discern four main periods in the development of welfare in Australia. These are the mid-to-late nineteenth century, the period from the early twentieth century to the Second World War, the postwar period, in which the welfare state became widely established and accepted, and, since the mid-1970s, a period of critique and pulling back.

Social responses to poverty in the nineteenth and early twentieth centuries

Much of the financial support and counselling assistance that we now associate with formal institutions and professions used to be provided within families and local communities. This largely meant that welfare was the responsibility of women: as carers of children, the sick, and the elderly; as managers of economic resources; and as voluntary charity workers. More affluent women participated in appropriate activities to support husbands in business or in running landed properties. They also ran church bazaars and, on occasion, visited the local poor with handouts of food and clothing (Connell and Irving 1979, pp. 123–7; Dickie 1979, pp. 87–92).

Aboriginal women were used as servants in White households, as well as trying to maintain traditional obligations to care for kinfolk (Huggins and Blake 1993, pp. 53–7). For White working-class women, charity 'began at home', supporting the often unreliable income of men and children by taking in laundry, cleaning others' houses, and even working in factories and shops. The dominant ethos was, therefore, one of *charity*. This was something to be dispensed by the wealthy and earned by the 'respectable' poor — that is, those who were not drunkards or gamblers, but orphaned, ill, or widows. Economic support was seen as a privilege, not a right, with the churches, government officials, and leading citizens promoting the goal of self-reliance.

However, several changes led to greater demands for government involvement. In the United Kingdom, the growth of industrial capitalism meant enormous social dislocation. People moved to cities in search of work, and local traditions of charitable support for the widowed or homeless collapsed. In Australia too, new social problems emerged, but with the differentiating factors of European immigration over longer distances, and the subsequent disruption of Aboriginal culture. These problems included urban overcrowding and poor living conditions, homeless and unruly street children, and problems providing clean water, food distribution, and effective disposal of sewerage (Dickie 1979, ch. 4; Reiger 1985, ch. 2; Connell and Irving 1979, pp. 113–35). Various inquiries led to demands that governments 'do something'.

The dominant philosophy until then had been that of a '*laissez faire*' or 'leave alone' state, meaning belief in individual self-reliance and minimum interference from government. The market was seen as the principal site of exchange of goods, talents, and property, and individual well-being should be secured there, thus leading to collective well-being. The State should only protect the population through external defence and internal policing. Nonetheless, by the late nineteenth century, the

Australian state was becoming increasingly involved in community life, through the conducting of censuses to measure the population, increased regulation of housing and health, and provision of education.

By the early twentieth century, therefore, important changes were afoot, and several factors laid the basis for an emerging system of social welfare. In both the United Kingdom and Australia, new ideas concerning social or collective provision for the poor accompanied the rise of the labour movement and conservatives' fear of industrial unrest (Connell and Irving 1979, ch. 4; Macintyre 1985, pp. 48–56). The philosophy of 'new liberalism', as it came to be called, accepted that the State had a role to play in overseeing economic well-being. Although the unions suffered defeat in the strikes of the early 1890s, the Australian Labour Party took up their cause in the new Federal parliament in the early twentieth century.

The beginnings of the 'welfare state'

In the first decade of the twentieth century Australia was seen as 'leading the world' with minimum wage provisions, and health and welfare legislation, including old age and some invalid pensions (Roe 1975; Macintyre 1985, ch. 3). These developments, however, were limited by a preoccupation with the rights and needs of White adult male workers. The introduction of the basic wage and of means-tested pensions was the result of a 'deal' made by some workers and employers. It was linked, on the one hand, to protection of local industry through government tariffs and, on the other, to the limitation of the working rights of non-Whites and women (Macintyre 1985, ch. 3; Garton 1990, ch. 4). The trade-offs done in these years formed the very character of social welfare in Australia. Francis Castles (1985) has called it a *male wage-earners'* welfare system: one in which it was assumed that employment was the main route to economic security for men, and that their wives and children could be dependent on them. Instead of income supports like pensions being allocated on the basis of one's rights as a citizen, as developed in Scandinavian models, the State's responsibility came to be seen only in terms of 'residual' or fall-back support.

This early twentieth century period can, nonetheless, be seen as the 'dawn' of social welfare provision by the State. It was accompanied by a variety of legislation affecting many aspects of everyday life, such as the introduction of children's courts, regulation of the age of sexual consent, and greater supervision of amusement venues. Middle-class 'ladies' from charitable and church organisations were particularly active in these developments. There were some contradictory measures for women however. In 1912 the Federal Government introduced the 'baby bonus': a payment of £5 on the birth of a child, paid directly to the mother, but only if she was a White woman (Kewley 1973, pp. 103–4.)

In the years between the wars, other maternal and child-health services were brought in, but Aboriginal women found themselves increasingly under the scrutiny of White missionaries and government officials. Under what was officially called 'protection', but what others have called 'welfare colonialism', their children were taken away and 'adopted' out to White families, in many cases merely as household or farm labour. The personal trauma, and the harm done to traditional family relationships, was worsened by moving more Aboriginal people into 'settlements'. Here they became 'dependents' of White officialdom (Huggins and Blake 1992, pp. 43–53). Their encounter with the developing system of 'welfare' continued to be damaging. As Jackie Huggins and Thom Blake comment in their discussion of the reserve system: 'People were taken from their "country", wives were separated from husbands, children taken from parents, and the elderly separated from their children and grandchildren ... Such forced removals are within living memory of many Aboriginal people today' (Huggins and Blake 1992, p. 45). In New South Wales alone, more than 5600 Black children were taken by force between 1883 and 1969, all under the claims of providing State care. The real government agenda was social control and preventing 'contamination' of the White race (Huggins and Blake 1992, p. 49).

The interwar years — during which such developments were most evident — saw the consolidation of basic social-welfare schemes. The promotion of charity and private philanthropy continued to be the preferred policy of governments. Even the impact of the Great Depression failed to bring about widespread schemes of financial support for the needy. Limited 'dole' schemes usually required recipients to work, often on public projects like road building. Many were merely given humiliating 'sustenance' hand-outs of food and clothing (Garton 1990, pp. 127–30; Macintyre 1985, pp. 73–8). At the same time, many working-class people found themselves at risk not only of having no, or minimal, income, but of being evicted from housing. They were also being 'watched' more by professionals such as doctors, infant welfare sisters, and housing reformers who were concerned about social problems. Women, as mothers and household managers, were especially a target of concern (Reiger 1985, ch. 2).

War, social welfare and postwar prosperity

The years of the Second World War and its immediate aftermath are usually identified as the real period in which the welfare state was established. Although varying in extent and character, systems of financial support became formally instituted in the United Kingdom, Australia, and most other Western countries (Bryson 1992, ch. 3). The pressures of maintaining civilian support for the war effort, combined with genuine visionary commitment to providing a better postwar world, motivated unprecedented expansion in government welfare activity (Beilharz et al. 1992, pp. 82–9; Watts 1987). Child Endowment, later Family Allowance, started in 1941; widows' pensions, a new maternity allowance, and funeral benefits in 1943; unemployment, sickness, and special dependent benefits in 1944; and free hospital and medical cover was promised in 1946. However, the opposition of the powerful medical profession, and the collapse of the Labor government in 1949 in the new cold war atmosphere of suspicion of 'socialist' schemes, halted this rush of activity. The Liberal Government under Robert Menzies, however, continued the basic measures that had already been established. They were paid for from general taxation and reflected the increase in Federal financial powers over those of the states that the Federal Government had won during the war (Watts 1987, ch. 5). Government departments at both Federal and state level became larger and the State welfare bureaucracy increased, as did non-government organisations.

However, it was relatively easy to maintain the concept of the 'wage-earners' welfare state during the boom years of the 1950s and 1960s. Industries and commercial activities were expanding rapidly; jobs seemed plentiful; and even the flood of immigrants, primarily from southern Europe at that stage, did not seem to challenge the basic premises upon which the system rested. If we look more carefully, though, it is clear that the prosperity was not evenly shared, and some people fell through the supposed 'safety net' of income supports. Postwar housing shortages affected many people on low-incomes; newly arrived migrants did not qualify for many benefits; welfare services were English-based; and Aboriginal families were still being broken up.

Uneven access of women and children to family income, along with violence and distrust of official services, made many vulnerable to poverty (Garton 1990, pp. 138–40). Some were at least given community support, taken in to others' homes during emergencies, and 'neighbours kept an eye out for well-dressed strangers, thought to be government inspectors' in order to warn the 'widowed and deserted mothers on a pension who worked under assumed names' (Garton 1990, p. 139). Women's feelings about their encounters with 'welfare', like those of the woman whose comments we started with in this chapter, were frequently ambivalent. They needed help with public housing, and with caring for children, but the increasingly powerful role of social workers and other professionals allowed them to make judgements that were often inappropriate. Mothers easily became stereotyped as 'bad', especially if their children had to be taken into foster care, where they were contrasted with 'good' care-givers (Voigt 1987, pp. 84–5).

Further reform — the Whitlam years

During the 1960s, the public perception was that the 'bad old days' of poverty and stigmatising charity had gone, replaced by benevolent government provision in a context of economic prosperity. Some alarm bells were sounded though by investigative journalists and reports from private welfare organisations, of which there were between 20 000 and 30 000 by 1970 (Garton 1990, p. 141). Poverty, they argued, continued to be a social problem, now further complicated by the specific difficulties of migrants and Aboriginal people. The enthusiastic, reforming Whitlam government gave voice to these concerns about social disadvantage.

The most significant exploration of poverty was the Henderson Inquiry, which reported in 1975, documenting the continuing problems of socially disadvantaged Australians (Beilharz et al. 1992, pp. 46–7). One of its legacies was the concept of a 'poverty line': an income level that, adjusted for family numbers and housing costs, was to provide a basic, even austere, measure. Using this measure, some Australians were pronounced to be at risk, especially the aged, the chronically ill, the unemployed, sole mothers, some immigrants, and most Aboriginal people (Commission of Inquiry into Poverty 1975). Many have criticised the poverty-line concept because it fails to take into account the overall distribution of wealth, and because it describes but does not explain the real reasons for the vulnerability of some groups, such as those on low wages, and of many women and children (Beilharz et al. 1992, p. 46; Garton 1990, p. 152; Bryson 1992, p. 192).

Both the Whitlam Government, and later governments who used Henderson's benchmark, proceeded to target these specific groups. In 1973 the Supporting Mothers' Benefit was introduced, becoming in 1977 the Supporting Parents' Benefit. Unemployment and sickness benefits were increased in 1973, and the Federal Government at last also assumed some responsibility for the financial support of child care. The most significant initiative, however, was in the field of health, with the introduction of a national hospital and medical scheme — the first Medibank. An enormous outlay in government social expenditure reflected these developments: 'spending rose from 14% of total economic resources in 1972 to 20.6% in 1975' (Beilharz et al. 1992, p. 90). However, their timing was a major problem.

The 'crisis' of welfare states

Not only in Australia, but in the United Kingdom and North America especially, the mid-1970s ushered in a different era of debates about social welfare. Whereas previously there had been general social consensus that the postwar welfare state was beneficial, it was increasingly argued that the State was overspending, that people should be more self-reliant, and that social welfare should be targeted to only the most needy. During the administrations of the Fraser Government in the late 1970s through to those of Hawke and Keating in the 1980s and 1990s, not to mention state governments, what has come to be called 'economic rationalism' or 'economic liberalism' has dominated. This suggests not only a financial or 'fiscal' crisis of welfare states, but also a crisis of their legitimacy or public acceptance (Beilharz et al. 1992, pp. 49–53, 90–1). The changing economic and social context helps make sense of the about-turn in ideas.

A rapid change in family patterns, particularly the rising divorce rate since the mid-1970s, has led to more women and children suffering a decline in living standards after divorce (Bryson 1992, pp. 192–3). Although men also suffer from the economic consequences of marital breakdown, they have more workforce resources and are less likely to have custody of children. There are now approximately 300 000 sole parent families reliant on State support, about 90 per cent of which are headed by women. Changes in gender roles, and greater recognition of problems such as domestic violence and youth homelessness, are part of other cultural shifts, especially in family and home–work relationships.

Official unemployment rates rose with the decline of the manufacturing industry, going from 2 per cent in 1972 to 7.4 per cent in 1978, and hovering around 8–10 per cent since then. A general period of recession was ushered in, Australia being only one player in the larger international capitalist context. One leading commentator, M. A. Jones, has blamed this growth in 'social dependency' on the decreased value placed on self-reliance, and increased expectations of State support in a period of financial restriction (Jones 1990, chs 4 and 5). He argues that the period since the mid-1970s has seen a more developed welfare state than existed before. Others, such as Lois Bryson (1992; 1993) and Stephen Garton (1992, ch 8), disagree, asserting that government attempts to target more precise 'needy' populations during the 1980s and 1990s indicate that there is no widespread acceptance of social welfare as a right. Instead, older ideas of 'residual welfare' remain dominant. As Mr Baldwin, Minister for Social Security, has argued, 'During recessions, people are prepared to accept the inevitability of a large number of people getting social security support ... but this relatively forbearing attitude dissipates' in conditions of economic recovery (*Age*, 24 March 1995, p. 4).

During the period from the 1980s to the mid-1990s, there have, however, been several important developments, most notably some of those arising from the major Review of Social Security carried out between 1985 and 1989 (Bryson 1993, p. 479). The Family Income Supplement, more recently the Family Allowance Supplement has eased the plight of many low-income families, and the Child Support Scheme has increased the amount paid by non-custodial fathers (Bryson 1993, p. 478). In general, the aims of government are clearly to reduce State expenditure, and this is most apparent in changes to unemployment assistance. Jobstart and Newstart programs aim to encourage retraining. However, for the increasing number of people unemployed for over a year, and with jobs themselves changing rapidly, there are more than economic issues at stake. As one woman said of her husband, 'he needs a job for his health, but now it's his health that's preventing him from working. He thinks about not having a job constantly. If anything goes wrong, he panics' (Trethewey 1989, p. 136).

Issues and debates

One of the main problems with popular debates on the welfare state, then, is that they concentrate only on financial costs. Even most official accounts direct attention to one aspect of State support for segments of the community, to the exclusion of other government measures. Just as a focusing on poverty, rather than exploring who holds wealth, how they hold it and why, only gives part of the picture, so too much concentration on the social welfare system obscures other government supported 'welfare systems'. Bryson draws attention to the problem of neglecting 'fiscal' and 'occupational' welfare (Bryson 1992; 1993, pp. 480–90).

The community does not regard financial support to industry or farmers, or the way the government regulates income through the tax system, as 'fiscal' welfare, as a 'drain' on resources or 'welfare'. Yet some people are more able to take advantage of the system than others, whether through actual avoidance of tax, or forms of company structuring that hide the real distribution of profits. Furthermore, there is 'occupational' welfare: rewards associated with paid work, such as superannuation, and extras like car allowances and cheap loans on top of ordinary pay. Traditionally, governments treated those with these benefits quite favourably. Again they have tended to be financially better off, and more often men rather than women (Bryson 1993, pp. 480–90; Sharp and Broomhill 1988).

The critical point made by Bryson and others is that these benefits are not seen as 'welfare' at all. Society views recipients of social-security payments differently from those benefiting from the other forms of fiscal or occupational welfare. As the pensioner in our opening example pointed out, benefits are stigmatised, as though they 'come out of the pockets' of politicians or welfare professionals. Similar sentiments are expressed by another single mother: 'Look if I could tell the Social Security department to stuff their pension, I would. I really would! I'd love to have the option to do that because, you know, it's humiliating, it's degrading, it's emotionally destructive because you just can't survive on it!' (Murdoch 1985, p. 28).

Social-security recipients also have to deal with the experience of being a 'client'. This entails an often humiliating reliance on others for information and resources, and standing around for hours in queues. A researcher for the Henderson inquiry into poverty commented that 'If you are an unmarried mother, deserted wife or unemployed person and you visit a government department, you will have to wait. You will be treated in an impersonal manner, you will be attended to by someone who will be unable to answer questions' (Cunnington 1977, as quoted in Watts 1988, p. 97).

How do we make sense of the experience of the supposed beneficiaries of the welfare state then? On the one hand, there are undoubtedly greater income support structures in place for single mothers, and unemployed or sick people are not at the same risk of starvation as they were in the late nineteenth century or even during the Great Depression. But there is still significant, even increasing, social inequality. Is the welfare state much of a solution? To answer this, we need to consider alternative possibilities.

Interpreting the welfare state

How should we assess the emergence and role of modern welfare states? Some writers have seen the increased role of the State in providing health and welfare services as a sign of an enlightened social conscience at work. This view assumes that reformers instigate changes in the interests of the community and to lessen some of the harsh consequences of the market economy (for example, Kewley 1973) Although, certainly, many of those who brought in housing reform, for example, or agitated for increased income supports for the poor, have been motivated by genuine concern about social problems, this is not the whole story. An exclusive focus on idealistic motivations neglects the complexity and role of political interest groups, such as was involved in the trade-off between White male workers and employers in the introduction of the arbitration system in the early twentieth century. It also plays down the partial and biased nature of many benefits, at least in their original form. A more critical analysis stresses the interplay of class, race, and gender as factors influencing who gets what from the welfare state, when they get it, and how. The efforts to improve working-class living conditions in the 1890s–1900s can be seen as arising from employers' fears of further industrial unrest and the possibility of a more radical uprising (Connell and Irving 1979; Macintyre 1985). As we have noted, Castles has argued that Australia's welfare provisions have continued to reflect their origins in serving male wage-earners' interests, rather than those of women, children, or minority groups (Castles 1985). Indeed, women and men stand in very different relationships to the welfare state, to the extent that Bryson has contrasted the *men's* with the *women's* welfare state (Bryson 1992, chs 5 and 6). Men are treated primarily as workers, unless ill or unemployed; their main connections to the State are through occupational and taxation measures.

Although, increasingly, women too are paid workers, they remain concentrated in the least secure, least remunerative jobs, vulnerable to dependency on a male breadwinner or the State. Ironically, however, it has been through the introduction of, first, the Widow's Pension and, then, the Supporting Parent's Benefit, that many women have been enabled to leave violent and troubled domestic arrangements. The funding of child care, refuges, and women's health centres, while currently under some threat of financial cut-back, has been something that groups of women struggled to achieve.

The complexity of power relations within the State suggests that no simple explanation of developments is possible, nor can we easily assess current developments. Some politicians and commentators argue that we should return to goals that encourage greater self-reliance, such as saving for old age, or caring for dependants within families (Jones 1990). Recent comments about 'tailoring the welfare product' (*Age*, 24 March, p. 4) reflect the economic framework that drives policy developments. Such concepts are too simplistic, however. Most of the social changes that have produced increased reliance on social security — such as the higher numbers of mothers rearing children alone, or the effects of industrial restructuring on labour market patterns — are not matters of individual choice. Instead, they indicate major structural change in Australian society, with debates about the welfare state struggling to keep up.

Discussion questions

1 Discuss the difference between seeing social welfare benefits as charity and seeing them as a right or entitlement.
2 Why has Australia been called a 'wage-earners' welfare state'?
3 Are there problems with the concept of a 'poverty line'? Explain.
4 In what ways are women and children especially affected by the welfare state?
5 What are the different types of 'welfare', and why are the distinctions important?

Recommended reading

Easy-to-read accounts of the everyday problems of Australians in poverty, along with their interaction with welfare professionals, are provided in:

* Edgar, D. et al. (eds) 1989, *Child Poverty*, Allen & Unwin, Sydney.
* McCaughey, J. 1987, *A Bit of a Struggle: Coping with Family Life in Australia*, McPhee Gribble, Penguin Books, Melbourne.

- McCaughey, J., Shaver, S., and Ferber, H. et al. 1977, *Who Cares? Family Problems, Community Links and Helping Services,* Macmillan and Sun Books, Melbourne.
- Trethewey, J. 1989, *Aussie Battlers: Families and Children in Poverty,* Brotherhood of St Laurence, Melbourne.

For more discussion of debates and theories concerning social welfare, not only in Australia, see:

- George, V. and Wilding, P. 1983, *Ideology and Social Welfare,* 2nd edn, Routledge & Kegan Paul, London.
- Graycar, A. and Jamrozik, A. (eds) 1989, *How Australians Live: Social Policy in Theory and Practice,* Macmillan, Melbourne.
- Travers, P. and Richardson, S. 1993, *Living Decently: Material Well-being in Australia,* Oxford University Press, Melbourne.

On gender issues and the welfare state, see also:

- Cass, B. 1983, 'The Changing Face of Poverty in Australia', *Australian Feminist Studies,* no. 1, summer, pp. 67–90.
- Cass, B. and Baldock, C. (eds) 1983, *Women, Social Welfare and the State,* Allen & Unwin, Sydney.
- Franzway, S., Court, D., and Connell, R. (eds) 1989, *Staking a Claim,* Allen & Unwin, Sydney.
- Montague, M. and Stephens, J. 1985, *Paying the Price for Sugar and Spice,* Report, Brotherhood of St Laurence, Melbourne.
- Watson, S. (ed.) 1991, *Playing the State: Australian Feminist Interventions,* Allen & Unwin, Sydney.

For more information on the so-called 'protection' of Aboriginal people by the State, see:

- Beckett, J. 1988, *Past and Present: The Construction of Aboriginality,* Aboriginal Studies Press, Canberra.
- Cummings, B. 1990, *Take this Child,* Aboriginal Studies Press, Canberra.

Chapter 16

The Australian Health System

Evan Willis

An Open Letter to the Victorian Minister for Health Services

Three and a half weeks ago I had a brain tumour removed and spent eleven days in the Neurology Ward. I am writing this letter genuinely, not to have a go at you personally, or your health policies, but because as excellent as parts of the health system were, I felt, experienced and witnessed a sufficient lack of focus on the reason for this system — the patient — me, and my friends in my room. I believe (and am constantly told) I had (still have) one of the best Neurosurgeons and his team; the hospital had the specialist equipment for diagnosing me; and I was under constant observation by the medical staff. I am utterly lucky and grateful that I live in Melbourne in 1994. In Melbourne 100 years ago or in some present day Third World countries I would be, or would soon be, dead. However, all of the above skills, expertise, technical equipment and observations weren't enough to fully encourage my wellness as a person, as a human being. I am left asking the following questions about the health system as I experienced it. Greater focus on these issues would, I believe, have assisted the other patients and myself to better health as human beings.

1   Why was it so *noisy* most of the time? Only on two of my 11 days did a senior nurse insist on the blinds going down and all visitors leaving from 1.00–2.00 pm. Only on one of these days did some lovely relaxing music play in the background. Why couldn't this have happened everyday? While I greatly appreciated my family and friends bringing me their love and strength, my now fragile being also desperately needed to be protected from our noisy world. Why in the recovery room did the young nurses chatter on about what sort of pizza they would order for supper and what club they were going to at the end of their shift? Post operation, I desperately needed peace and quiet or someone to talk gently to me. I know hospitals have to have their routines, but on it went. Blinds up at 6.00 am, the clanging breakfast trolleys, the cleaners polishing the lino, the corridor noise, the harsh light in the ceiling on until 10.00 or 11.00 pm, all

on top of the necessary frequent patient observation rounds during the day and night.

2   Why was the Neurology Ward (and probably the building it is part of) such a *physically depressing* place? Some colour, some pictures, some bright curtains, some carpet, some human touches would make so much difference. Two bathrooms for about 30 patients wasn't very good. My soul was nourished by the love and care of family and friends expressed in their beautiful flowers and cards. But the wider world could/should have added to my inner recovery.

3   Why, when I finally felt secure and comfortable in a window corner with two female friends (after already having been moved beds several times), did I have to resist three times when we were told we would all have to be split up and moved to other rooms? Feeling secure, comfortable and familiar (even if only for a few days) in my hospital environment was a necessary pre-condition for me to start my inner healing.

4   Why was it so difficult for the system to recognise the unique characteristics of 'Marla' my Croatian companion in the bed next to me and 'Barry' my Koori companion in the bed opposite? In the days before her operation 'Marla' desperately needed someone to talk to. After one day of talking very slowly 'Marla' and I could communicate some basics about our lives. The next day I was very tired and turned away on my pillow (I will never forget the look of rejection on her face). It was the week-end and I asked a nurse if an interpreter could be found so she could have someone to talk to between visiting hours. I was told that the interpreter service didn't operate over the week-end and when I enquired about the week-days I was told you have to book, it takes ages, and Croatian would be difficult anyway. I was told that 'we rely on the families'. But families aren't there 24 hours a day. The system also didn't allow for 'Barry's' uniqueness. He was 'mateyed' along to eat and drink and be a good boy. It was 'Barry' who was clearest and strongest about the Neurology Ward not focusing on individual human beings. He firmly told me that we weren't treated as people in this place and was very clear that the only place that he would recover would be amongst his own people.

5   Why are all the *nurses so young* and on one year or so contracts? Why were agency staff brought in over the weekend? Why did I have to tell the agency staff what was wrong with me, where the bathroom was, and what particular assistance they had to give me? Individually, I liked the young nurses, but sometimes I wondered about the appropriateness of some of their comments to

patients. One night we had an older agency nurse and while it may have been a quiet period, she came and asked my friend and me if we would like a cup of tea. She also asked what I had had done and how I was feeling. It was the first sign of TLC (tender, loving care). If the nursing staff is so young and insecure in their employment, I wonder if any real commitment to the Neurology Ward and empathy with us patients can be built up.

6   Why did I feel as though I was being pushed through the system? (Even though I in fact may not have been). I felt very vulnerable as I lay in the recovery room on the first post operation night hearing the nursing staff say they 'had three emergencies coming up, and Mrs Gow was the wellest to be moved down the Ward in the morning.' Perhaps I was, physically, the 'wellest' but my inner person needed comforting and looking after.

Since my diagnosis my life has been totally transformed. It is not for this space for me to write about my inner spiritual journey, my discovery of what love can do, why I believe my tumour grew, and a possible new road for me to travel on. However, since coming out of hospital I have strongly felt the need to write this letter and then move on. A friend in the health system said I should be sending this letter to the Chief Executive Officer of the hospital rather than you. I don't see it this way. I have written to you about my personal experience of care of the human being, of the person who needs to heal outwardly and inwardly. I believe that this is a wider health care issue that is beyond the, probably over stretched, resources of the hospital that I happened to end up in'.

Gow 1994

How do we begin to make sociological sense of an experience such as this one? My answer, following C. Wright Mills (1959), is that the key feature of a sociological explanation is a concern to relate the personal troubles that a letter such as this reflects to public issues. The public issues here relate to the organisation of health services — collectively known as 'the Australian health system' — in the late twentieth century in Australia. A sociological understanding of these events involves asking the question 'what is it about the way our society is organised that would explain an experience of the kind reported in this letter?'.

In this chapter, I shall argue that getting a sociological 'handle' on these personal troubles — detailed here as an example of the implications of the way health care is provided for the individual — involves looking at four sensibilities or elements of explanation (see Willis 1995): historical, cultural, structural, and critical elements.

In providing health care to the citizens of a nation-state such as Australia, the task is to 'provide reasonable access to effective care, supplied in a humane way, and to do so at a cost that society will accept' (Sax 1984, p. 236). The complexities of providing such care are enormous. Even if every Australian agreed with this overall goal, each element of this definition is nevertheless contentious. There are, for instance, no absolute definitions of what is reasonable access. Is having to wait an hour to be seen at the casualty department of your local hospital reasonable access? What is effective care? Does attention only to the physical aspects of recovery from surgery constitute humane care, or should it include attention to the emotional aspects also, as the letter-writer asks? How can it be determined what cost society will accept?

Historical issues

The answers to all the questions raised by Sid Sax's definition above are historically bound (that is, the answer to them will vary historically). As the writer of the above letter indicates, she is lucky that she did not live 100 years ago. What is considered effective, not to mention humane, care has changed enormously over that time. One example is childbirth. For your grandmothers, and certainly your great-grandmothers, maternal and infant mortality at childbirth was many times the rate it is today, and just getting through a childbirth with their own health and that of their child intact was counted as a successful outcome. In your own generation, however, a successful outcome to the childbirthing experience is likely to be defined not only as mother and baby being healthy, since deaths in childbirth are now, fortunately, exceedingly rare. With the physical threat to the lives of mother and baby now largely removed, child-birth is also supposed to be a satisfying emotional experience, and one allowing per-sonal growth and bonding experience. In other words, how a successful childbirth is defined, both in terms of effectiveness and humaneness, has changed historically.

Historically, a major social-policy consideration has been the question of how to ensure reasonable access to quality health across all sections of the population. The aim for governments has been to attempt some degree of equity of access to health care, so that access is based upon need rather than ability to pay. For those who are unable to afford health care, various schemes have been implemented to ensure rea-sonable access at a tolerable cost, usually funded from taxation revenues as part of a public health system (see Crichton 1990). The latest in a long line of these attempts is the current Federal system of Medicare: a national health insurance scheme funded from a levy on taxable income. Medicare is unusual among current government pro-grams in that benefits are provided on a universal basis. Health care is available to all permanent residents, regardless of their ability to pay as assessed by their income. Most other government benefits — like Austudy, for instance — are means-tested, which means that it is only available to those whose incomes are below a certain pre-determined level.

The consequences of the latest in a long line of schemes to restrain the cost of providing quality health care are felt by the writer of the letter. In the current eco-nomic climate, Sax's criteria of 'the cost the community will accept' appears to be changing, though of course it is not something on which the community as a whole has been asked its opinion. Rather, it is a consequence of an elected government being given a general mandate to reduce government expenditures in various areas, of which health is one. The letter-writer's feelings of being pushed through the system and of being required to make space for others when she felt her physical condition did not warrant being moved are both consequences of an administrative system directed to this end.

Indeed a historical awareness also allows us to consider whether, in fact, the historical wheel is turning full circle. Arguably, the last fifty years have been characterised by a move away from seeing the healing process as a purely physical one, to a situation in which attention has been given to the emotional side of what the letter-writer calls 'wellness'. Perhaps now, in the name of cost restraint, individuals are once again being 'pushed through the system' with little attention being paid to what the letter-writer calls 'the inner person'?

Cultural issues

How can a health system provide treatment in a humane way? The second of the sociological sensibilities essential to understanding the relationship between the individual and society, and to relating personal troubles to public issues, is a cultural or anthropological awareness. The need is to make provide culturally appropriate service. The letter-writer experienced a number of situations in which the treatment she and her fellow patients received was less than totally humane, in the sense, as she put it, of not recognising their unique characteristics. For her Croatian companion, 'Marla', the desperate need was for the interpreter service to be made more widely available. In times of cost restraint, not only was the interpreter service only available during normal weekday working hours, but also the range of community languages the service provided did not extend to less common languages, such as Croatian. Again, in the best of all worlds, interpreters for all community languages would be available at all times, but in reality this is probably not 'a cost the community would bear'. For her koori (Aboriginal) companion, 'Barry', the treatment was also less than totally humane, to the point at which, in fact, he felt he could only recover among his own people. A cultural awareness is also relevant in understanding the deprivation the letter-writer felt when moved away from her two female companions. Being deprived of the company of female friends makes no sense in terms of what might be called 'the culture of femininity'.

Structural issues

A structural sensibility seeks to explain personal troubles in terms of changes in the way society is organised as a whole. What changes are occurring in the structure of the Australian nation-state that are being reflected in the experiences of individual patients within the health system, such as the letter-writer? One important change has been in the organisation of the labour market. These changes, broadly directed at reducing labour costs, have resulted in significant changes in how health care is actually provided. According to the letter-writer, the nurses were young and, by implication, relatively inexperienced. This was reflected, for instance, in a certain degree of

perceived insensitivity, demonstrated by talking about pizzas and nightclubs in deli-
cate medical situations. All of these are the effects of changes in the labour market for
nursing, traditionally the largest component of the health workforce. Younger and
more inexperienced workers are cheaper to employ. Likewise, one of the means of
reducing costs is to employ casual nurses from nursing employment agencies to provide care during the times when penalty rates and overtime would need to be paid to
permanent workers, such as on the weekend. Can Sax's criteria of 'effective care' possibly be met when, understandably, temporary nurses have little understanding of
their patients' conditions or, indeed, where basic facilities like bathrooms are located?
What does this do for the concept of 'continuity of care', which has always been held
up as crucial to effective treatment? Other cost-cutting measures also undermine
effectiveness. Not long ago, nursing shifts used to be organised so that there was
what was called a 'change-over period'. This involved a system of overlapping shifts,
in which the nurses finishing their shifts spent a short time familiarising the oncoming nurses on the 'state of play' in the ward. In the interests of cost-saving, however,
the idea of overlapping shifts has been abandoned in most health-care settings.
Instead, as one study conducted by a postgraduate student at La Trobe University
found, change-over was supposed to occur with the finishing nurses making a tape
recording to familiarise the oncoming nurses. Frequently, however, the tape recorders
were not working. So it was possible, and did on occasion happen, that an agency
nurse turned up to take sole charge on a night shift, in a hospital in which she or he
had previously never set foot. The agency nurse was expected to take responsibility
for a ward full of sick people (since the faster throughput of patients meant the ones
present were sicker) with no information available other than the written charts on
what was happening in the ward (Bates 1994).

A structural sensibility is also useful in making sense of some other aspects of the
letter reproduced at the beginning of the chapter. During a period of funding cuts in
public hospitals, precious little funds are available to improve the physical environment of the ward and its surroundings, causing 'the lack of a human touch' to which
the letter-writer refers. Likewise, many of the routines of a hospital are organised
such that the work of cleaning and so on is done for the least cost, rather than the
least inconvenience for the patients. The same explanation applies to the situation in
which only two bathrooms are provided for thirty patients. All of these consequences
of the more threadbare approach to public health care can also be observed in a
wider global context. In a period of increasing globalisation (which is dealt with in
the final part of this book), governments everywhere, and of all political persuasions,
have been attempting to reduce levels of expenditure in attempts to enhance their
competitiveness in international markets. All areas of expenditure are targeted.
Likewise, schemes developed in other countries to reduce expenditure and hopefully
increase efficiency are being tried in the Australian context. 'Case-mix' funding is the
latest of these schemes: in brief, a scheme that reimburses hospitals for the number of
actual procedures performed, rather than on the basis of more generalised funding in
the form of block grants.

Critical issues

The sociologist Anthony Giddens has argued that a critical or reflexive orientation is important to sociology. Sociology is concerned not only with what is, but also with what might be; it is concerned with the role of 'alternative futures' in contributing to the 'critique of existing forms of society' (Giddens 1983, p. 26). Another way of saying this is that sociology is concerned with social policy — that the aim is not only to understand how society works, but also what can be done about it. It should be noted that no particular answer to this question is implied. There are likely to be several different answers given by sociologists. The point is that debating the alternatives is very much a part of the sociological enterprise. Having a critical sensibility involves asking 'how could it be otherwise?'. Are there alternative arrangements in providing health care, even within the context of funding constraints?

Seeking to make sociological sense of the personal troubles of the letter-writer involves relating the problems to broader public issues regarding the organisation of Australian society. Making a sociological analysis involves paying attention to historical, cultural, structural, and critical sensibilities. Sociologists enquire into the context in which health care is provided in the Australian nation-state. The question of how to provide 'reasonable access to effective care, supplied in a humane way, at a cost that society will accept' has been hotly debated throughout White Australian history. Inevitably, as one senior medical administrator commented, such issues are resolved in 'a political, ad hoc, learn-as-we-go fashion' (Stoelwinder, as quoted in Sax 1984, p. 236).

The political debate involves those organised groups that have a stake in how health care is provided. These are usually known as 'interest groups' and are usually made up of government and health administrators, and of occupational groups. The current shape of the health-care system is the outcome of conflict and contestation between these powerful groups, each of which advances an idea of how health-care services should be provided that is consistent with its own vested interests. Each group claims to be pursuing the health-care goals outlined by Sax, not in their own narrow self-interest, but in the best interests of the population as a whole, each member of which is a patient at some time. Yet the interests of patients themselves are only rarely represented. Only occasionally does dissatisfaction with the provision of health-care services, such as that expressed by the letter-writer, surface, and then notably in a consumer magazine.

However, the differences between the members of these elite interest groups should not be overemphasised. Most share the same class background; they have often been to the same schools and have a common interest in protecting their positions of privilege and power.

It should be remembered that the context of health care in Australia is one in which Medicare, in spite of its universal character, increasingly just provides a safety net for those who are not able, or the few who do not choose, to have private health insurance. From the earliest days of White settlement in Australia, health care has been provided through either a public system based upon taxation revenues or, alternatively, a private system based upon ability to pay. For those who have the ability and desire to avoid the public system experienced by the letter-writer, the context of health care is likely to be different. There is no 'two bathrooms for thirty sick people' in the private system, and no lack of paintings or fresh paint.

There is a parallel here with the education system. Significant numbers of 'clients' opt out of the public system of education, which is funded by taxation revenues, and enter a private system of education, funded not only by taxation revenues but also by fees. As a result, what might be called the 'political will' is lessened to ensure that the levels of funding for the provision of a public system of health or education are adequate to meet the needs of all.

The much vaunted 'choice', then, only exists for those who can afford to exercise that choice. For most, however, the consequence of being given a choice is the running down of public facilities, reflected in the sorts of personal troubles experienced by the letter-writer. Were everybody, including powerful members of society, to use these facilities it is unlikely that the sorts of situations that the letter-writer experienced would be tolerated for very long. The public issues, however, are the wider considerations concerning the direction in which our society is heading, especially with regard to the growing level of inequality between different groups.

Discussion questions

1 What, in your view, would constitute 'reasonable access to effective care'?
2 What are the most important considerations, in your view, in supplying health care 'in a humane way'?
3 What groups are the most important in shaping the Australian health system?
4 How might consumers have a greater voice in the determination of health-care policy?
5 Does Medicare have a future? Explain your answer.

Recommended reading

• Davis, A. and George, J. 1993, *States of Health: Health and Illness in Australia*, 2nd edn, Harper Educational, Sydney, especially pp. 94–108.
This is a good overall introduction to the Australian Health System.
• Ballis, P. H. 1994, 'Health', in B. Furze and C. Stafford, *Society and Change: A Sociological Introduction to Contemporary Australia*, Macmillan, Melbourne, pp. 147–68.
This is a very interesting account of the sociologist-author's experience of the Australian health system after a serious car accident.
• Lupton, G. and Najman, J. 1995, *Sociology of Health and Illness: Australian Readings*, 2nd edn, Macmillan, Melbourne.

This is an edited collection of useful readings. Three in particular are relevant: chapter 4, 'The Australian Health Care System', by John Dewdney, pp. 71–100; chapter 5, 'The Politics of Health in Australia', by Sid Sax, pp. 101–20; and chapter 17, 'The Sociology of Health and Illness', by Jake Najman and Gillian Lupton, pp. 365–78.

• Sax, S. 1984, *A Strife of Interests*, Allen & Unwin, Sydney.

Read selectively on the history of the health system (pp. 3–29 and part 2). See also chapter 9 (pp. 236–44) on 'The Inevitability of Continuing Strife'.

• Palmer, G. and Short, S. 1989, *Health Care and Public Policy: An Australian Analysis*, Melbourne, Macmillan, especially pp. 5–20.

This is an overview account of the Australian health system.

• Waters, M. and Crook, R. 1990, *Sociology One*, Longman Cheshire, Melbourne.

See chapter 14, 'Health and Medicine', for an overview of the field of medical sociology.

• Bates, E. and Linder-Pelz, S. 1987, *Health Care Issues*, Allen & Unwin, Sydney, especially ch. 1.

• Russell, C. and Schofield, T. 1986, *Where It Hurts*, Allen & Unwin, Sydney, especially chs 1–2.

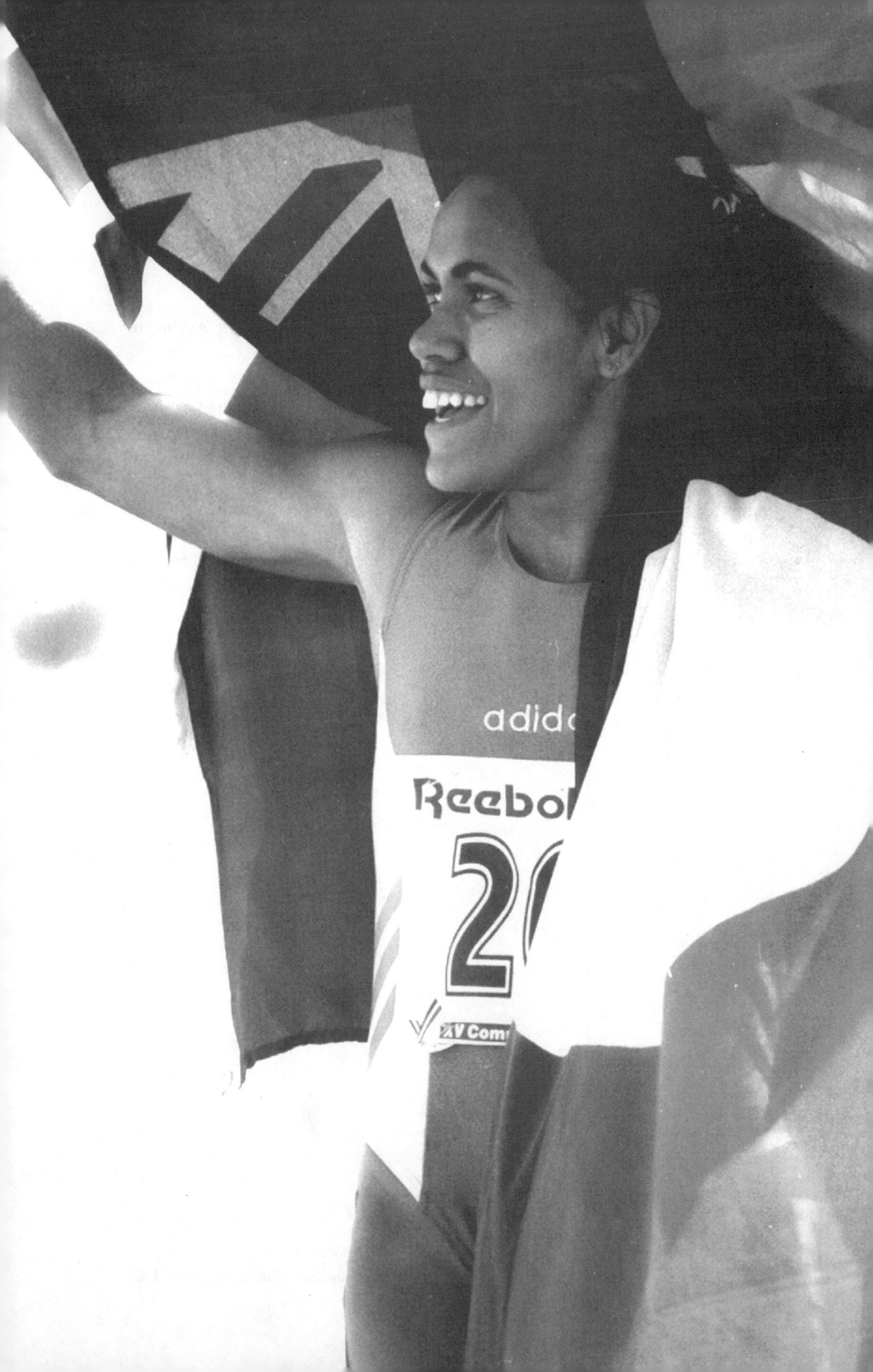
adida
Reebo
20
XV Comm

Chapter 17

The Politics of Settlement

Lucinda Aberdeen

> Throughout the Commonwealth Games, with the exception of Cathy, the image of your typical Australian sportsman and sportswoman continues the myth that this country's achievers are English or European.
>
> Nicola Joseph, *Sydney Morning Herald*, 26 August 1994

> Surely if we had a national flag that was inclusive of Australian Aborigines there would be no need for Cathy Freeman to carry *two* flags.
>
> Patricia Ryan, *Sydney Morning Herald*, 27 August 1994

If you were living in Australia in 1994, it is unlikely that the wide media coverage of Cathy Freeman's victory in the 400 metre individual race at the Commonwealth Games in Canada escaped your attention. Images of the athlete draped colourfully in both the Australian and Aboriginal flags as she jogged a victory lap were given particular prominence. So too was the response of the Head of Australia's Commonwealth Games Federation, Arthur Tunstall. He effectively censured Ms Freeman's behaviour in a subsequent public announcement, which stated that Australian athletes competed under the national flag only (*Age*, 25 August 1994).

Further media coverage of reactions to Tunstall's remarks followed, with public figures from both main political parties in Australia, such as the Labor Prime Minister and the Federal Leader of the Opposition, praising Ms Freeman's success and supporting her use of the two flags (*Weekend Australian*, 27–28 August 1994). Other public figures, such as the conservative Victorian Returned Services League Secretary, Bruce Ruxton, criticised Ms Freeman on the grounds that the only national flag was the Australian flag (*Age*, 25 August 1994).

No doubt, there were other Australians following these events in the media who would have dismissed the matter as a media 'beat-up'. Nevertheless, the significance of Freeman's display of the two flags — which she subsequently repeated when she won her second gold medal in the 200 metre individual race at the Games — cannot be dismissed. It symbolises, uncomfortably for some, the national strength of the Aboriginal and Torres Strait Islander Australians' struggle for recognition and justice. On a broader scale, it is a part of the complex nature of indigenous and ethnic identity to be found in Australian society in the latter part of the twentieth century. It forces us to consider the fundamental question of what constitutes the Australian nation.

This chapter aims to demonstrate that the Australian nation is not a fixed cultural identity about which all but a few wayward citizens agree. Rather, national identity is continually undergoing redefinition in a manner that involves conflict as well as agreement. Nowhere is this more evident than when we consider the politics of settlement over the past 200 years, and particularly the relationship between European settlers and the indigenous peoples, as well as between the descendants of both these groups. I will contend that central to this relationship is a continuing struggle over the recognition and position of Australia's indigenous population in the nation's identity. Furthermore, I will employ a number of sociological and anthropological concepts to explore why this is so, including colonialism, ethnocentrism, and racism.

Colonialism: invasion and settlement

Implicit in the criticisms of Cathy Freeman's celebratory behaviour is the assumption that Australian society is uniform (that is, homogenous) in values and aspirations, or that it should at least appear so. This overlooks the fact that modern Australia is the historical product of the British colonial invasion and settlement (colonialism) that began in 1788. If you are not an Aboriginal Australian, you may not have considered how colonialism is related to the controversy surrounding Cathy Freeman's victory lap, especially since political independence from colonial rule was achieved almost a century ago in the 1890s, when self-government was established throughout the various Australian colonies.

However, British colonialism in the eighteenth century involved not only the political control of one country over the people of another, but, by controlling the machinery of government, the colonial rulers also dominated the indigenous economy and culture of the countries they colonised. Moreover, they justified their actions through beliefs that can be classified as ethnocentric. That is, they judged other cultures by what they assumed to be the superior standards of their own. In Australia, this led to the cultural, economic, and political dominance of the British (or 'Anglo-Celtic') colonial settlers, who subordinated those who could not, or would not, conform.

Colonialism, ethnocentrism and *terra nullius*

Probably the first most identifiable evidence of ethnocentrism on the part of the British Government towards Australia's original inhabitants was its declaration that the Australian continent was *terra nullius* ('no man's land'). This declaration was based on the observations of Captain James Cook and botanist Sir Joseph Banks, on their sea voyage to Australia in 1770, that the country was an empty land. Apparently, from their European viewpoint, the indigenous inhabitants had not 'settled' the land because there was no evidence of regulated laws of land-ownership, fencing, cultivation of crops, or permanent dwellings, such as houses, to be seen. The course of history might have been different if Cook and Banks had lived at a later time, when they could have studied some anthropology or sociology before embarking on their travels. Such study would have equipped them to question, and think more systematically about, the influence of their own beliefs and values on their perceptions (that is, they could have engaged in critical reflection). They may have then considered the possibility that the semi-nomadic hunter-gathering inhabitants, whom they observed on the continent's coastal fringes, had another system of land tenure and usage, which was entirely different from contemporary European models.

Unfortunately for the indigenous population, the doctrine of *terra nullius* provided an expedient justification under the international law of the day for Great Britain to legally take possession of Australia without providing compensation for the Aboriginal people displaced by this occupation. Officially this occurred on 26 January 1788, when the captain of the First Fleet, Arthur Phillip, declared a penal colony at Botany Bay in the name of King George III. Later when the Australian colonies federated, this day officially became recognised as Australia Day and is still celebrated as such today. The dramatic, ongoing, and adverse effects that British colonialism had upon the continent's indigenous people has led Aboriginal people to rename this day 'Dispossession Day', and mark it with organised protest. The first such protest was held by the Aborigines Progressive Association in Sydney in 1938 to mark 'A National Day of Mourning and Protest' (see Lippmann 1981, p. 48). More recently, in the interests of reconciliation between indigenous and other Australians, official calls have been made for the Australian Government to choose an alternative day to 26 January as Australia's national day, and one that has the support of all Australians (Council for Aboriginal Reconciliation 1995, p. 15).

Not long after the very first Australia Day it became apparent that the doctrine of *terra nullius* was a legal fiction. The first colonial governor, Arthur Phillip, had originally been advised 'by every means possible to open an intercourse with the natives, and to conciliate their affections, enjoining all our subjects to live in amity and kindness with them' (Barton 1889, p. 485). However, this advice became unworkable as Aboriginal people did not readily cede the land they occupied to the British Crown, nor could they move easily elsewhere into 'unclaimed' land occupied by other tribal groupings. Instead they attempted to defend themselves and their land by engaging in guerrilla warfare (see Reynolds 1981). This resulted in frontier violence as settlers sought reprisals, which in turn triggered counter-reprisals. The response of the colonial authorities was to resort to a policy of 'dispersion'. This was literally the breaking up and driving away of indigenous people thought to be hostile to European expansion and settlement. Such an approach escalated the hostility between the two groups by providing the justification for massacres of Aboriginal people that lasted into the 1930s (see Elder 1988).

The impact of colonialism upon the continent's indigenous population was catastrophic. Denying Aboriginal people occupation and use of their land destroyed the basis and viability of their traditional social, religious, and economic arrangements. Frontier violence alone is estimated to have caused 20 000 Aboriginal deaths compared with approximately 1500 deaths on the European side (Broome 1994, p. 51). Yet under British colonial rule, indigenous inhabitants were denied any legal recourse, as they were not granted the rights of British subjects, even though they were subject to British law. (It was not until late in the following century that they were permitted to give evidence in courts in the colonies. See Bennett 1992, p. 49.) Their numbers dwindled largely through violent deaths, starvation, and introduced diseases to which they had no resistance. The result was that, as European invasion and settlement expanded, indigenous people became increasingly dependent as fringe-dwellers in camps on the outskirts of towns and on pastoral properties.

Ethnocentrism and racism

The dependence of indigenous people upon colonial settlement — especially where this dependence manifested itself in the form of begging, malnutrition, and alcoholism — helped to fuel racist behaviour towards, and racist thinking about, Aboriginal people. Racism can be classified as an extreme form of ethnocentrism. It occurs when one social group attributes negative characteristics (for example, foul odour, 'thieving', or low intelligence) to another group that is seen as being biologically distinctive (for example, in terms of skin colour, hair type, or facial features). Moreover, the biological features are alleged to somehow cause the negatively evaluated attributes or behaviour. These perceived associations are, in turn, used to justify discrimination against a group with regard to its access to resources and legal rights (Miles 1982; 1989).

Initially, colonial officials and settlers took an ethnocentric view towards Aboriginal people. They appeared to believe that, given adequate education, the continent's original inhabitants were capable of becoming 'Europeanised' and thereby 'civilised'. In this sense, indigenous people were seen as 'equal' to Europeans. Racist thinking became more evident in the colony, however, as frontier violence and expanding settlement took its toll, rendering Aboriginal people dependent on those who had undermined their independence. This dependency was widely perceived to be further proof of Aboriginal inferiority, rather than the result of colonialism. Any recognition of the significant contribution of Aboriginal labour to colonial exploration and development, particularly in the pastoral industry (see Reynolds 1990), was conveniently overlooked as a result of racism.

In the latter part of the nineteenth century such views were bolstered by the influence of Charles Darwin's ideas about evolution. If, as Darwin argued, the evolution of the species occurred through the 'survival of the fittest', then the decline and eventual demise of Australia's indigenous population was evidence of 'natural selection' at work. The indigenous 'races' would eventually be replaced by the supposedly superior European 'races'. It was this kind of racist thinking that informed colonial governments' Aboriginal policies, particularly at the end of the last century. One example of this is seen in the colonial policies of Aboriginal protection, which from the 1880s onwards were used to control and segregate the 'dying race' of indigenous people on reserves.

The idea that there exist separate biological groups of people who can be classed as 'races' has been discredited within science in the latter part of this century. Modern biologists would agree that all human beings belong to one species and that the genetic variations within our species are far more diverse than the superficial characteristics that were previously used to construct racial boundaries. Furthermore, there is no sound biological evidence linking the genetic determinants of things like skin colour (that is, phenotypes) with the causes of particular social behaviours. In fact, there appear to be just as many social and behavioural differences *within* each phenotypical group (Black, White, and otherwise) as there are *between* the so-called races. Nevertheless, the term *race* continues to be a popular and powerful tool in Australia for stereotyping indigenous people, whose appearance or behaviour is different from, and devalued by, the dominant Anglo-Celtic majority. The recent (and first) prosecution under New South Wales racial vilification legislation of a local government councillor for referring to Aboriginal people as 'half-breeds' and 'savages' illustrates the tenacity of racism in Australia today (*Age*, 20 May 1995).

The politics of settlement after federation

The dominant belief among European colonists that the indigenous population would eventually die out or fade away was evident at the time of the federation of the colonies into a nation in 1901. The Australian Constitution, which provided the legal basis for federation, prevented the Federal Government legislating for Aboriginal people. Moreover, 'aboriginal natives' were specifically excluded from being counted in any national census. Those who drafted the constitution appeared not to believe that indigenous people and their affairs were sufficiently significant, politically or culturally, to warrant being under the control of the new national government. No doubt, this attitude reflected 'the taken-for-granted assumption of the Australian nation essentially without Aborigines and Islanders' (Sharp 1994, p. 122), and without other non-Europeans, where possible.

It is worth noting that this assumption was clearly evident with regard to immigration, an area in which the new national parliament had jurisdiction. One of the first pieces of legislation that it enacted was the *Immigration Restriction Act* of 1901. By requiring unwanted immigrants to undertake a dictation test in any European language, the Act attempted to legally guarantee the new nation's so-called racial purity and White Anglo-Celtic dominance. It was the cornerstone of the 'White Australia' policy, which remained in place until 1967 (Castles et al. 1992, pp. 52–6).

At the time of federation, the particular circumstances of indigenous Australians varied according to the Australian state in which they lived, and the manner and time in which it had been colonised. Unlike European Australians, however, they shared a common heritage of dispossession and did not have the civil and political rights enjoyed by other Australians. Consequently, they were subject to systematic discrimination — particularly by government officials, police, and employers — but lacked any real political influence within 'White Australia' to challenge this. Some of the worst conditions in this regard were found on reserves, where Aboriginal residents could be subject to authoritarian controls and surveillance by White managers.

Although many White Australians expected that the Aboriginal population would 'die out', this did not happen. Throughout the first three decades of the twentieth century, there was a steadily growing group of people who had a mixture of both European and Aboriginal heritage and who chose predominantly to identify their cultural heritage as Aboriginal, not European. Moreover, during the 1920s and 1930s, some of these people were organising politically and drawing attention to the plight of Aboriginal Australians, especially on reserves in New South Wales.

Clearly such a development did not sit comfortably with the idea of a 'White Australia'. The response of the State authorities to the 'half-caste' problem, as it was known, was to introduce a policy of assimilation. This policy was agreed upon nationally in 1937 in a meeting of State and Federal officials and was to remain in effect for almost three decades. Efforts were to be directed at 'absorbing' those with 'mixed' heritage into the White Australian population. The ethnocentrism that informs assimilation is evident in a statement issued at the 1961 Native Welfare Conference:

> The policy of assimilation means in the view of all Australian governments that all aborigines [sic] and part-aborigines [sic] are expected eventually to attain the same manner of living as other Australians and to live as members of a single Australian community enjoying the same rights and privileges, accepting the same responsibilities, observing the same customs and influences by the same beliefs, hopes and loyalties as other Australians.
>
> As quoted in Gale and Brookman 1975, p. 72

The dominance of Anglo-Celtic values in Australian society was also evident in immigration policy. European immigrants arriving in Australia as part of the mass migration program that commenced after the Second World War in 1945 were also expected to 'assimilate'. This helped to reinforce the myth that the Australian nation was a fixed cultural identity. As Castles et al. have noted:

> For the entire period from the late 1940s to the mid-1960s migrants were allowed to present no threat whatsoever to a concept of national identity based firmly upon the supposedly shared British roots of the bulk of the population. Indeed, in a curious, even paradoxical, way the doctrine of assimilation, so vigorously espoused by the government of the period, did much to reinforce the sense of homogeneity and the sense of superiority of the anglophone population.
>
> 1992, p. 45

The policy of assimilation did not address the fact that, as indigenous people were denied the civil, political, and legal rights enjoyed by other Australians, they were paradoxically not recognised as citizens in their own country. Laws precluded most of them from activities such as voting, frequenting hotels, and consuming alcohol, and even permitted the forced widespread removal of children to 'training homes' from families thought by state agencies to be unable to assimilate (see, for example, Read 1982). To gain exemption from such restrictions a certificate needed to be obtained stating that the person concerned was considered to be civilised into the European Australian way of life. The insulting nature of this procedure meant that exemption certificates became known as 'dog licences' within indigenous communities.

In such a climate of opinion it is understandable that indigenous people chose to hide or disguise their ancestry and thereby escape the above strictures (see, for example, Morgan 1987). It would have been inconceivable at that time for Aboriginal athletes to celebrate their success in the manner in which Cathy Freeman did. In fact, little more than thirty years ago, in 1962, two Aboriginal athletes, Jeff Dynevor and Percy Hobson, won gold medals for high jumping and bantam weight boxing respectively at the Commonwealth Games in Perth, Western Australia. Neither athlete drew attention to their Aboriginal heritage. In Percy Hobson's own words, 'I didn't tell anyone [about my Aboriginal heritage]. You didn't in those days if you could get away with it ... Back then I was jumping as a white person with black coloured skin' (*Age*, 29 August 1994).

However, during the 1960s changes were occurring that were to see an official end to assimilation. By this time it was clear that, despite the aspirations of assimilation, Aboriginal people remained culturally distinct. Moreover, they continued to be the most disadvantaged Australians in terms of their levels of education, employment, health, and housing, as well as their experience of discrimination. The idea that such people could eventually be absorbed within the dominant White population seemed remote, if not naive.

Moreover, on a broader scale, the value and feasibility of constructing and presenting the image of Australia as a culturally homogenous society was being questioned within Australian society. International affairs played a role in this questioning. Australia as a nation was a foundation member of the United Nations organisation, which had been created after the Second World War in 1948. It had taken a leading role in the development of the organisation's first major statement on human rights, the Universal Declaration of Human Rights. Inevitably this drew attention to issues regarding the human rights, including cultural rights and freedoms, of those living within Australia's own borders. Organisations for Aboriginal advancement were particularly active in this respect. Largely as a result of their work, a national referendum to change the Federal Constitution was held in 1967. Its success enabled Aboriginal people to be counted in the census and gave the Federal Government power to legislate for Aboriginal people, paving the way to the granting of citizenship rights, such as voting, to indigenous people. In 1967, the same year as the referendum, the 'White Australia' policy ceased, with the acceptance of non-Europeans immigrants deemed to be suitably qualified.

During this time there was also a growing conviction among younger urban Aboriginal people and sympathetic Europeans that the remedy to Aboriginal social inequality lay in attending more to the issue of dispossession, particularly land rights, rather than social welfare measures alone. Their concern was brought to both national and international attention when a group of them established an Aboriginal Tent Embassy on the lawns of Parliament House in the national capital on Australia Day in 1972. The symbol they used to highlight their protest was the Aboriginal flag, which had been designed the previous year by an Aboriginal person from Central Australia, Harold Thomas. It was the same type of flag displayed by Cathy Freeman during her victory lap in Canada some two decades later.

By the early 1970s the term *assimilation* was increasingly being replaced by the then more acceptable term *integration* to describe indigenous, as well as immigration, policies. Major developments in national government policies and practices in the Aboriginal field did not occur, however, until after the election of the Whitlam Labor Government in 1972. Moreover, assimilationist thinking is still evident in Australian society today. Only as recently as 1993, for example, after publicly denouncing the occurrence of racism in football, the president of a Melbourne football club added that, 'as long as they [Aborigines] conduct themselves like white people, well, on and off the field, everyone will admire and respect them' (Broome 1994, p. 219).

The politics of settlement after 1972

In late 1972, the year prior to Cathy Freeman's birth, the Australian Labor Party came to power federally. The new Government's political agenda involved policies and programs aimed at achieving recognition of, and justice for, indigenous Australians. One important effect of these policies and programs was to broaden the nation's identity so that it began to include, rather than exclude, its indigenous population and their heritage.

In particular, Federal policy on Aboriginal affairs was changed from one of assimilation or integration to one of empowerment of indigenous people. The Prime Minister, Gough Whitlam, announced in 1973 that his government would 'restore to the Aboriginal people of Australia their lost power of self-determination in economic, social and political affairs' (Gale and Brookman 1975, p. 100). This policy encompassed an inquiry into Aboriginal land rights (the Woodward Commission), legislative and administrative reforms, and spending programs to redress Aboriginal and Islander disadvantage.

The policy of 'self-determination' was also bolstered by the new Labor Government commitment to the ratification of the various United Nations conventions on civil, cultural, economic, religious, and social rights and freedoms. On the international stage, Australia had already endorsed these conventions as a signatory prior to 1972. However, the conventions had remained ineffective domestically because they had not been ratified; nor had they been put into operation through national legislation. By undertaking the process of ratification, the new Government committed itself to guaranteeing the full range of human rights to all its residents, not just those who were European Australians. The first such piece of legislation to come into effect in this regard was the Commonwealth *Racial Discrimination Act* of 1975.

In the area of land rights, the Whitlam Government introduced the Aboriginal Lands Rights Bill into Parliament in 1975 before it was dismissed in the same year. The Bill was subsequently passed by the National–Liberal Coalition Federal Government as the *Aboriginal Land Rights (NT) Act 1976* (Cwth), which facilitated the return of vacant or Crown land in the Northern Territory to Aboriginal people who could prove attachment to it. The hope among indigenous people and their supporters that this entitlement could be extended to all indigenous Australians through national land rights legislation was not realised, although South Australia and New South Wales each enacted their own land rights laws.

In fact, from 1972 onwards and throughout the 1980s, national initiatives to bring about uniform policies and programs concerning indigenous affairs were impeded by political differences between State and Commonwealth governments, among other things. This situation was reflected in the ongoing and marked disadvantage experienced by indigenous Australians. In 1981 these circumstances were drawn to international and domestic attention as a result of the visit to Australia of the World Council of Churches' delegation to assess justice for Aboriginal people. The delegation's report made detailed recommendations that it believed needed to be considered urgently at an international, as well as Federal and state government, level in order to redress 'the plight of Aboriginal communities in Australia' (Adler et al. 1981, p. 60).

One aspect of this plight — that of Aboriginal deaths in custody — later became the subject of a Royal Commission. The Commission's investigation of ninety-nine such deaths found that there was no difference in the death rates between Aboriginal and non-Aboriginal people in custody, but that there was a vast overrepresentation of the Aboriginal population in custody and this was mainly the result of 'the disadvantaged and unequal position in which Aboriginal people find themselves in the society — socially, economically and culturally' (1991, p. 15). Put simply, the Commission saw this inequality as stemming originally from the dispossession of indigenous Australians, which was sanctioned by colonialism and underpinned by ethnocentrism and racism, both of which remain potent forces in Australia today.

The year in which the Commission released its findings, 1988, coincided with Australia's bicentenary celebrations. It is not surprising, then, that, in opposition to the official bicentenary celebrations, an estimated 40 000 people — both Aboriginal people and their supporters — marked this occasion with a 'March for Freedom, Justice and Hope' in Sydney on Australia Day that year. Such a demonstration clearly challenged the official representations of Australia as a nation with a single and cohesive identity. Since that time, however, there have been two developments that suggest the possibility of some consensus between indigenous and non-indigenous Australians regarding what constitutes their nation.

Reconciliation, *Mabo*, and beyond

One of the many recommendations of the Royal Commission into Aboriginal Deaths in Custody was its final recommendation to commence a process of reconciliation between Aboriginal and non-Aboriginal people (1991, pp. 107–8). The latter recommendation resulted in the formation of the Council for Aboriginal Reconciliation by the Federal Government in 1991. Officially, the Council's object is to enable the broader Australian community to appreciate the cultures and contributions of the Aboriginal and Islander population, along with developing a continuing commitment to assist in overcoming the disadvantage of the indigenous population. Symbolically, the Council's work is to be completed by the year 2001, the date of the first centenary of Federation.

In June 1992, the year after the formal reconciliation process was launched, the Australian High Court handed down a historic decision on the Mabo case, named after one of the five Torres Strait Islanders who originally brought the case before the Court. The decision overruled the doctrine of *terra nullius* and acknowledged the survival of pre-existing land rights (known as 'native title') to Crown land with which indigenous Australians had a traditional association. The decision raised fundamental questions about the basis of Australian nationhood, because it rejected the legal basis of British colonialism in Australia. This undermining of traditional assumptions about Australian nationhood was reflected in the intense debate that raged over the next fifteen months between conservative and Labor politicians, Aboriginal leaders, mining and farming interests, and others.

The Labor Prime Minister, Paul Keating, perceived the situation as a chance to correct the legal fiction of the Australian nation's foundations. He introduced the Native Title Bill into Parliament the following year by stating that, 'As *Mabo* was an historic judgement, this is historic legislation, recognising in law the fiction of *terra nullius* and the fact of native title. With that alone, the foundation of reconciliation is laid — because after 200 years, we will at last be building on the truth' (*Age*, 19 October 1993). The Bill was subsequently passed into law as the *Native Title Act* in December 1993, in the International Year of Indigenous People. It enables indigenous Australians to be granted communal native title over land to which they have traditional association or to which they hold pastoral leases. The Federal Labor Government plans to compensate those indigenous Australians who are excluded from native titles claims through a land fund, and to deliver a 'social justice package' to redress indigenous disadvantage. By June 1995 there had been no successful land claims made under the *Native Title Act*.

Conservative forces — typified by academics like Professor Geoffrey Blainey, business people like Hugh Morgan, and many Liberal politicians, like Western Australian Premier, Richard Court — see these legislative and social reforms as privileging indigenous Australians in ways that will divide Australia as a nation. Events such as Cathy Freeman's carrying of two flags at the Commonwealth Games are seen, from this perspective, as divisive and unpatriotic behaviour. On the progressive side of the debate are those who see reforms as necessary in order to unite a divided nation. From this perspective, Cathy Freeman's display of the Aboriginal flag along with the official Australian flag is viewed, therefore, as a symbolic recognition of the indigenous struggle that calls out for reconciliation with non-indigenous Australians.

Despite these conflicting perspectives, it is apparent that today, unlike in earlier times, Aboriginal and Islander people are a politically and culturally significant part of Australia's changing national identity. The question remains as to whether this significance can be effectively translated into enduring institutional reforms that will include, and do justice to, Australia's indigenous people. Such reforms are by no means secure and may yet be reversed by more conservative political agendas, whereby the legacy of colonialism, and the ongoing problems of ethnocentrism and racism would continue unabated.

Discussion questions

1 What is meant by 'colonialism'? How has the impact of British colonialism on Australia's indigenous people differed from its impact on non-indigenous Australians?
2 In what ways has ethnocentrism been evident in government policies on Aboriginal people throughout the past 200 years?
3 What is meant by the terms *race* and *racism*? Explain these terms with reference to the indigenous population and the politics of settlement in Australia.
4 What is the significance of Cathy Freeman's gesture at the Commonwealth Games in relation to Australia's national identity?
5 What is the significance of the *Mabo* decision and subsequent Federal Government initiatives?

Recommended reading

The following book deals with broad patterns of relations between indigenous and non-indigenous Australians from the time of European invasion and settlement to the present day:
• Markus, A. 1994, *Australian Race Relations: 1788–1993*, Allen & Unwin, Sydney.
A challenging reassessment of the conventional political and legal arguments that provided justification for the British invasion and settlement of Australia can be found in:
• Reynolds, H. 1994, *The Law of the Land*, 2nd edn, Penguin Books, Melbourne.
A fascinating and insightful anthropological analysis of the Australian High Court's historic *Mabo* decision is contained in:
• Sharp, N. 1996, *No Ordinary Judgement: Mabo the Murray Islander Land Case*, Aboriginal Studies Press, Canberra.
A comprehensive reference for Australian indigenous affairs, both past and present, can be found in:
• Horton, D. (ed.) 1994, *The Encyclopaedia of Aboriginal Australia: Aboriginal and Torres Strait Islander History, Society and Culture*, vols 1 and 2, Aboriginal Studies Press, Canberra.

The contribution that indigenous Australians are making to Australian society and Australian identity are discussed in the following book, which deals with various aspects of their everyday lives:

- Bourke, C., Bourke, E., and Edwards, B. (eds) 1994, *Aboriginal Australia: An Introductory Reader in Aboriginal Studies*, Queensland University Press, St. Lucia.

Readers particularly interested in the achievements of indigenous people in sport, and the racial barriers they have encountered in the process, should read:

- Tatz, C. 1994, *Obstacle Race: Aborigines in Sport*, University of New South Wales Press, Sydney.

The following book provides a detailed community study of social relations between Aboriginal and non-Aboriginal residents in an Australian rural town:

- Cowlishaw, G. 1988, *Black, White or Brindle: Race in Rural Australia*, Cambridge University Press, Melbourne.

First hand accounts of the experience of being an indigenous person in Australia are found in the following work, compiled by the late Aboriginal writer Kevin Gilbert:

- Gilbert, K. 1978, *Living Black: Blacks Talk to Kevin Gilbert*, Penguin Books, Melbourne.

Since the appearance of Gilbert's book, there have been a growing number of other autobiographical and biographical accounts of indigenous Australians' experiences. For example:

- Roughsey, E. 1986, *An Aboriginal Mother Tells of the Old and the New*, McPhee Gribble/Penguin Books, Melbourne.
- Ginibi, R. L. 1988, *Don't Take Your Love to Town*, Penguin Books, Melbourne.

Chapter 18

Economy and Government

Peter Beilharz

Imagine Australia, if you can, before the British invasion, before what White folks called the arrival of civilisation. Not more than two centuries ago the cities we call home were not there. Think of Melbourne and Sydney as raw topography, 'nature', no buildings of metal or concrete. Other people, earlier inhabitants, coped with everyday life and existence in different ways. Then White people came, bringing government and economy in packages.

Where did modern Australia come from? It is a good question to ask, because the answers throw into relief some of the peculiarities about Australia, its economy, and its government. Australia is a peculiar case for sociologists, for while it follows many European paths, it also differs from Europe, no less with matters to do with economy and government than with other issues. So we can usefully approach these themes comparatively, both across time — the past two hundred years — and laterally, against obvious parallels like the United Kingdom and the USA.

What makes Australia different? In the first part of this chapter, these themes of comparison and difference are picked up, and some working definitions of terms suggested. In the second part, the idea of modern Australia as a statist or state-dependent culture is extended, with reference to ideas like nation-building and citizenship. This, in turn, raises questions concerning which citizens governments privilege over others. Government in Australia has traditionally privileged producer groups, manufacturers, farmers, and workers over less publicly visible citizens, such as women working in the home or in sweatshops, aboriginal peoples, or ethnic minorities. This set of arrangements, involving extensive State support for various economic arrangements like economic protection and arbitration has survived for nearly one hundred years but now is being transformed. The third part of the chapter focuses on questions of the past, present, and future of economy and government in Australia.

Locating economy and government

Where did Australia as we know it come from? The short answer is simple: Britain. Australia as we know it has always been a hybrid society, even before the advent of mass immigration after the Second World War and then multiculturalism in the 1970s. Australia has not remained solely Anglo-Celtic, but its institutions, parties, unions, and legal system are still British in origin and inflection. But what the British established in the colonies was not capitalism, or at least not the images of capitalism we associate with the Industrial Revolution: smoke and dirt, paupers in rags,

Dickens, Birmingham. The British exported to Australia a penal system — a form of state that had as its primary purpose the regulation of offenders against British law — and only after that did Britain show any concern about the economy or the production of livelihoods. Australia's origins were less caught up in the struggle between democracy and money than were those of the USA. An economy was needed, of course, to provide the prison system with the means of sustaining life: food, clothing, and shelter. Yet the story of the Australian economy, told in schematic terms, is the reverse of the European experience, within which classical sociology has emerged. In the United Kingdom, to simplify, the capitalist revolution came first, industrial economy was established in textiles and metals throughout the nineteenth century, and the welfare state 'arrives' during the twentieth century, consolidating especially after the Second World War, and establishing a 'safety net' of social security to 'catch' those who cannot help themselves. In Australia, again to simplify, the British state established the basis of an Australian state without a capitalist revolution and without an industrial base. Little wonder that Europeans constructed the antipodes in their own minds as a topsy-turvy place: upside down and, like the platypus, remarkable but bizarre; more a freak than a typical example of modernity. For while capitalism generated its own state in the northern hemisphere, in the Australian case the State came first (Beilharz 1994b; cf. Polanyi 1944).

In the USA, again to compare, early attempts to establish democracy ran not only against the power of money, but also against the tradition of slavery, the legacy of which still dominates the USA today, making race the most visible cleavage within American society. Those who emigrated to the USA went not at the behest of the British state, but went either to sell their labour as wage-earners, or else to seek to accumulate capital. Entrepreneurial spirit was stronger in this frontier capitalist culture than in either the United Kingdom or Australia. Those things that, until recently, we used to associate with the State — railways, public transport, schools and hospitals, museums and galleries, libraries, and swimming-pools — were established in the USA by entrepreneurs or else by their philanthropic foundations, Carnegie, Mellon, or Ford.

But all this raises other questions, not least of which are those of definition. What do we mean by economy, and by government? Here the answers are not as simple. The conservative cliché is that economy makes money, and government spends it; the reforming riposte is that governments ought to set out to civilise capitalism, for markets favour the strong, and governments ought to protect the weak. Viewed organisationally, matters become even more blurred. For there are plainly some capitalist firms that work with a social conscience, just as there are instruments of State bureaucracy that bully and brutalise their clients. Looked at practically, an issue such as scale seems to have as great an effect on the behaviour of an organisation as whether an institution is called 'private' or 'public'. Even the issue of size cuts both ways, however, as larger firms with more resources can often afford to be better corporate citizens than the small capitalists running the corner store, while, at the same time, smaller local bureaucracies can often work far more positively than larger centralised offices.

Nineteenth-century definitions of the State were often minimal, and this, it is important to observe, is a trend that has been undergoing revivals in the USA, the United Kingdom, and Australia since the 1970s. The State, according to this minimalist view, should act as night-watchman, policing against crime on the domestic front and mobilising armed forces against the prospect of foreign aggression. This minimalist view of the State was popular into the second half of the nineteenth century, when some of the more desperate consequences of unregulated capitalist growth became more evident. During the second half of the nineteenth century, poverty became so powerful a presence that a conservative politician like Benjamin Disraeli wrote of the 'two nations', rich and poor, that happened to coincide with the population of the United Kingdom. By the turn of the century the State was increasingly looked upon as a guarantor — a provider for those who were victims of this new social system — though private charity still persisted, especially in the USA and in the United Kingdom. In the United Kingdom in particular, the State increasingly became involved in easing relations of conflict between the classes, in attempting to regulate the labour market to minimise unemployment, in educating the 'unwashed' masses, providing them even with school lunches, and in underwriting housing and health care provision. These kinds of developments were less advanced in the USA, and considerably more developed in Australia. For Australia and New Zealand together became known as leading State reformers into the twentieth century (Reeves 1902).

Look at the railways. In the USA they were financed by entrepreneurs. In Australia there were no such entrepreneurs, so the colonies built the railways, and the State established a shipping line, a second domestic airline, the national air carrier, the Commonwealth Bank, arbitration and conciliation, the basic wage (now gone), and the award system (still intact). Foreign visitors to Australia still find it difficult to cope with the fact that, because of these differences, you do not routinely tip in hotels or in taxis. In Australia, the State has, for better or worse, been associated with the idea of the public interest and has, until very recently, been a major actor in the lives of its citizens.

Let us return, then, to an even more elementary kind of definition. 'Economy' and 'government' are not always easy to distinguish. 'Economy' implies market, private property, private firms, and private interests. 'Government' implies State, parliament, courts, police, and has come also to imply welfare, health, housing and education, the public sphere, and public interest. In its earliest usage, the Greek *oikos* (economy), meant household; the public life, by comparison, is the life of the *polis*, the city. Modernity has brought about, for many people, the practical separation of home and work; the household becomes a sphere of consumption, while we routinely associate production with factories run by private firms. Looking briefly at, say, British, United States, and Australian experiences, however, makes one thing clear: different cultures deal with problems of economy and government in different ways. These cultural differences become manifest in everyday life. If we ask an elementary question, like 'Who will provide?', in these different cultures, we will get very different answers — answers that will also differ within nations, and across time and place.

In general, across the USA, the United Kingdom, and Australia, the short answer to the question 'Who will provide?' will be the same: the market. But then, in the United Kingdom and Australia, there will often also be another question to echo the first, a conditional response, which will ask 'If *not* the market, then who?'. It is a response that confers upon State, or community, or local government the responsibility of acting as fall-back provider. For if there is one thing we learn from the way our world works, it is that the mechanisms that we trust to provide will default, break down, fail to deliver, or deliver with unintended consequences. So governments often end up filling the gaps, 'holding up the tent', filling the gaps left by market absences or failures, or providing services that are unprofitable but thought to be necessary or desirable. In short, government, typically caricatured as the 'umpire', often also supplies the oranges, builds and finances the playing field, trains the players, and picks up the results when things go wrong. And it is not obvious, so far, that we know a better way of organising society. Markets provide some things, but not others. And markets, what is more, depend on states to reproduce them.

What, then, is government, or the State? During the twentieth century, governments have become more caught up with the defence and extension of rights. The problem with rights, in modernity, is that they are often contradictory. Your right to invest (as a capitalist) may infringe upon my right to a job (as a worker). Then, again, when things go wrong, the State appears in the form of unemployment benefits or training schemes. As indicated earlier, however, the distinction between government and economy is often blurred, especially in a statist culture, such as has been traditionally found in modern Australia. In Australia, the State has been a constant actor in everyday life, resulting in a statist culture, in which reliance on the State is common. In some parts of Australia the State even ran butcher's shops. Australian government or statutory corporations have often produced goods such as electricity, which elsewhere have been privately produced. The matter of 'locating' the State is even more difficult when we also consider its local aspects, for the State is not just some kind of massive bureaucratic monster based in Canberra. In Australia the coincidence of Federal, state, and local levels of government mean that the 'State' can often present as the local state, working on the ground at council or local level. So, while rights and duties can be conceived of as Federal, in terms of the national legislature and its workings, they can also have vital effects much closer to home. Government, like economy, is not just Federal or located in big cities; both are found all around us.

Living in a statist culture

Rights and duties have also been associated with the emergence of modern notions and practices of citizenship. Citizenship, in turn, has been caught up with the idea of nation-building. Nations, like modern economies, are relatively new phenomena: traditionally peoples' loyalties are to something closer — to locality or community — not to an abstract idea such as 'Australia'. At the same time, modern Australians have often been caught up in concerns to do with national identity.

Who are we: exiled Britons? a multicultural coalition? something else? Are we made what we are by our origins, by our environment here, or by some other influence? Historically, nineteenth-century Australia was viewed as a colony or set of colonies, even though the convicts inhabiting Australia were not free colonists. The idea of being British, by derivation, went together with that other sense of identity: that to be antipodean was to be completely different, upside down, matter out of place. Defined empirically, Australia is a population with multicultural loyalties — a population that is spread around the coastal regions of the continent, between suburb and city. If you define Australia essentially, as many have historically, it is a place, or a state of mind, to do with the outback or beach — a big place with a silently Aboriginal heart.

The point is that, when we talk about nation, there is an image or a myth, as well as a series of realities, at work. Governments not only recognise subjects or citizens, and valorise some of their rights and duties and not others, they also hold together the national mythology that allegedly makes us what we are (Anderson 1982; Hobsbawm and Ranger 1983). This has practical, as well as imaginary, effects. For the recognition of some citizens over others, or some rights over others, means, for example, that members of the returned services have been privileged over others, with internal or closed welfare systems being constructed to ensure that there is recognition, through repatriation, of national service in war (see, for example, Skocpol 1992).

In Australia, more generally, wage-earners have been recognised by states or governments over those engaged in domestic labour. Australia in the twentieth century has thus been characterised as a 'wage-earners' welfare state' (Castles 1985). Governments in Australia have not only built or financed infrastructure, like railways or universities, then; they have also set about regulating relations of conflict, actual or potential, such as those between the major classes. In the process they have favoured some citizens over others citizens who are publicly less visible or less vocal.

There are three schematic views of the relationship between classes and the State. Conventionally, some associate the State or government with the ruling class, and presume that government always works in the interests of those who own capital, the media, and so on. Conversely, some have argued over the years that the State works often, if not always, in the interests of the working class or the oppressed — legislating limits to the length of the working day, introducing health care and education reforms, or whatever. There is a third view, which is probably both the most interesting and the most persuasive. It suggests that the State is a third institutional terrain, occupied neither exclusively by rulers or the oppressed, the project of which is to work with and across classes, to pursue its own purposes, but also to regulate and manage the tensions and conflicts between the major classes. (Beilharz, Considine, and Watts 1992). In line with this way of thinking, Federation in 1901 helped create institutions like the Arbitration Court, which in 1907 heard Justice H. B. Higgins insist that there must be a basic wage (for men), and that firms who claimed they were unable to pay fair wages would be allowed to go under and, indeed, should not be in the market at all. Protection or tariffs would only be applied to those industries that paid decent wages, not at any cost.

What this indicates, among other things, is that the State can also make moral or ethical claims — claims to do with notions of what makes life, or way of living, good or decent. Organisationally, it also reminds us of the ongoing influence of British political culture, for the party system recognises a labour party as a major actor, and industrial law recognises the central place of a labour movement. Both of these features are in striking contrast to United States experience, where there is no labour party, less public acceptance of unions, and ritual use of union-busting techniques, including even the use of private police armies. To put it in different terms, parliamentary politics in Australia since the Great Strikes of the 1890s has increasingly conformed to the politics of producer groups. The three permanent actors — labour, conservative, and country parties — all represent producer groups: the labour movement, manufacturing (especially earlier), and agrarian producers or farmers. The effect of this has been both positive and negative. Representatives of major public producer groups can make their views heard with relative ease. Others — those located outside this system in the rank and file, or in the home, and those with different agendas (eco-politics, in the case of the Greens; Catholic principles or interests in the earlier case of the Democratic Labor Party) — have no such immediate influence, except to the extent that they can sometimes act as third-party brokers, holding the parliamentary balance of power between labour and the conservative–agrarian coalition. At the same time, it must be recognised that Australian feminists have been successful in unprecedented ways at accessing and intervening in the State. Indeed, 'femocracy' is an Australian invention (Yeatman 1990).

The result has been that, until fairly recently, country party elements have supported a kind of 'agrarian socialism'. Here the State has been expected to support the export of primary commodities over imports, and to socialise losses, while both capitalists and manufacturing workers have also expected protection, for example, of Australian-made cars, textiles, clothing, and footwear against cheap imports, usually from Asia. In other words, while the Arbitration Court has served to promote industrial peace between the unions and business, there has also been a kind of local compromise, in which it has been taken for granted that Australians would be paid decent wages, which they would then spend, in turn, on local products, which they also produced — on Australian cars and white goods, housing materials, and groceries. For the better part of the twentieth century, then, Australian government and political culture have promoted the idea of a relatively closed local manufacturing economy, exporting primary commodities like wool, wheat, and minerals, importing some goods, including luxury items, but simultaneously engaging in import-substitution, protecting local firms and their workers from external competition, and creating a government-sponsored and regulated internal economy, within which living standards were relatively high.

Governments of both persuasions — labour and conservative, with all their differences — have supported this pact, until recently. In fact, modern Australia entered the twentieth century with something like a historic compromise or settlement between the classes. It was a compromise that facilitated nation-building and rested on shared commitment to three principles: arbitration, protection, and 'White Australia' (Beilharz 1994; Kelly 1993). Arbitration would regulate class conflict and ensure the promotion of decent standards of living for conventional families. Protection would keep out cheap goods and promote local products to the same ends: Vegemite on every table, a Victa in every shed, Vacola jars in every pantry (men outside, women inside, suburbia expanding). 'White Australia' would do the same for racial purity: keep out cheap Asian labour, and preserve the image of Australia as 'Britannia down under'.

'White Australia' was the first of the three principles to go. By the 1960s the roots of multiculturalism were already established. White Australian culture was in the process of becoming more conspicuously differentiated. During the 1980s both economic protection and the idea of arbitration became more generally contested, and this, again, occurred on both sides of politics. In the USA and the United Kingdom the dominant politics associated with Ronald Reagan and Margaret Thatcher purported to return to the market and the small, or 'nightwatchman', state. In Australia the fashionable language became less that of 'rolling back the welfare state' than that of 'opening up' and becoming 'internationally competitive' by undoing protection and arbitration. The process, however, logically involves systematic attacks on living standards that the State has hitherto choreographed and maintained through mechanisms like arbitration and protection. Australia approaches the new century now with some of its British origins intact, with some of the desirable aspects of American society, with its difference and plurality expanding, but also with a new will to Americanise government and economy. Australia into the twenty-first century will look less and less like the social laboratory of the early twentieth century, and more and more like the USA today.

After regulation — what next?

What might this mean, this image of Australia and 'the USA today'? Defining the USA today is probably even more difficult than establishing what we mean by 'Australia'. The USA is, however, of central symbolic significance for us, because it has typically been identified with modernity, suburbia, mass consumption, supermarkets, the car society, film, television, and rock and roll. The USA is, symbolically, everything that modern societies want to be: free, fast, comfortable, driven. Yet, practically, the USA also represents the best and the worst of modernity. Its terrible inequality, racism, and homelessness, even just its vast scale, make it a reformist's nightmare. Consider, for example, the symbol of a universal health-care system, existent in the United Kingdom since 1948 in the form of the National Health Service, and since the 1970s in Australia as Medibank and Medicare. America has never achieved anything like this, and now, after the failure of Bill Clinton's health reforms, probably never will.

The reality of American modernity is a market-focused, economy-driven society — and the devil take those who cannot fend for themselves. They will live not in fibro Housing Commission boxes, but in cardboard constructions of their own manufacture. Those who can afford to buy the goods will encounter some version of the good society, but claims of community will become shallow, and levels of personal violence will increase. Why should Australia take this road?

Today common sense seems to indicate that social protection is a false fabrication, like tariff walls — a thing of the past. The Australian experiment of regulating society, of protecting economy and community against insecurity and unfair competition from more powerful nations, is widely viewed as over. The welfarist consensus — common in different forms to the USA, the United Kingdom, and Australia, and across major party lines — has increasingly been replaced by a sense that the less governments regulate economies the better. In Australia, this process has coincided with the arrival of economic rationalism in Canberra (Pusey, 1991). The peculiarity of the Australian story is that the process of deregulation and privatisation has been sponsored and steered by a Labor government. The Hawke and Keating Labor governments, which were in power from 1983 to 1996, have again offered a pioneering example of sorts, just as the earlier reformers like Higgins did after Federation. The difference is that, where Reagan and Thatcher claimed to feed economic growth actively by rolling back the welfare state, Labor in Australia has sought both to deregulate and to maintain some elements of commitment to welfare. The issue here is whether it is possible, in a small nation-state like Australia, to deregulate or 'open up' the economy while still regulating society in the ways traditionally associated with the image of the welfare state. The irony in this regard has always been that developed welfare arrangements depend on substantial economic growth to fund them, yet those arrangements themselves are less necessary when such economic growth occurs, as it did, say, in the period of sustained economic growth after the Second World War. The times when governments most need revenue — for example, to fund unemployment benefits — will also tend to be the periods when fiscal austerity reigns.

State and federal governments have responded to these difficulties by restricting or reducing their areas of involvement, most notably in seeking to privatise activities such as road-building, transport-provision, and the supply of electricity and water. Controversies over privatisation revolve around issues of whether users benefit, or of what the other consequences might be. Market institutions tend to be governed by the bottom line — by questions of short-term returns, which may generate adverse long-term consequences. Market institutions also tend to make everything pay, whereas other institutions (like, say, Telecom/Telstra) have traditionally used publicly useful strategies such as cross-subsidisation, where profits made in one area (for example, commercial telephones) are transferred to others (such as subsidising costs for ordinary country users). Together with the idea that 'markets rule' we now increasingly encounter the insistence that 'users pay', which again advantages some people (for example, drivers of cars) over others (those who, because of limited means, need to use public transport). This brings us back to the earlier observation that all modern societies need states because there are some things or services that markets cannot, or will not, provide. It also reminds us that not all services can, or will be, run at a profit. Public transport, most notoriously, is extremely difficult to run at a profit, yet there is a clear sense in which the quality of life in any city is related to its transport system: bad transport system; bad city, whether it be inner or outer suburbs, rail or road.

The effects of deregulation can be far more painful than just having to wait in desolation in the outer suburbs for buses to come, or feeling unsafe in inner-city trains. The shift away from arbitration and from the award system will increasingly mean that, if they want to survive, people have to take whatever wage they are offered. What this means, in sociological terms, is that there will be increasing activity in the informal economy — the cash-economy where things fall off the back of trucks and people trade in kind (sex for drugs or drug money; cars stolen and bought off the books), all outside the tax system, which again means that there will be less revenue in government funds to spend on socially necessary services.

The overall result of all this may not be a return to what Disraeli imagined as 'two nations', but it will certainly not be the 'one nation' imagined by Paul Keating either. 'Two nations' suggests a clear social divide — a wall between those who have and the outcasts. As you encounter cities like Melbourne or Sydney, or their suburbs, today, what you detect is something more mixed and messy than that. The extremity of contrasts is certainly there: besuited 'corporate cowboys' on mobile phones, homeless people drinking out of brown paper bags, the fashionably chic alongside mums with strings of kids and pushers with groceries. These people are all engaged in economies of some kind or another, whether they are selling stocks and bonds, or real estate, going home to cook, or purchasing second-hand Levis. They all have some relationship to government as well, though some will benefit more from tax-evasion than others, and some will expect State support for their social contributions while denying it to others, whom they will cast as parasites.

Imagine Australia, if you can, into the new century. The future of Australian society will not differ dramatically from the futures of other societies, in Europe, North America, or Central America. The process of globalisation will see more and more societies coming to share these kinds of problems to do with economy and government, wealth and poverty. In seeking to make sense of them, sociologists will need to continue to think in terms of similarity and difference, comparing different national experiences, and thinking in terms of historical comparison as well. The problems and advantages of living in Australia as this scenario unfolds may well be determined by issues of location and size. For Australians remain distant from some of the most desperate problems faced elsewhere, and they remain caught, in a sense, in the middle: small enough to lack sufficient wealth to grow but, at the same time, small enough to remain susceptible to the will to reform.

Discussion questions

1 How can we distinguish between economy and government?
2 What does it mean to talk about a statist culture?
3 How does the modern Australian path of development differ from other nations of comparable experience?
4 What was the Australian historic compromise? Why is it over?
5 What is the future of Australian government and economy?

Recommended reading

* Anderson, B. 1982, *The Imagined Community*, Verso, London.
* Beilharz, P. 1994, *Transforming Labor — Labour Tradition and the Labor Decade in Australia*, Cambridge University Press, Sydney.
This book attempts to locate recent developments within the broader context of the twentieth century and beyond.
* Beilharz, P., Considine, M., and Watts R. 1992 *Arguing About the Welfare State — The Australian Experience*, Allen & Unwin, Sydney.
This book consists of three critical essays, strung together to try to make sense of the Australian welfare state and the arguments surrounding it.
* Butlin, N., Barnard, A., and Pincus, J. 1982, *Government and Capitalism*, Allen & Unwin, Sydney.
A standard reference on the unusually strong state tradition in Australia and its role in the economy.
* Castles, F. 1985, *The Working Class and Welfare*, Allen & Unwin, Sydney.
A pioneering essay on the relationship between the labour movement and the State.
* Considine, M. 1994, *Public Policy — A Critical Approach*, Macmillan, Melbourne.
A lateral view of how states and public policy actually work, and dysfunction.
* Macintyre, S. 1989, *The Labour Experiment*, McPhee Gribble, Melbourne.
This precise and brief survey of some of the issues is a good place to start.
* Pusey, M. 1991, *Economic Rationalism in Canberra: A Nation Building State Changes its Mind*, Cambridge University Press, Sydney.
A highly controversial work in critical sociology and a major sociological contribution to public debate.
* Ward, R. 1975, *A Nation for a Continent*, Heinemann, Melbourne.
Browse through this for useful background by way of recent social history.
* Watts, R. 1987, *Foundations of the National Welfare State*, Allen & Unwin, Sydney.
The best short history of how national welfare consolidated during the 1950s.
* Yeatman, A. 1990, *Bureaucrats, Technocrats, Femocrats*, Allen & Unwin, Sydney.
A leading feminist work that sorts out the limits and prospects of working in, and against, the State.

Chapter 19

Nation: Experiences and Explanations

Peter Beilharz

> A nation is a soul, a spiritual principle. Two things, which are
> really only one, go to make up this soul or spiritual principle.
> One of these things lies in the past, the other in the present. The
> one is the possession in common of a rich heritage of memories;
> and the other is actual agreement, the desire to live together and
> the will to continue to make the most of the joint inheritance.
>
> Ernest Renan 1882

> What Disraeli meant ... was two nations of employers and
> employees, the exploiters and the exploited. Our society consists
> again of two nations. Only ours are nations of the seduced and
> the repressed; of those free to follow their needs and those forced
> to comply with the norms.
>
> Zygmunt Bauman 1987

What is a state? What is a nation-state? What is a nation? The answer to these questions is that they are various things for various people — this much already is apparent from the preceding chapters in this section. In his chapter, Brian Graetz indicates the way in which the nation is a kind of basic organisational unit, the system we take to be the basis of inequalities in income, wealth, labour markets, and life-chances like those provided by education. The nation-state does not generally create these inequalities, but it does license or reproduce them through, for example, particular policies concerning taxation, death duties or inheritance, schooling and training. As Graetz implies, the nation-state could follow different policies, but it chooses not to. Kerreen Reiger shows how the State both acts and decides not to act. In her chapter, the State is depicted as cutting both ways: it acts both as a potential enabling agent and as a powerful patriarch against those it constructs as marginal or immature — in this case, women and Aborigines. Evan Willis's discussion of health care reveals the tensions within a sub-system in a larger social system, again suggesting, like Graetz and Reiger, that with a different sense of purpose (or 'will-to-power') the nation-state could do a great deal more than it actually does to humanise the delivery of welfare services. In all these portrayals, then, the nation-state looks after economic and social policy concerning inequality, education, employment, family assistance, child care, and health care. All the contributors to this part, like myself, were born into the

Keynesian national welfare state; it is probably fair to say, on another level, that they are all 'children' of the Whitlam years of social reform. Here sociology is seen as a natural ally of social reform, and this largely within the framework of the nation-state as organisational unit and ideal model.

As Lucinda Aberdeen points out, it was the Whitlam period that saw a rethinking of social policy and the beginning of a reconsideration of national identity. This introduces a new twist on the idea of nation: that a nation is a people and has an identity. Arguments about national identity have been around at least since the period of the French Revolution, even though the French Revolution was not made by the French; rather, it made, or constructed, the nation of France, just as other apparently stable entities like 'Germany' and 'Italy' were forged as global maps were redrawn through the nineteenth century. Historically, Australian national identity was imagined as Anglo, White, British, and English-speaking, and it was built upon the legal fiction of *terra nullius*, or 'no man's land'. This introduces a further dimension of the modern state: that it rests, as Weber put it, on the claim to a legitimate monopoly of violence (Weber 1948, p. 78). In other words, citizens of modern states cannot legally take up arms against each other, but states, and their armies or police, can and do. Modern nation-states are based on categories of inclusion or exclusion; some people count for more as citizens than others. While some (like Vietnamese boat-people) will be excluded, others (like immigrants with professional skills or capital) will potentially be included. Increasingly, however, these kinds of matters become political issues, which is to say that — like national identity in the Cathy Freeman example — they become contested. For if there are multiple selves, as Fiona Mackie argues in the first part of this book, there are certainly also multiple identities within nations.

These kinds of paradox also inform my previous chapter. Ironically, what we call the modern nation-state is also pre-modern, for it often seems to presume that a national population is a given, fixed, and pre-existing community, language group, or race, and that a citizenry emerges in the twentieth century that could be homogeneous and harmonious. Nations are imagined to be made up of like, interchangeable citizens or subjects. States make it their business to administer populations, which means they also set out to construct them. The Australian nation-state, however, began as a state, before it had a capitalist economy; it was only in the 1980s that the relations between economy and state were restructured, making markets more dominant, but this also coincided with the newly vigorous processes of globalisation, which erode national sovereignty and place the nation-state (and thereby the welfare state) under question.

Note the significant linguistic slippage in all this. One moment we are talking about the 'state', and the next minute the 'nation-state'. This kind of identification is a sign of our times — of twentieth-century and postwar times. Inhabitants of the modern age presume that states work largely at federal levels, that citizens have largely national identities (I come from Australia, not Melbourne; I am Australian, not German-Australian), and that states can identify and measure social problems like health or unemployment and fix them. But all this, too, now looks like common sense under question. Radicals and reformers, people of good will in places like Australia after the Second World War especially, imagined that all subjects would become citizens, and that the outcast would be included and the goal of social harmony achieved. Today, again, these kinds of hopes are clouded, and so sociology's connection to the modern project of national reform is also cast in some doubt. This is largely because the sense of stability that we had about the nation-state is radically undermined by globalisation. But to acknowledge this sense of global displacement is also to ask what the connection was between nation and state in the first place. Earlier states, before modernity, were often city-states. The obsession with the nation as unit, and the common practice of using the terms *nation* and *state* interchangably, overlooks the fact that the state is a local and regional presence in our lives, not only a federal one. The focus on 'nation-state' when it comes, say, to the discussion of welfare also means that we risk losing sight of, for example, the welfare work done informally by women in the private sphere, as Reiger argues.

Where, then, do we place the nation? What is a nation? Is it the same as a 'society'? Probably most work in sociology defines its object as the study of society, not the nation; the nation is given a more political, institutional glaze, being associated with constitutions, governments, international affairs, and overseas trade. But the nation is also conjured up by politicians as though it were an imagined community, as in Paul Keating's assertion that, after years of Liberal disarray and divisiveness, the Labor Government would again make us 'One Nation'. Certainly it can be argued that we are not, and have never been, one nation; ask the Aboriginal nation whether they belong to the same nation as Paul Keating. Are we then one society? Yes, perhaps, but only in the sense of the organisational unit presumed by sociologists: a manageable unit of analysis, a unit of claimed political sovereignty and apparent economic autonomy. Even then, the concept of Australia becomes more complex once we question the notions of 'nation' and 'society'. What is Australia? Viewed practically, it is not the shape of the land mass on the tourist logos or the red heart some believe it to be, but a bunch of cities thrown up largely against the edge of the continent, a margin that winds around the periphery of the map. That, in any case, is where most of the people are. That is where, we might say, society is; but it is not clear that it is the nation-state, which we still, most of us, probably persist in identifying with Canberra. Society, at the very least, exists outside the State; the state could collapse, in principle, but society would still exist. In fact, it is society that holds together everyday life, upon which states rest. To this extent, nation-building (like Federation) may be seen in Australia as a game for boys, whereas civil society has disproportionately been built by female hands (see Grimshaw et al. 1994). To speak of nation or state, therefor, is also to raise issues of sex or gender.

What is a nation?

What is a nation? Let us engage now in a more general level of discussion, for ours is not the only nation, and the new global order we increasingly encounter is also, still, a world system of nation-states. The logical structure of this book is to shift through levels of increasing abstraction and size: self, community, nation, world system. The terms themselves all cross-refer; define one, and you begin almost inevitably to define another. Is a nation, then, a group of selves or individuals? The answer to this question is yes, but it does not much advance our understanding, except in the already observed sense that nations, like individuals, have multiple sources of identity. Is the nation then a community? Certainly some would identify or associate the two categories (Tönnies 1955). As Ken Dempsey observes, however, in Chapter 13, 'community' is also a loaded or essentially contested category; the whole reason we continue to be fascinated by terms like this in sociology is because different people persist in putting different values on them. Sociology itself is an essentially contested discipline, which is exactly what makes it interesting. Sociology is a discipline that questions. *Community*, as Dempsey shows, is a term used both prescriptively and actively: a community is a traditional group, like a settled country town or a bounded ethnic group, but, today, it is also something we actively construct — it is more fluid, like a social movement, or a group of enthusiasts for music or sport. Communities differ: some we inherit, others we elect to be part of, some we find constricting, others we feel free in. Significantly, as Dempsey points out, community is often valued, as signifying place, belonging, security, an escape route out of the uncertainties of modernity. 'Community' is often contrasted invisibly with 'city', where life is presumed to be lonely, alienated, isolated, and rootless. But cities are also places where many people feel free; and, as I suggested earlier, Australia's real identity is actually derived more from a bunch of cities and suburbs scattered around the edge of the continent than from settled inland communities, real or imagined. Ironically, perhaps, sociologists, until recently, may have spent more time worrying about community than city; yet inhabitants of the twentieth century are increasingly city-dwellers, and this is the case throughout the world system, from Mexico and Brazil to Perth and Sydney. Cities, we can reasonably expect, will become more, rather than less, prominent in everyday life, and therefore also in sociology. This is not least of all because, when it comes to 'national identity', we can usually expect that individuals to define themselves regionally as well as nationally (when I am in the USA, I come from Australia; when I am in Australia, I come from Melbourne).

So what is a nation? If it is not a bunch of selves, or a community, could it be a group of communities? The image of a group of communities may be helpful: it reminds us that Australia is now, and has, in fact, always been, multicultural (we associate cultures with communities, rather than with the nation-state). Yet there is also a cloud of other associations to do with identity, nation-state, and community. In the previous chapter I referred to recent and influential discussions that connect up nationalism with the ideas of the 'imagined community' and the 'invention of tradition'. Modern nations create narratives or myths in order to bond people together, sometimes through ritual, sometimes more passively through cultural media, like television, sport, or the press. A 'people' does not pre-exist, or evolve as a unitary group; it has to be created and reproduced as such, for modern societies generate disorder and disruption at the same time that they generate integration and stability. The idea of the nation, and of a world of nations, is a new idea and a phenomenon peculiar to modernity. Like much else that is new, however, it is constantly shadowed by tradition, just as we, as individuals, are ghosted by our pasts.

Is a nation then its geography? I have suggested that it is not; place matters, but Australia is a culture more than a landscape. In terms of the arguments about imagined communities, shared memory weighs heavily. We are held to belong to a nation if we share its secular religion, if we identify with its gains and losses, not least of all in wars between nations. We are held to be citizens if we behave loyally. Before the massive world wars of our century, nation was identified with culture (or community), with language-group, race, and religion. Nations were imagined as ethnically homogeneous groups (which of course, even then, they never were: Neapolitans come from Naples, not Italy, and the Welsh or Scots did not come from England). Even in the twentieth century, Australians were amusingly described as 'independent Australian Britons', as though somehow they were even more British than the British because they were independent; the Scots, Welsh, Irish, Indians, and Sri Lankans, by this criterion, were less British than Australians were. The icon of Anzac similarly points back to a view of nation as a masculine bond forged in the purgatory of war, in this case at Gallipoli. Even to suggest this connection raises the issue of the connection between nation and nationalism, which so often in the twentieth century has been deeply implicated with racism and chauvinism, even genocide. In the case of Nazism, to pick the most extreme example, notions of race, language, blood, and soil generated both assertions of Aryan supremacy and the anti-Semitism that killed six million Jews, along with various other 'alien' elements, such as gypsies, communists, and homosexuals. This is not to say that all nationalisms are the same, or of this pernicious, destructive kind; Australians of my generation, again, remember the Whitlam years as a moment of cultural nationalism, when a subordinate antipodean culture flowered in areas such as film, rock music, and writing. Nevertheless, after a century of slaughter in the name of civilised values, we still often, and rightly, twitch when talk of nation spills over into talk of nationalism.

Divided nations in a new world order

If nations are constructed units — symbolic groups often attracted to myths of foundation like revolution or war — they also manage to contain, and often suppress, difference. Nations, as we have seen, can be viewed as divided by gender or sex, by the difference of experience in worlds we call public and private. Nations can tolerate ethnic difference, but more often they seek to assimilate it, waiting, as White Australia's founding fathers did, for the Aborigines to die out and, less brutally, encouraging 'new Australians' after the Second World War to feel ashamed of their origins, to anglicise their names and take up football or mothers' clubs, to shut up and fit in. In addition to these kinds of distinctions, nations are divided into classes. Sociologists have traditionally viewed classes as national actors, if only because domestic politics has historically been conducted on national lines, and labour and capital have usually been major political interests, as well as economic forces. As

Brian Graetz points out in Chapter 14, class analysis has been one dominant tradition utilised by sociologists in making sense of national inequality.

Both Karl Marx and Max Weber focused on the national dimensions of class. Even though Marx claimed to have an internationalist politics — 'the working class know no fatherland' — his historical writing explained processes of class struggle in particular settings, such as France or England, and his general model of capitalist production in *Capital* also worked on the level of the nation, with two (or three) dominant classes. Weber, for his part, was a German nationalist who worried about the poor working and living conditions of marginal Prussian workers. Classes — or their organisations, like trade unions — then worked on a national level. Attempts at international organisation — like the International Workingmen's movement or, later, the International Labor Organisation — were like the United Nations: good ideas that never really came to much. Marx, however, was only half right when he viewed class struggle as central and potentially revolutionary : it was central, if not revolutionary. Rather than revolution, the common path into the twentieth century in Western societies was that of reform or compromise between the dominant competing classes. The postwar or Keynesian welfare state can be understood as one such compromise: the labour movement showed its loyalty to the nation by fighting in the world wars, and the welfare state — health care system, public housing, and so on — was part of the resultant trade-off. National loyalty held the welfare state and the nation-state together.

In other words, then, nations have also faced the task of generating social solidarity. Until recently some have followed the Durkheimian clue, and viewed high levels of male employment as the key to stability and order, generating the wage-earners' welfare state in the process (Durkheim 1893; Castles 1985). Others have sought to regulate class conflict through instruments of economic and social protection, like tariffs or arbitration, producing social contracts with regulated standards of living to secure relative harmony in social reproduction. Now this is another area in which the nation-state, or at least the postwar class compromise, is under threat. For, increasingly, capitalists and even working classes are scattered across the globe. Both money and those who control and own it have always been mobile, ready to chase profits wherever they might lead. The labour movements, by comparison, have been geographically fixed; when an Australian-owned firm relocates 'offshore' in South-East Asia, its previous workers are stuck here, unemployed and defenceless. At the same time — for example, in continental Europe or across the Mexican border of the USA — labour is increasingly mobile and without nation. Thus, for example, a thorough sociological analysis of what we call 'Germany' would also have to take into account what we call 'Turkey', because of the significant numbers of so-called Turkish 'guestworkers', labour without rights of citizenship, who have contributed to German economic growth. The same is true of Africans in France, or Mexicans in the USA. To put it more emphatically, parts of the Turkish working class are now in Germany, just as (by default) parts of the old Australian labour movement now have their work done in the Philippines. The recipient nation-state therefore not only benefits from disorganised, cheap immigrant labour, but also saves the State the expense of socialising and educating these workers before, and supporting them after, their working lives.

Is the nation-state then a thing of the past? Hardly. What is becoming increasingly obsolete is the neat, modular way of thinking that portrayed the nation-state as a clearly bounded and operational unit. Not all of this is negative. Into the new century, it is probable that individuals will identify more with regions, whether they be localities, like cities, or spheres, like the Pacific or Asia. Given the powerful and often nasty link between nations and punitive forms of nationalism, this may be no bad thing, though, of course, particular forms of local identity can also degenerate into tribalism like that associated with horrific activities such as 'ethnic cleansing'. Globalisation itself is also as exciting as it is threatening. What remains most important with regard to globalisation is that sociologists keep at it, casting off the illusions that they will periodically acquire, and arguing for reform wherever possible. The biggest shift to have taken place in our own times is arguably still a politically initiated shift of cultural horizons, made manifest in the now widespread sense that social problems cannot be overcome. This is a belief far more than it is a reality. We are located between nation-state and global system, and the challenge for sociology is to identify the room for manoeuvre between the two.

Discussion questions

1 What is a nation-state?
2 How are nation-states created and reproduced?
3 'The workers have no country'. Discuss.
4 If Australia's founding myth was established at Gallipoli, what does this mean for the nation today?
5 What does it mean to say that we are Australians?

Recommended reading

- Alexander, J. (ed.) 1988, *Durkheimian Sociology: Cultural Studies*, Cambridge University Press, New York.

An advanced, rather than introductory text, that picks up on the insights of Hobsbawm and Anderson in terms of cultural reproduction and ritual, following the idea that nation works, in a way, like religion.

- Beilharz, P. 1994, *Postmodern Socialism: Romanticism, City and State*, Melbourne University Press, Melbourne.

A brief analysis of future and past — with specific reference to globalisation and prospects for social reform — that asks 'Are we beyond the age of social reconstruction?'.

- Beilharz, P. 1996, 'Postmodern Citizenship', in W. Hudson (ed.), *Rethinking Australian Citizenship*, University of New South Wales Press, Sydney.

A discussion of citizenship after globalisation that asks 'Can we be citizens of regions?'.

- Carter, D. and Hudson, W. (eds) 1993, *The Republicanism Debate*, New South Wales University Press, Sydney.

An interesting and accessible collection of views about nation, identity, unity, and division, bringing together the views of sociologists and other scholars and politicians.

- Civic Experts Group 1995, *Whereas the People ... Civics and Citizenship Education*, AGPS, Canberra.

It would be useful to read this important report discussing citizenship, nation-state, and education in connection with 'Postmodern Citizenship' above.

- Coleman, P. (ed.) 1962, *Australian Civilization*, Cheshire, Melbourne.

A classic period Australian text; read it together with Nile and identify differences (and gaps) in both books. Ask yourself what it might mean to speak of Australian civilisation.

- Drew, P. 1994, *The Coast Dwellers: A Radical Reappraisal of Australian Identity*, Penguin Books, Melbourne.

An exaggerated but important case for the view that Australian identity primarily looks 'out' rather than 'in'; that we are more outward looking than provincial.

- Nile, R. (ed.) 1994, *Australian Civilisation*, Oxford University Press, Melbourne.

This book revisits the terrain covered by Coleman's writers in the 1962 collection of the same name; read the two together.

- Renan, E. 1882, 'The Nation as a Community', in A. Arblaster, and S. Lukes (eds) 1971, *The Good Society*, Methuen, London.

A classic text of early modern thinking that is deeply traditionalistic in identifying nation and community.

- Smelser, N. 1994, *Sociology*, Blackwell and UNESCO, Oxford.

A very useful handbook; chapter 7, on nations, offers some interesting historical and cultural views on European experience based on material by John Keane.

Globalisation

Some sociologists tell me that, as I get older, there will be fewer real revolutions to bump into. The dark forces of the new world order will nip real revolution in the bud; the postmodern conciousness of the young will be unable to sustain revolutionary action; or globalisation will mean that you and I, the rank and file of real revolutions, will not be able to locate and confront, still less overthrow, the world's ruling elites. Could that be so?

Rowan Ireland, Chapter 24

Chapter 20

Development

Alberto Gomes

Jeli is a small rural town in the north-eastern state of Kelantan in Peninsular Malaysia. Encircled by several farming communities that depend primarily on rice cultivation and cash-cropping of rubber and oil palm, it has experienced considerable growth in recent years, but it is still a relatively unknown town. This changed in April 1993 when it received mention in most of the national newspapers. On one fine April afternoon in 1993 the shocking news of the tragic slaying of three Malay farmers by a group of Malaysian Aborigines in a small hamlet nearby reverberated in this idyllic town.

As the story goes, an attempt by six Malays to evict about forty Aborigines from an area where the Aborigines had established their dwellings had ended tragically. Claiming that he had bought the piece of land, one of the Malay men demanded that the Aborigines move out immediately. The Aborigines refused, on the 'grounds' that they were residing on their hereditary homeland, which was within the recently state-designated Aboriginal reserve. After a prolonged argument, tempers flared and the situation became very tense. The Malays began to abuse the Aborigines and physically threatened them with their machetes. One thing led to another and, after a Malay man assaulted the village head, a scuffle broke out. When the dust settled, three dead Malays were found: one had succumbed to the injuries inflicted on him by the Aborigines, and two Malay men were found dead in their van a kilometre or so away, alleged to have been killed by blowpipe-propelled poisoned darts. The incident was reported to the police, and nine Aborigines were arrested and charged for manslaughter. The court trial is still in progress at the time of writing (February 1995).

I initially received the news of this incident with a certain degree of scepticism because such a display of violence was out of character for the Malaysian Aborigines, who I know well as a researcher. I have visited and stayed at the Aboriginal village near Jeli on several occasions since 1975, and not once have I ever witnessed any form of aggression by the people. In fact, as other anthropologists have noted, Malaysian Aborigines profess and practise non-violence. How, then, can we explain this act of violence?

Using a sociological imagination that penetrates beneath the surface of social behaviour, one might uncover the underlying factors or structures that direct or influence social practices. What, then, is the main underlying factor that could explain this

Aboriginal act of violence? Why was there conflict over land in the first instance? As I will demonstrate in this chapter, the answers to these questions may be found in an examination of the impact of development on, or the experience of modernity of, people such as the Malay farmers and Malaysian Aborigines. This chapter critically examines the concept and practice of development, focusing on the implications of development for people in the developing world. We will begin with the question 'What is development?'.

What is development?

Development means different things to different people. There is no clear consensus about the meaning of the term. One of the main reasons for this is that the theories or ideas informing the policies and practice of development vary. To put it in a some-what simple way, the theories may be classified into two types: liberal/neoclassical economy theories and radical/political economy theories. Development, as a concept, emerged after the Second World War, although developmental policies and practices have a much longer history. Colonial regimes — European as well as non-European — have in almost all cases intervened in the lives of their subjects in attempts to institute and engineer social, economic, and cultural changes in the colonies. The Romans were famous for implementing 'developmental' programs such as the construction of roads and canals, and the imposition of Roman law in their 'colonies' during the hey-day of the Roman Empire. Aryans did the same after they conquered part of what is known today as India, and since the fifteenth century the Europeans have trans-formed many of their colonies in the Americas, Asia, and Africa. Europeans attempted to morally justify their establishment of colonial rule in many parts of the world in terms of 'civilising mission' or 'White-man's burden'. The 'natives' were per-ceived and depicted as 'primitive' or 'backward' peoples desperately in need of civil-ising. Civilisation was defined almost without exception as Christian and European.

Global politics changed radically after the Second World War. Many of the colonies were able to break free from the direct domination of Europe and achieve independent status. They generally ceased to be viewed officially as 'backward' peoples, but became known as 'emerging' nations. Terms like 'civilising mission' and 'White-man's burden' were replaced by more neutral-sounding concepts, such as 'development' and 'modernisation'. One could argue that the concept of develop-ment emerged from the ruins of war-torn Europe as the guiding principle in the range of American initiatives — such as the Truman Doctrine, Marshall Plan, Point Four Doctrine — in the European Recovery Program. Several international agencies, such as the United Nations, the World Bank, and the International Monetary Fund, saw the light of day during this period. They have all played, and continue to play, a prominent role in the promotion and implementation of development.

Following the ideas of a French demographer, Alfred Sauvy, the world was divided into three: First, Second and Third Worlds. The First World comprised of nations perceived to be developed and democratic, which essentially included North America and most of non-communist Europe, while the Second World referred to the communist nations. The Third World is a residual concept, which includes a 'mixed bag' of nations that do not belong to the First and the Second Worlds. In describing the Third World, either one, or a combination, of such terms as *backward, undeveloped, emerging*, and *developing* were used. As a concept, the Third World is somewhat impotent, as it refers to a disparate group of nations with hardly any semblance of unity. Furthermore, the concept has been much criticised by 'Third World' leaders and scholars because of its association with other loaded terms, such as *backward* and *undeveloped*. Nowadays there seems to be a preference for terms such as *North* and *South* to refer to the North American/European nations and the Latin American/African/Asian nations respectively. There are also other new terms such as *less developed countries* (LDCs) and *newly industrialising countries* (NICs). In spite of this plethora of new labels, the concept of development as used in mainstream thinking or by international agencies seems unchanged. While there have been some concessions made with regard to issues related to culture and equity, particularly in terms of gender and ethnicity, the emphasis of development is firmly on economic growth and industrialisation. Furthermore, development is almost invariably measured primarily on the basis of economic criteria, such as income and mode of production, rather than social indicators, such as literacy, well-being, and equity.

Liberal and neoclassical approaches

During the 1950s and 1960s several theories, known collectively as modernisation theories, were prominent in influencing developmental thinking. One of the best known of these theories was outlined in Walt Rostow's *The Stages of Economic Growth* (1960). Like his modernisationist counterparts, Rostow conceptualised development as movement along a continuum of historical change, upon which all societies can be located. For Rostow, all developing societies had to pass through five stages: (i) traditional; (ii) pre-takeoff society; (iii) takeoff; (iv) the drive to maturity; and (v) mass consumption society. Other modernisation theorists simply view the process of modernisation as the transformation of traditional society into modern society, invariably represented by 'advanced' Western nations. Development is considered to occur through the diffusion of certain attributes of the developed nations. As one of the modernisation theorists, Shmuel Noah Eisenstadt (1966, p. 1), puts it, 'modernisation is the process of change toward those types of social, economic and political systems that have developed in Western Europe and North America from the seventeenth century to the nineteenth and have then spread to other European countries and in the nineteenth and twentieth centuries to the South American, Asian and African continents'.

Modernisation theorists have advocated or promoted changes that are seen as necessary for development (or takeoff, in Rostow's words) at several levels. Some of the more psychologically oriented theorists, such as Daniel Lerner and David McClelland, have prescribed the inculcation of what were seen as 'modern' values and personal traits, such as achievement orientation, empathy, and democratic ideals. McClelland (1962), for example, believed that the transfer of what he called the 'mental virus of n Ach' (need for Achievement) was the key to modernisation. Most modernisationalists, however, have stressed that changes should occur at the institutional and organisational levels. Influenced by the writings of Émile Durkheim, Max Weber, Ferdinand Tönnies, and Talcott Parsons, theorists such as Neil Smelser (1963), Berthold Hoselitz (1960), and Eisenstadt (1966) have prescribed the introduction or imposition of capitalist economic practices, markets, division of labour, bureaucratic rationality, modern state structures, and 'modern' technology as means of development or modernisation. In essence, these theories suggest that non-Western countries and people can achieve development by imitating Western social and economic values and practices. In other words, they will 'take-off on the road to maturity' if they adopt Western-styled capitalism and liberal democracy, and for this reason some refer to modernisation as Westernisation.

These theories were heavily criticised in the 1970s and 1980s, but they seem to be resilient and have re-emerged in new guises in the recent neo-liberal push. Today we hear governments and international agencies promoting development strategies based on a free-market principle and on economic rationality in their endeavours towards sustaining economic growth and industrialisation. How can we link such developmental thinking and practices to the sad event in Jeli? The incident may be traced to the implementation of modernisation policies in two state-sponsored development projects: development programs for 'marginal' communities and the green revolution.

Development for marginalised people

In almost every country there are people who are, or have been, marginalised as a result of their disadvantaged socio-economic and demographic position in relation to dominant or settler societies. The Australian Aborigines and the Malaysian *Orang Asli* (Aborigines) are examples of such people. Similar to other indigenous peoples all over the world, the Australian Aborigines and the *Orang Asli* are relatively much poorer (measured in terms of income and material possessions), have a higher rate of infant mortality, a lower rate of literacy, and a lower life expectancy than other people in their respective countries. It is on the basis of such facts that governments and international agencies have embarked on developmental programs, inspired by modernisation theories, to improve the living conditions of such marginalised communities. In Malaysia the government has implemented, since the early 1960s, several development programs for the *Orang Asli* aimed at drawing the people 'into the mainstream of society'. It has provided health, medical, and educational facilities, and sponsored rural development programs such as resettlement projects and the promotion of cash-cropping (Gomes 1990). A majority of the *Orang Asli* communities were engaged in hunting and gathering, and shifting cultivation at the time of Malaysia's independence in 1957, and now many are involved in cash-cropping of rubber, oil palm, and fruit, as well as wage labour. The government, from a typical modernisation perspective, views a lifestyle based on hunting and gathering as backward and outmoded. To 'develop' the people, the government has carried out resettlement projects, as a result of which *Orang Asli* living in small traditional settlements have been moved into Malay-styled villages.

Since the inception of the resettlement program in 1968, a little more than one-sixth (about 12 500 people) of the total *Orang Asli* population have been resettled. The Jeli *Orang Asli* are a case in point. In 1972, together with six other settlements, they were enticed to move out of their traditional homeland into a patterned village with a much reduced resource base. A health clinic and a national-type school were set up, and people were encouraged to grow cash crops. While the medical program was successful, the other developmental efforts produced more problems than benefits for the people. I shall discuss these problems later in the context of theories critiquing modernisation perspectives.

Green revolution

The improvement of agricultural systems was considered a priority by many newly independent nations. Famines and the high incidence of malnutrition in many of the 'Third World' nations were linked to the low productivity and relative inefficiency of traditional agriculture, and to the problem of rapid population growth. To solve the perceived problem of food shortage, governments, in conjunction with international agencies such as the World Bank and USAID (United States Agency for International Development), implemented agricultural development programs that involved the introduction of scientifically developed high-yield varieties (HYV) of food crops and the use of chemical fertilisers, pesticides, and machines like combine harvesters (Shiva 1991). Since the 1940s, scientists — particularly from the International Maize and Wheat Improvement Centre (CIMMYT), based in Mexico — have conducted research in order to create varieties of wheat that are high-yielding, rapid-growing, disease-resistant, and with short stiff stems. By the early 1960s they developed varieties that were subsequently cultivated in Mexico, and wheat production expanded by over 5 per cent annually; Mexico began to export wheat, rather than import as in the past. Such technology was exported to other countries, such as India, where the introduction of HYV in places like the Punjab resulted in remarkable increases in wheat production. This 'success' had inspired scientists to work on other food crops.

By 1966 the International Rice Research Institute, set up in Los Banos in the Philippines, released a high-yielding rice variety that yielded almost four times more rice than the traditional varieties. The green revolution started to gain momentum in the late 1960s, and by the 1970s it had spread around the globe. In Malaysia the government sponsored such programs in the rice-growing areas of the country along with its land-development schemes, which open up forested areas for settlement and cash-crop cultivation for mainly landless Malay peasants.

In terms of agricultural productivity, the green revolution was certainly a success. Food production expanded enormously, converting some countries from importers to net exporters of grain. As G. Conway and D. Barbier (1990, p. 20) indicate, per capita food production in the developing countries has grown by 7 per cent since the mid-1960s, and as much as 27 per cent in Asia. However, as researchers inspired by radical/political economy theories of development have argued, there are several problems and hidden costs associated with the green revolution.

Political economy theories of development

In the late 1950s several scholars, mostly Latin American specialists, began to formulate new approaches to understanding development. Drawing inspiration primarily from Marxist perspectives, these scholars sought to analyse 'Third World' economic woes such as development failures, unemployment, and debt crisis by applying a number of key Marxist concepts and methods of analysis, including surplus accumulation, exploitation, imperialism, and dialectical reasoning. In dialectical reasoning, an idea (referred to as a thesis) is counterposed with a differing or opposing idea (anti-thesis) in the process of reasoning in order to create a novel idea (synthesis), which contains elements of the thesis and anti-thesis. This method was applied to development to analyse critically the different ideas related to capitalism. Modernisation theorists view the imposition of capitalist economy into the 'Third World' as an important step in 'Third World' development. Capitalism is supposed to wipe out poverty and improve the general well-being of the developing world. To counter the modernisation thesis, neo-Marxists contend that capitalism, instead of alleviating, actually exacerbates poverty and social inequality. They go so far as to argue that underdevelopment and economic stagnation, as observed in much of the developing world, is a product of past colonialism and of modernisation since the 1950s, considered by some to be neo-colonialism.

In true Marxist fashion, political economy theorists of development assert that, for capitalism to thrive, it needs to accumulate surplus from production and exchange, commonly known as profits, which then serves as capital investment for further production and trading. Much capitalist surplus is accumulated through exploitation, which refers to the appropriation of part of a producer's labour or product by a non-producer on the basis of ownership or control of the means of production. Capitalism also accumulates surplus through imperialism (a concept developed by Lenin), which denotes the expansion of capitalism through monopolistic control of markets and production systems worldwide.

Political economy theories of development are of two types: circulationist and productionist. Those that fit into the circulationist category include Paul Baran (1957) and André Frank's (1969) theory of underdevelopment, Fernando Cardoso's and Enzo Faletto's (1979) dependency model, and Immanuel Wallerstein's (1979) world systems theory. These theories focus on international trade and on surplus-extraction by capitalist countries, sectors, and corporations (especially transnational corporations, or TNCs) via trade. In other words, they stress the impact of external relations on the developing world. Productionists, on the other hand, emphasise the implications of capitalism for the production systems in the developing sectors once capitalism begins to take root. They are more interested in the internal dynamics of the production system as it responds to the penetration of capitalism.

Despite this difference in focus, both the circulationists and productionists generally argue that underdevelopment is an outcome of the diffusion of capitalism through development and modernisation, which have plunged the developing world (called 'satellites' or 'periphery') into a state of dependence on, and indebtedness to, the capitalist centres (also referred to as either 'metropolis' or 'core' in the dependency literature). Such dependence accords the capitalist centre dominance over its periphery, giving it definite control of the market, the production system, and even financial institutions. This, in turn, is said to facilitate the centre's appropriation of economic surplus from the developing world through several means. These include the exploitation of 'Third World' labour by paying lower wages, the maintenance of unequal terms of trade by exchanging lower priced raw materials from the 'Third World' with higher priced manufactured goods from the centre, and giving out tied loans, which plunges the developing world into severe debt crisis. Every move of the centre in its relation with the periphery becomes a vicious cycle, throwing the periphery into ever-increasing dependence, indebtedness, underdevelopment, and poverty.

The Jeli incident revisited

In order to find an explanation for the Jeli violence, we would need to explore how development has affected the people at the centre of the tragedy in light of political economy theories. The Malaysian Aborigines, as a result of resettlement and State-sponsored agricultural projects, have had to cope with several lifestyle changes. Since they have been confined to an area much smaller than their traditional homelands, they have lost much of their resource base, leading to a decline in subsistence-oriented activities, such as hunting, gathering, and farming, which are longstanding primary sources of livelihood. Their increasing involvement in cash-cropping and wage labour has taken a further toll on subsistence production, which in turn has entailed a growing dependence on market-produced food. To meet this ever-increasing demand for externally produced food and manufactured goods, the Aborigines have had to work harder and longer to earn more money to pay the traders. They have become producers and consumers of commodities (which are things that can be bought and sold), a process known as 'commoditisation'. They have also become increasingly dependent on a market economy that is beyond their control.

In a study of another group of Malaysian Aborigines, whom I observed for a period of one year (from November 1982 to October 1983), I found that a sample of twelve individuals allocated three times more work time to commodity-production than to subsistence-production. Their quest for money stems primarily from their dependence on the market for almost all of their food supply. Sample households in the study village obtained 97 per cent, 88 per cent, and 93 per cent of their consumption of rice, meat, and fish respectively from the market. In this study I found that increased commoditisation, among other things, has engendered a shift from communal to private ownership of property and, concomitantly, a decline in the sharing practices that serve to level off wealth differences, leading eventually to a widening gap between rich and poor villagers (Gomes 1991). There was also a growing trend towards gender inequality, as development projects tend to favour males more than women. This finding complements numerous other studies, which indicate that development has engendered, among other things, greater impoverishment of women, increasing their workloads, while reducing their employment options and social status.

This Malaysian case, which is by no means unique, clearly illustrates the arguments made by political economy theorists of development. It is evident that development has resulted in general destitution among the Malaysian Aborigines by making them less self-reliant, more vulnerable to the whims of a market economy, and ultimately impoverishing the people by robbing them of much of their resource base. Studying the population dynamics of the Jeli Aborigines over a twelve-year period (from 1976 to 1988), I found that the mortality rate was increasing as a result of the higher incidence of transmittable diseases, such as dysentery and cholera. This, I have argued, is linked to their resettlement. Confining people into smaller areas than they are accustomed to has forced them to live in poor sanitary, and crowded, conditions, facilitating the transmission of diseases. Furthermore, their nutritional status has also declined. They no longer are able to obtain a balanced diet from their waning subsistence pursuits, and they do not earn enough money to buy market-produced nutritious food.

Similar depressing conditions are also to be found in rural communities affected by the green revolution. Increased mechanisation and the use of chemical fertilisers and pesticides have put people in a situation of growing dependence on transnational corporations for supplies of chemical inputs, on financial institutions for loans to buy machines and agro-chemicals, and on external agricultural expertise. This has compounded indebtedness, leading to a widening gap between rich farmers — who have been able to take advantage of their position to accumulate surpluses by buying more land and agricultural inputs — and poor farmers, who have simply accumulated more debts and fallen into misery, eventually losing their land, which is their primary source of livelihood. Several studies of the effects of the green revolution have reported increasing landlessness, unemployment, and social inequality as the result of such agricultural development.

How is this related to violence? Vandana Shiva (1991) illustrates this in her study of the impact of the green revolution in the Indian state of Punjab. In recent years Punjab has been thrown into turmoil as a result of ethnic conflict, which has left about 15 000 people dead between 1986 and 1991. The Punjab tragedy is commonly presented as an outcome of communal conflict between two religious groups — the Sikhs and the Hindus. Shiva, however, traces the conflicts and violence in contemporary Punjab to the ecological and political demands of the green revolution. She points out that agricultural development has left Punjab with 'diseased soils, pest-infested crops, water-logged deserts, and indebted and discontented farmers' (Shiva 1991, p. 12). The high level of frustration and discontentment culminated in acts of violence. Typically, people began to direct their anger towards members of other communities, escalating into ethnic strife and violence.

One could readily identify several similarities between the Punjab case and the Jeli incident. The scarcity of farming land resulting from the expansion of large-scale cash-crop plantations owned by capitalist corporations ('agribusiness'), the accumulation of land by rich farmers, and ecological degradation have created a class of landless peasants. The Malays involved in the Jeli incident belonged to such a class. To escape their predicament, they began to encroach on the ever-dwindling areas belonging to the Malaysian Aborigines. The Aborigines, having to cope with the growing pressures of entering the 'mainstream of society', have been pushed to unbearable limits, leading to a breakdown in their social norms — hence the uncharacteristic display of violence on that tragic April day in 1993.

Discussion questions

1   What do you understand *development* to mean? Explain the reasons for the different views on the meaning of *development*?
2   Compare and contrast neo-liberal and political economic theories of development.
3   How does development affect minorities such as indigenous peoples?
4   What is the green revolution? What are its implications for peasants in the developing world?
5   Explain how the Jeli tragedy is linked to developmental programs.

Recommended reading

For comprehensive and general discussion of development issues and theories, the following books are particularly useful:

*   Allen, T. and Thomas, A. (eds) 1992, *Poverty and Development in the 1990s*, Oxford University Press and Open University, Oxford.
*   Hettne, B. 1995, *Development Theory and the Three Worlds*, 2nd edn, Longman, Essex.
*   Sachs, W. (ed.) 1992, *The Development Dictionary: A Guide to Knowledge as Power*, Zed Books, London.
*   So, A. 1990, *Social Change and Development: Modernization, Dependency and World-Systems Theories*, Sage, Newbury Park.
*   Worsley, P. 1984, *The Three Worlds*, Weidenfeld and Nicholson, London.

The following deal with the impact of development on indigenous peoples and ethnic minorities:

*   Bodley, J. 1990, *Victims of Progress*, Mayfield, Mountain View, Calif.
*   Burger, J. 1990, *The Gaia Atlas of First Peoples: A Future for the Indigenous World*, Gaia Books, London.

For an overview of gender issues in development, you might find the following books helpful:

- Momsen, J. 1991, *Women and Development in the Third World*, Routledge, London.
- Mosse, J. 1993, *Half the World, Half a Chance: An Introduction to Gender and Development*, Oxfam, Oxford.

The following is a readable and interesting account of the impact of the green revolution with a focus on India:

- Shiva, V. 1991, *The Violence of the Green Revolution: Third World Agriculture, Ecology and Politics*, Zed Books, London.

Chapter 21

Urbanisation

Kerreen Reiger

Describing London in 1844 as 'the commercial capital of the world', Friedrich Engels commented that he knew 'nothing more imposing' than the view from the Thames: 'The masses of buildings, the wharves on both sides ... the countless ships ... all this is so vast, so impressive, that a man cannot collect himself, but is lost in the marvel of England's greatness before he sets foot on English soil'. Introducing his discussion of 'The Great Towns', he went on,

> But the sacrifices which all this has cost become apparent later. After roaming the streets of the capital for a day or two, making headway through the human turmoil and the endless line of vehicles, after visiting the slums of the metropolis, one realizes ... that these Londoners have been forced to sacrifice the best qualities of their human nature, to bring to pass all the marvels of civilisation which crowd their city.

> Engels 1982 (1845), p. 57

Countries in Latin America, Asia, and Africa are now going through similar social upheaval to that wrought by industrialisation and urbanisation in the late eighteenth and nineteenth centuries in the West. They do so in a very different political context, however — that of postcolonialism — and in a new era of technological development. In order to make sense of global urban developments, we need to trace continuities while recognising these significant differences. I will establish a historical context, which will include Australian patterns, from which to move to current international concerns, especially the rapid urbanisation of the 'developing' world (for further discussion of 'development', see Chapter 20).

Considering the processes of urban development raises many important issues. These include issues concerning economic structures (industry, transport, and trade, and the organisation of labour, including its sexual division); social and cultural aspects of life, such as effects on family life, and artistic and educational endeavours; and political questions, such as the role of the State in overseeing the spatial re-organisation of buildings, services, and population necessitated by urbanisation.

Pre-modern cities

Not all human societies have had towns, let alone cities — that is, large concentrations of people and their activities in relatively permanent geographical space. Archaeologists and historians indicate that recognisable centres of urban life date back about 5000–8000 years. Their origins and significance are the subjects of considerable debate (Abu-Lughod 1991, ch. 2). The cities of the ancient Middle East, of India and China, and some highly developed cities established by the Mayans and others in Central and South Americas were complex centres of economic distribution, religious and other cultural activities, and political power (Bairoch 1988, chs 2–4). The contradictions between some of these aspects of urban life continue to the present, giving rise to considerable mixed feelings about cities, especially our large metropolises. One of the most powerful discussions of the central contradiction on which cities are based has been that of Lewis Mumford. In *The City in History* (1961), he points out that the early roots of urban life lay in the community support system of the village, on the one hand, and the military functions of the citadel, on the other.

European developments

The growth of cities, or urbanisation, has had a chequered history. For the purpose of our brief overview, two points need to be made. The first concerns the influential role played by ancient cities in European history. Athens and Rome, in particular, were the political and administrative, as well as commercial, centres of great empires, drawing together diverse populations, including slaves. They were primarily supported by their colonies: the soil of North Africa, Rome's 'bread basket', was ruined by growing grain to feed towns people across the Mediterranean (Girardet 1990, p. 171). The cities of ancient Western civilisation, however, were also centres of political, religious, and intellectual life, giving rise to ideas of 'democracy', practices such as doctors' 'Hippocratic oath', and institutionalised Christianity.

The second important point concerns the period of rapid urban growth and change in Europe from the late fifteenth century. Earlier imperial cities were replaced by new centres of exploration and commerce on the Atlantic coast, such as Lisbon. By the end of the sixteenth century, the balance of power tipped towards northern Europe, to port cities like Antwerp, London, and Amsterdam. As the feudal system of land-owning and controls on internal trade broke down, the transport of goods such as cloth and foodstuffs within Europe increased, leading to other cities developing in geographically favourable locations.

Colonial expansion

In the sixteenth century, European traders and armies, particularly those of Spain and Portugal, expanded into the so-called 'New World' (North and South America), in the name of 'God or glory or riches, or more likely riches plus glory plus God' (Bairoch 1988, p. 384). They were amazed by the extensive, highly developed urban centres they found, such as Tenochtitlan, now Mexico City, with its sophisticated irrigation, streets, and ceremonial sites. They proceeded, however, to destroy the economic and cultural basis of this urban life through direct expropriation of resources and the imposition of Christianity. This process of imperial conquest, along with ventures in the South Asian area, increased the volume of goods entering Europe, providing resources for expansion there. Thus, the European stock of precious metals, especially gold and silver, at least doubled in the course of a century (Bairoch 1988, p. 131). Soon the trade in African slaves was established to provide further labour for the mines in Central America and for plantations to grow highly profitable cash crops, such as sugar (Bairoch 1988, p. 131).

One of the first stages in the enormous social change that brought about both the modern market economy of international capitalism and urbanisation in its modern forms involved changes in agricultural production. Crops grown to be sold for cash increasingly replaced production for the immediate use of the local population, at first in the West, then in other parts of the European colonised world. New agricultural products, made possible by new forms of technology and energy, allowed market towns to grow into larger commercial centres. The biggest of these also became the base for distributing goods from further afield, providing new services such as communication, transport, and finance.

They also became new political centres for the developing capitalist class — entrepreneurs who were challenging the political authority of the landed aristocracy. They needed the population of the towns as consumers, and town property was a source of investment. Moneyed interests increasingly came to dominate, and the capitalist entrepreneurs were less interested in property with aesthetic or timeless qualities. The focus on the needs of the market generated new urban forms that disregarded not only history, but also topography. Whereas the cities of the Middle Ages had grown primarily for cultural and religious reasons, such as towns that grew up around cathedrals, or political considerations, like fortified castles, these new cities were unashamedly commercial. They used space differently; entrepreneurs were more interested in straight streets, to provide efficiency of transport, than in historically significant buildings and the natural shape of the landscape (Mumford 1961, p. 416).

The impact of industrial capitalism

By the seventeenth century, this new market system was well established, bringing about a rapid increase in urban populations, especially in Northern Europe, and consolidating shifts in the balance of political power to owners of city commercial enterprises and property. The growth of the nation-state offered protection to international trade (Abu-Lughod 1991, p. 43), in turn contributing to the wealth-accumulation and technological development that made the Industrial Revolution possible.

Conditions under early industrialisation

The industrialisation that took place during the late eighteenth and nineteenth centuries meant that factory life came to dominate the urban landscape, and living conditions generally deteriorated. Rapid population growth, and disruption of agricultural production, brought about the migration of people to the new cities in search of jobs and a better life (Hay 1994). A wholesale transformation of the physical environment was brought about by mines, factories and railroads. While the factories took the best sites and spilled waste into waterways, the population had to find accommodation nearby, living in extraordinary conditions of overcrowding. Existing houses were turned into barracks, and dehumanising slums developed (Engels 1973, pp. 57–75). All in all, this new urban environment was 'Dark, colorless, acrid, evil-smelling' (Mumford 1961, p. 472).

The new urban dwellers faced contradictions: on the one hand, payment of individual wages gave some new freedom from family ties, and greater mobility. On the other, working and living conditions were frequently appalling, and traditional kinship and cultural bonds were disrupted. The effects on women have been widely debated, paralleling contemporary debates about their situation in developing countries. Edward Shorter (1976), for example, argues that many seized new opportunities, such as to control their fertility, whereas L. Tilly and J. Scott (1980) point out that even young single women remained constrained by sending money home to their families. Certainly family life changed considerably. Much traditional women's work, such as producing food and clothing, was taken over by the industrial sector. Although initially preferred as a labour force because they could be employed at lower wages, women became increasingly dependent on male breadwinners (Gittins 1985, pp. 6–33). Without individuals realising it, these changes in domestic relationships were inevitably linked to much larger historical, and international, processes.

The world system, urbanisation and European colonialism
Earlier forms of imperialism — including the Ottoman (Turkish) Empire, ancient Rome, or the first stage of European expansion — had established military and political control over subject populations. Although extracting resources through taxes and labour power, they largely left the existing economic and social system alone. However, the unseemly scramble of rival European powers to acquire Asian and African territory by the later nineteenth century was different (Magdoff 1982, p. 18). Its goal was the increased integration of the colonies into the capitalist system of production, reflecting a change from merchant to industrial capital as the driving economic force. This produced increased demand for raw materials, such as cotton, timber, jute, rubber, and metals. Foodstuffs to feed the increasing European population, especially in urban areas, were also needed; including basic commodities such as meat and grain, but also more 'xotic' ones, such as sugar, tea, coffee, and cocoa (Frost 1994, p. 22). Colonial expansion also provided markets for European manufactures (Roberts 1978, ch. 2; King 1990a, p. 39; Magdoff 1982, pp. 18–19).

The port cities became bases for colonists pushing further inland, frequently led by military power, and followed by improved communication and transport. In some countries, such as India, local industries like silk and cotton were run down in order to encourage importation of British products. On the whole though, while it varied greatly around the world, the main period of intense European colonialism up until the First World War, even until the Second World War, primarily involved change in agricultural production. The colonial cities provided the link between what have come to be called the 'core' capitalist countries and those on the 'periphery' (Alavi and Shanin 1982; King 1990b, pp. 27–43).

The Australian case

Although distinctive in many ways, it was within this international context that the Australian colonies developed during the nineteenth century (Berry 1983, p. 14; Frost 1994). Founded first as penal settlements, they were part of attempts to deal with problems of urban crime and disorder in Great Britain. They soon became like other 'outposts of empire', providing resources for British industry and markets for its products. By the 1860s the major cities, especially Sydney and Melbourne, had developed as commercial bases and administrative centres (Berry 1994, pp. 531–3). The extent of industrialisation was still minimal, as most manufactured products were imported, but the availability of primary products and the wealth associated with the gold rushes encouraged considerable investment.

The patterns of White settlement in Australia were fairly typical of urbanisation in many White settler societies of the 'New World' (Maher 1986, pp. 13–14). The harsh physical environment was another reason for the extraordinary dominance of Australian capital cities, and the high degree of urban or suburban concentration of the population in the more fertile coastal areas. Michael Berry (1983; 1994) has argued that Australian urbanisation is best interpreted as *dependent development*: part of the waves of expansion and contraction of the capitalist system, but with local class relations also affecting spatial outcomes.

Australia is one of the most suburbanised nations in the world, and cities in Australia have also been shaped by distinctive housing patterns (Davison 1994). Forms of mechanised transport, such as tramcars, horse-drawn vehicles, and, later, cars, allowed domestic dwellings to spread far afield from the central city. The ready availability of land and the widely held belief that individually owned homes are the best place in which to 'raise a family' were further factors. According to one real-estate company: 'To own your own home is the hallmark of *Good* citizenship. It marks you as one possessing the virtues of a *Real Man* ... *The joy of home ownership* is natural ...' (cited in Reiger 1991, p. 34).

By the 1880s (Davison 1978; Harris 1988), but more noticeably in the later suburban boom times of the 1920s and 1950s, this dream of home ownership had different implications for women than for men. As the cities of industrial capitalism developed in the United Kingdom and in other Western countries, the idea of a separate sphere of private life, associated with women and children, became literally built into the physical environment in the form of suburban homes and gardens (Davidoff and Hall 1987; Allport 1986; Game and Pringle 1983). According to urban designers, suburbs became so-called 'dormitory' areas, a label that ignored the fact that women actually did their daily domestic work there. This pattern of urbanisation produced class and ethnic divisions as well (Johnson 1994, p. 64). The wealthy, White, Anglo-Saxon elite could be separated off physically from the 'workers' and those seen as 'other', whether indigenous or immigrants (Harris 1988). In the years following the Second World War, Australian cities became even more socially differentiated. The mass migration to Australia from southern Europe, itself part of global processes, led to particular 'ethnic' concentrations in specific inner urban areas, setting up new symbols of urban and suburban life (Jupp 1983; Lozanovska 1994).

Urbanisation in the postwar decades

In both the 'old' capitalist or 'core' countries and those of the 'periphery' or developing countries, the period after the Second World War produced qualitatively different forms of urban development. These were the result of changes in the distribution of labour, the organisation of capital investment and industrial production, and shifts in the political balance of power in the period of neocolonialism and postcolonialism. In the so-called 'developed' world, there was rapid urban expansion, in terms of both the extension of new forms of industrial development and suburban housing. In the United Kingdom, the planners attempted to remedy the problems of older industrial cities by building whole 'New Towns'. In North America and Australia, the increased use of cars allowed rapid suburban sprawl, resulting in worse pollution, the decline of inner city areas, and further class and ethnic spatial separation. Many parts of United States cities are now characterised by walled elite enclosures with security guards, and similar environments are emerging in Australia.

Even by the 1960–70s considerable urban unrest resulted from this social polarisation. Protests and violent riots were a response to the poor housing and limited work opportunities experienced by many Blacks and immigrant people, such as Puerto Ricans in the USA and the ex-colonial populations of West Indians and Pakistanis in the United Kingdom (Abu-Lughod 1991, pp. 253–66; Rex and Tomlinson 1979). Most developed or 'core' capitalist countries built up their labour forces during the postwar years by encouraging immigration from poorer areas, reflecting the movement of labour that is characteristic of the world economy in the period of multinational corporations. It was a strategy that had direct consequences for their cities.

Australian developments

After the Second World War Australia continued to be dependent on overseas investment, but increasingly on investment from the USA rather than the United Kingdom (Connell and Irving 1979, pp. 292–7; Berry 1994, p. 47). Heavy industry, such as iron and steel manufacture, had been established during the interwar and war years, still mainly based on British investment. The new postwar industries that produced consumer goods, household appliances, cars, leisure products, and the electrical and chemical products supporting them (plastics, for example) had 'huge capital and skill requirements [which were] quite literally, monopolised by capitalists in the central economies', particularly the USA, and later Japan (Berry 1994, p. 47). The cities were rebuilt as part of closer integration into the world market, with investment going into office expansion in central business districts and rapid suburban growth (Connell and Irving 1979, pp. 296–7).

In recent decades, population has also moved to new areas of Western Australia and Queensland, both centres of mining and tourism (Mullins 1993, p. 536). Since the 1970s the process of 'de-industrialisation' in the capital cities, with manufacturing being moved off-shore, has led to increased unemployment and the decline of working-class inner suburbs. Many have become home, however, to recent immigrants who value denser forms of urban living, which allows them to create their own cultural ambience. Others have been taken over and redeveloped by the affluent, professional middle class, a process known as 'gentrification' (Howe 1994).

The movement of women into the labour market since the 1960s has changed some aspects of Australian suburban life. Women provide the main labour force for the growing service sector, and facilities such as child care and suburban shopping complexes have developed to meet their needs, as well as to encourage further consumption (Spearitt 1994, pp. 135–6). However, the Australian dream of the satisfaction of suburban home ownership is now affected by women's absence during the day. As one woman said, 'I say 'hello' but I really don't know anybody. I suppose I'm too busy! That doesn't sound too good does it? Everybody *works* here . . .' (Richards 1994, p. 125). Nonetheless, suburbia continues to be seen as the best setting for 'raising a family'. Urban sprawl, pollution, and maldistribution of educational and health services are left to government 'planners' to deal with, and, indeed, transport and unemployment problems loom large (Mullins 1993). But Australian concerns seem small in the face of the totally unprecedented pace and scale of urbanisation in Third World or developing societies.

The world market economy, urbanisation, and 'development'

Urbanisation in countries directly controlled, or indirectly influenced, by former European colonialist powers is part of the same international trend affecting Australia. The new 'global' order since the 1960s has involved increased international integration of capital investment, of labour, and of production and consumption. Most power remains concentrated in the multinational (or transnational) corporations of the developed world, generating specific patterns of urban growth in developing countries. A distinctively new form of city — the 'global city' — located in the 'core' capitalist nations, especially the USA and Japan, plays a central role.

Global cities

As multinational corporations have come to dominate the world economy, a few giant conglomerates, consisting of complex, interlocked corporations, deal in diverse products, from energy to electronics to foodstuffs. The international scale of their operations makes management of finance, communications, and technological innovation critical. Management remains strategically concentrated in the headquarters of the corporations, mainly in New York, Tokyo, and London (Sassen 1991, p, 5; King 1990b, p. 14–17).

In spite of very different histories, cities as diverse as these now share similar features. Their business districts have extremely high densities, and focus on finance, marketing, and communications centres. The large numbers of affluent technical specialists employed in these areas enjoy 'expensive restaurants, luxury housing, luxury hotels, gourmet shops, boutiques . . .' (Sassen 1991, p. 9). However, there is increased social polarisation. Services (for example, cleaning and food preparation) are provided by low-paid workers, especially women, immigrants, and, in the USA and United Kingdom, often non-Whites. New York can easily be seen as at least two cities, depending on one's vantage point in Manhattan: the area around Central Park is worlds away from Harlem, even if only a couple of kilometres separate them geographically. The concentration of specialised knowledge in global cities drains resources away from the regional cities of developed countries, and limits the knowledge and power available to developing countries.

Urbanisation and 'underdevelopment'

The economic growth and sustainable urbanisation of postcolonial countries have been seriously compromised by the enforced economic dependency of these countries. This is apparent not only with regard to industrial and urban development, but also in the rural sector, with which the fate of the cities is inevitably linked. Capitalist core countries' demands for cash crops and other products continue to disrupt agricultural production, leading to the importation of food into countries that were once self-sufficient or exporters themselves (Bairoch 1988, pp. 462–3). The rural dislocation contributes to a flood of immigrants to swell the cities, affecting traditional kinship and gender relations in many different ways.

In places where women used to be major rural traders, as in West Africa, or subsistence food producers, Westerners have favoured men when dispensing agricultural machinery and technical knowledge, thus undermining women's position (Ward 1985, p. 310). Many cities in developing countries show an odd sex imbalance, further contributing to social instability. In Latin America, for example, more women moved to seek urban factory and domestic labouring jobs because their role in peasant agriculture was less important than that of men. By contrast, in East Africa, developing cities have been largely populated by men. Encouraged by 'colonial and multinational officials' inducements and coercions for work in mines and urban areas' (Ward 1985, p. 307), men abandoned declining rural subsistence production. These gender differences in migration have consequences for family and social life generally, and for the economic position of women in particular.

The most significant aspects of urbanisation in contemporary developing countries are its speed and scale. These reflect seemingly impersonal global economic processes, but take on very human dimensions. As B. Roberts points out, 'in 1920, 4.8 per-cent of the population of Africa, 5.7 of that of South Asia, 7.2 per-cent of that of East Asia, and 14.4 per-cent of that of Latin America lived in places of 20,000 or more inhabitants; by 1975, the respective percentages were 18.1, 17.4, 23.7 and 40.5' (Roberts 1982, p. 367). The 'megalopolises' or giant cities — such as Mexico City, with over twenty million people — are becoming extremely difficult to manage, but only very few cities approach this size. The patterns and implications of growth are still matters of debate (Bairoch 1988, pp. 512–60; Roberts 1982; Rakodi 1990).

Explaining the complex patterns of urban life in developing countries, especially the glaring contrasts of poverty and wealth, requires analysis of the cities' relationship to their local and global environments, and the patterns of labour-force organisation. One of the consequences of 'the development of underdevelopment' has been very uneven urban growth. As Third World cities have generally grown up primarily as colonial and neocolonial commercial and service centres, they have lacked a solid local base in terms of food-production and manufacturing (Bairoch 1988, p. 462). Now, as centres of multinational-controlled production and consumption, they have extremely high rates of unemployment and underemployment (Roberts 1982, p. 367), although often the educated local elite form an affluent middle class. The economy is divided into the modern, technological sector and a sector comprised of informal, low-paid, family-based jobs, with poverty concentrated in the latter, generally unregulated, sector.

The distinctive characteristics of various cities in the developing world reflect not only differing local cultural traditions and rural economies, but also the occurrence of industrialisation at different times and rates. The implications of this for working conditions and housing vary for women and men. When so many men from rural areas lack employment, women have found it difficult to get jobs, but undertake many informal jobs in food and clothing production (Ward 1985, p. 311). By contrast, in the new growth industries that have developed since the 1980s, especially micro-electronics, young women have become a favoured source of cheap labour. They spend, however, a relatively short time in the labour market; their health, especially their eyesight, deteriorates under the strain of intensive assembly work (Ward 1985, p. 314), and they are then dispensed with, frequently disabled for life. Trade union power varies considerably, as does State regulation; the crucial threat is that the multinational company will simply move elsewhere if its requirements are not met.

Although men and children are also affected by poor housing conditions, women continue to carry the general domestic responsibility. Most Western commentators have noted the expansion of 'shanty towns' around the perimeters of Third World cities. Perhaps these shacks — made of tin, cardboard or whatever is at hand — should be compared with rural living conditions, and not only with more affluent urban dwellings; these dwellings can form a bridge into city life for rural immigrants (Bairoch 1988, pp. 472–3). The health risks and sheer poverty experienced by inhabitants of shanty towns are still very real. Many have begun as 'squatter' settlements, such as the 'favelas' around Sao Paulo in Brazil. Eventually, local groups have formed to organise the extension of services such as water, electricity and health facilities, suggesting an active and positive response by residents to their housing crisis (Roberts 1982, p. 374–7).

Global urbanisation: is there a sustainable future?

In recent years, traditional sociological debates about the relative effects of urban life compared with rural life have come under fire on the grounds that the experience of urbanisation in developing countries is very different from that of the developed world (Abu-Lughod 1991, pp. 74–6). Since the nineteenth century, European social theorists had been concerned about the perceived decline of kinship, friendship, and neighbourly relations in large, amorphous, and densely populated cities. However, in spite of the rapid growth of Third World cities, there is evidence to suggest an alternative picture. Family bonds and village ties continue to play an important role in finding jobs, accommodation, and mutual support. Furthermore, especially in Africa, food-production on domestic plots and sharing of resources continue to be more significant factors than Westerners have assumed them to be. This has considerable implications for the planning of future urban development (Hardoy and Satterthwaite 1990).

When Engels and others set out to reform conditions in the early industrialising cities, there was still the hope of achieving widespread growth and prosperity. The global economy now presents new dilemmas. Centrally controlled from the major world cities in the 'core' countries, economic and urban growth in developing countries is primarily in the interests of the powerful multinationals. Responsibility for urban pollution and housing problems, and services such as transport, education, health, and welfare, tend to get left to national and regional governments, which are dependent on capricious sources of external finance. Most significant of all are the ecological dangers presented by uneven development and 'hyper-urbanisation'.

As Henry Girardet points out, the 'metabolism' of cities depends on sustaining their environment. However, rural production, the maintenance of soil fertility, and the effective management of forest and water supplies is under widespread threat. And the 'urban and industrial rubbish dumps piled up over recent decades pose an environmental hazard whose scale is, as yet, inadequately understood' (Girardet 1990, pp. 171–3). The ecological and human dangers of gigantic 'megalopolises', and the danger of seeking only technological solutions, were already foreseen by Mumford (1961) in his insightful historical account of cities. He noted that 'significant improvements will come only through applying art and thought to the city's central concerns, with a fresh dedication to the cosmic and ecological processes that enfold all being' (Mumford 1961, p. 575). In 1844, when Engels juxtaposed his awe at the wonders of the modern city with his recognition of its dark underside, he was only considering Great Britain. Now nearly half the world's five billion people live in cities, and global urbanisation seems to be more a threat than a promise.

Discussion questions

1   What factors motivated European colonial expansion, and what effects did it have on urban life around the world?
2   How did industrialisation in Europe affect urban development and everyday life?

3 Why have Australian cities developed as they have?
4 Discuss the significance of global cities.
5 What have been the main influences on, and consequences of, urbanisation in developing countries?

Recommended reading

For more discussion of theories of urbanisation and urban life in Western countries, see:

- Holton, R. J. 1986, *Cities, Capitalism and Civilisation*, Allen & Unwin, Sydney.
- Kilmartin, L. and Thorns, D. 1978, *Cities Unlimited: The Sociology of Urban Development in Australia and New Zealand*, Allen & Unwin, Sydney.
- Kilmartin, L., Thorns, D., and Burke, T. 1985, *Social Theory and the Australian City*, Allen & Unwin, Sydney.

Australian developments, especially in suburbanisation and housing, are debated in:

- Stretton, H. 1970, *Ideas for Australian Cities*, Georgian House, Adelaide.
- Kemeny, J. 1983, *The Great Australian Nightmare: A Critique of Home Ownership Ideology*, Georgian House, Melbourne.
- Richards, L. 1990, *Nobody's Home: Dreams and Realities in a New Suburb*, Oxford University Press, Melbourne.

Issues of 'development', ecology, and urban growth are dealt with well in:

- Cadman, D. and Payne, G. (eds) 1990, *The Living City: Towards a Sustainable Future*, Routledge, London.

and at a more advanced level in:

- Knight, R. V. and Gappert, G. 1989, *Cities in a Global Society*, Sage Publications, London.

For some very 'readable' accounts of urban life in different conditions, see:

- Lewis, O. 1961, *The Children of Sanchez*, Random House, New York.
- Lewis, O. 1968, *La Vida: A Puerto Rican Family in the Culture of Poverty — San Juan and New York*, Random House, New York.
- Roberts, B. 1978, *Cities of Peasants: Explorations in Urban Analysis*, Edward Arnold, London.

On gender issues and urban space, see:

- Huxley, M. 1994, 'Space, Knowledge, Gender and Power', in L. Johnson (ed.), *Suburban Dreaming: An Interdisciplinary Approach to Australian Cities*, Deakin University Press, Geelong.
- Watson, S. 1988, *Accommodating Inequality: Gender and Housing*, Allen & Unwin, Sydney.

Chapter 22

Environment

Alberto Gomes

'Hamburger and a Coke, please' he said. The friendly person at the counter responded, 'Would you like some fries with that, sir'. 'No, thank you.' he replied. 'That will be $2.70'. Within minutes this everyday transaction is completed. A man walks out with a brown bag containing a hamburger wrapped in waxed paper and a paper cup filled with Coca-Cola. That is his meal, supplied within two minutes. It is fast, convenient, and relatively cheap. Everywhere in the world there are literally millions of people who perform this ritual. It is so commonplace that one might wonder what the big deal is in starting a chapter on something as serious as the ecological crisis with something as mundane as buying a fast-food meal. It has got to do with what has been dubbed as the 'hamburger connection'.

The hamburger connection

Almost everyone in the Western world knows what a hamburger is. Hamburgers are consumed in an ever-increasing number of places around the world, even in China. About four decades ago hamburgers were on the menu in just a few places in the world, but particularly in the USA. Today there are many fast food outlets like McDonald's and Burger King which have built their business and renown on the sale of hamburgers. Going to McDonald's or Burger King (Hungry Jack's) for a meal is such a familiar and common experience in our everyday lives that we consider everything we do in the outlet as 'natural'. At the entrance of a McDonald's one is greeted by a brightly coloured statue of a clown, readily recognisable as Ronald McDonald. The statue, the colourful decor, and the ever-smiling staff all give this place an 'atmosphere' of friendliness. Fast food has become very much a part of the lives of most Australians. It is a growing industry. There are more than 400 McDonald's restaurants in Australia, and if we add to this all the other fast food enterprises, such as KFC, Hungry Jack's, and Pizza Hut, we will end up with a staggering number of fast-food outlets in the country. On a global scale there are literally thousands of these outlets, all together churning out millions of hamburgers. Resembling an industrial production system, such as for motor car assembly, the fast-food production process is quick, efficient, and rationalised, making food service convenient and fast for the customer. Fast food is a social phenomenon that encapsulates and signifies simultaneously a whole range of social practices and perceptions associated with industrialism.

When we enter a fast-food outlet we allow ourselves to be enchanted by the trimmings and 'atmosphere' of the fast-food restaurant. We are so deeply enmeshed in the rites of ordering food, paying, and then consuming while engaging in the usual social banter that we lose sight of how something seemingly ordinary and commonplace, like patronising McDonald's or any other fast-food chain, can have far-reaching and dire consequences for humanity and nature. How can a simple act like eating a hamburger at McDonald's or any other hamburger joint have any impact on something so complex as the environment? Sociologists would deal with this question by going to the 'backstage', to study how fast food is produced, and then proceed beyond that context to find out what the effects and hidden costs of fast-food production and consumption are. At each stage of our intellectual 'journey', we ask questions and seek answers to them in order to unlock the hidden issues behind the practices.

We begin with a straightforward question: 'What is the usual hamburger made out of?'. A hamburger is a beef patty in a bun. Where does the beef come from? McDonald's insists that its beef supplies are from local (Australian) sources. This may be the case. However, as Norman Myers (1981) and several other researchers have documented, the ever-increasing North American demand for cheap beef arising out of its growing fast-food industry is met mostly by South American (Amazon) and Central American beef supplies. To cater for the growing demand for beef, nearly 40 per cent of forests in Central America have been cleared and converted into pasture land for cattle raising, and a staggering proportion of the Amazonian rainforests have been lost to cattle-ranching. So we could say that the growing fad in hamburger consumption has indirectly taken a heavy toll on rainforests. Deforestation has severe repercussions on the environment and humanity. Forests, particularly the dense and diverse tropical rainforests, serve as a 'green lung', absorbing carbon dioxide and other gases emitted by the burning of fossil fuels that are used heavily in our industrial enterprises and motorcars. The build-up of such gases in the earth's atmosphere is said to be the cause of global warming through what is known as the greenhouse effect. Carbon-dioxide and other greenhouse gases accumulate in the atmosphere, forming a dome over the earth that resembles the glass cover in a greenhouse, and like the glass cover, the greenhouse gases allow sunlight to pass through but prevent heat from radiating back into space. In the process the earth is warmed up gradually, leading to rising sea-levels as the ice caps begin to melt, and to the destruction of vegetation and farm crops. All this occurs because of our appetite for hamburgers? There is more.

We are frequently warned to keep away from the sun or to 'slip, slop, slap' some 15+ sun lotion to protect our skins from the harmful ultraviolet rays that are said to cause skin cancer. Just like our craving for hamburgers, 15+ lotions have become very much part of everyday life in Australia. It is widely known these days that the growing incidence of skin cancer is linked to the depletion of the ozone layer, which absorbs dangerous ultraviolet rays from the sun and, in the process, protects us from ultraviolet radiation. There are two main chemicals that destroy the ozone layer: chloro-fluorocarbons (CFCs) used as refrigerant gas, aerosol propellants, and in the manufacture of foam packaging; and methane, released in the process of decomposition of particular organisms and in enteric fermentation by ruminants such as cattle, sheep, and goats. Cattle are responsible for some 76 per cent of annual methane emissions.

Now the picture should become clearer. Greater use of refrigeration by the fast-food industry in the transportation and storing of meat and other ingredients, more air-conditioning to provide a cool 'environment' in the restaurants, and the expanded reliance on disposable foam packaging right through the different processes, from production to transportation to consumption, have all contributed to the accumulation of CFCs in the atmosphere. In addition, the increase in the number of cattle to meet the growing demand for hamburgers has resulted in more methane being emitted into the environment, all leading to a dangerous chemical concoction that is disastrous for the ozone layer. So it would not be altogether absurd to say that our skin-cancer problem is somewhat related to our desire for a hamburger. But there is even more.

What happens to all the packaging that is used for the convenience of the consumer, not to mention the restaurant (no dish washing needed)? The next time you are at McDonald's observe how often the large rubbish bins are emptied, and try to figure out where all this waste goes. It is because of the use of elaborate and environmentally 'unfriendly' (plastic and foam) packaging, and not just in the fast-food industry, that industrialised nations dump hundreds of millions of tonnes of rubbish each year. While some of this waste is biologically degradable, other waste, such as plastics and radioactive material, may take many years to disintegrate.

What this fast-food case study illustrates is the extent of interconnectedness of our practices and the processes of the natural environment. If an act as simple and common as buying a hamburger can have such an impact on the environment, just imagine how severe the impact of something like a large industrial complex or a nuclear plant would be. Accidents like those that occurred at Chernobyl, Bhopal, and Three Mile Island bring home the extent to which ecological damage from such complexes of the industrial age can occur, not to mention the loss and degradation of human life.

Environmental sociology

Humans have, for a long time, exploited their environment as though it were an inexhaustible resource, resulting in considerable environmental degradation and destruction. Before the industrial era, human impact on the environment was essentially local. The expansion of trading and the establishment of a global trading network from the sixteenth century onwards led to a more extensive human impact on the environment. This was the advent of what Alfred Crosby (1986) called 'ecological imperialism'. Humans began to transform nature to suit their lifestyles. For example, some places in the 'East' were transformed extensively to resemble English 'countryside', and botanical species were taken from their native sites and planted in distant lands, either for aesthetic reasons or for economic profit. With the advent of the industrial era, human impact on the environment increased, and nowadays the scale of the impact is said to be so extensive and global that some ecologists predict a bleak future for humanity. Since the 1970s there has been an unprecedented surge of interest in environmental issues in the wake of growing public awareness of environmental problems such as global warming, acid rain, ozone depletion, pollution, and deforestation. There is now more media attention given to environmental issues. Educators have incorporated lessons about ecology and environmentally friendly practices in school curricula, and even introductory sociology textbooks. Environmental movements (often referred to as 'greenies') and lobbying the government on environmental issues have become increasingly popular. In step with such public concern, or in response to the environmental lobby, governments and State bodies are supporting 'green' ventures, such as the recycling of glass and paper. At an international level there have been many conventions to deliberate on environmental issues and numerous attempts to solve or arrest ecological problems. In 1972 the United Nations held a convention in Stockholm to address issues such as environmental pollution, a decade after Rachel Carson's bestseller *The Silent Spring* had raised public concern over the implications of pollution for humanity. The outcome of the Stockholm convention was the establishment of the United Nations Environment Programme (UNEP) to monitor environmental degradation. More recently, heads of states met in Rio in 1992 to resolve some pressing environmental issues such as global warming, deforestation, and loss of biodiversity. One key question that seems to emerge at all these international conventions is who is to be blamed for environmental damage.

Only recently have sociologists demonstrated interest in environmental issues. A growing number of sociologists are devoting their scholarly attention to environmental problems, having recognised that these problems are closely related to sociological matters such as how societies are structured and their function, as well as societal development and change. They have shrugged off their preoccupation with the notion that 'social facts are to be explained in terms of other social facts' and have demonstrated a willingness to consider 'non-social' factors, such as the natural environment. Some of the issues with which sociologists have been concerned are the different perceptions people have of the environment, and their implications for human use or abuse of nature.

Perceptions of the environment

The way humans treat or interact with nature is intimately related to their perceptions of nature. People are more likely to transform the environment if they think of it as wild and useless. In contrast, people who have respect for the natural environment are more inclined to live in harmony with nature. Human perceptions of the environment vary considerably, but they may be grouped into four different types: romanticist, stewardship, utilitarian, and imperialist. Romanticist and imperialist views are at opposite ends of the spectrum, the former being extremely ecocentric or biocentric (that is, biased towards nature), and the latter taking an anthropocentric position (that is, placing more importance on human, rather than ecological, interests).

For romanticists, nature has intrinsic value. They appreciate, some even worship, nature as it is and advocate that it should be preserved in its pristine state. They draw some of their inspiration from the writings of the eighteenth-century French philosopher Jean-Jacques Rousseau, who was an ardent critic of Western civilisation, which he declared was achieved at the cost of alienating humanity from nature. He was drawn to the idea that humans would be better off if they re-established their harmonious relationship with nature along the lines of the lifestyles of people like the Native Americans, whom he portrayed as 'noble savages', living in harmony with their environments and showing immense respect towards nature. Many environmentalists, particularly 'deep ecologists', hold romanticist attitudes towards the natural environment. Some romanticists venerate nature as a deity. Following the lead of British scientist James Lovelock, an increasingly popular name for 'Mother Earth' among such environmentalists is 'Gaia', the Greek Goddess of the Earth. Romanticists generally promote the preservation of natural sites such as forests, rivers, mountains, and wild plants and animals.

While romanticists aver that humans should preserve nature as it is, those that subscribe to a stewardship view affirm that human societies have a responsibility to control and manage the natural environment. They find appealing the systems of land and resource control and management in some small-scale farming and forest-dependent communities. Some forest peoples, for example, regard the forests as communal property, and members of the social group serve as stewards, ensuring that the forests are managed or conserved properly for the benefit of the whole community. Environmental conservation strategies are usually based on a stewardship perception of the environment.

Utilitarians think of the environment as something that is there for the pleasure and satisfaction of everyone. It exists for the common good and is valued only if it can benefit humans in some way or another. Utilitarians, for example, may view forests positively if such environments are in some way useful to society. Unlike romanticists, utilitarians perceive the environment as having extrinsic, rather than intrinsic, value. For utilitarians, the environment need not be transformed or modified in order to attain value.

Imperialists, in contrast, see the environment as something that has value only after it is transformed into materials or resources needed by humans. They advocate human domination over nature, which they believe is to be subjugated and exploited for the benefit of humanity. This view is associated with industrialism, and it is widely accepted that such imperialist views about the environment underlie the ecological problems we are facing today. Does this mean that all we have to do is change our perception of the environment to solve the various ecological problems we have caused? The answer is no, because the way ecological issues and social factors are linked is so complex that there is no simple or straightforward solution to ecological problems. Some say that an important step towards solving ecological problems is the curtailment of the human population problem, while others argue that we need to eradicate poverty, which they link to environmental degradation. Why are humans destroying or degrading nature at such a rapid rate and on such an extensive scale?

Population and the environment

Is overpopulation the cause of global ecological problems? In his book, *The Population Bomb*, first published in 1970, the American scientist Paul Ehrlich warned that, if human population were to grow unabated, the earth would not be able to support humanity. Ehrlich's warning was echoed in an influential publication, *The Limits to Growth*, published in 1972 by the 'Club of Rome', a self-styled international group of researchers, business people, bureaucrats, and politicians who met in Rome in 1970 to discuss environmental problems. The Club of Rome concluded that growth — both population and economic — was limited by the earth's carrying capacity (that is, the amount of resources adequate for basic survival). They envisaged that the limits would occur at three levels — food supply, minerals, and environmental pollution — and advocated a scaling down of both population and economic growth to achieve a steady-state economy.

Such pessimistic views were by no means new. In 1798, Rev. Thomas R. Malthus, a British economist, published *An Essay on the Principles of Population*, which introduced his renowned theory of population. Malthus argued that human population tends to grow much more rapidly than does its capacity to produce food and the other necessities of life. Without actually providing supporting evidence, he asserted that population tends to grow geometrically (2, 4, 8, 16, 32) while food supply or economic production expands only at an arithmetic rate (2, 3, 4, 5, 6). This discrepancy between population and food production is said to keep widening the gap between population and resources until population growth is halted in one of two ways: natural (or positive) checks, such as famines and wars, or preventive checks, such as sexual abstinence (but not contraceptives, which he rejected on religious grounds). Malthus was against welfare programs for the poor because he felt that such initiatives would translate into population growth and, in the process, would simply prolong misery among the people. Today many policy decisions relating to population control are influenced by neo-Malthusian assumptions, which advocate family-planning programs to stop the mounting demands of growing population on resources and the environment. Several international conferences — notably the United Nations-sponsored Population Conventions of Bucharest in 1974, Mexico in 1984, and Cairo in 1994 — have been held to discuss ways of controlling population growth. Some governments have taken harsh and coercive measures to curb population increases in their countries. These include forced sterilisation programs in India and China's one-child restrictions. Several feminists have rightly criticised such family-control programs as attempts by a patriarchal system to control and dominate women, particularly those from poorer, developing countries.

The overpopulation-as-a-cause-of-environmental-degradation argument is flawed in a number of respects. First, the idea that human population will grow exponentially for ever is incorrect, as recent United Nations studies estimate that human population will grow steadily in the next few decades and then stabilise at ten billion around the year 2045. Will there be enough food to feed the world's growing population? With technological advances in food production, food supply has increased to the extent that there is plenty of food available to feed several times more than the current population. The existence of famines, which Neo-Malthusian theorists invoke as evidence of food shortage as a result of overpopulation, is more a consequence of poor distribution of food rather than a lack of it (Lappe and Collins 1988).

Second, studies of human impact on the environment have indicated that fewer people could cause more environmental damage than many people. For example, industrialised nations, which constitute about one-quarter of the world's population, contribute 80 per cent of the world's greenhouse gases (*New Internationalist*, April 1992). The USA, which has less than 5 per cent of the world's population, is responsible for 26 per cent of carbon dioxide emissions, 20 per cent of methane, and about 26 per cent of the world's CFCs (*New Internationalist*, April 1992). Some critics of the population argument have indicated that such a preoccupation with the demographics of human population and family-planning programs tends to divert attention away from the real culprits responsible for environmental deterioration: industrialism and consumerism.

Poverty and environmental degradation

The poor are often an easy scapegoat for problems usually created by the rich. Neo-Malthusians blame the poor for much of the population increase and, indirectly, for causing ecological problems. In a similar vein, governments and international agencies such as the World Bank link poverty to environmental abuses and unsustainable resource exploitation, resulting in deforestation, soil erosion, and desertification. The poor are seen as self-serving people who are prone to take any opportunity, even one that is ecologically unsustainable, just to survive. Poverty is believed to convert the impoverished into destroyers of commons such as forests, rivers, and oceans. Garrett Hardin has called this the 'tragedy of the commons'. He asserts that commons are destroyed because the individual gain to users from overexploitation of the commons will always outweigh the individual losses that users have to bear arising from the resulting degradation.

Development planners promote modernisation programs aimed at poverty alleviation in the belief that such programs will not only eradicate poverty, but in the process will also solve the ecological problems perceived to be caused by poverty. Such programs are not entirely successful, primarily because they are based on false premises. Many studies have shown that people have been defined as poor because they live frugally and engage in subsistence-oriented economic activities. Such frugality is actually good for the environment, but is seen as inimical to a modernised (or Westernised) lifestyle. In the process of modernising the 'poor', such ecologically sound lifestyles have been thrown into disarray, leading, rather ironically, to ecological disasters as the 'poor' are pushed, as a result of development, to overexploit the environment. As with the population issue, the poverty explanation is viewed by some commentators as simply a distraction from dealing with the primary culprit responsible for most environmental problems: industrialism.

Industrialism and environmental deterioration

On the eve of India's Independence in 1947, Mahatma Gandhi was asked whether India would embark on an industrialisation program to 'catch up' with the West. He remarked, 'God forbid that India should ever take to industrialism after the manner of the West. The economic imperialism of a single tiny island kingdom is today keeping the world in chains. If an entire nation of 300 million took to similar economic exploitation, it would strip the world bare like locusts' (as quoted in *The Ecologist*, July/August 1992, p. 139). Gandhi's warning was not heeded. Soon after Independence, India, like most of its 'Third World' counterparts, followed in the footsteps of the West, undertaking full-scale industrialisation, which was spurred on by postwar international agencies such as the United Nations and the World Bank. Development for most of these 'emerging nations' meant industrialism. Within a couple of decades, the whole world was entrapped in industrialism characterised by growth-mania, wanton surplus-accumulation, and frenzied consumerism. Linked to a world capitalist system, nations engaged in manufacturing for a global market. As earlier chapters indicate, the implications of industrialism for society were deep and radical. For one thing, people's perceptions, values, and actions in relation to the natural environment changed drastically. The environment was viewed as a resource valuable only if it could be utilised for the production of commodities, and nature had to be controlled and dominated to cater for human needs and aspirations.

In the quest for economic growth and surplus accumulation, industrial and industrialising nations have promoted the maximisation of output to meet increasing market demands, spurred on by growing consumerism. It is a chain reaction with dire environmental consequences, as more and more resources (fossil fuels, minerals, timber) are tapped and transformed into commodities. Since most transformation processes create waste, industrialism causes increasing atmospheric and water pollution, leading subsequently to ecological problems such as global warming, acid rain, the ozone hole, radioactive radiation, deforestation, soil degradation, and desertification.

The impact of industrialism on the natural environment is a pressing issue. Since the onset of the industrial era, numerous writers have drawn attention to the disastrous effects of industrialism on the natural environment. Much of the writings appeared only after the 1960s with the publication of Rachel Carson's *The Silent Spring*. Commentators such as Barry Commoner, Edward Goldsmith, Ivan Illich, Theodore Roszak, and E. Schumacher have linked ecological problems to industrialism, which, with its imperialist ethos, is viewed as ecologically unsustainable. As the Club of Rome declare, 'If the present growth trends in world population, industrialisation, pollution, food production and resource depletion continue unchanged, the limits to growth on this planet will be reached sometime within the next one hundred years. The most probable result will be a rather sudden and uncontrollable decline in both population and industrial capacity' (Meadows et al. 1972, p. 23).

Sustainable development?

Does this mean that the future of humanity is doomed because of the way we have destroyed, and continue to destroy, the planet? Many commentators have indicated that there is hope if we are prepared to change our lifestyle. In the 1980s the United Nations established a commission under the leadership of the Norwegian Prime Minister, Glo Brundtland, to deliberate on environment and development. The commission submitted its report, entitled *Our Common Future*, in 1987 advocating 'sustainable development', which it defined as 'development that meets the needs of the present without compromising the ability of future generations to meet their own needs' (WCED 1987, p. 43). Ever since the publication of the report, 'sustainable development' has become a popular catch-phrase in official rhetoric. While the Brundtland Report has mounted a challenge to materialist and consumerist values, critics wonder whether it challenges industrialism. Some argue that to prevent ecological catastrophe we would need to change fundamentally the values of industrialism. Perhaps our first step should be knowing how our actions, even something as simple as buying and consuming a hamburger, have ecological implications. Our second step would be to act in cognisance of this knowledge.

Discussion questions

1 Why has the environment become a pressing issue in recent years?
2 Outline the different perceptions of the environment, and indicate how they relate to the way humans treat their environments?
3 'Overpopulation is a cause of environmental degradation.' Do you agree or disagree with this statement and why?
4 How and why does industrialism lead to environmental deterioration?
5 How can sociology contribute to an understanding and resolution of environmental problems?

Recommended reading

The following are books that have had considerable impact in influencing the discussion of environmental issues:
- Carson, R. 1962, *Silent Spring*, Houghton Mifflin, Boston.
- Meadows, D. H., Meadows, D. L., and Behrens, W. 1972, *The Limits to Growth*, Pan, London.

This following book is an anthology of the writings of various 'environmentalists' and scholars concerned with ecological issues:
- Brennan, A. 1988, *Thinking About Nature*, Routledge, London.

A good general 'dictionary' for quick reference on various environmental issues is:
- Elsworth, S. 1990, *A Dictionary of the Environment*, Paladin, London.

The following provide comprehensive and general discussion of environmental issues from a sociological perspective:

- Martell, L. 1994, *Ecology and Society: An Introduction*, Polity, Cambridge.
- Silvertown, J. and Sarre, P. (eds) 1990, *Environment and Society*, Hodder & Stoughton/The Open University, London.
- Smith, P. and Warr, K. (eds) 1991, *Global Environmental Issues*, Hodder & Stoughton/The Open University, London.

The following are particularly useful for a discussion of sustainable development:

- Redclift, M. 1987, *Sustainable Development: Exploring the Contradictions*, Methuen, New York.
- WCED (World Commission on Environment and Development) 1987, *Our Common Future*, Oxford University Press, Oxford.

An excellent journal dealing with environmental issues is:

- *The Ecologist* (various issues).

Chapter 23

Social Movements

Kevin McDonald

Alan	Knowing who you are. That's the main thing!
Jim	If you know where you stand, then you're right.
Alan	It's whether you stand or not, you know.
Jim	Because we stand up ... for what we are.
Alan	A lot of cultures know their own language. We don't.
Jim	It was taken away from us. We wasn't allowed to speak it. We had to stay on missions and stuff.
Kerry	We have to learn now, so that we know.
Kevin	How are you doing that?
Rick	Research ... Going back to where we come from... going on camps where your ancestors were... going to the land.
Kerry	Go on walks, and that.
Rick	Go up the bush.
Alan	Our dances.
Ric	We've danced in High Street. We danced for Yarta Worta.
Jim	We know where we are going. But we just haven't got there yet.

This is a fragment from field work I was engaged in during 1993 and 1994. Kerry, Alan, Rick, and Jim are four Koori young people, aged between seventeen and twenty. They live in Melbourne's northern suburbs. They had been students at Northlands Secondary College, a school with an important Koori program, which had been closed down as a cost-cutting measure. At the time of this research, the school had been closed for two years.

Kerry, Alan, Rick, and Jim have a deep sense of the great wrong that has been done to their people. They are involved in what might at first seem small forms of action. They are building up networks between Koori young people in Melbourne, through sport and social activities. They are part of efforts to maintain contact with Koori communities in rural Victoria. They had been working for the reopening of their school, something that happened some months after the research. They are involved in a struggle to recover the ability to say who they are, to recover a past in order to claim a future. They speak of themselves as 'we'. They share a collective identity, not simply on the basis of their people's dispossession of their land, but on the basis of their shared struggle. They are not attempting to create a world of their own, a subculture; they are oriented towards the 'High Street', towards entering and transforming public space. Their action is often symbolic, incorporating forms of communication such as dance. They are aware that a great issue is at stake: they have to stand up and, in the process, discover who they are. They are part of a process of social creativity that is contesting forms of power in Australian society. Kerry, Alan, Rick, and Jim are part of a social movement.

We often have the impression that public life in Australia is nothing but economics. Television and radio seem taken up with endless debates on the subject, from foreign debt to underlying inflation and interest rates. Candidates for prime minister present themselves as potential general managers or accountants. The meanings of the political seem to be leaching out of our language. It almost seems that, as a culture, we are losing the capacity to explore other problems, that the way we make sense of experience is being relentlessly ground back to calculations of profit, loss, and economic growth.

But when we look closer, we can see the extent to which other debates and questions are well and truly part of our public conversation. Over the first half of the 1990s we saw the re-emergence of environmental and green groups, with forests being occupied from far-north Queensland to Tasmania. We also saw the timber industry and timber workers counter-mobilising, leading, in early 1995, to a spectacular blockade of Federal Parliament, and to a shutdown campaign in the timber towns of New South Wales and Victoria.

Aboriginal action continued. In Perth, Aboriginal groups struggled to stop the development of a former brewery site, claiming the land and its meaning as their people's. In South Australia, Koori women fought against the development of a bridge connecting Hindmarsh Island to the mainland, while, in Melbourne, Koori groups won a two year battle against the closure of Northlands Secondary College, a school that had developed a nationally acclaimed Koori education program. These Aboriginal actions were assertions of collective identity, of shared experience and meaning. The question of identity was also raised in Melbourne in February 1994, when 60 000 people marched against the Federal Government's recognition of the Former Yugoslav Republic of Macedonia, a massive community mobilisation that was part of a broader campaign that had mobilised the press and radio, and which had seen the fire-bombing of churches and social clubs.

Other forms of collective mobilisation were even more spectacular. Arguably the most prominent was the Sydney Gay and Lesbian Mardi Gras. This had begun in 1978 with one float and two hundred participants, with the first march ending in bashings and arrests at a time when homosexuality was illegal. By 1994 it was the largest cultural event in Australia, with over 3000 marchers and over half a million people in the streets supporting it. Other forms of action emerged. Disability-rights groups fought not only against discrimination, but also for social visibility — in Victoria they were at the centre of campaigns to maintain a public transport system to which they would have access. The shape of cities was on the agenda. Over the 1980s it seemed as if cities were to be determined by their place in global flows of capital, image, and information. State governments were busy winding back local democracy, and attempting to transform their capitals into entrepreneurial cities that could compete in the global flow. The 1990s saw the first mobilisations against this. In Melbourne scores of people were arrested for attempting to stop the redevelopment of Albert Park into a Grand Prix racing track, and people were once again mobilising against freeway extensions. In Sydney, which over the 1980s had established itself as Australia's global city, residents were regularly blockading the airport following the opening of a new third runway.

These forms of action point to new themes in Australia's public culture, new forms of action and identity. Significantly, over this same period, there were clear signs of the decline of work-based identities and action. Unionisation levels continued to fall, with only 40 per cent of Australian workers unionised in 1992 (ABS, 1994). Trade union leaders attempted to stem the exodus by forming 'super unions' based on service delivery to clients, offering retirement planning, financial services, cheap home loans, or holidays, with even the idea of a trade union airline being floated. The older model of solidarity between workers seemed less and less viable, increasingly being replaced by one of customer satisfaction.

All this suggests that there is more happening than the economic commentators who so dominate our culture would suggest. Older forms of action and identity, and an older language of social connection, seem to be in decline. At the same time new issues, new questions, and also new problems appear to be emerging. Can the concept of a 'social movement' be of any help in making sense of this? This is the question that we explore in this chapter.

We do so in four steps. First, we look at some of the conflicting ways the term has been used. Second, we explore the movement that has, without doubt, been the most significant over the past two decades: the women's movement. We cannot explore all the dimensions of this movement, but we can construct an idea of what a social movement is through engaging with this experience. Third, we explore the relationship between social movement and other forms of action. Finally, we look to see whether the concept of social movement can help us explore the questions of identity and action that appear central to the context we are increasingly calling 'globalisation'.

Conflicting meanings

Different sociological traditions have conceptualised social movement in radically different ways. American functionalism in the 1960s conceived of social movements in terms of 'collective behaviour' (Smelser 1963), as an expression of some form of 'social strain', such as an inability to cope with rapid social change. This approach owed a great deal to theories of crowd behaviour dating from the end of the last century (Le Bon 1960) and to that period's concern with social order. This functionalist analysis tended to place social movements in a continuum of often irrational responses to modern industrial society.

This view was shattered by the rise of movements and action in the 1960s. As a result, the idea that social movements reflect a more or less irrational response to the strains of modern life has been largely rejected in the USA. If anything, the pendulum has swung to the opposite extreme, with American sociology conceiving of social movements as forms of collective mobilisation that follow the same cost–benefit laws that govern economic activity. According to this logic, I will mobilise against a freeway development if the likely benefit (maintaining property values, quality of life, and so on) is greater than the cost involved (loss of time, income). The pendulum has swung from collective irrationality to the theory of 'individual rational action' that forms the base of American Resource Mobilisation Theory, which conceives of collective action as the sum of individually rational decisions (Zald and McCarthy 1987).

Neither of these approaches is satisfactory. Action is clearly more complex than either approach suggests. Recently we have witnessed the rise of an approach that conceives of social movements as attempts by elites to enter the political system. Jan Pakulski's work in Australia is a good example (Pakulski, 1991). He argues that the Green movement is essentially made up of middle-class educated elites who have been excluded from the 1980s tripartite negotiating table of business, labour, and the State. These thinkers conceive of social movements as essentially political actors, and have hence coined the term 'new politics' to describe their significance. This political emphasis has also become more important in the USA, where national political parties structured by programs have effectively ceased to exist, having been replaced by networks of groups mobilising in an attempt to enter the political system. Alan Scott (1990) in the United Kingdom also explains the development of European social movements in terms of this same 'political exclusion' thesis. He explores Sweden and Germany and argues that the Greens are a highly educated group of middle-class activists who are excluded by 'growth coalitions' of business, labour, and the State. Such approaches owe a great deal to the pioneering work of Charles Tilly (1978), who argued that the structure and relative openness of the political system is the prime determinant of the shape of what he calls collective mobilisations. Groups will mobilise into movement, he argues, when the doors of the political system are closed to them.

We can contrast these approaches with a more European tradition. Here sociologists such as Alain Touraine and François Dubet in France, or Alberto Melucci in Italy argue that contemporary social movements point to qualitative social transformations. Touraine was the first to argue that the student movements of the late 1960s pointed to what he saw as the development of a post-industrial society that would be characterised by new forms of power, new social actors, and new types of conflict and creativity, and he developed a research method, the sociological intervention, to engage directly with these forms of action. Touraine argued that industrial society was decisively shaped by a core social relationship between industrialists and the labour movement, arguing that patterns of social life and culture were produced through the conflict, compromise, and creativity at play in the relationship between these social actors. For Touraine, the central issues for the discipline of sociology were the decline of industrial society and the birth of a new post-industrial society (1974), and the way to engage with these issues was to engage with the movements and conflicts at the centre of this transformation. Over the 1980s he researched the student movement, the ecology movement, the women's movement, struggles for regional autonomy, and the labour movement. But after this decade of research, Touraine was less optimistic, seeing social life as being shaped more by the decomposition of industrial society than by the emergence of new forms of conflict and social creativity.

This research emphasised the complexity of movement action and identity, and above all, what Touraine (1987) called the 'two sides of identity'. On the one hand movements construct an experience and identity in terms of a language of creativity, a positive identity. In the labour movement, this was a central factor for the skilled workers who have led the labour movement throughout the world — affirming pride, skill, and the creativity of work, in opposition to the parasitic employer. This was central to the struggle of Solidarnosc, the Polish labour movement of the 1980s led by skilled workers from Poland's defence and metal industries, who opposed their creativity and productivity as workers to a parasitic bureaucracy living off them. But Touraine's research also underlined another face of identity, which, in the case of the labour movement, he called the 'proletarian' identity. This was based on the experience of deskilled work, of being subjected to the rhythm of the machine or the assembly line. Here work was not an act of creativity, but an experience of domination and loss of meaning. The action of these workers was qualitatively different from the first group. While skilled workers fought to defend the creativity and autonomy of work, those for whom work was an experience without meaning would often react through sabotage of the assembly line or withdrawal into apathy.

Separated, neither of these forms of action were the labour movement. Skilled workers were tempted towards a kind of corporatist defence of their own interests, while the unskilled were more likely to try to break with the world of work — through sabotage or drug-use — than transform it. When these forms of action came together, however, a language of creativity interacted with an experience of domination, and a social movement was born. This movement was not a 'response' to a situation, but action that both affirmed a form of social creativity and contested a form of power, namely employers' attempts to deskill work and to appropriate the meanings of work as their own.

This suggests that a social movement is not a 'thing', but a complex social dynamic involving social creativity and attempts to change power relationships. Movements can be seen as attempts to shift the boundaries of possibility, opposing the way dominant groups monopolise core cultural resources in a society — in this case the meanings and creativity of work. But they can also be defensive and heirarchical — sects with strong borders that divide the world into the 'pure' and 'impure' are radical examples. Let us explore this approach to social creativity and power by engaging with the most significant of contemporary social movements: the women's movement.

The women's movement

There is no doubt that women's organisation and action have a long history, but a series of events in the late 1960s point to a new development. In 1969 the Australian Arbitration Commission had given 'equal pay' to women, but only in industries in which men and women were doing the same jobs. The decision would mean nothing to women doing 'women only' work in industries like textiles, so on 21 October 1969 Zelda D'Aprano, a trade unionist, chained herself to the Commonwealth building and set in motion a process that would lead to the formation of a Women's Action Committee. Meanwhile, in November 1969, women who had been involved in the anti-war movement formed the Sydney Women's Liberation Group, and by May 1970 the first national Women's Liberation conference took place at the University of Melbourne. In 1972 the Women's Electoral Lobby was formed, aiming at influencing the outcome of the 1972 Federal elections, which saw the election of the Whitlam Labor Government (see Read 1994; D'Aprano 1977; Curthoys 1988).

Right from the beginning, the women's movement was shaped by core tensions and problems. As Katherine Read notes (1994, p. 209), socialists and radicals clashed: socialists arguing that the liberation of women was part of the liberation of the working class, while radicals emphasised the domination of men. Socialists looked to join and transform working-class organisations, while many radicals sought to create a world free from men. Where this option radicalised into lesbian separatism, it often came to be associated with increasingly authoritarian forms of

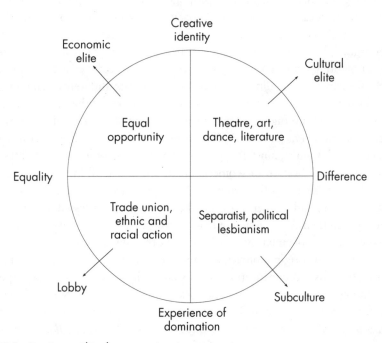

Figure 23.1 Tensions within the women's movement

politics (Read 1994, p. 209). Often the language of these debates drew on the categories of older social movements, and many of the debates were constructed in a language of 'revolutionaries' versus 'reformists'. It was only later that a clearer way of conceptualising the issues at stake would emerge: one exploring the tension between the demand for equality with men and the struggle to construct an experience different from the dominant masculine one.

The women's movement did not form an all-encompassing organisation or a political party, as the labour movement had done a century earlier, and the hopes for a unifying 'sisterhood' that were so important in the early period of action have disappeared. Parts of the movement appear to be associated with emerging business and cultural elites, who insist that a woman can do anything she wants in Australian society. This group is attracted to the 'power feminism' of American writers such as Naomi Wolf (1993). Others focus on the experience of woman as victim, and construct a picture of widespread violence against women. These tensions can be illustrated in graphic form.

Figure 23.1 suggests that the action of the women's movement can be explored in terms of being structured around two intersecting tensions. On the one hand, there is the tension between equality and difference, in which some groups will be aiming at achieving equality with men, while other groups will emphasise the difference of women's experience. The second axis reflects the tension between an identity constructed in terms of possibility and creativity, and one more shaped by the experience of domination.

Emerging business leaders and proponents of equal opportunity emphasise equality with men, affirming women's capacity to achieve their goals once the barriers are broken down. Socialist feminists also argued in terms of equality with men, but they argued that men and women were being dominated equally by a system that puts profit before people. These views illustrate the two sides of actions for equality. Similarly we can see two dimensions of action around difference. One experience emphasises the domination of men, and this is an important theme in groups organised around women's refuges and centres against sexual assault, which construct an experience of woman as 'survivor'. The meaning of difference here is constructed in the context of a fight against the power of men. The other face of difference is expressed in the celebration of women's creativity, above all in the domains of cultural production, in the affirmation of the importance of women's art, women's music and writing, and women's corporeal experience as expressed in dance.

Groups find themselves acting in fields constituted by these tensions. At the same time, the women's movement has encountered other significant struggles of the past twenty years: the Aboriginal movement and the action of ethnic groups. These have meant that the tensions constituting the movement have become more complex, and have destabilised the earlier social analyses of the movement. None of the groups pointed to above is *the* social movement: *the social movement is the process of social creativity that occurs between these groups as they attempt together to name their experience and transform the world of which they are part.*

Movements and other forms of action

The domains of action identified here can separate from the social creativity that the movement represents. In the case of the women's movement, this is represented by the arrows in the Figure 23.1. We can see that groups affirming equal opportunity can become absorbed within the structures of power: they stop critiquing forms of power and become transformed into a *modernising elite*. Similarly, forms of action affirming creativity and difference can become absorbed into the logics of literary and cultural worlds, and become a *cultural elite*. In both cases, these groups become disconnected from the experience of domination. In a similar way, the forms of action that affirm an experience of domination that is shared with men can become absorbed into the logic of trade unions, ethnic or racial groups, or, in some cases, movements of religious renewal, such that they disconnect from a sense of being part of the struggle of women to change the world. And finally, the groups and actors affirming an experience of domination and difference can reach the point of becoming a *subculture* — becoming a separate world rather than attempting to transform the world. Subcultures are characterised by hierarchy, and are defined by an experience of domination. Affirming their difference, subcultures tend towards dividing the world into categories of pure and impure — these then become sects. This was evident in the Australian labour movement in the early part of this century, where a logic of subculture developed and radicalised to the point of dividing the world into pure and impure. This has occurred in sections of the women's movement as well, where subcultural logics have radicalised into sectarian authoritarian cultures.

This process of disconnection leads to fragmentation of the social movement. It underlines the extent to which a social movement, rather than being an organisation, is above all a process of social creativity; it is action that attempts to name and contest forms of power, and the struggle to shift the boundaries of possibility while creating an experience of shared meaning. We can see the same process at work in other social movements — whether in the current revival of ethnic movements, in the environmental movement, or in the disability-rights movement.

Social movements and globalisation

We are now increasingly part of a global culture, and this is reflected in everything from music, television, and Coca-Cola to the growing of opium in Thailand and Colombia. This is a major issue for sociology, which had equated 'society' with the nation-state. Part of the globalisation debate has seen the re-emergence of a new form of technological determinism, with some authors arguing that, if the assembly line gave us one type of society, the global information network gives us another. Much is made of economic flows.

But the sociological problem does not lie in attempting to determine how far the economy is internationalised. The significance of 'globalisation' for sociology is that it points to the breaking down of borders within contemporary experience. It points to the end of a social world defined in terms of hierarchy, and to the dissolution of experience into flows — of image, of capital, of sound. It highlights the blurring of all sorts of borders in contemporary experience, whether they be between different kinds of art, between masculine and feminine, or between homosexual and heterosexual.

The issue at stake is not the percentage of exports in the gross domestic product, but the shift from social models based on hierarchy to those based on flows and networks. This represents a move from a social world characterised by cohesion and integration to one of weak borders and uncertainty. Once a culture that valued sameness, we now value difference. But what social form this difference will take is not decided in advance. A society of *difference* can easily become one of *indifference*, in which the sense of social connection weakens, the natural form of social life becomes a market in which everything can be bought and sold, and the older forms of social solidarity and connection at the base of the welfare state are not as strong.

Questions of identity are becoming increasingly urgent in this new context, and these are at the centre of social-movement action. In the older social model, 'who we are' was largely defined by our place in the social system, with sociologists often equating the personality with the social roles that people occupied. Now who we are is defined less and less by our place in the social structure, but is increasingly something that we have to invent in order to navigate in increasingly uncertain global flows. We are moving from a culture of socialisation to one of self-creation — symbolised by the pop stars who are known only by their first name, having no need of parents and family history to define them.

We are in the middle of this transition at the moment, and so the most innovative sociology is open to the new — it is questioning rather than certain. Just as the rise of the industrialists and their culture of progress pointed to the birth of industrial society, it may be possible to point to the emergence of a new dominant model of creativity, in which the self becomes a resource to be mobilised, and experience is increasingly the raw material of new post-industrial systems of production. This is evident in the changing experience of growing old — increasingly the raw material for financial and techno-medical industries — and also in an experience of place that is increasingly shaped by global networks of capital and power.

Just as the labour movement of a century ago contested the dominant shaping of industrialisation, and constructed a language of possibility and an ethic grounded in the solidarity of work, so today's fragmentary social movements may be pointing towards a recomposition of social life — to new debates at the centre of a postindustrial experience. On the one hand, this involves constructing a new ethic: one grounded more in the respect of the person than in a confidence in progress. The ambiguity in social movements underlines the ambiguity of the current context. As the forms of identity and connection of the older industrial society weaken, we may move towards a new social life and widened democracy. Or society may fragment into increasingly disconnected subcultures.

We can see these tensions in contemporary ethnic identities and movements. On the one hand, these movements can be read as attempts to reclaim memory, as a fight against the dissolving of experience into the market, as attempts to ground forms of connection and identity within a narrative or meaning constructed from human experience. On the other hand, they can point towards intolerant communitarianism, to what sociologists such as Michel Maffesoli have called the 'return of the tribe'.

The current hold of economics on our culture underlines a social crisis of imagination. This is reflected in political life, in which political parties appear increasingly as shells — as vehicles for personal ambition rather than instruments that societies can use to construct political debate. The new movements that have emerged have not sought to form political parties, as labour movements throughout the world did a century ago. But they may nonetheless represent the renewal of our culture so that new political debates can be constructed, and eventually new types of political organisation can emerge. The environmental movement opens up the question of the relationship of humanity with the natural world. Ethnic movements underline the struggle for identity; these can become defensive and closed, tempted by racism and the search for sameness, but they can also represent the attempt to construct memory and to give meaning to human experience, a recognition of incompleteness and the value of the encounter with the other. The disability-rights movement represents a struggle for the value of the person, and is increasingly important in a culture torn between respect for the individual, and the celebration of performance and achievement. The women's movement underlines the tension between equality and difference, while the Aboriginal movement claims the right to a past and a future.

These movements are involved in reconstructing our culture. All can fragment into subcultures, new elites, or authoritarianism. But all represent attempts to shift the boundaries of the possible, to make forms of power visible (Melucci 1989). They underline and amplify core tensions within our social world. Despite their day-to-day confusion, these movements are attempting to represent our world and culture, and to articulate the core dilemmas with which we are faced. They may be our best chance for democracy as we move into the next century.

Discussion questions

1   What is your experience of social movements? Do you feel that, in some way, you are part of a form of struggle to change society? If you do, what does that mean to you in terms of identity — of who you are?
2   Dominant groups involved in reconstructing our society and culture? Do they represent an image of creativity — a new culture? What does it look like?
3   Do social movements in some way represent a counter-model to emerging dominant models of self and society? Are these movements essentially nostalgic, wanting to return to the past, or are they attempting to articulate a different future? Give examples.
4   Do you think that social movements point to and amplify core dilemmas confronting us? If you do, what are examples of this?
5   What are the main strengths and weaknesses of the different sociological approaches to social movements?

Recommended reading

There are a number of different approaches to exploring contemporary social movement experiences. An excellent overview of current international debate is:

- Maheu, L. (ed.) 1995, *Social Movements and Social Classes: The Future of Collective Action*, Sage/ISA, London.

In Australia, a very good overview is provided by:

- Pakulski, J. 1991, *Social Movements: The Politics of Moral Protest*, Longman Cheshire, Melbourne.

Arguably the most important sociological exploration of social movements, linking field research and theoretical work, has been developed by Alain Touraine in France:

- Touraine, A. 1974, *The Post-Industrial Society*, Wildwood House, London.
- Touraine, A. 1987, *Return of the Actor: Social Theory in Postindustrial Society*, Minneapolis University Press, Minneapolis.
- Touraine, A. 1988, *The Workers Movement*, Cambridge University Press, Cambridge.
- Touraine, A. 1989, 'Is Sociology Still the Study of Society?', *Thesis Eleven*, vol. 23, pp. 5–34.

Important Italian texts exploring mobilisation, identity, and social creativity are:

- Alberoni, F. 1984, *Movement and Institution*, Columbia University Press, New York.
- Melucci, A. 1989, *Nomads of the Present: Social Movements and Individual Needs in Contemporary Society*, Radius, London.

American work generally explores processes of mobilisation, with an emphasis on resource mobilisation:

- Tilly, C. 1978, *From Mobilisation to Revolution*, Addison Wesley, Reading, Mass.
- Zald, M. N. and McCarthy, J. D. (eds) 1987, *Social Movements in Organisational Society*, Transaction Books, New Brunswick.

While there are many texts on feminism, there are very few explorations of the women's movement. A good overview of the Australian movement is:

- Read, K. 1994, 'Struggling to be Heard: The Tension between Different Voices in the Australian Women's Liberation Movement in the 1970s and 1980s', in K. P. Hughes (ed.), *Contemporary Australian Feminism*, Longman Cheshire, Melbourne.

An important account of the birth of the contemporary women's movement in Australia is an autobiographical account by one of the key people involved:

- D'Aprano, Z. 1977, *Zelda: The Becoming of a Woman*, self-published, Melbourne.

Chapter 24

Social Revolution

Rowan Ireland

The concept of revolution is the centrepiece of all theories about society.

Kimmel 1990

Revolution is the sex of politics.

Mencken 1927

The sexual revolution is over.

Age, 27 February 1995, p. 3

Some books in my university library with 'revolution' in the title:
The Sexual Revolution
The New Revolution: The Impact of Computers on Society
Modern Latin American Revolutions
The Quiet Revolution: The Electrification of Rural Ireland,
1946–1976

Reflections on a revolutionary life

I might have been born on the 'quiet continent' in Melbourne 1940, but all my life I have been bumping into revolutions. Through later primary and into secondary education, I was forever being located in relation to revolutions. I was heir to the industrial revolution, without which my life would have been nastier, more brutish, and short. My political freedom had been won for me by the English Revolution back in the seventeenth century and by the sensible bits of the French Revolution in the eighteenth; though I was reminded that all this was under threat from the witting and unwitting agents of the Russian Revolution (1917) and the Chinese Revolution (1949). In the 1960s I learnt that the hormonally driven excesses of my generation constituted a sexual revolution. But, while negotiating that, I was becoming a social scientist, and that, as Michael Kimmel (1990) implies, involved a lot more bumping into revolutions — which was, as Mencken's (1927/1990) observation would lead you to expect, exciting. At one point, in the early 1960s, however, that career, and indeed the whole world, nearly came to an end as the superpowers of the day locked horns over whether the Cuban Revolution should continue or not.

It, and my career, did. Pursuing the latter, I took up the study of Latin America as a special interest. That meant learning at some depth about the Mexican Revolution (1910), the Bolivian Revolution (1952), the Cuban Revolution (1959), and the Nicaraguan Revolution (1979). When I went to Brazil, on and off from the late 1960s to the mid-1980s, I encountered what purported to be a revolutionary military government that had taken power, its spokesmen said, to stop subversive Leftists fomenting a revolution against national security. Some of my friends at that time risked their lives attempting what they called a peaceful revolution for justice and peace against the military's national security regime. Meanwhile, back in Australia, I was beginning to teach about social movements and reviewing claims that the green revolution and the revolution against patriarchy, as well as a further stage of the sexual revolution, were in the making.

Some sociologists tell me that, as I get older, there will be fewer real revolutions to bump into. The dark forces of the new world order will nip real revolution in the bud; or the postmodern consciousness of the young will be unable to sustain revolutionary action; or 'globalisation' will mean that you and I, the rank and file of real revolutions, will not be able to locate and confront, still less overthrow, the world's ruling elites. Could that be so? Is the electrification of rural Ireland about as close as we will come to real revolution in the future?

The notion of revolution

These questions about the demise of real revolutions beg a lot of other questions. What on earth, or in the mind of a sociologist, could the real revolution be? That is the question examined in this first section of this chapter. In the second section we ask what sociology has to do with real revolution and how sociologists have approached the study of revolutions. In the third section we ask a potentially embarrassing question, which fortunately has an encouraging answer: what have sociologists discovered about revolutions? In the final section we return to those questions about the future: what does sociology have to tell us, as students and citizens, about the future of social revolution?

Scanning the revolutions I have bumped into, they seem a mixed lot. Let us place them in groups and examine them for their differences before we search for common features or delve into how they figure in sociology. First, there are those revolutions — at base, breakthroughs in the technology of production, exchange, and communications — that I have been educated to see as the turning points between historical epochs. The industrial revolution is one of this set, along with the preceding urban and agrarian revolutions, and the variously called automation, computer, or telecommunications revolution that is supposed to have succeeded it. These are the great historical punctuation marks that social scientists have devised to bring order and coherence to the rambling prose of history. Some sociologists (for example, Galtung 1971, ch. 1), in applying the sociological imagination to the work of archaeologists and historians, have tried to piece together how the technological breakthroughs have set off transformations of social structure, political institutions, economic systems, and even deep cultural changes. Individual, or even collective, human actors (for instance, peasants, as well as other social classes) are curiously absent from accounts of these epochal revolutions: they are revolutions that seem to happen to people. On the other hand, the combined legacy of epochal revolutions, gathered together and given meaning in the great eighteenth-century revolution of the mind known as the Enlightenment, is seen by many sociologists to have created the conditions for revolutions sought and consummated by human actors.

Among these are the great state-centred social revolutions of modern times, from the French Revolution (1779) through the Mexican, Russian, Chinese, Cuban, Iranian, and Nicaraguan revolutions. The story of these revolutions is usually focused around decisive political events, the conquest and transformation of the State by revolutionary forces. Where the accounts of epochal revolutions are faceless, devoid of human actors, each of the social revolutions is associated with named individuals who are seen variously to have seized the revolutionary moment or orchestrated the whole revolution. Robespierre, Zapata, Lenin, Mao Dzedong, Fidel Castro, and the Ayatollah Khomeini come to mind. At the same time, these revolutions are said to involve much more than the takeover, or attempted takeover, of the State by revolutionary heroes. Each of these revolutions is described by participants, and often by observers and analysts as well, as involving deep transformations in the relations of class, status, and power. Further, these revolutions involve change in culture: the discrediting of old myths of the nation's past, and the successful diffusion of new myths and new images of its emerging future, such that the postrevolutionary citizenry are disposed to accept the new order and the projects of the new regime as legitimate.

There is at least a third set of revolutions: the identity and lifestyle revolutions. The sexual revolution, and the revolutions both discerned and sought by the so-called 'new social movements' (for example, the feminist movement, or the ecological or Green movement) belong to this set. For those who think of the state-centred social revolutions of modern times as the real thing, these often appear too ephemeral, too dissociated from concrete political processes and struggles, too fragmented, to deserve the mantle of revolution. Though protagonists of these revolutions will sometimes pressure the State for policy change, they do not seek to capture State power itself. They are more interested in changing the hearts, minds, and practices of ordinary citizens. As such, those who seek to transform the identity of women, or human relations to the natural ecology, or the use and development of urban space, are often characterised as self-limiting — as holding back from the comprehensive, linked transformations of the political, economic, and social systems already achieved, or prefigured, in real revolutions (Kauffman 1990).

For the moment, though, we should continue to consider the identity and lifestyle revolutions as contenders for designation as real social revolutions, even if they are still in the making, and their protagonists are self-limiting. Some sociologists urge us to do so on the grounds that, in our 'postindustrial' world, deep, comprehensive change is no longer to be achieved in and through the nation-state, but precisely where the identity and lifestyle movements are located: in 'civil society', and in the cultural realm in which the symbols that provide meaning in everyday life are produced (Melucci 1989). Others point out that significant actors in some of the new social movements are not so self-limiting after all. Some analysts of the Green movement point out that the movement as a whole seeks change in the dominant political, economic, and social projects that have been embraced around the globe at the same time as its components battle to save a forest in New South Wales or an endangered species in the Brazilian rainforest (Hutton 1987). In Chapter 23, Kevin McDonald gives several examples of how Australians, creatively constructing and asserting social identity in local networks, may effectively contest forms of power in Australian society.

The three sorts of social revolution, then, may be distinguished on a number of grounds. They differ in the degree to which they are consciously planned and prosecuted; they differ in the extent to which the modern state is centrally involved; they differ in geographical scope and historical location. But in some of their common features, and in the consequences that one type of revolution may have for others, they suggest what real social revolution might be. Each of the types involves *comprehensive* social change: not just change in the social relations of production and exchange, but also related changes in political relationships, in social arrangements, and in the norms, values, and ideologies that orientate members of a society in everyday life. Each of the types involves *decisive* social change: there may be partial restoration of pre-revolutionary social relations, or these social relations may survive in some sections of the population, but the revolutionary transformations are relatively permanent. Real social revolutions are decisive because the various social changes are institutionalised and consolidated. For most members of the society, the new ways of managing economic and political relationships, and of ordering society, become normal and proper.

These qualities of real social revolutions are captured well in what has become the most widely quoted definition of revolution in the social sciences. The political scientist Samuel Huntington has defined revolution as 'a rapid, fundamental, and violent domestic change in the dominant values and myths of a society, in its political institutions, social structure, leadership and government activity and policies. Revolutions are thus to be distinguished from insurrections, rebellions, revolts, coups and wars of independence' (Huntington 1968, p. 264). As the sociologist Charles Tilly has pointed out (Tilly 1978, p. 193), this definition has its shortcomings. It brings successful revolutionary outcomes into sharp focus, but at the expense of specifying revolutionary situations and the social processes that may result in revolution. Further, it is a fair description of only a very few grand revolutions — the French, the Russian, and the Chinese, perhaps — and it privileges the state-centred revolutions of modern times over both the epochal revolutions and the identity or lifestyle revolutions.

Huntington's definition is worth using nonetheless. To have the characteristics of grand revolution so clearly defined, and the interdependence of those characteristics so sharply suggested, helps us analyse *any* process of complex social change. We can compare any such process — achieved or in the making — with Huntington's definition of grand revolution, and this can be an important step towards better understanding of the process. The military revolution that I found in Brazil, while it transformed the lives of those who lost their political rights or who were tortured, is misunderstood if the analyst classifies it uncritically as a revolution. This becomes clear when we compare its features with the terms of Huntington's definition. The military took over rapidly in 1964, but they neither sought nor achieved rapid and fundamental change in the dominant values and myths of the society. They did not change and develop new political institutions, but closed down the old set, allowing their gradual restoration in the 1980s. There was certainly a change in political leadership, but it amounted to a sort of changing of the guard within existing elites, rather than the assumption of power by a new political elite. Systematic comparison with the terms of our definition shows the events in Brazil to have been a coup rather than a revolution. And having established that, we can move on to investigate the profoundly anti-revolutionary character of the military regime.

The same exercise, performed on the Green revolution-in-making, may challenge the conventional wisdom that the word *revolution* is merely figurative when used to characterise what Greenpeace or the Wilderness Society are on about. Up to a point, this conventional wisdom would seem to be confirmed: none of the organisations that comprise the Green movement wishes to achieve 'rapid ... and violent domestic change' in political institutions and political leadership; nor are any of them within cooee of achieving the sort of state-focused revolution that Huntington had in mind. On the other hand, some sociologists and Green activists would argue that the Green movement as a whole *is* bringing about 'fundamental ... change in the dominant values and myths' around the globe and in several national societies (Hutton 1987, ch. 1). Drew Hutton argues that the Green movement embodies an alternative 'ecological paradigm' that comprehensively challenges the core values, the economic and political projects, and the social structures of the 'dominant paradigm'. If that argument can be supported by the results of research on the development of the Green movement itself, and on changing attitudes and practices in the community at large, then we might conclude that the Green movement was closer to achieving real social revolution than the Brazilian military revolution ever was.

You will find it instructive to perform the same exercise in relation to the sexual revolution. The article in the *Age*, quoted from in the epigraph, suggests that, if the values and practices that were thought to constitute the revolution could wither away so fast, there could not have been much of a revolution in the first place. It would also seem that the sexual revolution, unlike the Green revolution, ended up being non-comprehensive: it was so exclusively concerned with sexual identities, interests, and practices that it never developed that broad challenge to the dominant myths, values, and institutions of society that Huntington's definition suggests is an essential characteristic of real social revolution. You may come to a different conclusion, as Jeffrey Weeks (1985) does when he links the sexual revolution to a much broader set of social, economic, and political changes. Were you to conclude that the sexual revolution is as much a real social revolution as the Green revolution or any of the grand revolutions, you would probably be well on your way to abandoning Huntington's definition as your touchstone for recognising real social revolution. His narrowly conceived focus on the State and on politics would have become too restrictive for you. Moving along these lines, you rapidly find yourself at the frontline of change in sociology itself.

Sociology and the study of social revolution

Sociology and the grand state-centred social revolutions of modern times are intimately related. Sociology was born of the French Revolution of 1789, the associated cultural changes referred to as modernity, and the changes in European political economies referred to as modernisation. The historian Robert Darnton (1989) has referred to one of the crucial phases in the French Revolution and later nineteenth century as the phase of 'possibilism'. This is the phase when revolutionary leaders and the mobilised population are united in the fervent belief that anything is possible now that the old order has been destroyed and a new, more just order can be established by the new state. On the basis of the at least partial success of the French Revolution, 'possibilism' became a theme in modern cultures, and a theme rendered all the more plausible by the achievements of science and industrial capitalism. Sociology grew on the hopes and fears generated by 'possibilism'. It is only from the perspective of 'possibilism' — the perspective that profound social change may be wrought by human beings who have discovered how society works and how it might be managed — that the central activities of classical sociology, the new science of society, make sense.

So sociology became especially attuned to the study of precisely the kind of grand revolution that nurtured it — to the study of how revolutions are made and how their consequences might be managed. That is one sense of the Michael Kimmel quotation (1990) in the epigraph. The sociology of Karl Marx is the attempt to uncover the processes leading to revolutionary situations, in which men and women of the revolutionary classes learn how to achieve the ultimate revolution for a classless society. Émile Durkheim was centrally concerned with how the gains of the French Revolution might be institutionalised so that progress in liberty, equality, and fraternity might be attained without social, and consequent individual, disintegration. Well into the twentieth century, much of sociology was devoted to what we might call 'revolution-spotting': detecting the sources and signs of revolution with an eye to heading it off (the counter-revolutionary agenda) or helping it along (the revolutionary agenda).

Sociologists who study particular national revolutions (The French, the Cuban, and so on), and those who attempt the comparative study of a number of grand revolutions, divide the topic into several areas of enquiry and sometimes specialise in one area. One of these is the enquiry into the development of revolutionary situations — the factors that increase the likelihood of grand revolution. Thomas H.

Greene (1990, p. 178) has helpfully assembled many of these factors in his list of current hypotheses concerning revolutionary potential. The factors listed include population-growth in relation to material resources; the level of exploitation of peasant labour in relation to the provision of basic services to the peasantry; the rate of economic development in relation to the capacity of the political system to adapt; the relationship between a society's class, status, and power rankings; the relationship between expectations about mobility and opportunity for mobility; and the relationship between an upwardly mobile class and other classes threatened by that class. When these relationships are out of kilter or change suddenly, then the potential for revolution is thought to increase. Some sociologists — James Davies (1969), for example — have argued that there is a single common factor in revolutionary situations: revolutions are most likely to occur when a sharp decline in well-being follows a long period of improvement.

Other areas of enquiry include the study of the dynamics of the revolutionary situation as it develops (or fails to develop) into grand revolution; the study of leaders and the groups that are mobilised to participate in revolution; and the factors involved in the success or failure of revolutions. In all of these areas, until fairly recently, what we might call a 'structural' or 'systems' analysis has dominated. In the structural analysis of revolution, large-scale structural forces — like the State, social classes, national and international economic trends, and demographic patterns — figure as the units of analysis. Thomas Greene's list of hypotheses, noted above, emphasises these factors and is itself an example of structural analysis. More recently, 'action analysis' has come to the fore. Action analysis emphasises the role of human action in revolutionary processes over impersonal forces: it puts revolutionaries — as real people, making choices in terms of their interpretations of particular situations — back into the study of revolution. Where structural analysis examines material circumstances, structural systems, and events in the determination of comprehensive structural change, action analysis focuses on the competing goals and visions of individual people, on complex processes of decision-making, and on revolutionary outcomes as humanly constructed, creative acts. In my own field of special interest, Eric Selbin (1993) has recently revivified the study of Latin American revolutions using, and arguing the merits of, action analysis.

What do we know about social revolutions?

The answer is that we know a lot about grand state-centred social revolution and the sorts of questions raised by structural analysts. Action analysts tend to argue that there is still much to learn about revolutions as human constructions, and they seek further understanding of social revolution by shifting focus from the State to the social relations of everyday life. Nevertheless, structural analysis has had its achievements. Theda Skocpol and other structural analysts have demonstrated how revolutionary situations arise from the failure of political institutions to accommodate new demands and absorb challenges that arise during the modernisation process (Skocpol 1979).

Careful comparative study of structural factors has taught us a lot about the conditions under which the chances of moving from a revolutionary situation to successful revolution will be maximised. An English sociologist, Krishan Kumar, has noted that four structural features were present in all successful past revolutions. First, 'in all cases revolutions occurred in societies in which only a minority … of the population live in cities and towns'. Second, 'these were societies where the technical means and organisation of coercion possessed by government were never so totally superior to those of the insurgents', as they are in most modern societies. Third, successful revolution occurred 'in societies where the integration of political authority was never very complete … where the opposition, however conceived, could collect its forces and bide its time' (Kumar 1976, pp. 251–2). The final factor was deep division within the ruling groups over the very shape and direction of the society. Greene (1990, p. 73) and Galtung (1974) extend this point, asserting that alliances between disaffected members of elite groups (Galtung identifies them structurally as 'rank disequilibrated elites') and mobilised sectors of the exploited classes are essential to successful revolution.

The same sort of careful comparative study has helped clarify the conditions necessary for sustaining successful revolutionary overthrow of the old regime so that comprehensive social transformation may be achieved. It appears that one, or some combination, of two conditions are necessary for sustained success. The first condition, paradoxically enough, is that the old regime need to be centralised, well organised, and powerful. The revolutionary regime, to realise the aims of the revolution, will need to have at its disposal the organisational means to effect national transformation, and one source is the available governmental machinery of the old regime. Charles Tilly (1978) explains the sustained character of the French Revolution — as opposed to the failures of several revolutionary takeovers in nineteenth-century Spain — in these terms. The French revolutionary coalitions of 1789–94 overthrew the most powerful state in world history up to that point: 'They were able to use that great power, in fact, to destroy the juridical structure of feudalism, effect large transfers of wealth, subjugate the Church, build a mass army. The nineteenth-century revolutionaries who repeatedly seized control of the Spanish state grabbed an apparatus whose extractive and repressive capacities were insufficient to any task of national transformation' (Tilly 1978, p. 221). The alternative condition is exemplified by the Chinese case: 'The Chinese experience indicates that in the course of a long mobilisation revolutionaries sometimes build alternative institutions which are potentially stronger than the existing state, and serve as the infrastructure of a strong new state when the revolutionaries come to power' (Tilly 1978, p. 222). These conditions are hard to come by, which helps to explain why cases of sustained revolution are rare. Indeed the accumulated structuralist studies of attempted and successful state-centred revolutions show that revolution, even in 'the age of revolution', is unlikely and fragile. The 'normal', even when some of the conditions for the development of a revolutionary situation are in place, is powerfully counter-revolutionary. Crane Brinton, one of the best known analysts of revolution, argues that, because most ordinary citizens hanker after the normal in periods of revolutionary disturbance, the greater the degree of violence and turmoil in the overthrow of the old regime, the less the comprehensiveness and depth of revolutionary transformation (Brinton 1963).

Conclusions: the future of social revolution

Looking to the future, the sorts of studies we have been reviewing suggest those who hope that a better world might be born of state-centred social revolution will be disappointed. S. N. Eisenstadt (1978) has summed up the features of 'late modern societies' that, he argues, greatly reduce the chances of grand revolutions occurring in them. These include the absence of a closed, exclusive centre, which can become a common target for the relatively excluded and underprivileged; the softening and blurring of class divisions through the interventions of the State so that, despite continuing inequality, class conflict declines as the main engine of social change; and new forms of conflict concerning status divisions of ethnicity, gender, age-group, and lifestyle that have come to the fore, variously replacing, cutting across, and defusing the class divisions out of which grand revolution once grew. At the same time, in these societies, the State has responded to the great crises of war and economic depression in the twentieth century. In so doing, it has developed the means for ever more discrete, but ever more effective, social control and repression, so that revolutionary situations are rapidly defused, and the groups that foster them are quickly nipped in the bud.

Structuralists argue that, in less modernised societies, various features of globalisation undermine even movements for peaceful revolution. Manuell Castells (1983) has examined such movements in the 'dependent cities' of Latin America, where he has found many of the conditions that, in other times and places, have generated revolutionary situations. And he has found small groups of citizens among the urban poor practising new forms of participatory politics, attempting new forms of economic exchange, building new forms of communal life, and struggling to realise their own alternative cultural values. But citizens engaged in these movements for comprehensive change (arguably, true revolutionaries) find that they are limited to bringing about change in neighbourhoods; decisive power to shape the economic, political, and social projects of the city and the society increasingly resides in transnational companies and the emerging, superpower-dominated institutions of the world economy. Local movements, unable to engage with decentred, de-spatialised, transnational structures, inevitably come to be seen, by the urban poor they seek to mobilise, as ineffective in the struggle for survival. And so the movements themselves shrink until they are nothing more than isolated groups of idealists. End of revolution. The revolution is also likely to end should the idealists take to arms. For then the superpowers of the new world order will flatten them with 'low-intensity conflict' or high-technology blitzkrieg.

That is the future, or lack of it, for state-centred revolution, seen from the perspective of structural analysis. But there are other possibilities for social revolution, perhaps the better appreciated as we continue that revolutionary life, the future of which seemed to be so uncertain.

Postscript: a revolutionary life continues into the twenty-first century

I continued teaching into the first decade of the twenty-first century. And though some of the predictions of my structuralist colleagues came to pass, social transformations of such comprehensiveness and decisiveness that they could only be called revolutions continued to take place — even in Australia and Brazil. What is more, some my former sociology students from La Trobe, along with sociology students from all over the world, figured prominently in these social revolutions.

They are an interesting new breed, these sociologically informed revolutionaries. Prepared by sociology, they were quick to learn that the application of economic rationalism on a global scale generated revolutionary situations the world over, even in societies where revolution was presumed by Eisenstadt to be dead. But they have taken much from structuralist analysis, and, unlike some romantics of my own generation, they have taken on board the fact that millions were slaughtered in revolutionary struggles and millions more as revolutionary regimes turned totalitarian. So they are properly sceptical about the chances for achieving state-centred revolution and inclined to believe that a revolutionary state is an oxymoron. From the analysis of twentieth-century state-centred revolutions, they understand that revolutionaries in power have been profoundly and ruthlessly hostile to social movements. But these social movers call themselves revolutionaries nonetheless. And though they work mainly at the level of local communities, they are also virtuosi in the use of twenty-first-century information highways to inform and mobilise communities all over the world, as they effectively challenge and bring to account the powers that be at national, regional, and world-system levels.

Kind to an old teacher, they tell me that sociology has set them off and sustained them in their revolutionary careers. These young revolutionaries tell me that, where one line of structural analysis —analysis of failed and successful revolution — showed them how little room there was for responsible moving and shaking, another line prepared them to understand the new forms of global class conflict and the revolutionary situations that developed at the end of the twentieth century as free markets turned out to be incompatible with free political institutions. At the same time, they say, action analysis helped to draw them out of a sort of pessimistic apathy by showing them how initially small groups, developing images and appropriate practices for more deeply human social life, might in time transform the practices of whole societies. For example, action analysis showed them that modern telecommunications were not only a means of manipulation and control by global elites, but were also a means for enabling and sustaining new global social networks, able to contest the projects of the rich and powerful. Action analysis, it seems, taught the best of this generation how to keep the best of the revolutionary tradition alive.

Ah well, perhaps that image I used to have of myself as merely bumping into revolution was not so apt after all. My students are telling me that, teaching sociology, I have been a bit of a revolutionary all along.

Discussion questions

1 How might we compare and contrast social revolution with each of the following:
   - a national strike over wages and conditions
   - rallies mobilising a million marchers in Australian capital cities in protests against woodchipping
   - a military coup
   - a completely new type of popular music that tops all the charts, causing a new generation of 'musos', disk-jockeys, and promoters to take over?
2 Why have consciously organised attempts at social revolution occurred only relatively recently in human history?
3 What are the preconditions for revolution uncovered by structuralist analysis of revolutions?
4 What are the arguments for and against the claim that the age of social revolutions has ended?
5 In what senses are the 'new social movements' (for example, the Green movement) seeking social revolution, and what are the factors affecting their chances of achieving it in the contemporary world?

Recommended reading

On the concept of revolution, see:
- Kimmel, M. 1990, *Revolution: A Structural Interpretation*, Temple University Press, Philadelphia, pp. 4–7.

This book considers a number of definitions of revolution. On pages 15–25 Kimmel outlines Karl Marx's notion of revolution and the dynamics of revolution in industrial capitalist societies. Pages 162–3 summarise Anthony Giddens' arguments that revolutions are possible only within the historical epoch known as modernity.

Another useful survey of concepts and models of revolution is to be found in:
- Calvert, P. 1990, *Revolution and Counter-revolution*, Open University Press, Buckingham, pp. 1–19.

On social revolutions as *modern* phenomena:
- Giddens, A. 1985, *The Nation State and Violence*, University of California Press, Berkeley, pp. 17–31, 313–25.

On the structural preconditions of revolution:
- Greene, T. H. 1990, *Comparative Revolutionary Movements*, 3rd edn, Prentice Hall, Englewood Cliffs, NJ, ch. 11.

For an outline and discussion of the major structuralist accounts of modern revolutions, see:

- Tilly, C. 1978, *From Mobilization to Revolution*, Addison Wesley, Reading, Mass., ch. 7.

On the argument that the age of social revolutions has ended, see:

- Eisenstadt, S. N. 1978, *Revolution and the Transformation of Societies*, Free Press, New York, ch. 10.

A subtly different argument is advanced in:

- Kumar, K. 1976, 'Revolution and Industrial Society: An Historical Perspective', *Sociology*, vol. 10, no. 2, pp. 245–69.

On the comparison of 'new social movements' with 'old' revolutionary movements, see:

- Scott, A. 1990, *Ideology and the New Social Movements*, Unwin Hyman, London, ch. 1.
- Pakulski, J. 1990, *Social Movements: The Politics of Moral Protest*, Longman Cheshire, Melbourne, pp. 25–31, 32–42, 60–76.

Chapter 25

Globalisation: Experiences and Explanations

Trevor Hogan

> A child sobs because her rugby hero has been bought by Rupert
> Murdoch's super league. Another textile factory closes in
> Brunswick because it can no longer compete with Chinese wages.
> Another power station is sold off to foreign interests. Moody's
> credit rating agency warns that Australian governments must keep
> cutting taxes and services, or else. The Queensland Government
> slashes share transaction taxes and every other State must follow.
> What is the magic word which unites all these actions?
> Globalisation.
>
> Wiseman 1995, p. 5

Globalisation is an awful word about awesome powers, structures, and processes. Rather than start with technical definitions and conceptual discussions about abstract global forces, I begin with a set of stories and examples of Australia's place in the world. To write about the world is to speak about our own experience of the world. To write about Australia is to draw our attention to Australia's relation to wider forces, structures, and processes. We are forever experiencing and reflecting across time, across borders, across cultures. These wider forces not only provide contexts for understanding ourselves, but also help shape us. From a discussion of Australia's place in the world, I turn to the vexed question of definition and the contested explanations of globalisation. I will look at how sociologists have been contributing to these debates and adding their own interpretations. Australia is an ideal place to engage in cross-cultural and historical comparison, and to think about the meanings and impacts of 'globalisation', for we live 'down under', where everything else in the world looks upside down.

Australia's changing place in the world

Australia has always been supremely conscious of the outside world, more often than not as a violent place that is potentially hostile to our own welfare. Thanks in part to the Vietnam Moratorium movement in the 1960s, and to the Whitlam government in the 1970s, the generation of men born in the 1950s — my generation — is the first in six not to have fought in active combat overseas. Australian men and women have been involved in wars in nearly every part of the world: South Africa in the Boer War, Europe, Northern Africa, and the Middle East in the two world wars, Asia and the

Pacific in the Second World War, Korea and Malaysia in the 1950s, and Vietnam in the 1960s. If there were no 'reds under the beds', there were always the 'yellow hordes' ready to disturb 'our' sleep. The Korean and Vietnam wars put the two colours together, creating a potent mixture of cold-war politics and racial hostility.

War was not the only way young Australia learnt about the world. Primary-school geography lessons in the 1960s still involved colouring large parts of the world map in the pink hues of the British Empire-turned-Commonwealth. The 1960s was also the time when an Australian prime minister could proclaim — at the opening ceremony of the joint Australian–United States communications base at North West Cape in Western Australia — that Australia's foreign policy was 'All the way with LBJ' (Lyndon B. Johnson was then President of the USA). If Australia felt anxious about its near neighbours and the state of world politics, it has always managed to align itself with the world's two largest superpowers: first the United Kingdom and then the USA. In the 1960s Donald Horne suggested that these alliances helped to make us a 'lucky country', born into the richest and most powerful 'family' of the nineteenth century, and a first cousin of the nation that has dominated the twentieth century. For most of our national history since federation, we have viewed the world with bifocal spectacles: though the lenses of transatlantic/Anglo-American loyalties and cold-war suspicions (capitalism versus communism; liberal democracy versus totalitarianism). With the collapse of the Berlin Wall and the implosion of the Soviet empire, we have a historic opportunity to choose new spectacles with which to view the world. However, it is not just our means of viewing that has changed: we the viewers have also changed.

Since the 1960s Australia's place in the world has become rapidly and progressively more complex. As Fiona Mackie and Susan Harvey have shown in their chapters, successive waves of immigration from all corners of the world have transformed the term *multiculturalism* from an ideological prescription or normative ideal to a description of everyday social reality and experience. Eric Bogle (a Scottish immigrant) was still able to satirise Anglo-Australian prejudices in the 1970s when he sang 'I don't like Wog food, I eat Chinese Take-away', but in the 1990s Australian cuisine is not only marked by an extraordinary diversity of 'ethnic restaurants' (in city and country locations alike), but a growing number of cosmopolitan cuisines, which mix and match East and West with eclectic flair. My Irish and English grandparents remember the introduction of pumpkin and tomatoes to their dinner plates; my parents first saw pasta in the 1950s, garlic and espresso coffee in the 1960s, zucchini and aubergine in the 1970s, and avocados and tropical fruits in the 1980s. In the 1980s and 1990s, Anglo-Australians of my generation unselfconsciously use Indian, Thai, Vietnamese, Indonesian, and Japanese spices and recipes. The diversification of food stuffs, and the increased sophistication of palates, is not only a function of increased socio-economic living standards and the fashion-fixated pretensions of the upwardly mobile professional middle class, but also a reflection of our increased everyday interaction with the world beyond our shores. Unlike the empire-building European nations of the sixteenth through to the nineteenth centuries, whose tastebuds were stimulated by global conquest, the world has not been brought back home to us so much as it continues to arrive on our doorsteps, dinner plates, and television and computer screens. Australia is both colonised by global culture and a cultural coloniser of global markets and technologies. It is both peripheral and central to globalisation.

To meet the communication needs of increasingly diverse ethnic populations, the Australian Government established the Special Broadcasting Service (SBS) in the mid-1970s. SBS's subsequent transmutation into a global communications network, which promises to 'Bring the World Back Home', is in itself symbolic of the rapidly changing nature of Australia, of Australian identities, and of Australia's location in the world. A further indication of these shifts is the number and frequency of Australians travelling abroad. Just as the volume of trade between Australia and the Asian-Pacific region has been growing rapidly, so too has tourism, employment, and education abroad. One index of the increasing predilection for travel has been the exponential rise in 'backpacker' travel, epitomised by the emergence of the 'Lonely Planet' travel guides.

Each generation seems to forget what its forebears struggled to learn. No sooner were we free of the spectre of conscription and war, and in possession of a university education, than we were to be found wandering the planet, ignorant, for the better part, of Australia's cultural, economic, and political place in the world order. We were post-Bazza MacKenzie types, but only just so, for we were also heirs to Richard Neville's 'Hippie-Hippie Shake' generation. London was no longer the ultimate destination, the metropolitan centre of our provincial imaginations. In the 1970s, New York, Los Angeles, Berlin, Tokyo, and Bangkok were alluring alternatives. As it emerged later, we were pioneers of a new type of tourist market, giving a new twist to the historic romantic ideal of the 'Grand Tour'. We were the first to travel overland to Europe via Asia, our 'Lonely Planet' guides in our backpacks. Now the whole world has caught on. Today, 'Lonely Planet' guides constitute 90 per cent of Australia's export market in books, many of which are available in other languages (reported in the *Australian*, August 1995).

Australian nationals have always been nomads, and not only the indigenous peoples; after all, we are a nation of immigrants and their offspring. But the destinations, purposes, and modes of our travel have changed over time — not out of material necessity, as in the past, but born of spiritual restlessness and market innovation. My grandparents were migrants who travelled out of economic necessity and a sense of adventure; Australia and New Zealand *had* to be better than anything on offer in England and Ireland. Within Australia, they were fortune-seekers, following the paths of employment and excitement generated by land settlements, gold rushes, and railway construction. Only after the Second World War, with the development of the consumer revolution, the emergence of the dormitory suburb, the weekend, and four weeks of annual leave, were my grandparents able to become tourists (see Whitwell 1989). Their holidays consisted of trans-Australian rail trips to the 'eastern states'. My parents took their three children on caravan holidays around Western Australia. At the end of their working lives, in the late 1980s, they took to the skies, courtesy of lump-sum superannuation and an inheritance from a recently deceased Aunt. With credit cards, rolling suitcases, and videocam in hand, the world of prepackaged tours became their reality — for one year at least. Revolutions in transport over the past one hundred and fifty years — trains, cars, and planes — have reshaped our sense of time and space, compressing them and reshaping our sense of ourselves (Harvey 1989).

Australians are not only bringing the world back home via holiday snapshots and trinkets, but the world of tourism has arrived here in a big way too, especially at the obligatory destinations of Sydney, Surfers Paradise, the Great Barrier Reef, and Uluru, or wherever native fauna are to be found (Phillip Island, Monkey Mia, Hervey Bay). As the whole world becomes a tourist destination, so too each place is re-created as a privatised theme park. As Jonathan Raban once observed, each city in the USA now has at least one iconic tourist object so that busy commercial travellers on a one night stopover are provided with an instant memory and memento to take back 'home', or to satisfy them at least until the next stopover (Raban 1990). So too in Australia, every town is busily inventing an image and erecting a monument to attract tourists. As Humphrey McQueen recently commented in the *Australian* (August 1995), for post-conquest Australia's lack of antiquity, we substitute monumentalism: big bananas, big pineapples, big worms, not to mention dogs on tucker boxes and an array of colonial gold-mine towns, waterworlds, filmworlds, and tomorrowlands. The tourist no longer visits a place that takes time and a disposition to experience the locality on its own terms; instead one is shown 'a tight cluster of artfully manufactured symbols' (Raban 1990, p. 245).

Tourism in Australia has become a gauge of our new relationship to Asia, especially the emergent world powers of Japan and China. A T-shirt worn by a Japanese tourist at Surfer's Paradise displays this prize specimen of instant pop wisdom: 'Go West Fuzzy Duck and have pumping nice time like fluffy freedom of Baudrialard's [sic] poetry' (reported in the *Independent Monthly*, July 1993). This caption is a playful pastiche of global culture. While, to native speakers, the English used may seem comical, the 'otherness' of its texture is experienced by English- and non-English-speakers alike. Sly references to Baudrillard (the cool auteur of 'po-mo' — post-modern to the uninitiated), the coy alliteration, and the sexual innuendo suggest that the author of the text was probably Japanese and knew what she or he was doing; many of the Japanese T-shirt wearers, whose English vocabulary might be limited, probably do not. As the first generation of Japanese youth to have large disposable incomes, a penchant to spend them, and a desire for all things 'Australian' continues to visit our shores in increasing numbers, close encounters of a new kind between the two nations will take place. The increasing encounters with otherness experienced by the nationals of Australia and Japan are not encounters between two discrete groups, but rather they involve (in Australia's case at least) already multicultural, multi-voiced populations (see Chapter 1). Moreover, as the cultural interactions increase, so too the cultural, political and economic landscapes of a place called Australia will continue to be revolutionised before our very eyes.

The impact of globalisation processes on Australian cultures is contributing, in turn, to the growing complexity of Australian national political culture. Witness the political acrobatics of Paul Keating in his promotion of Mabo, a 'postmodern republic', 'Asianisation', *and* a 'community of true believers'. The advent of the first Hawke government in 1983 signalled some major changes in the nation's political and public culture. Back in the mid-1980s, when the Labor government was trying to whip up a little national enthusiasm to compensate for its embrace of the dictates of economic rationalism, Bob Hawke used prime-time television to nominate four Australian heroes: Paul Hogan, Joan Sutherland, Greg Norman, and Ben Lexcen. They were chosen because they were all high achievers, having risen from relatively modest socio-economic backgrounds to become internationally recognised in their fields of endeavour. They were therefore presented as inspirational models fit for emulation by all Australians. They were signs of their times in more ways than Hawke was ready to admit, however. Of the four nominees, three were living overseas at the time, and all four were working in post-industrial cultural activities, which involved international markets organised in the Northern hemisphere: Hollywood films, opera, golf, and yachting (the America's Cup no less). One is reminded of the contemporaneous pop song that has subsequently become an advertisement for Australia's ex-national airline: 'I Still Call Australia Home'. It was first sung by Peter Allen, also an expatriate Australian who — before dying of the quintessential postmodern global disease, Aids — used to live in North America. Allen was also famous for his self-declared inclination to 'Go to Rio', the international Mardis Gras city.

To gauge the extent of the shift that has taken place in Australia's place in the world and in the nation's identities, compare the sentiment of 'I Still Call Australia Home' with what remains the most popular choice for national anthem: 'Waltzing Matilda'. 'Waltzing Matilda' is a subversive political fable with a mythic twist. It celebrates loyalty, mateship, and a community of unemployed nomadic workers over and against the parasitical squatters, settler capitalists, and the police state. The troopers are depicted as protecting the interests of the squatters (sheep, no less) before the basic needs and rights of the worker. In contrast, 'I Still Call Australia Home' evokes 'Australia' as lost community, as elsewhere in time and place; it is an elegy for a mobile generation condemned only to know that home is some place elsewhere. 'Waltzing Matilda' is a song about the heroic stoicism and defiance of the losing battler, whose only victory is that others continue to sing his song. 'I Still Call Australia Home' sells the idea of community as synonymous with an act of consumption (see Chapter 6). Is it any surprise then that the Australian Labor Party has, by the end of the twentieth century, transmuted from being the party of the down-and-out worker on the open road into a party of backslapping bonhomie and hobnobbing with entrepreneurial global squatters and globe-trotters of finance capitalism? What better hero, then, for Bob Hawke to choose than Paul Hogan — the working-class bloke who sells to North America the idea of 'Australia' as a land of prawns on the 'barbie', sheep in the paddock, and Crocodile Dundees in the bar?

The struggles between market and community, capital and labour, and globalism and place are epitomised, likewise, in current fights over sport. Here Australia has the dubious honour of being a world-leader in the transformations of team sports. The curious struggles between media barons, corporatist sporting commissions, unionising professional players, and community supporters mimic and promote all that we mean by 'globalisation'. While these struggles have occurred in all sports for many years, the genuinely novel transformation of late-twentieth-century sport is the modification of the game to deliver consumers to markets via international media networks — in this case, sport as pre-packaged entertainment. It is the media barons who are currently redefining the social meaning of sports, first by restructuring the ownership of clubs and players, and second by changing the rules to meet the technological requirements of the new media and the kinds of markets they are endeavouring to build. First in was Kerry Packer with his 'world series cricket revolution' in the late 1970s, and now it is Rupert Murdoch with 'world super league' rugby league, and Packer again with his attempt to form a 'world rugby corporation'. The Australian Rules football code has yet to face such a takeover, but the Australian Football League (AFL) commission itself is fully committed to the dictates of globalisation logic.

The technological capacity of global communications will not necessarily lead to global cultural homogenisation but, rather, can make a local tradition a global event. The process of converting a local tradition into a global event, however, has involved a transformation of the form, the content, and the meanings of the tradition. The world over, local governments and corporations compete to host and present global events. Some are world events such as the Olympic Games, Expos, and World Cups. Others are place and genre specific, such as the Wimbledon tennis tournament, motor-racing Grands Prix, and cultural events, such as the Cannes Film Festival, the Sydney Gay and Lesbian Mardi Gras, the Edinburgh Fringe Festival, and the opening seasons of musical theatrical extravaganzas (*Phantom of the Opera*, *Beauty and the Beast*, and *Miss Saigon*, for example). Global events are part of the inter-urban competition to become 'global cities', a struggle that transcends and fragments nation-states (Sassen 1991; see Chapter 21).

The communications revolutions brought about by fax machines, mobile phones, personal computers, the internet and information highway, videos and compact discs, virtual realities, and theme parks have not only fed popular culture, but now also reshape the meanings and experiences of popular culture. Allan Kellehear (Chapter 1) and Chris Eipper (Chapter 8) use pop culture references, as I have done here, to help us understand our experiences of everyday reality. As Beryl Langer (Chapter 6) demonstrates, consumer capitalism is good at removing our loyalty to place and community, repackaging the ideals, and selling them back to us as commodified needs (see also Seabrook 1985). Popular culture is not the simple outcome of technological change and consumer capitalism. Nor is its globalisation further evidence of sociology's oldest lament — that we are experiencing the end of community — as first argued by Ferdinand Tönnies in his '*Gemeinschaft–Gesellschaft*' dichotomy and continuum, and as implied by David de Vaus in Chapter 9 and Ken Dempsey in Chapter 13. Rather, popular culture continuously reconstitutes the meanings and experiences of both 'community' and 'society' alike. Rock and pop music cultures, for example, were born locally out of an eclectic mix of local traditions from different parts of the world, but which themselves soon became global phenomena, and not only because of market imperatives and technological capacity. Rock music is a social revolution of the 1950s, 1960s and 1970s, but is now mutating into new forms of cultural production as a result of the very same global structures and processes that made its invention and dissemination possible in the first place. If we ignore, for the moment, the parodic irony of revivalism (demonstrated, for instance, by the emergence of tribute albums and bands) and nostalgia (surrounding bands such as Abba and the Rolling Stones), the technologies that first made the sounds possible are now reshaping the noise produced. Moreover, the aural medium is now crossing over into multimedia. Madonna, Michael Jackson, Peter Gabriel, Pink Floyd, and U2 are global performers who have been sensitive monitors of these changes at all levels of pop culture and technological change on the street and in the air.

War, migration, food, travel and tourism, transport and communications, sport, and pop culture are just a few of the many possible indices of the major shifts that have occurred in Australia's identity and place in the world over the past fifty years. Post-conquest Australia was born modern; it has always been acutely conscious of the wider world, as both threat and promise. In recent years, the rhetoric has embraced the promise of absorption, through globalising forces, into global economy and global culture. Our past has given us an acute awareness of both the dangers of globalisation and the need for a helping hand from parental superpower figures. In an era in which the USA appears to be losing its grip on the mantle of 'superpower *numero uno*', and in which Germany and the European Union, Japan, China, and the USA all appear to be jostling for the title, Australia has moved from a stance of 'mastering risk' (White 1992) to becoming a 'high-risk society' (Beck 1992). As a nation-state, Australia has moved from a cultural 'politics of domestic defence' (Castles 1989) — of protection against the outside world — to a starry-eyed embrace of 'globalisation' (Beilharz 1994a and 1994b; see also Chapters 18 and 19). But what is this brave new world that our nation appears to be embracing with enthusiasm for the first time in its relatively short history? How are we to understand and interpret the key terms that continue to be bandied around in academic and popular discourse, as if their meanings are self-evident? What do the terms *global economy*, *global politics*, *global culture*, and *globalisation* mean? How do we make sense of the giddy changes in the landscape of Australia's own public life, some of which have been traced by Peter Beilharz and others in the chapters on 'nation' and by all of the authors contributing chapters on 'globalisation'?

Globalisation: definitions and explanations

Globalisation must be the ugliest buzzword of the 1990s.

Wiseman 1995, p. 5

Globalisation as a concept refers both to the compression of the world and the intensification of consciousness of the world as a whole.

Robertson 1992, p. 8

As is demonstrated by our discussion of Australia's changing place in the world, *globalisation* is best appreciated as a term still in search of a concept. Its incipient universalism encompasses a plethora of meanings and uses. Its very ambiguity and opacity — like that of *postmodern* and its cognate terms — looks set to guarantee its longevity in academic discussions, and its ubiquity in public and popular discourses. This is not a cynical point but, rather, a sociological observation in itself. For all its ugliness, the term does indicate something about the world around us that suggests the need for further investigation. We need the signifier (word), even if we do not yet know the precise nature of the signified (the thing referred to by the word). The term's open-ended nature provokes us to think further about those contemporary global changes that we are still struggling to understand.

If defined in terms of 'a growing international economic interdependence with radical improvements in transport and communications' (Dewberry 1995, p. 11), then *globalisation* is essentially a new buzzword for an older concept called 'development', already succinctly outlined by Alberto Gomes (Chapter 20). As Gomes has demonstrated, development debates have centred on two competing models or approaches used to explain the emergence of a worldwide economic, technological, and political system: modernisation theories and political economy theories. Both approaches, however, have a common historical source in eighteenth-century and early nineteenth-century political economy discourses, which emphasised the emergence of modern transnational and international commercial societies, and the emergence of material cultures that, because they were cosmopolitan, acted as a civilising process on humankind. Until the eighteenth century, the world was most frequently interpreted in cosmological terms (focusing on the world religions) and/or in terms of the geopolitical struggles of aristocratic national leaders and/or ethno-linguistic groups. With the rise of political-economy discourses, a new kind of argument developed, which emphasised the place of wealth-accumulation, of commerce, of free trade between peoples, and which purportedly transcended and cut across religious, ethnic, linguistic, cultural, and political differences. Therefore, commerce and wealth-accumulation, as ends in themselves, were granted primacy of place as the shapers of advancing European civilisation. It was in the eighteenth century that concepts such as 'civilisation', 'universal history', 'world literature', and 'wealth of nations' were first developed and popularised.

The so-called classical nineteenth-century exponents of modern social theory —
Karl Marx, Max Weber, and Émile Durkheim — were all heavily indebted to these
ways of thinking of the world as a whole: all started with the material processes of
society-formation, although each emphasised different aspects. Marx followed the
Scottish political economists by focusing on the emergence of a world economy called
capitalism, especially from the side of production. Weber and Durkheim, on the other
hand, emphasised the novel social formations arising from the rationalisation of the
world through the scientific and technological revolutions, and the specialised division of labour developed in the organisation of industrial capitalism.

By the end of the nineteenth century and the onset of the First World War in
1914, the initial enthusiasm for modern globalising forces turned to apocalyptic
despair. Tönnies lamented the loss of community, Georg Simmel spoke of 'the
tragedy of culture', Weber explored 'the iron cage' of rationalisation processes, and
Ernst Troeltsch explored the outer limits of historicism as relativism and Euro-
peanism. Oswald Spengler, meanwhile, predicted the decline and fall of Western civilisation. While continental thinkers were emersed in romantic despair as they came to
terms with the limits of European enlightenment, European modernisation, and European imperialism, theorists from the brave new worlds of the Americas rethought the
terms of globalisation, extending them beyond Europe.

Twentieth-century modernisation theorists, in part following the lead of Talcott
Parsons, turned the classical theories of eighteenth-century political economy and
nineteenth-century social theory into an explanatory model of cause and effect for
the total social order. In turn, their ambition extended from explanation to encom-
pass policy-prescription. It was hoped that the historical example of Europe could
be applied as a norm and technique to be emulated by all nations throughout the
world, irrespective of their own historical, religious, cultural, economic, and political differences and traditions. Europe was to be not only the origin of world history
and world civilisation, but its destiny also. As Gomes demonstrates in Chapter 20,
modernisation theory in the 1950s and 1960s quickly turned from description to
explanation to prescription.

Modern political economy, largely derived from Marxist-Leninist models of
development, also followed the same path, first emerging as critique and then as
alternative utopia — that of the total society of planned rationality, of communism.
While the dominant traditions of Marxist social theory offered stringent critiques of
modernisation theories, their own utopias were also modernist. While social democ-
rats looked to twentieth-century Sweden and Germany, Marxists advocated the
Russian, Chinese, and Cuban revolutionary paths to, and through, modernity. If the
latter revolutions were thought to be inadequate, it was not because they were recognised as fatally flawed in conception and execution, but because they were seen as
unfinished business. They would remain incomplete until the modern West learnt to
see 'reason in history' as necessarily leading to the good society of communism.

The modernisation theories of liberal sociologists and social democratic political
theorists, as well as the Marxist traditions of interpreting the contemporary world

order, have played themselves out, both as explanation and prescription. On the one hand, the past two decades have witnessed the collapse of economic certitudes, whether they be of the Keynesian liberal-capitalist variety or the Marxist command-economy variety. Of those communist societies that still exist, such as China, Vietnam, and Cuba, experiments in 'market socialism' abound, and on an ever-increasing scale. The social democratic capitalist nations, however, have lost their own confidence in theories and policies for organising international capitalist markets, and flows for social goods and social welfare, within nation-state boundaries, not least because of the growing sense of disbelief in the mechanisms for governing these economic globalising forces. This apparently ubiquitous loss of certainty has spawned any number of economic brands of fundamentalism, of quack prophets and false profits. The persistence of world poverty and ecological desecration, and (even more damning) the collapse of social orders within rich, 'First World' nations (not least as a result of rapidly rising disparities between rich and poor within these nations) perennially call forth proclamations of 'crisis' and apocalyptic visions of doom (Kaplan 1994). When considered together, world poverty and ecological disorder suggest that globalisation processes have run amok with economic theories if not preventing their continued application. At the very least, we now need to admit our confusion by using ambiguous terms such as *globalisation* in the place of old shibboleths such as *development*. The modern dream of conquering nature through 'development' has returned to us as a postmodern nightmare of ecological crises (see Chapter 22). 'Globalisation', unlike 'development' and 'modernisation', is not yet burdened with prescriptive and deterministic connotations, and thereby allows discussions of social movements — such as religious, anti-nuclear, and environmental movements — in non-pejorative terms.

To our anxieties about the loss of economic certainty, we must add the collapse of political certitudes about international relations and the world order of the nation-state system. Since 1989 we have witnessed not only the fall of the Berlin Wall and the implosion of the Soviet Empire, but also the collapse of our hopes in new forms of liberal internationalism (witness the United Nations' peacekeeping initiatives in the Balkans, for example), and in claims that there is a historical and necessary relationship between liberal democracy and free-market capitalist regimes. Revolutions continue to occur, but the crazy patchwork quilt of the world defies easy description or theoretical explanation (see Chapter 24). As we try to junk our cold-war armoury and drop the obsolete language of 'First', 'Second', and 'Third' worlds, of 'East' and 'West', of 'developed', 'less developed', and 'underdeveloped', of 'modern' and 'traditional', and so on, we are battling to adequately describe various contemporary phenomena. How are we to describe and explain the new nomads (see Kevin McDonald's discussion of social movements in Chapter 23); the millions of refugees and immigrants (as discussed by Harvey in Chapter 11, and by Gomes in Chapter 20); the international division of labour (see Doug Ezzy's discussion of work in Chapter 10); the massive and seemingly inexorable shift of the world's population from the country to the cities (see Kerreen Reiger's discussion of urbanisation in Chapter 21); or the 140 nation-states (out of 190) who are but nation-states in name alone, having been rent asunder by uncivil wars between rival organised crime syndicates, each equipped with their own private armies (Camilleri and Falk 1992)?

What these trends and troubles tell us is that the origins of the world economy and the modern nation-state system are to be found in the West — in Europe — but that the processes, forces, and structures are no longer mere reflections and implications of the West. As the world becomes united at the global level through economic and technological means, the organisation of its component parts are not necessarily systematically integrated. How the world, as it moves into the next century, will work as one world, and yet as many worlds of cultural difference, is currently a key theme of critical reflection among world historians and sociologists of globalisation.

Of the great many participants in these debates, I can only briefly mention here two representative figures in the sociology of globalisation. Anthony Giddens (1990) argues that globalisation is a function of the institutional and systemic dimensions of modernisation, of which there are four: the world capitalist economy; the world military order; the international division of labour; and the nation-state system. Each of these dimensions of globalisation, he argues, is the logical consequence of the institutional dimensions of modernity. The world capitalist economy is an outcome of the accumulation of capital in the context of competitive labour and product markets. The world military order derives from the control of the means of violence in the context of the industrialisation of war. The international division of labour is the consequence of industrialism itself, which has involved the transformation of nature by the development of the 'created environment' (that is 'manufacture'). And finally, but not least, the nation-state system is the consequence of the constant modernisation of the means of policing, watching, controlling, and supervising domestic populations (Giddens 1990; see also Harvey 1989).

Roland Robertson (1992), however, argues that such a schematic and boxed picture of globalisation fails to account for the longevity of globalisation processes and structures, which predate the modern epoch, and the cultural or social nature of human societies. According to Robertson, Giddens provides an adequate and insightful account of modern systems, structures, and institutions, and of their consequences for globalisation, but is unable to explain what people think, believe, do, and create. Robertson, as befitting a sociologist of religion, argues that globalisation is not only about the emergence of global unity and global compression in political, military, and economic terms, but is also about different cultural identities: different civilisations, different traditions, different epochs. As Robertson and others have demonstrated, globalisation processes and structures do not necessarily lead to global 'convergence' or 'homogenisation', as was once popularly believed by some sociologists in the 1960s. Nor are we witnessing only a one-way cultural process of 'Westernisation', of 'modernisation', of 'secularisation', or of any other single-factor '-isation' and '-ism'. To understand globalisation as being more than the modern consequence of time–space compression, we need also to understand the 'rise of global consciousness' which leads to ever-new expressions of local identities and traditions, in ever-new configurations and reconstructions of the modern, the pre-modern, the counter-modern, and the postmodern (Kung 1991; Robertson 1992).

Conclusion: the end, and new beginnings

As we approach the dawn of the third millennium, we live in a world that is rapidly becoming compressed into one world system. We continue to describe, understand, and interpret how this is so. Our explanations, however, will never be adequate to our experiences and stories. Nor must our theories be allowed to become statements of fate, of necessity. To link the economic and the political, or the historical and the cultural, in these globalisation processes is an act of the critical and interpretive imagination. To link them together in order to interpret social action is an act of the sociological imagination. To link them back to personal experience and identity, and to the embeddedness of our everyday lives in specific places and times, is an act of the moral and spiritual imagination. We continue to interpret our world from the antipodean margin. Australia's place in the world lies neither in an uncritical embrace of globalisation and of the romance of revolutionary change and risk-taking, nor in the provincial rejection of cultures, nations, and traditions different to our own. We will need to continue to look both ways, to value the global and the local, to critically evaluate the metropolitan centres of global power and the peripheral margins of the provinces, and to see that 'bringing the world back home' involves an awareness of where home is to be found in the first place. However much we look and travel elsewhere, and however much the world is brought back home, some of us still call Australia home — a place in which we live. Nonetheless, the term *globalisation*, at the very least, makes us more aware that, along with the prescriptive slogan 'think globally, act locally', there must be added the critical observation that we also 'think locally, act globally'.

Discussion questions

1   What does Robertson (1992) consider to be an adequate sociological definition of 'globalisation'?
2   What does Anthony Giddens (1990) identify as the main global dimensions and systemic consequences of modernity?
3   Why are the nation-state and the nation-state system thought to be under threat by globalisation processes? In Chapter 19, Peter Beilharz suggests that there is 'room for manoeuvre between nation-state and global system'. Where do you think this 'room to manoeuvre' is to be found with regard to Australia?
4   'Think globally, act locally' or 'think locally, act globally'? Discuss with reference to debates about the future of community as locality, as outlined by Ken Dempsey in Chapter 13.
5   What are the consequences of globalisation for the formation of the social self as outlined by Allan Kellehear in Chapter 7?

Recommended reading

When the topic is as big and complex as the world and the terminology is as clumsy as *globalisation*, the literature is bound to be difficult and at times formidable. The latest, but not necessarily the best, social theories of 'globalisation' include:

- Giddens, A. 1990, *The Consequences of Modernity*, Polity, Cambridge. Recommended for its clarity and brevity.
- Harvey, D. 1989, *The Condition of Postmodernity*, Blackwell, Oxford.

There are lots of pictures, diagrams, and tables to break up the text. Harvey usefully relates political economy to popular culture and historical sociology debates.

- Robertson, R. 1992, *Globalisation*, Sage, London.

Robertson has been the chief propagandist of globalisation as the proper and future unit of analysis for sociology.

- Waters, M., Hindess, B., McDonald, K., Yeatman, A., and Holton, R. J. 1994, 'Globalisation, Multiculturalism, and Rethinking the Social — A Symposium', *The Australian and New Zealand Journal of Sociology*, vol. 30, no. 3, November, pp. 229–54.

A lively interchange that provides Australian perspectives on globalisation debates.

On global culture, see:
- Featherstone, M. (ed.) 1990, *Global Culture*, Sage, London.

This book contains important articles by Roland Robertson, Johann Arnason, and Immanuel Wallerstein.

Look through and compare the following journals for ongoing discussions on globalisation:
- *Theory, Culture and Society*.
- *Thesis Eleven*.
- *Arena*.

On capitalism as world-system, see:
- Wallerstein, I. 1983, *Historical Capitalism*, Verso, London.

Perhaps one of the easier books by a prolific author who is always lucid and fascinating, but who is single-mindedly pushing an architectonic research project.

- Seabrook, J. 1985, *Landscapes of Poverty*, Blackwell, Oxford.

If Wallerstein is the synoptic mind as structure, Seabrook is the synoptic mind as narrative; both are fired by a moral imagination that interprets world order from the perspective of the poor, the marginalised, and the oppressed. Seabrook offers some fascinating, although disturbing, stories.

On politics, the nation-state system, and international relations:
- Camilleri, J. A. and Falk, J. 1992, *The End of Sovereignty?: The Politics of a Shrinking and Fragmenting World*, Edward Elgar, Aldershot, Hants.

A survey of contemporary crises, trends, and debates relating to international politics, this book offers a systematic overview of historical and theoretical perspectives, economic organisation, technological change, security systems, and ecological crises. In doing so, the authors argue that the doctrine of national sovereignty is defunct in fact, and is soon to be dumped in theory as well, and they search for new forms of politics in the post-nation-state system. They place their greatest hopes in the new social movements that are discussed by McDonald in Chapter 23. It is an excellent handbook, but perhaps an over-'stated' thesis.

- Kaplan, R. D. 1994, 'The Coming Anarchy', *The Atlantic Monthly*, February, pp. 44–76.

The subtitle says it all: 'How scarcity, crime, overpopulation, tribalism, and disease are rapidly destroying the social fabric of our planet'. This is 'apocalypse now' journalism at its best and worst. It is fascinating for its rich array of stories and information, but its interpretation of this material is highly controversial.

On possibilities for the emergence of a global ethic, see:

- Kung, H. 1991, *Global Responsibility: In Search of a New World Ethic*, SCM Press, London.

A succinct synthesis of contemporary social, political, and economic issues, with a persuasive argument for the importance of ethics and the world religions (for example, Judaism, Islam, Christianity, Hinduism, and Buddhism) in the search for world peace. His two slogans are 'No World Peace without Religious Peace' and 'No Religious Peace without Religious Dialogue'.

Appendix

When I look back at the particular
jobs I have had, it was true of every
one of them that, in the actual job-
selection process, condsiderable
weight was given to my general
s6ciological training. Certain of these
employers would have been pretty
well stuck if I had asked them what
sociology is about … In all the jobs I
have had, I was continually made
aware of just what a great asset my
sociology background was.

'Andrew' talking to Katy Richmond,
pp. 428–9

What Do Sociologists Do

Katy Richmond

The aim of this section is to identify employment prospects for sociology graduates or those with a substantial number of sociology subjects in their arts or social sciences degrees. After some introductory remarks, I will outline the careers of six young sociologists. I will then discuss some of the competencies acquired by arts and social sciences graduates, and how these are seen by employers. I will then analyse in more detail the specific skills acquired by graduates in sociology. The final section discusses what can be gained from doing an honours degree, how graduates can be accepted for postgraduate work, and what academic work as a sociologist is all about. Also included is some information about The Australian Sociological Association.

The demand for sociologists

It is evident in our society that the nature of work is changing, and that employment prospects are opening up in some areas and closing off in others. The good news for sociologists is that employment is increasing in the tertiary sector of the economy, where those with sociological skills are commonly employed. The need for sociology has increased as services in the areas of housing, education, health, and social welfare have expanded. There are now many more jobs for a variety of social-policy planners and researchers, not only in state and Federal bureaucracies, but also in governmental agencies. The main governmental agencies relevant to sociology graduates as potential employers are the Australian Bureau of Statistics; the Australian Institute of Family Studies; the Bureau of Immigration, Multicultural and Population Research; and the Australian Institute of Criminology.

Six case studies

The sorts of careers sociology graduates may have in the workforce are illustrated by the following six case studies. One graduate works in Canberra; the other five work in Melbourne. Two are graduates of Monash University, three are graduates of La Trobe University and one is a graduate of the University of Queensland. All have completed sociology degrees in the past fifteen years.

'Andrew', who completed his honours degree in sociology in 1982, first worked at two TAFE colleges (one in the city, one in the country) as a statistical planning officer. In these positions he analysed student-enrolment statistics and made predictions about the nature of future student populations. Andrew learnt a great deal from the computing component of these jobs, and found that the skills he learnt in these jobs were ones that other employers were seeking. He then took a research position at the Australian Institute of Family Studies, before returning to the university sector to work in another planning officer position.

'Karen' completed her honours degree in sociology in 1991. She gained a Commonwealth Government graduate cadetship, which was designed to give her brief experience in a variety of bureaucratic positions, and she was placed in seven positions in three years. She now works in a service-oriented Commonwealth Government department as a project officer, where her job is to evaluate welfare programs. Recently she decided she wanted to gain some specialist skills, and so she phoned one of her former sociology lecturers for advice about a suitable course. She has now begun a part-time Diploma in Program Evaluation, and she is thinking of making contact with the Australian Evaluation Society to attend their conferences.

'Phillip' completed an honours degree in 1983. He first worked as a market-research officer with a tourism promotion organisation, carrying out consumer attitude surveys. He took a job as a research officer in a Commonwealth Government department. He said that he found what he had learnt in his university statistical methods course very useful when he was asked to collect, compile, and model data relating to the allocation of welfare and health resources. With this experience, he was then able to move into a position as a policy analyst in the private hospitals industry, doing market and industry forecasting. He then took a research position in a private sector 'think tank' organisation, where he analysed migration and health policy. He now works part-time in this organisation in a management capacity, where one of his jobs is looking for funding. Recently he set up his own research consultancy business. One project was to find out how doctors choose hospitals for their patients. He also writes for magazines and journals.

'Peter' left university in 1987 with strong methodological skills. His first two jobs were for two medical research foundations: the Sudden Infant Death Research Foundation and the Haemophilia Foundation. He is now working for the National Australia Day Council as a senior project officer. His job is to develop and implement new programs to celebrate both Australia Day and the Centenary of Federation in 2001. The National Australia Day Council wanted someone with a broad understanding of the political and social make-up of Australian society and 'an ability to tease out emerging social issues'. Peter said that his sociology background was considered particularly relevant for this job.

'Catherine' completed an honours degree in 1981. She works as a program evaluator with the Aboriginal and Torres Strait Islander Commission in Canberra. Her job involves fieldwork all over Australia. Essentially, what her job entails is working out whether her clients get value for money and whether particular government programs benefit clients in the way they were intended to. She says that every day in her job she uses skills she learnt in her sociology course.

'Meredith', who graduated with honours in 1984, is employed by a large welfare organisation. Her first job there was as a social researcher working on a survey of homeless young people. Her current job involves helping to place the long-term unemployed in positions that are part work experience, part training. She and two other people work as a team, canvassing employers to see what positions are available, and then trying to fit their clients to these positions.

Skills acquired from university training

It is important to say at the outset that the term *sociologist* is not widely recognised in the community, and very few employers refer to the word *sociologist* in job advertisements. This does not mean, however, that graduates with sociology majors do not get jobs. Meredith says that it often may seem as though skills acquired at university are not directly applicable to work situations. However, the skills learnt in sociology courses directly relate to many policy-writing and research positions, but, as she says, 'you are not on a path where you get there directly'. It is important to remember that, though the subject matter of a particular job might seem new, graduates in sociology are more adept than they realise in analysing social issues.

Arts and social sciences degrees are, by their nature, somewhat of a smorgasbord — a rich mix of disciplinary studies. Graduates tend to pick up bits and pieces of knowledge in areas that interest them. Often graduates underestimate the value of the skills they acquire, particularly when they compare themselves with very goal-directed graduates in high-status degrees, such as medicine, law, and computer science.

The first thing to remember is that university courses are not specifically designed to teach 'facts', but more generic and longer-lasting skills. In arts and social sciences courses, such skills include how to think constructively about a topic; how to search for evidence; how to evaluate and analyse information; how to organise ideas and arguments; and how to place concepts and theories in a broader perspective.

Students rarely understand the importance of being able to write well. This is not simply a matter of having a good grasp of grammar and punctuation, and being able to spell. Good writing means being able to organise ideas in sequence, and to argue clearly and logically, with an appropriate respect for evidence. A survey of some United States employers in the 1980s indicated that 'the most critical skill is writing — the skill most likely to be appreciated by the broadest range of potential employers' (Garrison 1987, p. 127).

However arts and social sciences graduates learn more than the ability to write. They learn how to organise work, and how to do things within time limits. They develop valuable analytical and problem-solving skills. They learn how to read quickly and how to take a set of succinct notes. They learn how to communicate effectively, how to argue without closing off discussion, how to lead a discussion so that a resolution is reached, how to motivate others to contribute to a discussion, and how to negotiate. They develop a high tolerance of ambiguity and uncertainty. Their confidence gives them the ability to make decisions intelligently. Above all, social science graduates generally have something called 'intellectual curiosity'. They are not likely to be satisfied with simple, pat solutions to problems, and for this reason they are especially valuable to employers.

Having good writing skills means that arts graduates can move into employment areas in which concise and rapid report-writing is required. Graduates can fill research and policy positions in government departments (both state and Commonwealth). They can also fulfil similar roles in many non-governmental agencies, such as professional associations, trade organisations, and health research, religious, charity, and welfare groups. At the more junior stages in their careers, they make good research assistants and speech-writers for parliamentarians. They can write media releases for trade unions. They can also — with appropriate postgraduate qualifications — move into radio, television, or newspaper journalism. Their writing abilities can also be utilised in advertising and marketing agencies.

Sociology graduates acquire a number of specific skills, some theoretical, some methodological. Employers often see merit in employing graduates with a broader understanding of the world. Probably without fully realising it, sociology graduates develop some sensitivity to a wide range of people and their backgrounds, and a realisation that perceptions can differ, that people come into situations with different ideas about what is appropriate.

A sociology graduate has these general skills:

1 Effectively communicates (i.e. clearly explains self both orally and in writing).
2 Demonstrates an ability to think critically (i.e. points out potential problems, expands issues by asking questions, making comments).
3 Demonstrates problem-solving skills (i.e. looks to the consequences of proposals, finds alternative solutions).
4 Demonstrates an ability to make decisions (i.e. does things without constantly being told).
5 Shows a capacity for growth (i.e. seeks out new experiences and responsibilities).
6 Shows a capacity to cope flexibly with the unexpected (i.e. demonstrates confidence in responding to new situations and ideas).
7 Takes advantage of opportunities to contribute ideas and information (i.e. offers ideas, opinions, solutions).
8 Demonstrates leadership skills (i.e. can influence others, can develop ideas, and can delegate and coordinate responsibilities).
9 Can articulate a personal point of view (i.e. demonstrates viewpoints which are clear and which have been thought through).
10 Is responsible and dependable (i.e. shows up when expected and carries out given tasks by the due date).
11 Gets along well with others (i.e. demonstrates a positive working relationship with fellow workers, fosters team work).
12 Reflects self-confidence (i.e. volunteers for new assignments, hesitates little when deciding, accepts criticism well).
13 Shows an ability to gain the confidence of others (i.e. others seek opinions from this person).

Source: Watkins 1978

Sociology provides a means of seeing the world from a diversity of cultural perspectives. This ability gives sociologists an edge over other graduates in work situations where an understanding of cultural diversity is required — for example, in workplaces where equal-opportunity issues need to be addressed. Sociology also gives graduates an awareness of injustice and inequality, and some sympathy with the point of view of the underdog. Sociology graduates learn to respond sensitively to people and to issues, and to be alert to the underlying social context of problems. They start from the premise that individual problems have social causes. They develop the capacity to deal sympathetically with people, and they have an understanding of the value of self-help groups and of the need to allow social-welfare recipients to organise their responses to their problems in their own way. They are conscious of consumer issues, and have some understanding of the rights of the individual. For these sorts of reasons, sociology graduates are often employed in ethnic organisations and migration-research centres. Their understanding of the issues relating to equal opportunity means that they are useful in the personnel and industrial-relations units of business and government agencies.

Andrew had this to say:

> When I look back at the particular jobs I have had, it was true of every one of them that, in the actual job-selection process, considerable weight was given to my general sociological training. Certain of these employers would have been pretty well stuck if I had asked them what sociology is about. But they felt that a sociology background was extremely valuable in all aspects of a job requiring the assessment, or balancing, of different viewpoints, personal interaction with people from varied backgrounds, a capacity to communicate well with people, and the ability to appreciate different sets of values held by different people. In all the jobs I have had, I was continually made aware of just what a great asset my sociology background was.

Turning now to methodology, sociology graduates learn to 'do research'. Even without undertaking highly specialised methodology courses, most graduates, by the end of their degrees, understand what 'research' is and how to do it. They learn how to tease out 'the essence' of a particular problem, where to go to find previous research in the area, and how to design a research project from beginning to end. Sociology graduates also learn a number of highly relevant survey skills, especially if they take sociological methods courses. In these sorts of courses, they learn how to construct questionnaires, how to gather a sample, how to undertake systematic interviews, and how to analyse the data they have collected. Often graduates may acquire particular skills with computer software. One especially relevant piece of computer software for sociological research is called SPSS — Statistical Package for the Social Sciences. This software processes information from social-survey data, and allows easy and quick organisation of it so that a series of statistical tests can be conducted. Most sociology courses include one course on SPSS.

At a more general level, sociology graduates also develop some participant-observation skills. They learn to observe and investigate social groups such as the family, schools, small communities, and work groups. These observational skills are not only relevant in a research context, but they also have a wider applicability. Through the development of these sorts of skills, sociology graduates develop the capacity to carefully watch how others behave and what their body language is saying. Employers find such skills very valuable in the workplace, particularly at the management level.

Sociology graduates with strong methodology skills can be employed in market research, or in areas requiring social research. For example, employers might be local government agencies, regional authorities, welfare agencies, or government departments. In their first jobs after graduation, graduates who take on research-oriented positions will most probably be employed to undertake interviews, possibly face-to-face, but often by telephone. As they gain experience, they will be able to fill positions in which they design questionnaires, analyse data, and write reports. Positions for sociologists with considerable methodological training are sometimes available in Canberra at the Australian Institute of Criminology and the Bureau of Statistics, and in Melbourne at the Institute of Family Studies, and Bureau of Immigration, Multicultural and Population Research. In addition, many Australian states have bodies with names like The Centre for Urban Research and Action, or the Institute for Applied Economic and Social Research.

Sociology graduates are not limited to jobs that specifically require the ability to undertake research. Methodological skills are also of value in many government jobs that are not directly related to research. For example, most government departments need to evaluate their programs that are designed to give people access to housing, education, and health care. There are also many non-profit organisations that require people with some sociological methodology training, especially those that bring together particular client groups, such as the Sudden Infant Death Research Foundation and the Haemophilia Foundation.

An understanding of sociological methodology — how to do research, how to collect data — gives graduates not only specific skills, but also some more diffuse skills. Catherine says that her sociology background has given her a more rigorous approach to evaluating people's statements. She says that she is now able to stand back and see things from a distance. When people come to her and tell her that that they 'know' something, she is able to ask important questions about evidence. She has learnt to sift anecdotal data from more concretely based information. If she feels that information she is given is well founded, she is able to develop arguments about why certain information should be accepted as a basis for policy and governmental action. She also has the confidence to admit ignorance and to go off to find more data.

Sociology graduates also develop some important intellectual skills relating to the ability to sort out elements of a social situation with clarity, but without losing a grasp on the complexities. Undoubtedly, one factor in the ability to analyse social processes is the grasp of a package of central concepts. Sociology graduates often find, to their amazement, that they have learnt a new language. Several of the graduates whom I interviewed for this section mentioned how important they thought sociological concepts and sociological theory were in their work. Catherine said, in relation to her program evaluation work, that she thinks about 'power' and 'class' every day. She says that these concepts are 'fundamentals which most people don't talk about', but that they are essential to her in her job. Karen, doing a similar job in a different government department, says that she draws on sociological theories about power and social structure all the time. She says sociology has been invaluable to her, because it enables her to understand what power is and how power is used by gatekeepers in social groups.

Sociology graduates can rarely call themselves 'sociologists' in their chosen field of employment. But this has an unexpected spin-off. Because they lack a clear sense of professional ownership of a particular methodology, sociologists work particularly well with people from other disciplinary backgrounds. Bernie Jones — an American sociologist working as a consultant — reports that he developed a 'willingness to work in interdisciplinary groups of professionals, not all of whom either understood or appreciated the role of the sociologist' (Jones 1987, p. 187). Karen, who works in a service-oriented government agency, told me that, where she works, her employers deliberately create interdisciplinary teams. Her ability to 'mix' with other professionals is something her boss appreciates about her. But she insists that her job requires her active participation. There is no 'sitting back' and letting others talk. One of the obligations of her job is that she 'thinks aloud' and that she contributes actively to the debates about policy and its implementation. She is paid to discuss. But she also knows it is important not to dominate. Because she works in a team with people from a variety of disciplines, she has to be 'inclusive' and to let others speak.

Undertaking additional study

Most people advise graduates — especially graduates in the humanities and social sciences — to undertake additional study. Such study need not be undertaken immediately after graduating. Many people continue on to graduate and postgraduate study in their thirties and forties. It is important to remember, too, that some study can be undertaken outside the tertiary education sector. There is a summer program in social research methods run by the Australian Consortium for Social and Political Research Incorporated (ACSPRI), for example. These courses are arranged through the Social Science Data Archives, Australian National University, each January and February.

These days there is a huge variety of postgraduate diplomas and degrees from which to choose. Not all university courses require campus attendance — some are available through distance education, and some are intensive summer-school programs The most common postgraduate diploma undertaken by arts and social sciences graduates used to be in education, but the number of jobs available for teachers has been reduced in recent years. In any case, a sociology background has never had directly relevance for teachers since sociology is not taught in most secondary school curriculums. However, in the last decade, the range of graduate and postgraduate programs in the social sciences has widened considerably, especially in welfare, law, and industrial relations. Many sociology graduates take up additional degrees or diplomas in social work, law, industrial relations, labour studies, criminology, management, tourism, youth studies, recreation, and so on. There are also a number of specialist courses covering equal opportunity, race relations, and the like.

If you are looking for a full list of diplomas and degrees, each state has a 'tertiary admissions centre' (Victoria has VTAC, NSW has UTAC, and Queensland has QTAC, for example). The relevant organisation will be able to provide a guide to all tertiary courses in your state. Furthermore, each university has a careers office, which will be able to give you more detailed help. For a list of some of the most relevant graduate diplomas and postgraduate degrees for sociology graduates, see the latest edition of *Sociology in Australian Universities*, published by the Australian Sociological Association. This can be found in the reference section of most university libraries.

It is particularly advisable to continue on to a fourth year (or an honours year) in sociology. Having an honours degree will make you more acceptable to employers and more likely to gain entry to postgraduate degrees and diplomas. Doing that fourth year and getting an honours degree enables you to write 'BA Hons' after your name, but that is not all. Employers look particularly favourably on graduates with honours degrees. Having an honours degree demonstrates that you have the capacity to commit yourself to four years, rather than just three years, of study. It also means (usually) that you have undertaken a specific piece of research, and that you are someone whom your university teachers regard favourably. You have been picked out from the crowd, as it were.

How to become an academic sociologist

Here I want to provide an account of the 'academic game'. Universities in Australia are largely modelled on British universities (though there are some differences). In order to obtain an academic job, the requirement of a PhD has become virtually mandatory. The usual academic path is as follows (but check with your university about its specific requirements).

If you want to do a minimum university course, you study for three years and gain a Bachelor of Arts degree (a 'BA'). This is called 'taking out a pass degree'. If you want to continue on with studies, and your marks are good enough, you can undertake a fourth year of study in sociology called your 'honours year'. (Some universities may ask you to do some special subjects in order to be eligible for this fourth year of study.) In most universities, your honours year work includes writing a thesis and attending some lectures. For a new sociology student, writing 15 000 words may seem a mammoth task, but most students learn to write essays of 5000 or 6000 words, so that by fourth year the jump to 15 000 words is manageable. Remember that you will have a whole year to research and write it, and you will be writing your thesis under the close guidance of a supervisor, who is generally someone of your choice. Most honours theses are 'theoretical' rather than based on new research.

Mostly there is not time to do the necessary preparatory work for a piece of empirical research, though often honours students are able to use empirical data collected by members of the academic staff in the university where they are studying, and sometimes they have access to computerised sets of survey data or to census data.

Doing an honours degree generally allows you to move on to a Masters degree (an MA) and, ultimately, a PhD. There is an alternate way to get into a Masters program in most universities, but that alternate is less prestigious, and it has the added disadvantage that, although you do the same work, usually, as fourth-year honours students, you cannot describe yourself as having a 'BA Hons'. This alternative is called doing an 'MA Prelim.', which stands for Master of Arts Preliminary. (Sometimes it is called 'a qualifying year', which means that you are qualifying to do an MA.) You can enter an MA Prelim. program by applying to the department or school of sociology of your choice, and this means that you can swap universities if you wish. Your undergraduate degree needs to include a reasonable amount of sociology. However, there is one important thing to know: having completed an MA Prelim. year, you cannot write 'MA Prelim.' after your name. Neither universities nor employers see the MA Prelim. as having the same value as an honours degree. Your MA Prelim. year is really only useful if you want to get into an MA program at the same university (it is usually not transferable). The rules about honours and the MA Prelim. vary from university to university, so you should check the requirements carefully.

Now let us look at the MA and PhD systems. There are some MAs in sociology that are 'coursework' MAs. A coursework MA requires only a short thesis (perhaps 15 000–20 000 words). In addition, you are required to do perhaps three or four units of conventional study (attending lectures or seminars, writing essays, and perhaps sitting for examinations). These MA coursework programs do not generally allow you to 'upgrade' to a PhD, though again the rules vary from university to university. What this means is that you have to finish the MA coursework completely, and graduate, and then apply to start a PhD. There is nothing wrong with this approach, if that is what you want to do, but if you suddenly discover that you are a person with real research ability, it will take you many years to graduate with BA (Hons), an MA, and finally a PhD. So, though coursework MAs have their place, it is important to realise their limitations: you generally will not be able to transfer up to a PhD halfway through an MA coursework program. Again, check the rules at your university.

A conventional MA — not a 'coursework MA' but an 'MA by thesis' — involves writing a thesis of perhaps 60 000 words. This can be done in a year full-time, if you work hard, but most students take longer, perhaps eighteen months or two years. However, the important thing to know is that, if you start an MA by thesis, and if your supervisors feel that your MA thesis work indicates that you have strong research ability, you can usually upgrade to a PhD. The upgrading process differs from university to university. The requirements are often stringent. Generally, two or three chapters of your MA thesis are assessed to determine your ability to complete a PhD.

You can complete your PhD in three years full time, but this is unlikely; most people take longer. A lot depends on your ability to attract financial support: either a scholarship or a bursary from an employer. Many PhD students have access to employment as part-time university tutors, which is rewarding, interesting, and looks good on your curriculum vitae, but it does not pay well. Doing a PhD (also known as 'getting your doctorate') in minimum time requires concentrated effort, an ability to work largely in isolation, and some luck with choosing a topic that has 'boundaries'.

What happens after you do a PhD? Most people who graduate with a PhD aim to publish their thesis in article and/or book form very quickly, so that they can indicate to future employers that they can 'publish'. Publications, even very short publications, are remarkably valuable, even outside academia, because they indicate an ability to write independently and to follow through with a project to completion. Many people who get their PhDs aim to be academics. Universities are market-places that are fraught with difficulties for would-be academics. Academic jobs are not easy to acquire these days, and even for full-time Level A lectureships (the old 'tutoring' positions) in sociology and anthropology, a PhD and publications are generally required.

However, PhDs are very valuable outside academia. A PhD will probably gain you entry into the upper echelons of the Commonwealth or state public services, and you may also be welcomed in many research and policy positions (for example, in market research or in governmental research agencies, such as the Bureau of Immigration, Multicultural and Population Research). For instance, several recent PhD graduates have found places in Canberra in the Commonwealth Department of Foreign Affairs.

What do academic sociologists do?

What does the job of a university lecturer in sociology involve? Most undergraduate students see academics as teachers, but undergraduate teaching is only part of an academic's job. Academics are also required to do research and to publish, and often this means writing one or two articles a year, or writing a book every second or third year. Organising research, especially if it involves surveys, is very complex. In addition, most academics have a sizeable postgraduate load, and postgraduate supervision is very time-consuming. If they can, academics try to get their papers accepted at overseas conferences, which are often more prestigious than local conferences, which generally lead to better publication opportunities, and which certainly allow academics to meet others writing in the same field. Academics also have to do some administrative work (some of which, believe it or not, is interesting and even fun). They also edit journals, run conferences, and take part in the organisation of professional associations.

Sociological associations

The main sociological association in Australia is The Australian Sociological Association (TASA). It was founded in 1960, and in 1965 it began to publish a journal called *The Australian and New Zealand Journal of Sociology* (which we abbreviate to *ANZJS*). This journal is issued three times a year and is available free to members of the association. Members also receive the association's newsletter, which is called *Nexus*, and a Membership Directory (enabling members to contact other sociologists around Australia). Membership of the association is available to any interested person (some professional associations only allow you to join if you have passed a specific set of examinations, but this is not true of TASA). The payment of an annual membership subscription entitles you to three issues of the journal, four issues of the association's newsletter, and information about the annual conference. There is a reduced membership fee for students.

TASA also publishes a guide to sociology departments or schools in Australia called *Sociology in Australian Universities*. This guide is published biennially and is particularly valuable for sociology graduates wanting to find a suitable university at which to do their MA or PhD. The guide lists all staff members in sociology (and related departments) in Australian universities, and gives information about scholarships and postgraduate study programs. It is available at a reduced rate to members of the association.

Professional associations mostly concentrate on two central tasks: editing journals and organising conferences. Journal editors change every four years (approximately), and their job is to vet papers for publication. Mostly people who submit papers for publication are given advice on how to improve their work, and sometimes honours graduates publish their honours theses in article form. Even undergraduate students sometimes manage to get their essays published. See, for example, Dorothy Broom, Marguerite Byrne, and Lily Petkovic's (1992) article on women who play pool in a student union. This article started out as a third-year sociology essay.

The TASA sociology conference is held in the first or second week of December each year at a different Australian university. Undergraduate and postgraduate students are welcome to attend these conferences. Reduced registration fees are available for students, as well as often very cheap accommodation. Sometimes there is also a subsidised transport scheme. Some students give papers at the conference.

TASA is not the only association in Australia that you might like to join. There is also the Australian and New Zealand Criminology Society, the Australian Evaluation Society, the Australian Women's Studies Association, the Australian Cultural Studies Association, and many others. There are also a number of overseas sociological associations. The most important of these are the American Sociological Association (the ASA's conference is in August, and its journal is the *American Sociological Review*) and the British Sociological Association (the BSA's conference is in April, and its journal is *Sociology*).

Conclusion

It is useful to end with the words of the famous sociologist C. Wright Mills. He is often quoted because he loved sociology and he knew the value of having sociological skills in an increasingly complex world. What we talk about as 'learning sociology' he calls 'developing your sociological imagination':

> the sociological imagination ... is the capacity to shift from one perspective to another — from the political to the psychological; from examination of a single family to comparative assessment of the national budgets of the world ... It is the capacity to range from the most impersonal and remote transformations to the most intimate features of the human self — and to see the relations between the two ... By its use [people] often come to feel that they can now provide themselves with adequate summations, cohesive assessments, comprehensive orientations ...
>
> Mills 1959, pp. 7–8

And armed with these cohesive assessments and comprehensive orientations, people get jobs.

Recommended reading

- Broom, D., Byrne, M., and Petkovic, L. 1992, 'Off Cue: Women Who Play Pool', *The Australian and New Zealand Journal of Sociology*, vol. 28, pp. 175–91.

This article is fun to read, and it also shows how a student essay can be turned into a valuable piece of academic research.

- Demerath, N. J., Larsen, O., and Schuessler, K. F. (eds) 1975, *Social Policy and Sociology*, Academic Press, New York.

This is an American book that contains articles written by academics about how to produce sociology graduates who are useful to employers (there is not an equivalent Australian book).

- Dent, O. and Illy, A. 1980, 'Career Prospects for Sociology and Related Social-Behavioural Science Graduates', *The Australian and New Zealand Journal of Sociology*, vol. 16, pp. 82–9.

This is a useful study of the instances in which 'sociologists' were mentioned in Australian job advertisements in 1978–79.

- Garrison, H. 1987, 'Preparing Students for Nonacademic Employment', in J. M. and M. Iutcovich (eds), *The Sociologist as Consultant*, Praeger, New York, pp. 121–32.

This is an American commentary on sociology graduates' employment prospects.

- Jones, B. 1987 'Operating a Nonprofit Consulting Corporation in the Business Environment', in J. M. and M. Iutcovich (eds), *The Sociologist as Consultant*, Praeger, New York, pp. 185–92.

Geared more to an experienced sociologist than to a new graduate, this article provides a useful response to the question 'What is a consultant?'.

- Kellehear, A. 1990, *Every Student's Guide to Sociology*, Thomas Nelson, Melbourne.

This is a brief guide to sociology, which is written for first-year students. It also contains some basic career information for graduates.

- Mills, C. Wright 1959, *The Sociological Imagination*, Oxford University Press, New York.

This book is one of the most quoted sociological works written in the twentieth century.

- Richmond, K. (ed.) 1994, *Sociology in Australian Universities 1995–96*, The Australian Sociological Association, Melbourne.

This book, updated every second year, lists sociology departments and their staff around Australia. It contains useful names, addresses, email addresses, phone, and fax numbers, and details of many relevant postgraduate courses.

Bibliography

ABS. See Australian Bureau of Statistics.

Abu-Lughod, J. 1991, *Changing Cities: Suburban Sociology*, Harper Collins, New York.

Adler, E., Barkat, A., Bena-Silu, J., Duncan, Q., and Webb, P. 1981, *Justice for Aboriginal Australians: Report of the World Council of Churches Team Visit to the Aborigines, June 15 to July 3, 1981*, Australian Council of Churches, Sydney.

Aggar, B. 1991, 'Critical Theory, Poststructuralism, Postmodernity: Their Sociological Significance', *Annual Review of Sociology*, vol. 17, pp. 105–31.

Alavi, H. and Shanin, T. (eds) 1982, *Introduction to the Sociology of 'Developing Societies'*, Monthly Review Press, New York.

Alder, C. 1991, 'Victims of Violence: The Case of Homeless Youth', *Australian and New Zealand Journal of Criminology*, vol. 24, March, pp. 1–14.

Alder, C. and Sandor, D. 1989, Homeless Youth as Victims of Violence, report available from Criminology Department, University of Melbourne.

Allport, C. 1986, 'Women and Suburban Housing', in J. B. McLoughlin and M. Huxley (eds), *Urban Planning in Australia: Critical Readings*, Longman Cheshire, Melbourne.

Anderson, B. 1982, *The Imagined Community*, Verso, London.

Anderson, I. 1993/1994, 'Reclaiming Tru-ger-nan-ner: De-colonising the Symbol', *Art Monthly Australia*, no. 66, pp. 10–12.

—— 1994, *Black Bit White Bit*, ed. G. Papadellianis, Republica, Angus & Robertson, Sydney, pp. 113–22.

Araeen, R. 1987, 'From Primitivism to Ethnic Arts', *Third Text*, vol. 1, Autumn, pp. 6–25.

Austin, D. J. 1984, *Australian Sociologies*, Allen & Unwin, Sydney.

Austin, T. 1993, *'I Can Picture the Old Home So Clearly': The Commonwealth and 'Halfcast' Youth in the Northern Territory 1911–1939*, Aboriginal Studies Press, Canberra.

Australian Bureau of Statistics 1993a, *Australia in Profile*, Cat. no. 2821.0, ABS, Canberra.

—— 1993b, *1990 Survey of Income and Housing Costs and Amenities: Income Units Australia*, Cat. no. 6523.0, ABS, Canberra.

—— 1993c, *1990 Survey of Income and Housing Costs and Amenities: Housing Occupancy and Costs*, Cat. no. 4130.0, ABS, Canberra.

—— 1994a, *Labour Force Status and Educational Attainment, Australia — February 1994*, Cat. no. 6235.0, ABS, Canberra.

—— 1994b, *Labour Statistics Australia, 1993*, Cat. no. 6101.0, ABS, Canberra.

—— 1994c, *The Labour Force, Australia — December 1994*, Cat. no. 6203.0, ABS, Canberra.

—— 1994d, *Australian Social Trends, 1994*, ABS, Canberra.

—— 1995, *The Labour Force, Australia — January 1995*, Cat. no. 6203.0, ABS, Canberra.

Bacchi, C. 1990, *Same Difference: Feminism and Sexual Difference*, Allen & Unwin, Sydney.

Bairoch, P. 1988, *Cities and Economic Development*, Mansell Publishing, London.

Baran, P. 1957, *The Political Economy of Growth*, Monthly Review Press, New York.

Barker, M. 1981, *The New Racism*, Junction Books, London.

Barton, G. B. 1889, *History of New South Wales from the Records*, vol. 1, Government Printer, Sydney.

Barwick, D. 1964, 'The Self-Conscious People of Melbourne', in M. Reay (ed.), *Aborigines Now*, Angus & Robertson, Sydney, pp. 20–31.

—— 1985, 'This Most Resolute Lady: A Biographical Puzzle', in D. Barwick, J. Beckett and M. Reay (eds), *Metaphors of Interpretation: Essays in Honour of W. E. H. Stanner*, Australian National University Press, Canberra, pp. 185–239.

Bassnett, S. 1986, *Feminist Experiences: The Women's Movement in Four Cultures*, Allen & Unwin, London.

Bates, S. 1994, Hands for Hire: Contracting and the Nursing Labour Process, unpublished MA (Health Studies) thesis, School of Sociology and Anthropology, La Trobe University, Melbourne.

Bauman, Z. 1987, *Legislators and Interpreters*, Polity Press, Oxford.

Baxter, J., Emmison, M., and Western, J. (eds) 1991, *Class Analysis and Contemporary Australia*, Macmillan, Melbourne.

Beck, U. 1992, *Risk Society*, Sage Publications, London.

Becker, H. 1963, *Outsiders*, The Free Press of Glencoe, Toronto.

Beckett, J. 1988, 'The Past in the Present; the Present in the Past: Constructing a National Aboriginality', in J. Beckett (ed.), *Past and Present: The Construction of Aboriginality*, Aboriginal Studies Press, Canberra, pp. 191–217.

Beilharz, P. 1991a, 'Karl Marx', in P. Beilharz (ed.), *Social Theory: A Guide to Central Thinkers*, Allen & Unwin, Sydney, pp. 168–74.

—— 1991b, 'Max Weber', in P. Beilharz (ed.), *Social Theory: A Guide to Central Thinkers*, Allen & Unwin, Sydney, pp. 224–30.

—— 1994a, *Postmodern Socialism: Romanticism, City and State*, Melbourne University Press, Melbourne.

—— 1994b, *Transforming Labor — Labour Tradition and the Labor Decade in Australia*, Cambridge University Press, Sydney.

Beilharz, P., Considine, M., and Watts, R. 1992, *Arguing About the Welfare State — The Australian Experience*, Allen & Unwin, Sydney.

Bell, C. and Newby, H. 1971, *Community Studies: an Introduction to the Sociology of the Local Community*, George Allen & Unwin, London.

—— 1976, 'Community, Communion, Class and Community Action: the Social Sources of the New Urban Politics', in D. Herbert and R. Johnston (eds), *Spatial Perspectives on Problems and Policies*, 2nd edn, Wiley, London.

Benjamin, J. 1988, *The Bonds of Love: Psychoanalysis, Feminism, and the Problem of Domination*, Pantheon Books, New York.

Bennett, S. 1992, *Aborigines and Political Power*, Allen & Unwin, Sydney.

Berger, J. 1972, *Ways of Seeing*, Penguin Books, Harmondsworth.

Berger, B. and Berger, P. 1976, *Sociology: A Biographical Approach*, Penguin Books, Harmondsworth.

Berger, P. and Luckmann, T. 1966, *The Social Construction of Reality*, Penguin Books, Harmondsworth.

Berry, M. 1983, 'The Australian City in History', in L. Sandercock and M. Berry (eds), *Urban Political Economy*, Allen & Unwin, Sydney, pp. 3–33.

—— 1994, 'The Political Economy of Australian Cities', in L. Johnson (ed.), *Suburban Dreaming: An Interdisciplinary Approach to Australian Cities*, Deakin University Press, Geelong.

Beynon, H. 1973, *Working for Ford*, Penguin Books, Harmondsworth.

Billings, D. B. and Urban, T. 1982, 'The Socio-Medical Construction of Transsexualism: An Interpretation and Critique', *Social Problems*, vol. 29, pp. 266–82.

Blackmore, S. 1993, *Dying to Live: Science and the Near-Death Experience*, Grafton, London.

Blau, P. M. and Duncan, O. D. 1967, *The American Occupational Structure*, John Wiley, New York.

Bleier, R. 1987, 'Science and Belief: A Polemic on Sex Differences Research', in C. Farnham (ed.), *The Impact of Feminist Research in the Academy*, Indiana University Press, Bloomington.

Blyton, Enid 1972, *The Folk of the Faraway Tree*, Deans & Sons, Somerset.

Bodrow, A. (ed.) 1977, *The Worker in Australia*, University of Queensland Press, St Lucia.

Bolton, G. 1972, *A Fine Country to Starve in*, University of Western Australia Press, Perth.

Bottomley, G. 1979, *After the Odyssey: A Study of Greek Australians*, University of Queensland Press, St Lucia.

—— 1992, *From Another Place: Migration and the Politics of Culture*, Cambridge University Press, Cambridge.

Bottomley, G. and De Lepervanche, M. (eds) 1984, *Ethnicity, Class and Gender in Australia*, Studies in Society, no. 24, Allen & Unwin, Sydney.

Bottomley, G., De Lepervanche, M., and Martin, J. 1991, *Intersexions: Gender, Class, Culture, Ethnicity*, Allen & Unwin, Sydney.

Bourdieu, P. 1984, *Distinction*, Routledge & Kegan Paul, London.

Bowles, P. 1972, *Without Stopping: An Autobiography*, G. P. Putnam's Sons, New York.

Box, S. 1981, *Deviance, Reality and Society*, 2nd edn, Holt, Rinehart & Winston, London.

—— 1983, *Power, Crime and Mystification*, Tavistock Publications, London.

Brake, M. 1980, *The Sociology of Youth Culture and Youth Subcultures*, Routledge & Kegan Paul, London.

Braverman, H. 1974, *Labor and Monopoly Capital*, Monthly Review Press, New York.

Brewer, G. 1980, *Out of Work, Out of Sight*, Brotherhood of St Laurence, Melbourne.

Brinton, C. 1963, *The Shaping of Modern Thought*, Prentice-Hall, Englewood Cliffs, NJ.

Broom, D., Byrne, M., and Petkovic, L. 1992, 'Off Cue: Women Who Play Pool', *The Australian and New Zealand Journal of Sociology*, vol. 28, pp. 175–91.

Broom, L. and Jones, F. L. 1976, *Opportunity and Attainment in Australia*, Australian National University Press, Canberra.

Broom, L., Jones, F. L., McDonnell, P., and Williams, T. 1980, *The Inheritance of Inequality*, Routledge & Kegan Paul, London.

Broome, R. 1994, *Aboriginal Australians: Black Response to White Dominance 1788–1994*, 2nd edn, Allen & Unwin, Sydney.

Bryson, B. 1989, *The Lost Continent: Travels in Small Town America*, Abacus, London.

Bryson, L. 1992, *Welfare and the State*, Macmillan, Melbourne.

—— 1993, 'Welfare Issues of the 'Nineties', in J. M. Najman and J. S. Western, *A Sociology of Australian Society: Introductory Readings*, 2nd edn, Macmillan, Melbourne.

Burdekin Report. See Human Rights and Equal Opportunity Commission 1989.

Burgmann, V. 1993, *Power and Protest: Movements for Change in Australian Society*, Allen & Unwin, Sydney.

Burnley, I., Encel, S., and McCall, G. 1985, *Immigration and Ethnicity in the 1980s*, Longman Cheshire, Melbourne.

Calvert, P. 1990, *Revolution and Counter-revolution*, Open University Press, Buckingham.

Camilleri, J. A. and Falk, J. 1992, *The End of Sovereignty?: The Politics of a Shrinking and Fragmented World*, Edward Elgar, Aldershot, Hants.

Cardoso, F. and Faletto, E. 1979, *Dependency and Development in Latin America*, University of California Press, Berkley.

Carney, T. and Hanks, P. 1986, *Australian Social Security Law, Policy and Administration*, Oxford University Press, Melbourne.

Carson, R. 1962, *Silent Spring*, Houghton Mifflin, Boston.

Castells, M. 1983, *The City and the Grassroots: A Cross-cultural Theory of Urban and Social Movements*, Edward Arnold, London.

Castles, F. G. 1985, *The Working Class and Welfare*, Allen & Unwin, Sydney.

—— 1989, *Australian Public Policy and Economic Vulnerability*, Allen & Unwin, Sydney.

Castles, S., Cope, B., Kalantzis, M., and Morrissey, M. (eds) 1992, *Mistaken Identity: Multiculturalism and the Demise of Nationalism in Australia*, 3rd edn, Pluto Press, Sydney.

Castles, S., Kalantzis, M., Cope, B., and Morrissey, M. (eds) 1990, *Mistaken Identity: Multiculturalism and the Demise of Nationalism in Australia*, 2nd edn, Pluto Press, Sydney.

Castles, S. and Miller, M. J. 1993, *Age of Migration: International Population Movements in the Modern World*, Macmillan, London.

Chodorow, N. 1978, *The Reproduction of Mothering: Psychoanalysis and the Sociology of Gender*, University of California Press, Berkeley.

Clarke, J. et al. 1976, 'Subcultures, Cultures and Class: A Theoretical Overview', in S. Hall and T. Jefferson (eds), *Resistance through Rituals*, Hutchinson, London.

Cohen, A. 1988, *The Symbolic Construction of Community*, Tavistock Publications, London.

Cohen, S. 1972, *Folk Devils and Moral Panics*, MacGibbon & Kee, London.

—— 1989, *Visions of Social Control*, Polity Press, Cambridge.

Commission of Inquiry into Poverty 1975, *Poverty in Australia*, First Main Report (Prof. R. F. Henderson, Chairman), AGPS, Canberra.

Connell, R. W. 1977, *Ruling Class, Ruling Culture*, Cambridge University Press, Melbourne.

—— 1986, 'Theorizing Gender', in N. Grieve and A. Burns (eds), *Australian Women: New Feminist Perspectives*, Oxford University Press, Melbourne.

Connell, R., Ashenden, D., Kessler, S., and Dowsett, G. 1982, *Making the Difference*, Allen & Unwin, Sydney.

Connell, R. W. and Dowsett G. W. 1992, '"The Unclean Motion of the Generative Parts": Frameworks in Western Thought on Sexuality', in R. W. Connell and G. W. Dowsett (eds), *Rethinking Sex: Social Theory and Sexuality Research*, Melbourne University Press, Melbourne.

Connell, R. W. and Irving, T. 1980, *Class Structure in Australian History*, Longman Cheshire, Melbourne.

Conway, G. and Barbier, D. 1990, *After the Green Revolution: Sustainable Agriculture for Development*, Earthscan, London.

Council for Aboriginal Reconciliation 1995, *Going Forward: Justice for the First Australians*, AGPS, Canberra.

Cowlishaw, G. 1990, 'Helping Anthropologists: Cultural Continuity in the Constructions of Aboriginalists', *Canberra Anthropology*, vol. 13, no. 2, pp. 1–28.

Cowlishaw, G. 1987, 'Colour, Culture and the Aboriginalists', *Man*, vol. 22, pp. 221–37.

Crichton, A. 1990, *Slowly Taking Control? Australian Governments and Health Care Provision 1788–1988*, Allen & Unwin, Sydney.

Crosby, A. 1986, *Ecological Imperialism: The Biological Expansion of Europe 900–1900*, Cambridge University Press, Cambridge.

Crow, G. and Allan, G. 1994, *Community Life: An Introduction to Local Social Relations*, Harvester Wheatsheaf, London.

Cupit, G. 1994, 'Much to View About Nothing', in F. Briggs (ed.), *Children and Families*, Allen & Unwin, Sydney, pp. 160–81.

Curthoys, A. 1988, *For and Against Feminism*, Allen & Unwin, Sydney.

D'Aprano, Z. 1977, *Zelda: The Becoming of a Woman*, self-published, Melbourne.

Daniel, A. 1983, *Power, Privilege and Prestige: Occupations in Australia*, Longman Cheshire, Melbourne.

Darnton, R. 1989, 'What Was Revolutionary about the French Revolution?', *New York Review of Books*, vol. 35, nos 21–2, January 19, pp. 3–10.

Darwin, N. 1986, *The History of Ford in Australia*, Eddie Ford Publications, Newstead, Vic.

Davidoff, L. and Hall, C. 1987, *Family Fortunes: Men and Women of the English Middle Class 1780–1850*, Hutchinson, London.

Davies, J. C. 1969, 'The J-Curve of Rising and Declining Satisfactions as a Cause of Some Great Revolutions and a Contained Rebellion', in H. S. Graham and T. R. Gurr (eds), *Violence in America*, US Government Printing Office, Washington, pp. 690–730.

Davis, A. and George, J. 1993, *States of Health: Health and Illness in Australia*, 2nd edn, Harper Educational, Sydney.

Davis, J. 1993, *Boy's Life*, Magabala Books, Broome.

Davis, K. and Moore, W. E. 1945, 'Some Principles of Stratification', *American Sociological Review*, vol. 10, pp. 242–9.

Davis, N. 1993, 'Systemic Gender Control and Victimisation among Homeless Female Youth', *Socio-legal Bulletin*, no. 8, Summer, pp. 22–31.

—— 1994, Students Welfare Co-ordinators' Responses to Homeless Students in the South Eastern Educational Region, unpublished MA thesis, University of Melbourne.

Davison, G. 1978, *The Rise and Fall of Marvellous Melbourne*, Melbourne University Press, Melbourne.

Davison, G. 1994, 'The Past and Future of the Australian Suburb', in L. Johnson (ed.), *Suburban Dreaming: An Interdisciplinary Approach to Australian Cities*, Deakin University Press, Geelong.

De Lepervanche, M. and Bottomley, G. (eds) 1988, *The Cultural Construction of Race*, Sydney Studies in Society and Culture no. 4, Meglamedia, Sydney.

de Vaus, D. 1990, *Surveys in Social Research*, Unwin Hyman, London.

Deloria, V. 1973, 'Custer Died for Your Sins', in T. Weaver (ed.), *To See Ourselves: Anthropology and Modern Social Issues*, Scott Freeman and Company, Glenview, Ill.

Dempsey, K. 1983, *Conflict and Decline: Ministers and Laymen in an Australian Country Town*, Methuen, Sydney.

—— 1990, *Smalltown: A Study of Social Inequality, Cohesion and Belonging*, Oxford University Press, Melbourne.

—— 1991, 'Inequality, Belonging and Religion in a Rural Community', in A. Black (ed.), *Religion in Australia: Sociological Perspectives*, Allen & Unwin, Sydney, pp. 63–77.

—— 1992, *A Man's Town: Inequality between Women and Men in Rural Australia*, Oxford University Press, Melbourne.

Dewberry, T. 1995, 'Responding to Globalisation', *Frontline*, vol. 26, July, p. 11.

Dickie, B. 1979, *No Charity There: A Short History of Social Welfare in Australia*, Nelson, Melbourne.

Dilnot, A. W. 1990, 'The Distribution and Composition of Personal Sector Wealth in Australia', *Australian Economic Review*, vol. 90, pp. 33–40.

Dixson, A. 1986, 'Adrian Finds his Avalon', in G. Wotherspoon (ed.), *Being Different*, Hale and Iremonger, Sydney, pp. 51–81.

Duncan, O. D., Featherman, D. L., and Duncan, B. 1972, *Socioeconomic Background and Achievement*, Seminar Press, New York.

Durkheim, É. 1933 (1893), *The Division of Labour in Society*, trans. G. Simpson, Free Press, New York.

The Ecologist, vol. 22, no. 4, July/August 1992, special issue: 'Whose Common Future?'.

Ehrlich, P. 1970, *The Population Bomb*, Ballantine Books, New York.

Eisenstadt, S. 1966, *Modernization: Protest and Change*, Prentice-Hall, Englewood Cliffs, NJ.

—— 1978, *Revolution and the Transformation of Societies*, Free Press, New York.

El Saadawi, N. 1982, *The Hidden Face of Eve: Women In the Arab World*, trans. and ed. S. Hetata, Beacon Press, Boston.

Elder, B. 1988, *Blood on the Wattle: Massacres and Maltreatment of Australian Aborigines since 1788*, Child & Associates, Sydney.

Elias, N. and Scotson, J. 1965, *The Established and the Outsiders*, Frank Cass, London.

Elkin, A. P. 1931, *Understanding the Australian Aborigine: A Lecture Delivered at a Meeting Arranged by the Association for the Protection of Native Races*, held at Science House, Sydney, 23 June 1931, The St Johns College Press, Sydney.

—— 1959, 'Historical Background to the Present Problem', *Proceedings of Conference on N.S.W. Aborigines*, May 1959, Adult Education Department, University of New England, Armidale, pp. 3–27.

—— 1960 'The Background of Present Day Aboriginal Policies', *Proceedings of Conference on Welfare Policies for Australian Aborigines*, May 1960, Adult Education Department, University of New England, Armidale, pp. 2–23.

—— 1974, *The Australian Aborigines*, Angus & Robertson, Sydney.

Emmison, M. 1991, 'Wright and Goldthorpe: Constructing the Agenda of Class Analysis', in J. Baxter, M. Emmison, and J. Western (eds), *Class Analysis and Contemporary Australia*, Macmillan, Melbourne, pp. 38–65.

Encel, S. 1970, *Equality and Authority: A Study of Class, Status and Power in Australia*, Cheshire, Melbourne.

Encel, S. 1984, 'Sociological Education: The First 25 Years', *Alumni Papers*, UNSW, vol. 1, no. 3, pp. 4–9.

Engels, F. 1982 (1845), *The Condition of the Working Class in England*, trans. Institute of Marxism and Leninism, Moscow, Granada, London.

Evans, L. 1994, 'Fancy Footwork', *Good Weekend*, 2 June, pp. 11–14.

Evans, R. and Saunders, K. (eds) 1992, *Gender Relations in Australia: Domination and Negotiation*, Harcourt Brace Jovanovich, Sydney.

Ewen, S. 1976, *Captains of Consciousness: Advertising and the Social Roots of Consumer Culture*, McGraw-Hill, New York.

Fink, R. 1957/1958, 'The Caste Barrier: An Obstacle to the Assimilation of Part-Aborigines in North-West New South Wales, *Oceania*, vol. 28, no. 1, pp. 100–10.

Fishman, J. and Nahirny, V. 1966, 'Ukrainian Language Maintenance Efforts in the United States', in J. Fishman (ed.), *Language Loyalty in the United States*, Mouton, The Hague, pp. 318–57.

Fiske, J., Hodge, B., and Turner, G. 1987, *Myths of Oz*, Allen & Unwin, Sydney.

Ford, H. 1923, *My Life and Work*, Angus & Robertson, Sydney.

Foucault, M. 1981, *Discipline and Punish*, Random House, Vintage Books, New York.

Frank, A. G. 1969, *Latin America: Underdevelopment or Revolution*, Monthly Review Press, New York.

Freud, S. 1973, *Introductory Lectures on Psychoanalysis*, Penguin Books, Harmondsworth.

Frith, S. 1981, *Sound Effects*, Constable, London.

Fromm, E. 1968, *The Sane Society*, Routledge & Kegan Paul, London.

Frost, L. 1994, 'Nineteenth Century Australian Cities', in L. Johnson (ed.), *Suburban Dreaming: An Interdisciplinary Approach to Australian Cities*, Deakin University Press, Geelong.

Gale, G. F. and Brookman, A. (eds) 1975, *Race Relations in Australia — The Aborigines*, McGraw-Hill, Sydney.

Galtung, J. 1971, *Members of Two Worlds*, Columbia University Press, New York.

—— 1974, *A Structural Theory of Revolutions*, Rotterdam University Press, Rotterdam.

Game, A. and Pringle, R. 1984, 'The Making of the Australian Family', in A. Burns, G. Bottomley, and P. Jools (eds), *The Family in the Modern World*, Allen & Unwin, Sydney, pp. 80–102.

Gans, H. 1962, *The Urban Villagers*, Free Press, New York, pp. 95–118.

—— 1968, 'Urbanism and Suburbanism as Ways of Life', in R. Pahl (ed.), *Readings in Urban Sociology*, Pergamon Press, Oxford.

Gardner, H. (ed.) 1992, *Health Policy: Development, Implementation and Evaluation in Australia*, Churchill Livingstone, Melbourne.

Garrison, H. 1987, 'Preparing Students for Nonacademic Employment', in J. M. and M. Iutcovich (eds), *The Sociologist as Consultant*, Praeger, New York, pp. 121–32.

Garton, S. 1990, *Out of Luck: Poor Australians and Social Welfare*, Allen & Unwin, Sydney.

George, V. and Wilding, P. 1983, *Ideology and Social Welfare*, 2nd edn, Routledge & Kegan Paul, London.

Giddens, A. 1982, *Sociology: A Brief but Critical Introduction*, Macmillan, London.

—— 1990, *The Consequences of Modernity*, Polity Press, Cambridge.

Girardet, H. 1990, 'The Metabolism of Cities', in D. Cadman and G. Payne (eds), *The Living City: Towards a Sustainable Future*, Routledge, London, pp. 170–80.

Gittins, D. (1985, *The Family in Question: Changing Households and Familiar Ideologies*, Macmillan, London.

Goffman, E. 1967, *The Presentation of Self in Everyday Life*, Allen Lane, London.

Goldthorpe, J., Lockwood, D., Bechnofer, R., and Platt, J. 1968, *The Affluent Worker*, Cambridge University Press, Cambridge.

Gomes, A. 1990, 'Confrontation and Continuity: Simple Commodity Production among the Orang Asli', in T. K. Lim. and A. Gomes (eds), *Tribal Peoples and Development in Southeast Asia*, University of Malaya, Kuala Lumpur.

—— 1991, 'Commodification and Social Relations among the Semai', in N. Peterson, and T. Matsuyama (eds), *Cash, Commoditisation and Changing Foragers*, Senri Ethnological Studies, no. 30, National Museum of Ethnology, Osaka.

Gow, H. 1994, 'Reader's Letter', *Health Forum: Journal of the Consumers' Health Forum of Australia*, no. 32, December, pp. 24–5. (Slightly abridged and reproduced with permission of the author).

Graetz, B. and McAllister, I. 1994, *Dimensions of Australian Society*, 2nd edn, Macmillan, Melbourne.

Grant, C. and Lapsley, H. 1991 *The Australian Health Care System 1990: Studies in Health Administration*, no. 71, University of New South Wales, Sydney.

Grant, J. 1993, *Fundamental Feminism: Contesting the Core Concepts of Feminist Theory*, Routledge, New York.

Greene, T. H. 1990, *Comparative Revolutionary Movements*, 3rd edn, Prentice-Hall, Englewood Cliffs, NJ.

Grimshaw. P., Lake, M., McGrath, A., and Quartly, M. 1995, *Creating a Nation: 1788–1990*, McPhee Gribble, Melbourne.

Grint, K. 1991, *The Sociology of Work*, Polity Press, Cambridge.

Hall, R., Thorns, D., and Willmott, W. 1983, *Community Formation and Change*, Working Paper No. 4, Department of Sociology, University of Canterbury, New Zealand.

Hardoy, J. E. and Satterthwaite, D. 1990, 'Urban Change in the Third World: Are Recent Trends a Useful Pointer to the Urban Future?', in D. Cadman and G. Payne, *The Living City: Towards a Sustainable Future*, Routledge, London, pp. 75–110.

Harvey, D. 1989, *The Condition of Postmodernity*, Blackwell, Oxford.

Harris, D. 1988, 'A Great Ring of Landlords?', in V. Burgmann and J. Lee (eds), *Making a Life*, McPhee Gribble, Melbourne, pp. 39–55.

Hassan, R. 1990, *Unlived Lives: Trends in Youth Suicide*, Working Paper No. 10, Sociology Discipline, The Flinders University of South Australia, Adelaide.

Hay, D. 1975, 'Property, Authority and Criminal Law', in D. Hay (ed.), *Albion's Fatal Tree*, Allen Lane, London.

Hay, R. 1994, 'The British Nineteenth-Century Industrial City', in L. Johnson (ed.), *Suburban Dreaming: An Interdisciplinary Approach to Australian Cities*, Deakin University Press, Geelong.

Hayes, B. 1990, 'Intergenerational Occupational Mobility among Employed and Nonemployed Women: The Australian Case', *The Australian and New Zealand Journal of Sociology*, vol. 26, pp. 368–88.

Hearn, J. 1992, *Men in the Public Eye: The Construction and Deconstruction of Public Men and Public Patriarchies*, Routledge, London.

Henderson Report. *See* Commission of Inquiry into Poverty.

Hillery, G. 1955, 'Definitions of Community: Areas of Agreement', *Rural Sociology*, vol. 20, no. 2, pp. 111–23.

Hobsbawm, E. and Ranger, T. 1983, *Inventing Tradition*, Cambridge University Press, Cambridge.

Holton, R. 1994, 'Social Aspects of Immigration', in M. Wooden, R. Holton, R. Hugo, and J. Sloan, *Australian Immigration: A Survey of the Issues*, AGPS, Canberra, pp. 158–217.

Horne, D. 1971, *The Lucky Country*, Penguin Books, Melbourne.

Horowitz, D. 1975, 'Ethnic Identity', in N. Glazer and P. Moynihan, *Ethnicity: Theory and Experience*, Harvard University Press, Cambridge, Mass., ch. 4, pp. 111–40.

Hoselitz, B. 1960, *Theories of Economic Growth*, Free Press, Glencoe, Ill.

Howe, R. 1994, 'Inner Suburbs: From Slums to Gentrification', in L. Johnson (ed.), *Suburban Dreaming: An Interdisciplinary Approach to Australian Cities*, Deakin University Press, Geelong.

Huggins, J. 1987/1988, '"Firing on in the Mind": Aboriginal Women Domestic Servants in the Inter-War Years', *Hecate*, vol. 13, no. 2, pp. 5–23.

Huggins, J. and Blake, T. 1992, 'Protection or Persecution', in R. Evans and K. Saunders (eds), *Gender Relations in Australia: Domination and Negotiation*, Harcourt Brace Jovanovich, Sydney.

Huggins, R. and Huggins, J. 1994, *Auntie Rita*, Australian Studies Press, Canberra.

Human Rights and Equal Opportunity Commission 1989, *Our Homeless Children*, Report of the National Inquiry into Homeless Children, (B. Burdekin, chairman), AGPS, Canberra.

Huntington, S. 1968, *Political Order in Changing Societies*, Yale University Press, New Haven.

Hutton, D. (ed.) 1987, *Green Politics in Australia*, Angus & Robertson, Sydney.

Ibsen, H. 1965, 'The Lady from the Sea', in *The League of Youth, A Dolls' House, The Lady from the Sea*, trans. P. Watts, Penguin Books, Harmondsworth.

Isaacs, H. R. 1975, 'Basic Group Identities', in N. Glazer and P. Moynihan, *Ethnicity: Theory and Experience*, Harvard University Press, Cambridge, Mass., ch. 1, pp. 29–52.

Jacobs, J. 1961, *The Death and Life of Great American Cities*, Vintage Books, New York.

Jahoda, M. 1981, 'Work, Employment and Unemployment: Values, Theories, and Approaches in Social Research', *American Psychologist*, vol. 36, no. 2, pp. 184–91.

James, K. 1979, '"The Home: a Private or Public Place?": Class, Status and the Actions of Women', *The Australian and New Zealand Journal of Sociology*, vol. 15, no. 1, pp. 36–42.

Jamrozik, A. 1991, *Class, Inequality and the State: Social Change, Social Policy and the New Middle Class*, Macmillan, Melbourne.

Jennings, K. 1993, *Sites of Difference: Cinematic Representations of Aboriginality and Gender*, Australian Film Institute, Sydney.

Johnson, L. (ed.) 1994, *Suburban Dreaming: An Interdisciplinary Approach to Australian Cities*, Deakin University Press, Geelong.

Jones, B. 1987, 'Operating a Nonprofit Consulting Corporation in the Business Environment', in J. M. and M. Iutcovich (eds), *The Sociologist as Consultant*, Praeger, New York, pp. 185–92.

Jones, F. L. and Davis, P. 1986, *Models of Society: Class, Stratification and Gender in Australia and New Zealand*, Croom Helm, Sydney.

Jones, M. A. 1990, *The Australian Welfare State: Origins, Control and Choices*, Allen & Unwin, Sydney.

Joseph, J. 1991, 'Warning', in S. Martz (ed.), *When I am an Old Woman I Shall Wear Purple*, Papier Mache Press, Watsonville.

Jupp, J. 1983, 'The Politics of "Ethnic" Areas of Melbourne, Sydney and Adelaide', in J. Halligan and C. Paris (eds), *Australian Urban Politics*, Longman Cheshire, Melbourne.

Kalantzis, M. and Cope, B. 1990, 'Multiculturalism and Education Policy', in G. Bottomley and M. De Lepervanche (eds), *Ethnicity, Class and Gender in Australia*, Studies in Society, no. 24, Allen & Unwin, Sydney, pp. 82–97.

Kaplan, R. D. 1994, 'The Coming of Anarchy', *The Atlantic Monthly*, February, pp. 44–76.

Kauffman, L. A. 1990, 'The Anti-Politics of Identity', *Socialist Review*, vol. 21, no. 1, pp. 67–80.

Kellehear, A. 1990, *Every Student's Guide to Sociology*, Thomas Nelson, Melbourne.

Kellehear, A. 1993, *The Unobtrusive Researcher: A Guide to Methods*, Allen & Unwin, Sydney.

Kellehear, A. 1996, *Experiences Near Death: Beyond Medicine and Religion*, Oxford University Press, New York.

Kellehear, A. and Fook, J. 1989, 'Sociological Factors in Death Denial by the Terminally Ill', in J. L. Sheppard (ed.), *Advances in Behavioural Medicine*, vol. 6, Cumberland College of Health Sciences, Sydney, pp. 527–37.

Kelley, J., Bean, C., and Evans, M. D. R. 1992, *Religious Belief and Religious Behaviour in Australia, 1992*, International Social Science Survey, Canberra.

Kelly, P. 1993, *The End of Certainty*, Allen & Unwin, Sydney.

Kewley, T. H. 1973, *Social Security in Australia, 1900–72*, Sydney University Press, Sydney.

Kimmel, M. 1990, *Revolution: A Sociological Interpretation*, Temple University Press, Philadelphia.

King, A. D. 1990a, *Urbanism, Colonialism and the World Economy*, Routledge, London.

—— 1990b, *Global Cities*, Routledge, London.

King, D. 1987, 'Social Constructionism and Medical Knowledge: The Case of Transsexualism', *Sociology of Health and Illness*, vol. 9, pp. 351–77.

Kloss, H. 1966, 'German American Language Maintenance Efforts', in J. Fishman (ed.), *Language Loyalty in the United States*, Mouton, The Hague, pp. 206–12.

Kriegler, R. 1980, *Working for the Company*, Oxford University Press, Melbourne.

Kriegler, R. and Stendal, G. (eds) 1984, *At Work*, Allen & Unwin, Sydney.

Kumar, K. 1976, 'Revolution and Industrial Society: An Historical Perspective', *Sociology*, vol. 10, no. 2, pp. 245–69.

Kung, H. 1991, *Global Responsibility: In Search of a New World Ethic*, SCM Press, London.

Langer, B. 1989, 'Commoditoys: Marketing Childhood', *Arena*, no. 87, pp. 29–37.

—— 1990, 'The Continuing Trauma of Refugee Settlement — the Experience of El Salvadoreans', in P. S. J. Hosking, *Hope After Horror: Helping Survivors of Torture and Trauma*, UNIYA, Sydney, pp. 69–85.

—— 1991, 'Émile Durkheim', in P. Beilharz (ed.), *Social Theory: A Guide to Central Thinkers*, Allen & Unwin, Sydney, pp. 70–5.

—— 1994, 'Born to Shop', in F. Briggs (ed.), *Children and Families*, Allen & Unwin, Sydney, pp. 142–50.

Langford, R. 1988, *'Don't Take Your Love to Town'*, Penguin, Melbourne.

Langton, M. 1993, *Well, I Heard It on the Radio and I Saw It on the Television . . .*, Australian Film Commission, Sydney.

Lappe, F. and Collins, J. 1988, *World Hunger: 12 Myths*, Earthscan, London.

Le Bon, G. 1960 (1895), *The Crowd*, Viking, New York.

Lemert, E. 1951, *Social Pathology*, McGraw-Hill, New York.

Lenski, G. 1963, *The Religious Factor: A Sociologist's Inquiry*, Anchor, New York.

Lester, H. 1986, *A Porcupine Named Fluffy*, Macmillan, London.

Lippmann, L. 1981, *Generations of Resistance: The Aboriginal Struggle for Justice*, Longman Cheshire, Melbourne.

Loos, N. 1982, *Invasion and Resistance: Aboriginal–European Relations on the North Queensland Frontier 1861–1897*, Australian National University Press, Canberra.

Lozanovska, M. 1994, 'Abjection and Architecture: The Migrant House in Multicultural Australia', in L. Johnson (ed.), *Suburban Dreaming: An Interdisciplinary Approach to Australian Cities*, Deakin University Press, Geelong.

Lyons, G. 1983, 'Official Policy towards Victorian Aborigines 1957–1974', *Aboriginal History*, vol. 7, pp. 61–81.

McCaughey, J., Shaver, S., Ferber, H. et al. 1977, *Who Cares? Family Problems, Community Links and Helping Services*, Macmillan and Sun Books, Melbourne.

McClelland, D. 1962, *The Achieving Society*, Van Nostrand, Princeton.

McGrath, A. 1987, *'Born in the Cattle': Aborigines in Cattle Country*, Allen & Unwin, Sydney.

McGregor, R. 1993, 'Representations of the "Half-Caste" in the Australian Scientific Literature', *Journal of Australian Studies*, vol. 36, pp. 51–64.

Macintyre, M. 1986, 'Female Autonomy in a Matrilineal Society', in N. Grieve and A. Burns (eds), *Australian Women: New Feminist Perspectives*, Oxford University Press, Melbourne.

Macintyre, S. 1985, *Winners and Losers*, Allen & Unwin, Sydney.

Mackie, F. for the Department of Immigration and Ethnic Affairs 1983, *Structure, Culture and Religion in the Welfare and Muslim Families: A Study of Immigrant Turkish and Lebanese Men and Women and Their Families Living in Melbourne,* , AGPS, Canberra .

Mackie, F. 1984, 'Blind Ethnocentrism', *Arena*, no. 67, pp. 93–104.

—— 1991, 'Blind Ethnocentrism', in K. Eggerking and D. Plater (ed.) for Australian Centre for Independent Journalism, *Signposts: A Guide to Reporting Aboriginal, Torres Strait Islander and Ethnic Affairs*, University of Technology, Sydney.

—— 1975, 'Networks, Values and Cultural Change', in C. Price (ed.), *Greek in Australia*, Australian National University Press, Canberra, pp. 72–111.

McLellan, D. 1971, *The Thought of Karl Marx*, Macmillan, London.

MacLeod, S. 1981, *The Art of Starvation*, Virago, London.

McRobbie, A. 1978, 'Working Class Girls and the Culture of Femininity', in Women's Study Group Centre for Contemporary Cultural Studies, University of Birmingham (ed.), *Women Take Issue: Aspects of Women's Subordination*, Hutchinson, London, pp. 96–108.

—— 1991, *Feminism and Youth Culture*, Macmillan Education, Hampshire.

Magdoff, H. 1982, 'Imperialism: A Historical Survey', in H. Alavi and T. Shanin (eds), *Introduction to the Sociology of 'Developing Societies'*, Monthly Review Press, New York, pp. 1–10.

Maher, C. 1986, 'Australian Urban Character: Pattern and Process', in J. B. McLoughlin and M. Huxley (eds), *Urban Planning in Australia: Critical Readings*, Longman Cheshire, Melbourne, pp. 13–31.

Mannheim, K. 1976, *Ideology and Utopia: An Introduction to the Sociology and Knowledge*, Routlege & Kegan Paul, London.

Marks, G. N. 1992, 'Ascription Versus Achievement in Australia: Changes over Time 1965–1990', *The Australian and New Zealand Journal of Sociology*, vol. 28, pp. 330–50.

Martin, B. 1981, *A Sociology of Contemporary Cultural Change*, Basil Blackwell, Oxford.

Martin, J. I. 1972, *Community and Identity: Community Groups in Adelaide*, ANU Press and the Academy of the Social Sciences in Australia, Canberra.

—— 1978, *The Migrant Presence: Australian Responses 1947–1977*, Research Report for the National Population Inquiry, Studies in Society No. 2, Allen & Unwin, Sydney.

—— 1981, *The Ethnic Dimension: Papers on Ethnicity and Pluralism*, Allen & Unwin, Sydney.

Marx, K. 1909, *Capital*, vol. 3, Charles Kerr & Co, Chicago.

—— 1918, *Capital: A Critical Analysis of Capitalist Production*, trans. S. Moore and E. Aveling, ed. F. Engels, S. Sonnenschein, London.

—— 1938, *Capital*, vols 1 and 2, Allen & Unwin, London.

—— 1964, *Economic & Philosophical Manuscripts of 1844*, ed. D. J. Struik, International Publishers, New York.

—— 1975, *Early Writings*, trans. R. Livingstone and G. Benton, Penguin Books, Harmondsworth.

Maushart, S. 1993, *'Sort of a Place Like Home': Remembering the Moore River Native Settlement*, Fremantle Arts Press, Fremantle.

May, D. 1994, *Aboriginal Labour and the Cattle Industry: Queensland from White Settlement to the Present*, Cambridge University Press, Melbourne.

Mead, G. H. 1934, *Mind, Self and Society*, ed. W. Morris, University of Chicago Press, Chicago.

Mead, M. 1981, *Growing Up in New Guinea*, Penguin Books, Harmondsworth.

Meadows, D. H., Meadows, D. L. and Behrens, W. 1972, *The Limits to Growth*, Pan, *New Internationalist*, London, April 1992.

Melucci, A. 1989, *Nomads of the Present: Social Movements and Individual Needs in Contemporary Society*, Radius, London.

Mencken, H. L. 1927, *American Mercury* (magazine), November, p. 379, as quoted in M. Du Basky 1990, *The Gist of Mencken*, The Scarecrow Press, Metuchen, NJ, p. 483.

Miles, R. 1982, *Racism and Migrant Labour*, Routledge & Kegan Paul, London.
—— 1988, 'Beyond the 'Race' Concept: The Reproduction of Racism in England', in M. De Lepervanche and G. Bottomley (eds), *The Cultural Construction of Race*, Sydney Studies in Society and Culture, no. 4, Meglamedia, Sydney, pp. 7–31.

Miller, J. B. 1976, *Toward a New Psychology of Women*, Penguin Books, Harmondsworth.

Mills, C. Wright 1959, *The Sociological Imagination*, Oxford University Press, New York.

Minar, D. and Greer, S. 1968, *The Concept of Community*, Aldine, Chicago.

Minichiello, V., Aroni, R., Timewell, E., and Alexander, L. 1990, *In-depth Interviewing*, Longman Cheshire, Melbourne.

Mishra, R. 1984, *The Welfare State in Crisis*, Wheatsheaf Books, Brighton.

Morgan, S. 1987, *My Place*, Fremantle Arts Centre Press, Fremantle.

Mullins, P. 1993, 'Decline of the Old, Rise of the New: Late Twentieth Century Australian Urbanisation', in J. M. Najman and J. S. Western, (eds), *A Sociology of Australian Society*, 2nd edn, Macmillan, Melbourne, pp. 524–53f.

Mumford, L. 1961, *The City in History : Its Origins, Its Transformations and Its Aspects*, Harcourt Brace, New York.

Murdoch, A. 1985, 'Secured in the Welfare Trap', *Age*, 26 June.

Murphy, R. 1986, *Cultural and Social Anthropology: An Overture*, 2nd edn, Prentice-Hall, Englewood Cliffs, NJ.

Nandy, A. 1983, *The Intimate Enemy: Loss and Recovery of Self under Colonialism*, Oxford University Press, Delhi.

Narogin, M. 1990, *Writing from the Fringe. A Study of Modern Aboriginal Literature*, Hyland House, Melbourne.

Newby, H. 1980, *Community*, Open University Press, Milton Keynes.

Newby, H., Bell, C., Rose, D., and Saunders, P. 1978, *Property, Paternalism and Power: Class and Control in Rural England*, Hutchinson, London.

Nisbet, R. A. 1966, *The Sociological Tradition*, Heinemann, London.

Okely, J. 1978, 'Privileged, Schooled and Finished: Boarding Education for Girls', in S. Ardener (ed.), *Defining Females: The Nature of Women in Society*, Croom Helm, London, pp. 109–39.

Oxley, H. 1978, *Mateship in Local Organization*, 2nd edn, University of Queensland Press, St Lucia.

Pakulski, J. 1991, *Social Movements: The Politics of Moral Protest*, Longman Cheshire, Melbourne.

Palmer, G. and Short, S. 1989, *Health Care and Public Policy: An Australian Analysis*, Macmillan, Melbourne.

Papastergiadis, N. 1986, 'Culture, Self and Plurality', *Arena*, no. 76, pp. 49–61.

Parsons, T. 1954, *Essays in Sociological Theory*, Free Press, New York.

Pearson, G., 'Goths and Vandals', in M. Fitzgerald and D. F. Greenberg, (eds) 1981, *Crime and Capitalism: Readings in Marxist Criminology*, Mayfield Publishing Company, Palo Alto.

Peterson, N. 1990, '"Studying Man and Man's Nature": the History of the Institutionalisation of Aboriginal Anthropology', *Australian Aboriginal Studies*, no. 2, pp. 3–20.

Pettman, J. 1991, 'Racism, Sexism and Sociology', in G. Bottomley, M. De Lepervanche, and J. Martin (eds), *Intersexions: Gender, Class, Culture, Ethnicity*, Allen & Unwin, Sydney, pp. 187–202.

Pixley, J. 1993, *Citizenship and Employment*, Cambridge University Press, Cambridge.

Plomley, N. J. B. 1977, *The Tasmanian Aborigines*, N. J. B. Plomley in association with the Adult Education Division, Launceston.

—— 1987, *Weep in Silence; A History of the Flinders Island Aboriginal Settlement*, Blubberhead Press, Hobart.

Plomley, N. J .B. and Henley, K. 1990, 'The Sealers of Bass Strait and the Cape Barren Island Community', *Tasmanian Historical Research Association Papers and Proceedings*, vol. 37, pp. 37–127.

Poiner, G. 1990, *The Good Old Rule: Gender and Other Power Relationships in a Rural Community*, Sydney University Press, Melbourne.

Polanyi, K. 1944, *The Great Transformation*, Beacon Press, Boston.

Porter, J. 1975, 'Ethnic Pluralism in Canadian Perspective', in N. Glazer and P. Moynihan, *Ethnicity: Theory and Experience*, Harvard University, Cambridge, Mass., ch. 9, pp. 267–304.

Potts, D. (ed.) 1988, *In and Out of Work*, History Institute of Victoria, Melbourne.

Presdee, M. 1989, Youth and 'Law and Order' in Australia: Class and the Criminalisation of Culture, unpublished paper presented to the American Society of Criminology Conference, Chicago.

Price, C. A. 1963, *Southern Europeans in Australia*, Oxford University Press, Melbourne.

Probert, B. 1989, *Working Life*, McPhee Gribble, Melbourne.

Pusey, M. 1991, *Economic Rationalism in Canberra: A Nation Building State Changes its Mind*, Cambridge University Press, Sydney.

Raban, J. 1990, 'New World (Part Three)', *Granta*, vol. 31, Spring, pp. 231–46.

Rakodi, C. 1990, 'Can Third World Cities Be Managed?', in D. Cadman and G. Payne, *The Living City: Towards a Sustainable Future*, Routledge, London, pp. 111–24.

Read, J. 1982, *The Stolen Generation: The Removal of Children in New South Wales, 1883–1969*, occasional paper no. 1, NSW Ministry of Aboriginal Affairs, Sydney.

Read, K. 1994, 'Struggling to Be Heard: The Tension between Different Voices in the Australian Women's Liberation Movement in the 1970s and 1980s', in K. P. Hughes (ed.), *Contemporary Australian Feminism*, Longman Cheshire, Melbourne.

Reay, M. (ed.) 1964, *Aborigines Now: New Perspectives in the Study of Aboriginal Communities*, Angus & Robertson, Sydney.

Reay, M. and Sitlington, G. 1948, 'Class and Status in a Mixed-Blood Community (Moree, NSW)', *Oceania*, vol. 18, no. 3, pp. 179–207.

Reeders, E. 1988, 'The Fast Food Industry', in E. Willis (ed.), *Technology and the Labour Process*, Allen & Unwin, Sydney, pp. 142–54.

Reeves, W. P. 1902, *State Experiments in Australia and New Zealand*, Macmillan, Melbourne.

Reiger, K. M. 1985, *The Disenchantment of the Home: Modernizing the Australian Family*, Oxford University Press, Melbourne, 1985.

—— 1991, *Family Economy*, McPhee Gribble, Melbourne.

Renan, E. 1882, 'The Nation as Community', in A. Arblaster, and S. Lukes (eds) 1971, *The Good Society*, Methuen, London.

Rex, J. and Tomlinson, S. 1979, *Colonial Immigrants in a British City*, Routledge & Kegan Paul, London.

Reynolds, H. 1981, *The Other Side of the Frontier: An Interpretation of the Aboriginal Response to the Invasion and Settlement of Australia*, James Cook University of North Queensland, Townsville.

Reynolds, H. 1990, *With the White People: The Crucial Role of Aborigines in the Exploration and Development of Australia*, Penguin Books, Melbourne.

Rice, P., Ly, B., and Lumley, J. 1994, 'Childbirth and Soul Loss: The Case of a Hmong Woman', *Medical Journal of Australia*, no. 160, pp. 577–8.

Richards, L. 1994, 'Suburbia: Domestic Dreaming', in L. Johnson (ed.), *Suburban Dreaming: An Interdisciplinary Approach to Australian Cities*, Deakin University Press, Geelong.

Ritzer, G. 1993, *The McDonaldization of Society*, Sage, Thousand Oaks, Calif.

Roberts, B. 1978, *Cities of Peasants: Explorations in Urban Analysis*, Edward Arnold, London.

Roberts, B. 1982, 'Cities in Developing Societies', in H. Alavi and T. Shanin (eds), *Introduction to the Sociology of 'Developing Societies'*, Monthly Review Press, New York, pp. 366–86.

Robertson, R. 1992, *Globalisation*, Sage, London.

Roe, J. (ed.) 1975, *Social Policy in Australia: Some Perspectives, 1901–1975*, Cassell Australia, Sydney.

Root, J. 1984, *Pictures of Women: Sexuality*, Pandora Press, London.

Rostow, W. 1960, *The Stages of Economic Growth*, Cambridge University Press, Cambridge.

Rowley, C. 1970, *Outcasts in White Australia*, Penguin Books, Harmondsworth.

Rowse, T. 1993, *After Mabo: Interpreting Indigenous Traditions*, Melbourne University Press, Melbourne.

Royal Commission into Aboriginal Deaths in Custody 1991, *National Report: Overview and Recommendations*, AGPS, Canberra.

Ryan, L. 1981, *The Aboriginal Tasmanians*, University of Queensland Press, St Lucia.

Saïd, E. 1978, *Orientalism*, Routledge & Kegan Paul, London.

Sassen, S. 1991, *The Global City*, Princeton University Press, Princeton.

Saunders, P. 1989, *Social Class and Stratification*, Routledge, London.

Sax, S. 1984, *A Strife of Interests*, Allen & Unwin, Sydney.

Scheff, T. 1974, 'The Labelling Theory of Mental Illness', *American Sociological Review*, vol. 39, pp. 444–52.

Schmalenbach, H. 1961, 'The Sociological Category of Communion', in T. Parsons et al. (eds), *Theories of Society*, vol. 1, Free Press, Glencoe, Ill.

Schutz, A. 1970, *On Phenomenology and Social Relations*, University of Chicago Press, Chicago.

Scott, A. 1990, *Ideology and the New Social Movements*, Unwin Hyman, London.

Scutt, J. 1983, *Even in the Best of Homes: Violence in the Family*, Penguin Books, Melbourne.

Seabrook, J. 1982, *Unemployment*, Quartet Books, London.

—— 1985, *Landscapes of Poverty*, Basil Blackwell, Oxford.

Selbin, E. 1993, *Modern Latin American Revolutions*, Westview Press, Boulder, Col.

Sharp, N. 1991, 'A Landmark: The Murray Island Case', *Arena*, no. 94, pp. 78–93.

—— 1992, 'Scales from the Eyes of Justice', *Arena*, no. 99/100, pp. 55–61.

—— 1993, *Stars of Tagai: The Torres Strait Islanders*, Aboriginal Studies Press, Canberra.

—— 1994, 'Native Title in Reshaping Australian Identity', *Arena*, no. 3, pp. 115–47.

Sharp, R. and Broomhill, R. 1989, *Shortchanged: Women and Economic Policies*, Allen & Unwin, Sydney.

Shiva, V. 1991, *The Violence of the Green Revolution: Third World Agriculture, Ecology and Politics*, Zed Books, London.

Shorter, E. 1976, *The Making of the Modern Family*, Basic Books, New York.

Sjoberg, G. 1965, 'Community', in J. Gould and W. Kolb, *Dictionary of Sociology*, Tavistock, London.

Skocpol, T. 1979, *States and Social Revolution*, Cambridge University Press, Cambridge.

—— 1992, *Protecting Soldiers and Mothers: The Political Origins of Social Policy in the United States*, Harvard University Press, Cambridge, Mass.

Smelser, N. 1962, *Theory of Collective Behaviour*, Routledge & Kegan Paul, London.

—— 1963, *The Sociology of Economic Life*, Prentice-Hall, Englewood Cliffs, NJ.

Spearitt, P. 1994, 'I Shop, Therefore I Am', in L. Johnson (ed.), *Suburban Dreaming: An Interdisciplinary Approach to Australian Cities*, Deakin University Press, Geelong.

Spivak, G. C. 1990, *The Post-Colonial Critic: Interviews, Strategies, Dialogues*, ed. S. Harasym, Routledge, New York.

Stacey, M. 1969, 'The Myth of Community Studies', *British Journal of Sociology*, vol. 20, no. 2, pp. 134–47.

Swain, T. and Rose, D. (eds) 1988, *Aboriginal Australians and Christian Missions*, The Australian Association for the Study of Religions, Adelaide.

Sykes, R. 1989, *Black Majority*, Hudson, Melbourne.

Tawadros, G. 1989, 'Beyond the Boundary: The Work of Three Black Women Artists in Britain', *Third Text*, vol. 8, no. 9, Autumn/Winter, pp. 121–50.

Thompson, E. P. 1971, 'The Moral Economy of the English Crowd in the Eighteenth Century', *Past and Present*, no. 50, February, pp. 76–136.

Thomson, J. (ed.) 1989, *Reaching Back: Queensland Aboriginal People Recall Early Days at Yarrabah Mission*, Aboriginal Studies Press, Canberra.

Tilly, C. 1978, *From Mobilization to Revolution*, Addison Wesley, Reading, Mass.

Tilly, L. and Scott, J. 1980, 'Women's Work and the Family in Nineteenth-Century Europe', in M. Anderson (ed.), *Sociology of the Family: Selected Readings*, 2nd edn, Penguin Books, Harmondsworth.

Tolstoy, S. 1975, extracts from her diaries, as reproduced in M. J. Moffat and C. Painter (eds), *Revelations: Diaries of Women*, Vintage Books, New York, pp. 138–47.

Tönnies, F. 1955 (1889), *Community and Association*, trans. C. P. Loomis, Routledge & Kegan Paul, London.

Touraine, A. 1974, *The Post-Industrial Society*, Wildwood House, London.

—— 1987, *Return of the Actor: Social Theory in Postindustrial Society*, Minneapolis University Press, Minneapolis.

Trethewey, J. 1989, *Aussie Battlers, Families and Children in Poverty*, Brotherhood of St Laurence, Melbourne.

Troeltsch, E. 1931, *Social Teachings of the Christian Churches*, trans. O. Wyon, Macmillan, New York.

Veblen, T. 1953 (1899), *The Theory of the Leisure Class*, Mentor Books, New York.

Vidich, A. and Bensman, J. 1960, *Small Town in Mass Society*, Doubleday, New York.

Voigt, L. 1987, 'Welfare Women', in H. Marchant and B. Wearing (eds), *Gender Reclaimed: Women in Social Work*, Hale and Iremonger, Sydney, pp. 80–92.

Wallerstein, I. 1979, *The Capitalist World Economy*, Cambridge University Press, Cambridge.

Ward, C. 1974, *Utopia*, Penguin Education, Harmondsworth.

Ward, K. 1985, 'Women and Urbanisation in the World System', in M. Timberlake (ed.), *Urbanization in the World-Economy*, Academic Press, London.

Warren, R. 1966, *Perspectives on the American Community*, Rand McNally, Chicago.

Waters, M. 1990, *Class and Stratification: Arrangements for Socioeconomic Inequality under Capitalism*, Longman Cheshire, Melbourne.

Watkins, E. 1978, 'Footnotes', *Newsletter of the American Sociological Association*, Autumn, p. 6.

Watts, R. 1987, *Foundations of the National Welfare State*, Allen & Unwin, Sydney.

—— 1988, 'As Cold as Charity', in V. Burgmann and J. Lee (eds), *Making a Life: A People's History*, McPhee Gribble, Melbourne, pp. 85–100.

WCED. See World Commission on Environment and Development.

Weber, M. 1948, *From Max Weber*, Routledge, London.

Weber, M. 1968, *Economy and Society*, Bedminster Press, New York.

Weber, M. 1976, *The Protestant Ethic and the Spirit of Capitalism*, trans. T. Parsons, George Allen & Unwin, London.

Weeks, J. 1985, *Sexuality and its Discontents*, Routledge & Kegan Paul, London.

Weller, A. 1981, *The Day of the Dog*, Allen & Unwin, Sydney.

—— 1986, *Going Home: Stories*, Allen & Unwin, Sydney.

Western, J. 1983, *Social Inequality in Australian Society*, Macmillan, Melbourne.

—— 1991, 'Dimensions of the Australian Class Structure', in J. Baxter, M. Emmison, and J. Western, (eds), *Class Analysis and Contemporary Australia*, Macmillan, Melbourne, pp. 66–85.

Western, M. 1991, 'Class Structure and Demographic Class Formation', in J. Baxter, M. Emmison, and J. Western (eds), *Class Analysis and Contemporary Australia*, Macmillan, Melbourne, pp. 166–201.

Wheatley, N. 1981, 'The Disinherited of the Earth?', in J. MacKinolty (ed.), *The Wasted Years?*, Allen & Unwin, Sydney.

Winefield, A., Tiggemeann, M., Winefield, H., and Goldney, R. 1993, *Growing up with Unemployment*, Routledge, London.

White, C. 1992, *Mastering Risk: Environment, Markets and Politics in Australian Economic History*, Oxford University Press, Melbourne.

Whitwell, G. 1989, *Making the Market: The Rise of Consumer Society*, McPhee Gribble, Melbourne.

Wild, R. 1974, *Bradstow*, Angus & Robertson, Sydney.

—— 1978, *Social Stratification in Australia*, Allen & Unwin, Sydney.

Williams, R. 1977, *Marxism and Literature*, Oxford University Press, Oxford.

Williams, T., Long, M., Carpenter, P., and Hayden, M. 1993, *Entering Higher Education in the 1980s*, AGPS, Canberra.

Williamson, B. 1982, *Class, Culture and Community: A Biographical Study of Social Change in Mining*, Routledge & Kegan Paul, London,.

Willis, E. 1995, *The Sociological Quest: An Introduction to the Study of Social Life*, Allen & Unwin, Sydney.

Willmott, P. 1986, *Social Networks, Informal Care and Public Policy*, Policy Studies Institute, London.

Wilson, B. 1982, *Religion in Sociological Perspective*, Oxford University Press, Oxford.

Wilson, B. and Wyn, J. 1987, *Shaping Futures*, Allen & Unwin, Sydney.

Wiltenberg, J. 1992, *Disorderly Women and Female Power in the Street: Literature of Early Modern England and Germany*, University Press of Virginia, Charlottesville.

Winant, F. 1976, 'Dyke Jacket', in *Dyke Jacket: Poems and Songs*, Violet Press, New York.

Wiseman, J. 1991, 'Beyond Safety Nets and Springboards: The Challenges of Australian Income Security Policy', in R. Batten, W. Weeks, and J. Wilson (eds), *Issues Facing Australian Families: Human Services Respond*, Longman, Melbourne, pp. 69–77.

—— 1995, 'Globalisation is Not Godzilla', *Frontline*, vol. 26, July, pp. 5–6.

Wolf, N. 1993, *Fire with Fire: The New Female Power and How It Will Change the 21st Century*, Random House, New York.

Wooden, M., Holton, R., Hugo, G., and Sloan, J. 1994, *Australian Immigration: A Survey of the Issues*, AGPS, Canberra.

World Commission on Environment and Development 1987, *Our Common Future*, Oxford University Press, Oxford.

Wright, E. O. 1985, *Classes*, Verso, London.

—— 1989, 'Women in the Class Structure', *Politics and Society*, vol. 17, pp. 35–66.

Yeatman, A. 1990, *Bureaucrats, Technocrats, Femocrats*, Allen & Unwin, Sydney.

Young, M. and Willmott, P. 1957, *Family and Kinship in East London*, Routledge & Kegan Paul, London.

Zald, M. N. and McCarthy, J. D. (eds) 1987, *Social Movements in Organisational Society*, Transaction Books, New Brunswick.

Zaleski, C. 1987, *Otherworld Journeys: Accounts of Near-Death Experiences in Medieval and Modern Times*, Oxford University Press, New York.

Index

imperialism 226, 233, 234, 249, 283
individual, the 15–17, 261
    emergence of psychology and 16–17
    modern 13
    roles and 18–19
    welfare state and 170
    work and 15
    see also self
individualism 130
    traditional community versus modern
            society and 103
    see also self
individuality see self
industrial capitalism 283
industrial revolution 35, 233, 264
industrialisation 231, 235
    community and 5
    labour movement and 260
    nineteenth-century 5, 233
    postwar 236–7
    Third World 223
    urbanisation and 236
    work and 234, 239
industrialism 202, 243, 249, 255–6, 260
    ecological damage and 244, 246, 248–9
    international division of labour and 285
inequality 207, 228
    Aboriginals and 197
    education and 161–4
    gender and 36
        in the Third World 228
    income and 154–5, 159
    nation-state and 211
    social class and 153–67
    wealth and 155–7
    welfare state and 169–77
institutions
    social 57, 131

Kimmel, Michael 263, 268
Kooris 252–3
    see also Aboriginals
Kumar, Krishan 270

labelling theory
    defined 72

Labor Party see Australian Labor Party
labour market
    Australian
        and women 237, 239
        work and the 158–9
labour movement, the 256, 261
    Australian 259
    industrialisation and 260
Lenski, Gerhard 93, 102

Mabo judgment 40, 198, 277
MacLeod, Sheila 29
McRobbie, Angela 28–9, 135
Malaysian Aborigines see Orang Asli
Malthus, Thomas 247
Mannheim, Karl 37, 42
market economy
    urbanisation and 233
    world 237–40
Marx, Karl 5, 38, 65–6, 86, 113, 283
    class theory and 163–4, 216
    sociology of 268
Marxism 123
    the Third World and 226
masculinity 24, 31, 32
    learning of 27–8, 29
Mead, George Herbert 35, 36, 37, 58, 59,
        63, 64, 71
Mead, Margaret 66
media 189, 205, 214, 277
    globalisation of sport and 280
migrants see immigrants
Miller, Jean Baker 26
Mills, C. Wright 3, 61, 181
modernisation 224–5, 282, 283
    agriculture and 225
    globalisation and 285
    poverty and 248
    social revolution and 269
    sociology and 268
    theory 223–4
    urbanisation and 231
    see also development
modernity 35, 36, 38, 40, 204, 213, 283
    ethnic self and 37, 39–40, 42
    ethnocentrism and 40

social class and 96
structural nature of 98–9
religious
community, defined 104–5
denominations 100–2
sects 99–102
views about death 74–5
revolution 284
communications 280, 281
Marxist 164, 216
industrial 35, 233, 264
sexual 263, 265, 267–8
transport 277
see also social revolution
Rice, Pranee Liamputtong 74
Robertson, Roland 285
Rostow, Walt 223
Rousseau, Jean-Jacques 246
rural community 143, 145
Kooris and 252
rural sector 238, 239, 240
effect of cities upon 85

Sax, Sid 182, 184, 185
school
work and 110
science 38
capitalism and 38
Scott, Alan 255
Seabrook, Jeremy 113–14
Second World War 1, 119, 172, 213, 215,
222
urbanisation and 236–7, 277
welfare state and 202
self, the 13–20
Aboriginality and 45–55
consumerism and 57–66
creativity and 260
as a social process 58
developing a sense of 23–5
gender and 35–6
premodern culture and 14
see also ethnic self; identity; individuality;
social self
sex *see* gender
sexual revolution 263, 265, 267–8

sexuality 29–30
see also heterosexuality; homosexuality;
transsexualism
social change 266–7, 268, 271
social class 37, 123, 136, 203, 205, 216,
235
class conflict and 216, 271
consumerism and 60
inequality and 153–67
Marxist theory and 163–4
nation-building and 207
religion and 96
social construction of femininity and masculinity and 26–30
social revolution and 265, 269, 270
State and 205–6
Weber and 164–6
youth subculture and 134, 135
social control 132–3
social Darwinism 15, 16, 39
social inequality and 16
social mobility 37, 166–7, 269
social movements 252–61, 265, 266
Aboriginal/Koori 252–3, 261
cities and 253–4
defined 258
differing concepts of 254–6
ethnic 258, 260, 261
European 255–6
functionalism and 254
globalisation and 259–61
post-industrial society and 255–6, 260
social creativity and 256, 259
social revolution and 272
student 255
social revolution 263–72
economic rationalism and 272
factors contributing to 269
future of 271–2
most widely quoted definition of 266
social change and 266–7
social class and 265, 269, 270
State-centred 265, 270, 271, 272
structural features of 270
social roles 260
social sciences 2